Vasilii Shukshin in the 1972 film *Pechki-lavochki* (*Stoves and Benches*). Photograph provided by Mark Volotskii, Director, Gorky Film Studio Museum.

Prodigal Son

VASILII SHUKSHIN IN SOVIET RUSSIAN CULTURE

John Givens

NORTHWESTERN UNIVERSITY PRESS / EVANSTON, ILLINOIS

Northwestern University Press
Evanston, Illinois 60208-4210

Printed in the United States of America

ISBN 0-8101-1770-3

10032444609

Library of Congress Cataloging-in-Publication Data

Givens, John.
    Prodigal son : Vasilii Shukshin in Soviet Russian culture / John Givens.
        p. cm. — (Studies in Russian literature and theory)
    Filmography: p.
    Includes bibliographical references (p.) and index.
    ISBN 0-8101-1770-3 (alk. paper)
    1. Shukshin, Vasiliĭ Makarovich—Criticism and interpretation.   I. Title.
    II. Series.
    PG3487.U5Z67   2000
    891.73'44—dc21   T   00-008699

For Laura, with love

In memoriam Deming Brown

Contents

Preface

When reading Vasilii Shukshin, you are first struck by the liveliness of his language and the dynamic subjects of his stories. His frequently humorous, even boisterous tales of Siberian peasants at home in the village or newly arrived in the big city are colorful, compact, and surprisingly unlike much of what was written during the Brezhnev period. You get the feeling that you have encountered one of the unique short-story voices of Russian literature. Like Gogol' in the 1830s, Chekhov at the turn of the century, and Zoshchenko and Babel' in the 1920s, Shukshin was a master of the short form whose language and character types became emblematic of his times. Indeed, of all of the short fiction of the post-Stalinist period, Shukshin's stories have the most enduring value and are likely to be read and enjoyed for many decades to come. In them we encounter a narrative voice as confident and distinctive, at times as rough and unrefined, as those of the characters he describes. It is the voice of Shukshin's protagonists telling the story of their lives, and there is a compelling honesty and authenticity about it that moves Shukshin's work into the realm of the universal, where all great storytellers abide.

The initial impulse to write this book originated not only in Shukshin's fine talents as a short-story writer but in his unique position in Soviet Russian culture as a popular actor and film director as well. Even before his premature death in 1974 made him almost a cult figure among Soviet readers and audiences, his success in three careers was often referred to as the "Shukshin phenomenon." This term has added resonance for a post-Soviet reading of the writer and his works, for in his pursuit of three careers Shukshin altered some of the paradigms through which we have traditionally understood Soviet writers and Soviet literature. In Shukshin we have an artist who blurred boundaries: between cinema and literature, creation and performance, middlebrow and high culture, and between popularity and elite appeal.

Shukshin acted in over twenty films from 1958 until his death and directed five films, all of which brought his own prose to the wide screen and made him a popular figure with movie audiences. It also influenced his writing, for Shukshin always wrote with a broad audience in mind. Unlike Iurii Trifonov, Valentin Rasputin, Chinghiz Aitmatov, and other talented and published Soviet writers, Shukshin made significant inroads into the mass readership of the Soviet 1960s and 1970s. The popularity of his work, however, was distinct from that of the Socialist Realist potboilers of Party hacks like the infamous Vsevolod Kochetov, whose large print runs were more a reward for services rendered than a reflection of reader demand. It also differed from that of the well-liked detective and spy novels of Iulian Semenov, the historical adventure novels of Vladimir Pikul', or the science fiction fare typically popular with readers. The usual limiting factors do not seem to hold for Shukshin: his wide readership did not signal concessions made to the authorities, his popularity did not indicate low quality or lack of sophistication, and he retained his integrity despite success in the worlds of cinema and literature.

In many ways, Shukshin himself made the case for this book because of his unique position in Soviet culture. In addition to his prolific acting and directing, he was remarkably productive as a writer during his fifteen-year career, with over 130 short stories, ten novellas for stage and screen, and three full-length novels. He reached more people in more media than perhaps any other Soviet artist after 1953, and this fact alone would attest to the value of a study of Shukshin's works for understanding this period in Soviet culture. Neither his works nor the artist himself ever disappeared from the cultural scene, as did so many other writers as a result of dissidence, emigration, or creative silence. On the contrary, Shukshin remained a highly visible artist throughout his career. All of these factors made Shukshin an attractive subject. I wanted to understand the works and provenance of a person who crossed so many boundaries and who challenged many preconceived notions about Soviet culture.

I was also fascinated by the legend of Shukshin's arrival at the Moscow film institute (VGIK—Vsesoiuznyi gosudarstvennyi institut kinomatografii) because it struck me as an important narrative for understanding not only the artist's life and works but post-Stalinist society as well. While the legend is an enjoyable story that illustrates a popular truth in Russia—that of the resilience and resourcefulness of the *narod,* or Russian common folk, a part of Shukshin's legend that informs his artistic strategy as well—it also departs significantly from the famous origin stories of other Soviet writers of humble background, such as Maxim Gorky, Sergei Esenin, Nikolai Ostrovksy, and Mikhail Sholokhov. Shukshin's legend reflects an important demographic change in post–World War II Russia: that of the massive migration from the village to the city and the sense of displacement

and alienation this migration caused. As such, it illustrates the tension between urban and rural that would inform the most important social and cultural debate of the Soviet 1960s and 1970s: between tradition and progress
and between preserving Russia's rural heritage or leaving it behind. This
debate was famously carried out in and around the phenomenon of Village
Prose, "the most aesthetically coherent and ideologically important body
of published literature to appear in the Soviet Union between the death of
Stalin and Gorbachev's ascendancy."[1] Shukshin thus embodies a central
dichotomy in Soviet Russian culture and society from the 1950s through the
1970s, and the duality he experienced was both a personal burden and the
driving force of his art.

For a number of reasons, Shukshin's legend seemed an appropriate
critical construct and a productive way of understanding both his appeal
and the importance of his canon for Soviet and post-Soviet times. At the
end of the twentieth century, the matter of canons is a particularly vexing
one. All of the categories by which we have understood twentieth-century
Russian literature (prerevolutionary, émigré, Soviet, dissident, returned,
and so on) and which were brought together in the mid-1980s now need to
be sorted out again. Typologically and stylistically, where does Shukshin belong? Are his literary bloodlines predominantly Russian or Soviet? As a
"writer of the Soviet epoch,"[2] to what extent did he conform to or cooper-
ate with the prevailing political order? Is he a writer primarily concerned
with moral, aesthetic, social, or historical questions? What will be his lasting contribution to Russian culture? Are his main achievements a laconic
narrational style and rough idiom, credited with revitalizing the short-story
form in Soviet literature?[3] Or do those famous character types comprise his
primary cultural legacy? These are some of the questions this book attempts to answer.

During his lifetime, it was Shukshin's language and his literary types
that accounted for his appeal. He had an ability to get through gaps in the
censorship more earthy and honest writing than many other literary figures
of his day. But just as he never used popularity as an excuse to forgo artistic experimentation, he also never used censorship as the basis to motivate
certain literary devices. There are remarkably few subtexts in his prose,
perhaps because he valued accessibility over the frisson members of the intelligentsia got from reading between the lines. His concerns are more obvious—mainly the petty conflicts and wounding confrontations arising from
misunderstandings, missed opportunities, mistreatment at the hands of bureaucrats and philistines, or maladjustment to a new milieu. While these
are safe, even common, targets to be sure, Shukshin somehow made them
more authentic concerns. People could relate to Shukshin's characters, their
passions, quarrels, and the salty language they often spoke. There was a
hominess to his stories, a warmth and emotional energy that were attractive

to readers and helped to explain their affection for the writer. Like his readers, Shukshin's characters were not so much concerned with changing the structure of Soviet society as with changing their wives' or neighbors' opinions of them, or adapting to a changing social landscape. Like the vast majority of Soviet citizens, they pursued their own private fancies and obsessions with little thought about effecting political change. Yet it is perhaps precisely in this way that Shukshin is an important writer, for his prose reflected the lives and aspirations of the most ordinary segments of Soviet society, the same people whose children now cope with the challenges of post-totalitarian Russia.

Shukshin's own story, like those of many of his heroes, is that of a prodigal son, prodigal in the sense that he left his village home for a more comfortable life in the city, only to realize, too late, that the peasant heritage he thus forfeited could never be regained. The fact that Soviet agricultural policy—collectivization, dekulakization, rural purges, and widespread mismanagement—was chiefly to blame for driving people from the village did little to alleviate the conflicted feelings many had in abandoning their rural birthplaces. In Shukshin's case, the guilt he felt over leaving his Siberian home only grew as he became more successful. If there is a metanarrative to this book, it is this story, for it is implied in a complex way in Shukshin's search for *volia* (freedom, liberation) in his personal and artistic life. It explains, on the one hand, the large number of Shukshin's characters caught between the city and the countryside and, on the other hand, the author's privileging of "soulful" rural protagonists who have not left the village and have managed to achieve there a degree of the freedom Shukshin himself sought. These are the country innocents and eccentrics "not of this world" who act as the repositories of spiritual goodness, creative independence, and playful buffoonery. It also explains the late appearance of Shukshin's grotesque character types, whose distorted personalities mirror the disorder in Shukshin's own soul over his lost rural heritage, his father who disappeared in the rural purges, and the compromises Shukshin felt he made with his past.

In the end, it may not be possible to answer definitively how Shukshin will be remembered. In his life and especially in the progression of his works there is no single, major "cursed" question that is asked or answered, just a number of smaller, often almost domestic, questions. This is not Dostoevsky asking why childern suffer or Tolstoy questioning his own mortality. When Shukshin's heroes pose global questions, they are often absurd, such as: why is perpetual motion an impossibility, or why has mankind not killed off all of the microbes so that people will live longer lives? Although his characters do question the meaning of life and death from time to time, they are more frequently concerned with why a wife has run off with an officer or why a clerk in a store has mistaken them for drunken troublemakers.

Shukshin often wrote about transition, even as he was experiencing it himself, and he forged his works and his style as he moved along. While not all of his prose and movie experiments were successful, Shukshin never gave up searching for the best way to use his creative energies. And he was searching very much on his own, not even sure of the optimal artistic medium. Was he primarily an actor? A writer? A director? No one could answer this question for him. He had to figure it out for himself, along the way. And so he alternately acted, wrote, and directed. Toward the end he even contemplated giving up his Moscow apartment and moving back to his native Siberian village. He was in transition his whole life, and then he died young. Had he lived longer, we do not know what he might have been like. Would he have joined the rural writers and become involved in nationalist politics? Would he have achieved even greater success as a filmmaker? In a real sense, Shukshin only had half a career, and obviously it was the first half, not the mature period. He is, to some degree, the *podrostok*, the raw youth of post-Stalinist Soviet literature, a writer in transition during transitional times who died before completing his journey. He is one of Russia's many promising but unfinished creative projects. What we have of him, though, is substantial and very promising—Shukshin did more with the half career he was given than many whose careers extend into their old age.

Beginning in 1985, Russia once again embarked on a period of major transition. During this time of tremendous social, political, and economic changes, Russian audiences have continued to turn to Shukshin. Twenty-five years after his death, his greatest film triumph, *Kalina krasnaia* (*Red Kalina Berry*), is still being shown regularly on Russian television, where it continues to elicit strong public reaction,[4] and sold in Russian video stores, where it shares shelf space with the newest films from Hollywood. New editions of his works continue to be published and read. His canon—the subject of intense scrutiny immediately following his death—continues to attract the attention of scholars and critics, who seek new contexts in which to understand him.[5] As many in the West are now finding out—and as many Russian readers could have told us—there was a lot more going on in Soviet Russian literature than it seemed in the 1960s and 1970s, and it was going on above ground. Millions of people had access to significant artistic works, and many people's lives were enriched and sustained by what was available. Shukshin played a major role in this above-ground cultural production. Indeed, his work as an actor and movie director made him, as it were, stick farther above ground than many of his literary peers.

Like Shukshin, I will offer no grand conclusions at the end of this book, except to say that for some writers we need to either expand cultural paradigms or put them aside and simply focus on the person and listen to his creative voice. In this sense, *Prodigal Son* is neither a cultural nor a literary biography, but a case study through which larger questions of Soviet

Acknowledgments

I have incurred many debts over the years in my work on Shukshin, and it is a pleasure to acknowledge them here. My greatest debt of gratitude is also my most recent, to my colleague Kathleen Parthé of the University of Rochester, whose commentary on successive drafts of this book has been thorough, thoughtful, and astute. From her uncanny ability to discover just the article or citation I needed to our numerous discussions about Shukshin and Soviet culture over the last several years, I have benefited greatly by her close contact and collegial guidance. Galya Diment, mentor through the greater part of my two graduate degrees and my dissertation advisor, deserves a special thank you as well for her ever-generous counsel through the years and her patient and insightful readings of different drafts of this book. Anna Maslennikova of the University of St. Petersburg provided critical readings of several of the chapters that helped shape my arguments as well as much-needed personal encouragement. Daniel Rancour-Laferriere and Davor Kapetanič were helpful commentators on my work on Shukshin at various stages of my graduate years, and I thank them, too. I reserve a special debt of gratitude for Deming Brown, whose seminar on contemporary Soviet prose at the University of Washington was not only an important early influence but led to an academic and personal relationship that continued through the writing of my dissertation and my first steps as an assistant professor. This book, for all of its inadequacies, is offered in part to honor his memory as well as to recognize his special role in my academic formation and his distinguished contribution to the Slavic field.

Research for this book was supported in part by a grant from the International Research and Exchanges Board (IREX), with funds provided by the National Endowment for the Humanities, the United States Information Agency, and the U.S. Department of State, which administers the Russian, Eurasian, and East European Research Program (Title VIII) as well as by a Fulbright-Hays dissertation fellowship. I would like to thank my advisor in Barnaul, Professor Svetlana Mikhailovna Kozlova of the Altai State

University, for her personal and academic counsel, and Igor Korotkov and Tamara Varaksina of the Altai Regional Museum of the History of Literature, Art, and Culture for their invaluable assistance. In Moscow, Mark Volotskii of Gorky Film Studio gave me free access to the archives of the Studio Museum and spent many hours with me discussing Shukshin and Soviet cinema. Ketia Klevitskaia kindly coordinated my research efforts at the All-Union State Institute of Cinematography (VGIK). My thanks also to Robert Mann for sharing with me his transcription of *Kalina krasnaia* and for putting me in contact with Shukshin's widow, Lidiia Fedoseeva-Shukshina. In addition, I profited greatly from participation in the Summer Research Laboratory on Russia and Eastern Europe during the summers of 1994 and 1996 at the University of Illinois, Champaign-Urbana. I would also like to acknowledge a junior faculty leave supported by the University of Rochester in the spring of 1997, which gave me the crucial period of uninterrupted time necessary to complete the manuscript.

This book has taken shape over the years ever mindful of the works of other researchers and critics of Shukshin's prose, most of whom are listed in the bibliography. Three "muses" in particular were influential and inspirational. Svetlana Kozlova, in various articles and her book *Poetika rasskazov V. M. Shukshina* (*The Poetics of Shukshin's Stories*), opened my eyes to the deep structure of Shukshin's works and the subtle turns of his psychology. Diane Nemec Ignashev was one of the first Western critics to devote serious attention to Shukshin, and her dissertation "Song and Confession in the Short Prose of Vasilij Makarovič Šukšin: 1929–1974," which she generously shared with me when I began my own work, remains the most thought-provoking and comprehensive discussion of the writer's short stories to date. Finally, Lev Anninskii, the author of numerous articles and the important commentaries accompanying Shukshin's collected works, has made the task of everyone who studies Shukshin easier and more rewarding.

Further thanks go to Hugh McLean, Caryl Emerson, and an anonymous reader for Northwestern University Press, who evaluated the manuscript with keen but kind critical eyes and lent their support to the project. In that most delicate task of assessing a scholarly work in its still vulnerable penultimate version, all three commentators were thorough, objective, insightful, and above all professional and tactful. They made final revision and rewriting a fruitful and enjoyable process. Susan Harris, editor in chief of Northwestern University Press, has been a sympathetic and enthusiastic supporter of the project from the earliest stages of her involvement with it, and she deserves a special thank you, too.

Finally, I thank my parents, Marian and Calvin Schwenk, my sisters Susan, Deanne, and Joni, and my twin brother, Jim, for their unflagging support and confidence in me. They always knew I could do it even when I thought that I could not. My wife and favorite translator, Laura, was my biggest support and mainstay. She survived both Siberia and the Shukshin book and remained throughout it all my most tireless reader and selfless consultant. Her name should be on the cover, but she only let me put it on the dedication page.

Parts of Chapters One, Two, and Six appeared as "Vasily Shukshin: A Storyteller's Story," in Vasily Shukshin, *Stories from a Siberian Village*, trans. Laura Michael and John Givens (DeKalb: Northern Illinois University Press, 1996), and are reprinted here by kind permission of the press. Chapters Seven and Eight appeared in slightly altered form in, respectively, *Russian Review* 58, no. 2 (April 1999) and a special issue of *a/b: Auto/Biography Studies* ("Rethinking Russian Autobiography," edited by Marina Balina) 11, no. 2 (Fall 1996) and are reprinted with the generous permission of those journals.

A Note on Sources

All references to Shukshin's fictional works—stories, novellas, scripts, and novels—are cited parenthetically in the text by volume number and page from the definitive "Literaturnoe nasledie" edition of his collected works: Vasilii Shukshin, *Sobranie sochinenii,* 5 vols., compiled and with commentary by Lev Anninskii, Galina Kostrova, and Lidiia Fedoseeva-Shukshina (Moscow: Panprint, 1996).

With the exception of names that are widely known outside of Russia whose popular spellings I have retained (e.g., Gorky), I have followed the Library of Congress transliteration style for all Russian words.

Introduction

WHEN ASKED WHY a writer should aspire to be an actor and director as well, Vasilii Shukshin responded in a way that captures the power and allure of the cinema for any artist. "Tell me," he said,

> what author would refuse to appear with his program in front of an audience of millions? What author would refuse to enter into the closest contact with the public who—right there, not stirring from their places—give him proof of their approval, comprehension, sympathy (or perplexity and incomprehension) . . . What artist could resist the temptation to stand before such a judge in order to know who he really is?[1]

Close contact with an audience of millions and the instant gratification and validation this gives are what make the movies such an attractive vehicle for writers wishing to promote their own artistic programs in the broadest possible way and with the most immediate—if sometimes transitory—results. Shukshin understood this well, carving out his three careers with all of the gusto of an overachiever, as if to embrace every possibility for contact with the public on a host of issues. And by 1974, shortly before his death, he had succeeded beyond his wildest expectations when over sixty million Soviet moviegoers flocked to see his last film, *Kalina krasnaia*.

A clear example of the kind of upward mobility enshrined in the mythology of the "classless" Soviet society, Shukshin was a backwoods Siberian whose unlikely acceptance into film school and subsequent success in film and fiction became the basis of a legend told both during and after his lifetime. His tripartite creative identity, however, was as conflicted as it was celebrated. As an actor and a director, Shukshin had one foot in the world of popular cinema, while as a writer, he had the other in the more serious and (in Russia) more prestigious world of literature.[2] As much a split as it was a synthesis, Shukshin's multifaceted persona won for the artist a broader audience, even as it kept him from achieving greater success in any one of his chosen careers. At his best, Shukshin the short-story writer has been ranked alongside Anton Chekhov, Raymond Carver, John Cheever,[3] and Erskine Caldwell,[4] while his films have been credited with revitalizing auteur

1

cinema in the Soviet Union.[5] Yet Shukshin died neither a major writer nor a major filmmaker. Rather, he died as something less and yet more than either of those things—he died a cultural sensation: an artist of seemingly endless talents and great personal appeal, a jack-of-all-trades who represented one of the more memorable "rags-to-riches" stories in the history of Soviet culture, even a kind of folk hero beloved by millions. He was, as Edward J. Brown asserts, "that rare phenomenon, an original and powerful writer with a broad popular following and the complete support of the regime."[6]

Shukshin's striking combination of talents, interests, and outlooks struck a rare chord in Soviet readers and movie viewers of the 1960s and 1970s. Along with the actor and guitar poet Vladimir Vysotskii, Shukshin was the closest thing Soviet Russian culture had at that time to a popular artist for the working class, and this was one reason for his great appeal.[7] His themes, like those of Vysotskii, were closely linked to the lives of average citizens—the working masses and the so-called technical intelligentsia—and were conveyed in a simple, salty, and expressive vernacular. Readers and moviegoers felt that they could trust him, that he was telling *their* story and telling it the way it was. In the years following his death, Shukshin's name became synonymous with honest, truth-telling prose. Even in post-Soviet rereadings, he is seen as a symbol of conscience in a compromised, corrupt age.[8]

Since his death, some critics have come to view Shukshin as one third of a troika of artists who represented the best fiction to be published in the Soviet Union during the Brezhnev period. Iurii Trifonov and Valentin Rasputin—writers of so-called Urban and Village Prose, respectively—are the other two artists.[9] Together all three writers conveniently represent the main developments of Soviet literature after Stalin, with Shukshin occupying a prominent middle ground not only thematically (his works chronicle the transition from country to city life) but artistically as well (Shukshin's stories did not make the demands—in terms of complexity, length, and style—upon readers that Trifonov's and Rasputin's did). Shukshin's prose had the appeal and accessibility of his movies and was therefore widely read. Thus to the possible approaches toward understanding Soviet culture of the Brezhnev era, Shukshin added a significant category of his own: popularity.

Shukshin cultivated his broad appeal, in many ways gearing his entire artistic program toward that essential contact with "an audience of millions." As such, his art extends into the realm of Soviet popular culture—that broad band of artistic activity of differing degrees of cultural pretension, artistic depth, accessibility, and ideological conformity—even as he strove to be much more than just a popular artist. Anatoly Vishevsky places Shukshin in the category of "intellectual popular culture,"[10] although it is equally clear that the Shukshin phenomenon would have been impossible without the huge audience of average moviegoers that Shukshin's films brought him. Without the visibility afforded by his acting and directing, the writer simply would not have gained the wide audience he did. Moreover, the lessons of the popular cinema—authentic dialogue, quick tempo, dynamic scenes, broad appeal—were the secrets of the writer's success as well. Shukshin the writer needed Shukshin the actor and director.

In a certain sense, Shukshin can be considered the perfect embodiment of both traditional and modern notions of popular culture in Russia. With his origins in the "common folk," he stands for popular culture in the original sense—art of and for "the people"—even as he worked in the entertainment industry as an actor and movie director, the quintessential spheres of popular culture in the modern, urban sense. He described himself as a "folk storyteller" straight out of the village, and yet he told those rural stories in movies and in the pages of journals and literary weeklies. He thus describes—and personifies—an important intersection between the common folk of rural Russia and the mainly urban consumers of culture, popular or otherwise.

Obviously, there are huge differences in the growth, development, and impact of popular culture in the Soviet Union as opposed to its evolution and influence in the West, not the least of which have to do with differences in economic structure, and we should be clear as to the nature of Soviet popular culture and Shukshin's relation to it. Whereas Western popular culture has been shaped by consumer interests and industries, Soviet popular culture developed in close relation to political forces and at a far greater distance from fad and fashion. Accordingly, Soviet popular culture—primarily music, movies, and novels meant mainly as diversionary entertainment, to a lesser extent style and fashion—was never as varied as its Western cousin, which reflected a far greater range of popular interests and trends that, moreover, changed and developed much more quickly than they did in the Soviet Union. Also, as Richard Stites points out, Soviet popular culture betrays a much greater presence of "themes, conventions, and commonplaces . . . traceable to folklore and high culture" than does Western popular culture.[11] Popular culture in the Soviet Union as a whole had a more mixed pedigree than it did in the West.

During Stalin's "cultural revolution" of the 1930s, in particular, an effort was made to erase distinctions between high and low culture in order to replace them—by force—with a single, homogenized tradition. Katerina Clark notes, for instance, how the development of the Soviet novel since the late 1920s was conditioned by a "closing not only of the gulf between the literature of the Party press and other varieties of committed literature but the gulf between high culture and popular culture as well—between highbrow literature and Party rhetoric."[12] While this gulf was never fully bridged, the consequent blurring of boundaries actually elevated the importance of popular (or low) culture in the Soviet context as another potentially important sphere of ideologically correct entertainment and education.

Shukshin's art, like much of Soviet culture, is situated somewhere between folk culture, with its roots in tradition, and high culture, whose sophisticated aesthetic language makes demands of its audience that go well beyond mere entertainment value or popular edification. Neither his films nor his stories ever pretended to be art with a capital A. Like many artists whose names we associate with popular culture, Shukshin was heavily invested in reaching and being understood by the largest number of people. And yet Shukshin can only marginally be considered part of Soviet popular culture proper. While the notions of popular taste, general appeal, mass contact, and aesthetic accessibility guided the whole of Shukshin's artistic program, it is only his film career that truly brought him into the realm of popular culture.

Born and raised in the village, Shukshin grew up knowing both kinds of culture: the folk culture of the village, such as it had survived into the 1920s and 1930s, and the more popular fare of Soviet Socialist Realism that he read in school and borrowed from the village library. He also read, of course, the approved classics of Russian literature from the nineteenth century: Pushkin, Gogol', and Tolstoy. But it was the lessons of folk and popular genres that Shukshin so effectively synthesized in his own aesthetic.

Shukshin's synthesis of popular and folk culture, however, neither promoted urban culture and diversionary entertainment nor advocated a return to rural traditions. His position within and between cultural realms reflected his uprooted life and made him a unique barometer with which to measure the changes in the cultural atmosphere in the first decades after Stalin. He spoke for that sizable segment of the population that was migrating from the countryside to the city—25 million people between 1939 and 1959,[13] another 21 million from 1959 to 1970[14]—for whom social and cultural mobility were bound together with the rural/urban dichotomy. Shukshin's art, serving simultaneously as his own means of cultural mobility and cultural critique, gave voice to the very stratum of Russian society from which he, as a successful artist, had become distanced. In the final analysis, the Shukshin phenomenon seems to propose its own terms for rereading post-Stalinist culture, terms having to do with the notions of demographic displacement, class difference, popular genres, mass audiences, and synthesis of the arts.

Shukshin's formative years as an artist coincided with the years of the Thaw in Soviet culture (roughly, 1953–63), whose spirit guided his early development and informs his entire oeuvre. A brief summary of the period will allow us to place Shukshin within the larger context of post-Stalinist culture, for he began his training at film school in 1954 during the early days of the Thaw and made his debuts in film and fiction during the on-again, off-again decade of reforms that followed.

4

Joseph Stalin's death in 1953 ushered in a bewildering period of revelations and the relaxation of prohibitions in many spheres. By comparison with the previous thirty years of Soviet culture, the Thaw period heralded an unprecedented time of cultural openness. Indeed, the mechanisms of cultural control loosened during the Thaw were never fully tightened afterward during the Brezhnev period of stagnation. In the thirty-year interval between Stalin and Gorbachev, the Soviet culture industry afforded outlets for nonconformity on all levels.

Into the stylistic vacuum of the culture of the Stalin era burst a flood of Western writers and artists as varied as Monet, Kafka, Sartre, and Picasso.[15] There were also increased translations of popular Western authors (Hemingway, Salinger, Bradbury), a proliferation of Western jazz and popular dances, cautious rehabilitations of suppressed Russian and Soviet classics (Dostoevsky, Bunin, Babel', Platonov, and Bulgakov), and heightened emphasis on entertainment value in movies, which increased in number in the 1960s to an average of 150 a year shown in 151,000 movie theaters and 138,000 clubs. The advent of television in the late 1950s and its spread from 2.5 million homes in 1958 to 30 million a decade later[16] also gave Russians a new and unprecedented variety of cultural choices.

The Thaw opened up new possibilities for understanding and interrogating Soviet culture, possibilities played out largely in the realm of popular fiction, film, and music. Ol'ga Berggol'ts's article "A Conversation about Lyric Poetry" in April 1953 and Vladimir Pomerantsev's essay "On Sincerity in Literature" eight months later were the first volleys in the new battle for true sentiment, sincerity, and openness in the arts that helped give rise to new currents of lyricism, nonconformity, and social criticism in poetry, prose, and film.[17] The rapid proliferation of voices and movements that followed made for an especially exciting decade of change on the cultural scene, which would permanently alter how artists understood their role in Soviet society.

A new wave of lyrical prose appeared in the 1950s, led by Iurii Kazakov, whose poetic short stories of love, loss, and individual isolation helped clear essential artistic space for other movements. His loners, eccentrics, and individualists were the immediate forerunners of Shukshin's own protagonists and of the rebellious heroes of Youth Prose (1960–65) as well, whose practitioners (Vasilii Aksenov, Anatolii Gladilin, and Andrei Bitov, among others) depicted the conflict between generations in a style influenced by imported popular culture and propelled by jargon, slang, and an attitude of skepticism and sarcasm. The generational conflict at the center of much of Youth Prose was bound up in the spirit of social inquiry and cultural change that characterized the Thaw, pitting the values of the fathers and mothers compromised by years under Stalin against those of their offspring breathing the air of reform. Youth Prose reflected, in part, the aspirations of the so-called *stiliagi* (urban dandies).[18] It shared their Western sympathies, irreverence, and belief in the liberating powers of fad and fashion.

Partly in response to Youth Prose, partly as an outgrowth of essays on conditions in the countryside, and partly inspired by Kazakov's bittersweet contemplation of loss and of the natural world, Village Prose, a child of the Thaw, also emerged in the early 1960s. Its leading writers (Fedor Abramov, Viktor Astaf'ev, Vasilii Belov, and Valentin Rasputin) focused on their native realms, nature, and their nostalgia for what Kathleen Parthé calls the "radiant past" of rural life,[19] contrasting Russian folk traditions and folk culture to the failed policies of Stalinist agriculture reform and the illusory promises of Western culture, especially popular culture. Village Prose (1960–80) countered Western cultural imports and Soviet internationalism with a dose of Russian nationalism, almost exceeding the threshold of what was allowable. In the process, it turned up the heat on debates in the 1960s and 1970s over the relative value of culture—high, popular, and folk—and raised questions about national identity.

Many of the works of Youth Prose straddled the line between stories for a mass readership and a more serious art that attracted critical attention. Its main outlet—the journal *Iunost'* (*Youth*), founded in 1956—boasted a circulation of 500,000 by 1961 (reaching 1.5 million by 1965)[20] and was extremely popular among readers. To publish in *Iunost'*, according to Anatolii Gladilin, was to "set all the bells ringing."[21] Village Prose, on the other hand, was popular in a different sense: by championing traditional Russian rural culture, it sought to return cultural hegemony to the people—the Russian common folk. Both movements laid claim to the domain of Soviet culture even as each understood it in different ways; both sought to redefine culture in the 1960s in their own likeness and, in so doing, to define themselves and their resistance to the monoculturalism practiced by the Soviet cultural establishment. Shukshin, as we shall see, was influenced by both movements but remained outside either of them throughout his career.

The Thaw was also a time in which poets and cosmonauts vied to capture the popular imagination, sparking a public debate about who society needed more: *liriki* (lyricists) or *fiziki* (physicists). While Iurii Gagarin circled the earth in 1961 as the foremost of the *fiziki*, the immensely popular *liriki* Evgenii Evtushenko, Andrei Voznesenskii, and Bella Akhmadulina recited poetry to crowds at the monument to Vladimir Maiakovskii and even to entire soccer stadiums. It was a time of increased mobility in a variety of senses: as newly amnestied prisoners made their way west from Stalin's gulag, thousands of young folk headed east, participating, by choice or obligation, in Khrushchev's Virgin Lands program and contributing to a new romanticizing of Siberia. The whole nation was engaged in a reappraisal—limited, to be sure—of the past, and the air was thick with the promise of a new openness, even as the Thaw alternated with periods of political and cultural "frosts."

Although events of the 1960s—the ascendancy of Brezhnev, the trials of the poet Joseph Brodsky in 1964 and of the writers Iulii Daniel and Andrei Siniavskii in 1966, the invasion of Czechoslovakia in 1968—eventually marked a return to neo-Stalinist policies, the Thaw had already left its imprint on a generation of writers, artists, filmmakers, and poets. Moreover, Soviet culture, high and low, had become a battleground of ideas and styles, a more successful means of resistance and subversion than it had been at any other time since before the days of high Stalinism.

This was the environment in which Shukshin took his first steps as an artist, an environment which made possible his rise in Soviet cinema and literature. Shukshin was a direct product and beneficiary of the increased mobility in society and culture after Stalin's death, completing a journey from Siberia to Moscow to finish his education and moving in dramatic fashion from a life as an obscure provincial teacher in 1953 to successful debuts in literature and film over the next ten years. Indeed, the Shukshin phenomenon stands in part as testimony to the possibilities of social and creative mobility in the Soviet Union after Stalin, a topic to which we will return.

This book attempts to fill a gap in post-Soviet assessments of Russian culture of the Brezhnev era by looking at one of its most popular artists, someone who embodied both the opportunities and contradictions of his times. Here the myths and legends of the artist's bold appearance before the well-known director Mikhail Romm at the state film institute recall the legend of the young poet Sergei Esenin's visit to Aleksandr Blok upon his arrival in St. Petersburg. In each case, the meeting reveals a clash of cultures and identities—rural/urban, peasant/intellectual, outsider/establishment—that highlights important aspects of each artist's legend, the world of their art, and their society. Like Esenin, Shukshin was a highly visible and beloved figure whose very personality entered into the cultural history of his country.

As a product of his times, Shukshin embodies equally conflicted aspects of his country's social and political history. A Siberian peasant by heritage, Shukshin abandoned his rural roots to achieve success in the worlds of cinema and literature. The son of an enemy of the people, Shukshin was a member in good standing of the same Communist Party responsible for his father's death. Although he joined the Party after 1953 and during a decade of reforms, his status as a Communist was clearly also a weight on his conscience. Finally, Shukshin was a first-generation intellectual who suffered from the usual inferiority complexes, a fact that made him perennially highstrung and class conscious. These issues reverberate throughout Shukshin's art and endow it with a social relevance immediately recognizable to his audience.

Prodigal Son assumes a general familiarity with Soviet history—in particular, the post-Stalinist period—in order to focus more closely on Shukshin and his works. In this first English-language monograph on the artist, I have tried to encompass the whole of Shukshin's production—short stories and films as well as novels and plays. My goal is straightforward: by understanding the works of an author of the Soviet mainstream, an author associated with the mass literature of the period of stagnation,[22] we will better understand the workings of Soviet culture and the social forces of the time. Shukshin's art and personality can thus shed light on the still understudied features of the cultural terrain of post-Stalinist Russia.

My first chapter will look at the legends surrounding the artist and the provincial polemic to which they give voice. We will see how the popular myth about the writer both reflects his abiding provincial complex (with its attendant antiestablishment undertones) and reveals a central feature of his art: that of folk buffoonery, in which the lower body—understood both figuratively and literally—of Russian culture triumphs over the upper and asserts its right to autonomy and difference. I will trace the reenactment of the legend in several of Shukshin's works and link this pivotal moment to the subsequent course of his life and art. Chapter One establishes issues that reverberate throughout my study. The second chapter addresses how Shukshin merged folk notions of art with the aesthetic demands of film and fiction. I will show how Shukshin's characterization of himself as a "popular" or "folk" storyteller describes an important dialogic relationship between the artist and both his public and his characters.

Russian literature has always taken very seriously what kinds of enduring literary types a writer creates, and it has assigned Shukshin his own prominent place in its typology. Shukshin's signature type has long been considered to be the "oddball" or eccentric (*chudik*), a fact inevitably mentioned in references to the writer.[23] Since Shukshin's hero was so often at the center of critical debate during his lifetime as well as afterward, I devote considerable attention to the question of Shukshin's character typology, its origin, and its evolution. It is in these chapters that I deal at greatest length with his short stories. I begin in Chapter Three by looking at Shukshin's earliest protagonists, his "bright souls," and how they met or challenged the expectations raised by the Thaw period in Soviet culture. Concepts important for understanding all of Shukshin's works emerge from these early stories, though their presence there is muted.

Chapter Four examines Shukshin's famous *chudiki*, the artist's conscious revival of the potent figure of the fool in Russian culture. Country innocent, carnival buffoon, and folk artist, the *chudik* also embodies the physical and spiritual resilience of the masses from which he comes. He was

Shukshin's most important contribution to Soviet literature as well as to the tradition of the fool in world literature. In Chapter Five, I discuss Shukshin's move away from the figure of the fool toward unattractive, even grotesque, character types—the distorted incarnations of social ills satirized in his 1972 collection of short stories *Kharaktery* (*Characters/Types*) and in a series of novellas. These late negative characters, often overlooked in studies of the Shukshin, reflect his own sense of crisis over the state of Soviet society and anticipate the darker heroes that would appear in Russian prose of the 1980s and 1990s. They also reveal a submerged discourse of self-accusation, as Shukshin confronts his own choices and compromises as an artist and an émigré from the village.

Chapter Six places Shukshin in the broader context of the political controversies and literary polemics of the 1960s and early 1970s. Here Shukshin's frequently stormy relationship with the critics is discussed at length, with particular attention paid to the ideological, cultural, and stylistic conflicts that came to define the artist and his achievement. Chapter Seven is devoted to Shukshin's most famous work, *Kalina krasnaia* (a 1972 novella and 1974 film), which enjoyed spectacular popular success and conveys "some idea of what a Soviet best-seller is like."[24] It is in the triumph of *Kalina krasnaia*, a success that transformed Shukshin from a "cult figure" into a "popular hero,"[25] that we glimpse most clearly the intersection between Shukshin's artistic program and his investment in the power of popular cinema.

The final chapters examine Shukshin's novels, Books One and Two of *The Liubavin Family* and his novel about the Cossack rebel Sten'ka Razin, *I Have Come to Give You Freedom*. Less successful and less popular (in both senses of the word), these novels reveal the side of the artist that aspired to *bol'shaia literatura* ("big" or significant literature). Nevertheless, as Virginia Woolf has noted, the second-rate writing of first-rate writers often reveals the most about a writer's program.[26] In this case, *The Liubavin Family* novels offer insight into Shukshin's split identity: citified Siberian/maladjusted Muscovite, son of a purged kulak/Communist Party member, provincial rebel/successful Moscow artist. Similarly, the Razin novel rereads the personality of the folk hero and historical personage in terms of the search for *volia*, illuminating an important concept for understanding Shukshin's art and cultural critique. It also revisits and revitalizes the Cossack myth as an artistic and metaphysical ideal. The conclusion returns to the Shukshin legend to explore how it has been reread since 1974, especially during the culture wars that began in 1985.

Like Chekhov, Shukshin saw his task as "to entertain, to stimulate, to respond to public demand with well-crafted stories and plays"[27] (in Shukshin's case, with films). He never lost sight of the fact that he was writing and making movies for a wide audience. As V. Kardin wrote in 1986, "popularity"—

"what people were reading and who they were reading"—was the one category critics consistently neglected in their attempts to classify Soviet Russian literature.[28] Vasilii Shukshin fits this category, in certain ways he *fills* this category, for he was an artist who appealed to virtually all segments of Soviet society: average readers and moviegoers, conservative and liberal critics, dissidents and Party functionaries. As Carl and Ellendea Proffer have noted, Shukshin's "naive (but not phoney) sentimentality accounts for his popularity among such different kinds of readers as Brezhnev and Solzhenitsyn."[29] That Shukshin can be found on both Joseph Brodsky's reading list and that of the Communist politician Gennadii Ziuganov[30] testifies to his power to transcend borders and transmit different messages to different audiences, making him a crucial piece in the puzzle of Soviet Russian culture, high and low.

Chapter One

The Shukshin Legend

> [M]any force fields emanating from the capital
> and from the village intersect in the provinces,
> and the stormy discharges formed in the process
> can turn out to be powerful, dramatic, and
> unanticipated.
> —Anatolii Bocharov, "Counterpoint: The
> Common and the Individual in the Prose of Iuryi
> Trifonov, Vasilii Shukshin, and Valentin
> Rasputin" (translation modified)

LEGEND

Vasilii Shukshin's legacy in Russia is a paradoxical one, as befits those whose fate is explained in terms of legends. On the one hand, his appearance has been hailed as "one of the most significant events in the literary life of the 1960s"; he has been credited with "unexpectedly resurrecting the Chekhov tradition" of the short story in Russian literature; and his legacy was so strongly felt after his premature death in 1974 that the decade of the 1970s passed "under the sign of Shukshin."[1] On the other hand, Shukshin was a "diamond in the rough" who rushed to finish his stories and films, whose works were uneven in quality, and who tramped on social etiquette and literary propriety with oversized rural boots. In posthumous evaluations, Soviet writer Leonid Leonov called Shukshin a "sure and large talent" but likened him to a "big ruby, only very unpolished," while Fedor Abramov complained that many of Shukshin's stories were "written on the fly, in a hurry."[2] The critic Igor' Dedkov captured Shukshin's provocative roughness in a different analogy: "Sometimes it's as if Shukshin is stomping around in blacked boots on sparkling parquet." This, of course, was also part of Shukshin's fascination, as Dedkov acknowledges: "There is a certain anti-literariness, anti-elegance to Shukshin that is almost programmatic, and there is an appropriateness in this."[3] The writer Veniamin Kaverin put it this way: Shukshin "did not slick things down, did not polish, and was awkward and bold. His sincerity was touching, militant, and gentle."[4]

Shukshin's paradoxical appeal—the rough edges of his art that lent it both its freshness and its unevenness—was hard to explain within the traditional categories of Soviet literary criticism. Initially read, according to one critic, as "amusing fables" and the "little études of a dilettante," Shukshin's stories belied attempts to tuck them away neatly into one or the other development or school in Soviet prose. Where this literary phenomenon had come from and where it was going was a question that stymied the critics. Shukshin "not only did not fit into other conceptions, but gradually raised doubts about them merely by his existence in literature."[5] Unsuccessful attempts to look at Shukshin exclusively within the parameters of the literary process of the 1960s and 1970s, debates over Village Prose, or the ethical consequences of the NTR (*nauchno-tekhnicheskaia revoliutsiia,* the scientific-technical revolution) prompted one critic to ask, "Which is to blame for our not being able to subordinate Shukshin to the literary context of the 1960s and 1970s: Shukshin or the context?"[6] Kathleen Parthé explains Shukshin's "virtual absence" from her own book on Village Prose by acknowledging that he "has one of those utterly distinctive voices in literature that defies the efforts of scholars and critics to place it within any other context than its own."[7]

Shukshin's fundamental elusiveness is one reason why I believe that if he is to be classified at all, he should be put in the broad category of "popular artists," where the vagueness of the term accurately reflects the fluid, tripartite identity of its subject. In this regard, the legend of his journey from Siberia to Moscow is attractive because it expresses the paradoxes, enigma, and peculiar charm of the artist and the place he occupies in Soviet culture. The story of how the talented Siberian hick beat the odds and won admission to one of the most prestigious institutes of higher learning in the capital offers a neat explanation of both his rough qualities and his refreshing originality. It speaks to the victory of the individual over the system, the triumph of the ordinary man over the larger powers that seek to categorize and control him.

Traces of the Shukshin legend can be discerned as far back as the ecstatic reviews of his first film, *Zhivet takoi paren'* (*There's This Guy,* 1964), where his successful debut as a director was linked to his previous triumphs as an actor and writer and read as the outcome of the unlikely path he had traveled to become a filmmaker. He was praised as a self-made man: an ordinary Siberian of peasant descent and a latecomer to the world of art who had overcome all obstacles by dint of his will and originality.[8] Shukshin's friend and fellow Siberian writer Iurii Skop expanded on this common perception in 1968 in a well-known article in *Literaturnaia gazeta.* Claiming to be quoting Shukshin, Skop recounts the latter's now legendary appearance in 1954 before the entrance committee at the Institute of Cinematography (VGIK). Shukshin, who for want of better clothes wore his military fatigues at the examination, stood out from his rivals. His unlikely attire and rural accent—the trappings of an ignorant Siberian hick—supposedly inclined the committee to treat him less than seriously. Instead of the usual queries, Shukshin was allegedly asked a series of patronizing, even mocking questions. One committee member, for instance, asked him to show how a Siberian behaves in a bitter frost. Shukshin stomped his feet, patted himself, and shivered but forgot, as his interrogator pointed out, to make his nostrils stick together from the cold. Another supposedly asked Shukshin whether he knew where the nineteenth-century Russian literary critic Vissarion Belinskii was currently living, to which Shukshin answered (in a thick, rural accent): "You mean, the critic? Ain't he already kicked the bucket?"[9]

In Nicholas Galichenko's account of the examination, Shukshin "came looking like a *muzhik*" and shocked the committee by his ignorance of Tolstoy's works. When the committee next asked him whether he had ever heard of the famous nineteenth-century civic poet Nikolai Nekrasov, Shukshin supposedly answered in a rage, "I had a few drinks with him. He was a personal acquaintance."[10] Soviet director Aleksandr Mitta adds in his reminiscences that the committee pleaded with Mikhail Romm, the well-known Soviet filmmaker who led the VGIK studio where Shukshin eventually studied, not to take "this teacher from Siberia" who would only "make trouble for the whole class." Romm ignored their objections and instead asked the applicant whether he had ever read *War and Peace*. "No," Shukshin was said to have answered with a pun, "it's a very thick [*tolstaia*] book." "So," Romm supposedly answered, "you don't like thick books?" "No, *Martin Eden* is a thick one I like. It's a real book." The answer allegedly impressed Romm: "This is undoubtedly a gifted person. Now I'm convinced of it. He's independent—that's a sign of real talent."[11] Aleksandr Pankov retells the legend in this way:

> He played up to the pedagogues, pretended to be some "rube," some naive duffer, a man off the street. Tolstoy? Never read him. Why are you applying? Just because. I saw an ad. And as if throwing in an aside, he cooked up a story about some event that spurred him to walk through the door. The commission listened and didn't realize that the applicant was making everything up as he went along.[12]

In all these accounts, Shukshin's nerve and his ability to "play along" with the committee's patronizing questions were enough to carry the day.

Nearly everyone who mentions some variant of this legend implies that it helps us to understand the writer's personality and his works. Critic Lev Anninskii was the first to view Shukshin's appearance before the entrance committee as an exercise in mutual provocation and improvisation.[13] Those who repeat one or another version of this tale, however, rarely comment on the implications this "creation myth" holds for understanding either Shukshin or his art, nor has careful attention been paid to which account is privileged. Other factors that played a role in Shukshin's acceptance into VGIK—such as the quota guaranteeing a place to a certain number of applicants of rural or proletarian origins[14] or Shukshin's candidate membership in the Communist Party[15]—are ignored as they lie outside the parameters of the legend. The written and oral examinations Shukshin had to pass before being allowed to appear for his final interview also go unmentioned. Instead, a narrative foregrounding the sly peasant who wins over his more cultured urban antagonists by exaggerating the liabilities of his rural background is the version preferred by friends, biographers, and critics alike.

Even Shukshin's own version of this event, first published in 1969, encourages such an interpretation:

> The year was 1954. The entrance examinations were under way at VGIK. My preparation left much to be desired, I wasn't blessed with any special erudition and everything about my appearance evoked perplexity on the part of the entrance committee. [. . .] [Everyone] was stunned by whom Mikhail Il'ich [Romm] had recruited. After all, I noticeably stuck out from the others around me by my Neanderthal backwardness and uncouthness. The chair of the committee asked ironically:
> "Have you heard of Belinskii?"
> "Yes," I said.
> "Where does he live?"
> Everyone in the committee fell silent.
> "Vissarion Grigor'evich? He kicked the bucket," I said and began to prove with unruly fervor how Belinskii had "kicked the bucket."[16]

To speak of self-mythologizing, image creation, or a constructed self may be to overstate the significance of Shukshin's VGIK legend. Nevertheless, Shukshin clearly helped to promote and circulate the story, first in 1968 in Skop's article and then a year later in his own account. It was possibly even these publications that encouraged Aleksandr Mitta to repeat his own version in 1971. Shukshin never commented on Mitta's account nor did he ever refute it. Since then, and particularly after Shukshin's death, the legend has become a commonplace in Shukshiniana.

A legend can be understood in two ways: as a folk story about a real person or as a key to a map. In Shukshin's case, both definitions are applicable. The map in this instance depicts Shukshin's journey to Moscow; the key that tells us how to read this map is the folk tale describing his entrance into film school, which encapsulates some essential truths about the social-cultural environment he sought to enter. The significance of the legend has to do with distance: the geographic, cultural, social, and political distance that lies between Shukshin's early life in the Altai region of Western Siberia and Moscow, where he became famous and spent most of his adult life. While hyperbolic, Shukshin's legend also contains important truths, all tied to this relationship between the center and the periphery and to the issue of mobility between realms. But how do we proceed to read Shukshin's legend without uncritically conflating legend with life and life with art?

In his essay "Literature and Biography" (1923), Formalist critic Boris Tomashevskii argues that biographical legends have value for the reader or the critic only insofar as they possess "literary functions" concomitant to an artist's work. Tomashevskii is concerned with "how the poet's biography operates in the reader's consciousness" (thus affecting reception) and how "the juxtaposition of the texts and the author's biography plays a structural role" in an author's work (thus affecting composition).[17] According to Tomashevskii, the "literary work plays on the potential reality of the author's subjective outpourings and confessions. Thus the biography that is useful to the literary historian is not the author's curriculum vitae or the investigator's account of his life" but "the biographical legend created by the author himself. Only such a legend is a *literary fact*."[18]

The obvious difficulty in Tomashevskii's approach, as Svetlana Boym writes, is how to distinguish between documentary biography and biographical legend. "The documentary facts and the literary facts are co-dependent," she explains. "[T]hey often intrude into one another's territory and blur the frontiers between the poet's 'life' and 'art.'"[19] In Shukshin's case, it is even hard to tell which came first: did the perception of Shukshin's biography in movie and book reviews and his "on-set" interviews give rise to the legend,[20] or did Shukshin himself circulate the legend prior to these reviews? How much is journalistic hype to blame? Why did Skop and Shukshin choose to relate the VGIK story themselves? Was it simply an amusing anecdote, or was it some sort of a game with those who, according to Viktor Gorn, made Shukshin the perpetual target of "gossip" and "humiliating conversations" about how "Neanderthal" he was when he arrived to study in Moscow?[21] These questions complicate our application of Tomashevskii's theory, for in the absence of any further statement from Shukshin on this topic, it is unclear to what extent the artist was actually creating and promoting a legend about his life.

However the legend arose, it had circulated so widely by 1974 that an article surveying Shukshin's career that year in *Novyi mir* criticized both the artist and the critics for mentioning it so often, complaining: "It is surprising how much we love to astound the public's imagination with news about someone's 'simple origins,' as if everyone else were born of counts and privy councillors."[22] At the same time, the article gives us some indication of how Shukshin's creation myth might have affected reception of his works: "In the context of the persistent mention of Shukshin's village roots, he has become in the consciousness of the readers of these interviews the modern variant of the jack-of-all-trades, who will build you a stove, repair your accordion, and then play a tune on it."[23]

The effect of the legend on the reception of Shukshin's works is still felt in critical works about the artist, despite protestations against the "fad"

15

that has arisen of repeating it.[24] Indeed, even those who protest against it seem to fall under its spell. Although critic Gennadii Bocharov complains about the "malicious fables making the rounds about how Shukshin looked as a VGIK applicant, about his clumsy manners," he himself unwittingly contributes to the legend when he admits that Shukshin's "simple and difficult rural life" made the artist "awkward" and "excitable," leading to "explosions" at VGIK (including one fistfight with a policeman).[25] He even offers up a similar fable about how Shukshin looked at VGIK through his inclusion of director Sergei Gerasimov's account of Shukshin's oral exam, complete with Gerasimiov's description of Shukshin's attire: "First he reminded me of a young Fadeev. Even his clothes were the same. A soldier's blouse, belted at the waist, riding breeches. . . . But the fact that he appeared precisely in that attire, with its rural maximalism, so to speak, made a strong impression on all of us."[26]

In a similar way, the assessments by Leonov, Dedkov, and Kaverin cited earlier also betray the influence of the legend. The terms in which they describe Shukshin—"unpolished ruby," "blacked boots on sparkling parquet," "awkward, bold, militant"—are as reminiscent of the main features of his legend as they are of the chief qualities of his heroes, one reason, perhaps, why the VGIK legend, and not the more mundane aspects of Shukshin's vita, is so often highlighted as the key to the artist's personality and works. Life is not as important, or as convenient, as legend.

And yet, while the legend may have affected how Shukshin's works were received by readers and critics, how much the artist was actually influenced by it while writing or making films—thus joining the ranks of artists known for their *zhiznetvorchestvo* (life-creation)—is difficult to know with any exactitude. Unlike the rural peasant Sergei Esenin, it does not appear that Shukshin tried to "play the part of the peasant" in real life, even though, from his institute years on, Shukshin often dressed in the demonstratively un-urban attire central to the story about his VGIK entrance exam, indication perhaps that the rural maximalism it bespoke was more than the colorful costuming of legend.

Leonid Kuravlev, a VGIK classmate who later starred in Shukshin's first two films, recalls how Shukshin stood out from the crowd at film school by his "unusual" and "austere" clothing: "a soldier's blouse, riding breeches, and boots. And this at the film institute of all places!"[27] Cameraman Valerii Ginzburg, who worked with Shukshin on his first three films, remembers how Shukshin arrived at the set of the movie *When the Trees Were Tall* (*Kogda derev'ia byli bol'shimi*) in 1961 wearing a "jacket over a soldier's blouse with his pants tucked into his boots and a cap. . . . I quietly told the head of wardrobe that I liked how they had costumed the actor. I received the following answer: 'We haven't costumed him yet. He came dressed that way.'"[28] Evgenii Lebedev, who starred in Shukshin's third film *Strange Peo-*

ple (*Strannye liudi,* 1969), makes a similar comment: "Looking at Shukshin, you would think you were looking at an electrician, a scaffolder, a lighting technician, any studio worker at all but not an actor and a director."[29]

A comparable confusion existed on location during the filming of *Kalina krasnaia* in 1973, where, according to one observer, Shukshin looked "more like a crew member on location" and a regular "working stiff" than the film's director and lead actor.[30] In these and other instances we can detect what seems to be a carefully preserved split in the artist's identity between the successful urban intellectual that he aspired to become and the provincial "working stiff" that he always kept within him, an at times uneasy coexistence that is reflected in the class consciousness of the Shukshin legend itself. Shukshin's refusal to dress "like a movie director" or "like an actor" was one way of maintaining an allegiance with the common man and a link with the village he left behind.

Here, perhaps, is where we can begin to discern the value of Shukshin's creation myth for understanding the man and his art, for it not only testifies to the provincial complex that plagued Shukshin throughout his life but, more important, suggests how the writer sought to triumph over these complexes through his art. Tomashevskii stresses that legends are useful only when they become "literary facts"—when they function *formally* within a literary work or within an artist's modus operandi. For Shukshin, text and biography meet as literary fact precisely where the writer's class and cultural inferiority complexes become implicated in the poetics and themes of his art. Simply put, the legend helps reveal how Shukshin's provincial complex suggests discursive strategies important for understanding his works; it is these discursive strategies that are the literary fact latent in the legend.

Shukshin emphasizes three things in his legend: difference, distance, and discrowning (in the Bakhtinian sense of "casting down," where all hierarchy is made unstable and top and bottom are inverted). These are the elements that drive Shukshin's art as well. Whether we take Shukshin's story of his entry into VGIK at face value or not, the *artistic strategy* that Shukshin promotes in his accounts—particularly in the version quoted by Skop—is one to which he would return time and time again in his prose and films. In the legend, the "unruly fervor" with which Shukshin proves that Belinskii had "kicked the bucket" lays bare the social and cultural stereotypes being perpetuated. It also reveals an important feature of his art: its polemic with cultural and social hierarchies and its proclivity for unmasking falsehood. In the best tradition of folk buffoonery (*skomoroshestvo*), Shukshin plays the fool, but in so doing he transforms himself from the accused into the accuser. The sly peasant reveals the arrogance of his urban interrogators' questions and thus disarms them. Romm alone understood Shukshin's position. "The whole time Romm kept quiet and listened," says Shukshin.

"His infinitely kind eyes kept looking at me from over his glasses, slightly ironic, slightly smiling."[31]

The legend thus emphasizes the director's eye for spectacle, the actor's talent for role-playing, and the writer's celebration of difference. Shukshin shows his readiness to don the mask of the fool, whose function, according to Bakhtin, is to "see the underside and the falseness of every situation" and to exploit any position he chooses, "but only as a mask."[32] These masks

> grant the right *not* to understand, the right to confuse, to tease, to hyperbolize life; the right to parody others while talking, the right to not be taken literally, not "to be oneself"; the right to live a life in the chronotope of the entr'acte, the chronotope of theatrical space, the right to act life as a comedy and to treat others as actors, the right to rip off masks.[33]

Like Bakhtin's fools and like the writer depicted in the legend, Shukshin's provincial oddballs, eccentrics, and antiheroes exercise their "right to be 'other' in this world, the right not to make common cause with any single one of the existing categories that life makes available."[34] In a similar way, their conflicts—played out in the theatrical space of the Russian domestic *skandal*—reveal the bitter truths about life. This is the heart of the Shukshin legend, and it encapsulates much of the writer's universe: the little people fighting for volitional space against an immutable social hierarchy; the oddballs, fools, and eccentrics who rip off the masks of arrogance, pride, greed, and intolerance; the small rebellions carried out against prejudice and petty injustice; the homespun artists and philosophers who fling down challenges before science, the status quo, and common sense. These are Shukshin's heroes, and they are the reasons Soviet readers turned to his prose, for in the spectacle of his characters' famous rows and rebellions, the truth peeped through.

Shukshin makes this link between folk buffoonery and his own art explicit in his novel about Sten'ka Razin, *I Have Come to Give You Freedom* (*Ia prishel dat' vam voliu,* 1974), where he inserts a variation on his own biographical legend into the text. In the novel, Razin pays a peasant *skomorokh* (a type of Russian medieval jester and folk artist) to impersonate exiled Patriarch Nikon of the Russian Orthodox church, whose "appearance" in Razin's host was designed to increase popular support for the campaign. When Razin asks the *skomorokh* about his origins, we find out that the peasant artist hails from a little village called Shuksha, where, if this legend is to be believed, the name Shukshin supposedly originates, thus linking the *skomorokh* with the writer's distant relatives.[35] The effect is to associate Shukshin—and his art—with the *skomorokh*, who, in a metatextual sense, is both an ideal metaphor for Shukshin's own creative identity as actor, writer, and director and a reflection of the fool/jester from the artist's legend. The truth-telling art of the buffoon-*skomorokh* is thus revealed as a source and inspiration for Shukshin's own, a connection that, for some critics, is the defining feature of his art.[36] Like Shukshin's stories in Soviet times, the ribald, often risqué performances of the *skomorokhi* were at once a celebration of the earthy lives of peasants and an affront to the clerical and ruling classes; they often bore within them the seeds of social critique.[37]

The more we read, the more we find that many of Shukshin's most important characters—Pasha Kolokol'nikov from his first film, "oddball" Vasilii Kniazev from his 1969 film *Strange People,* the tractor driver Ivan Rostorguev from the film *Pechki-lavochki (Peasant Stoves and Benches,* 1972), Ivan the Fool from his novella *Till the Cock Crows Thrice (Do tret'ikh petukhov,* 1974), to name a few—are just such truth-telling fools and eccentrics as the writer in the legend or the *skomorokh* in the novel, in whose apparent self-abasement there hides an accusation. A Shukshin hero, like his creator, is "free and independent by nature": "someone who uses every possible means and all his eccentricities to defend his natural right to be himself, to have his own opinions, and to apply his intelligence and experience to everything under the sun."[38] They are marginalized types, or *kharaktery* (the title of Shukshin's fourth collection of stories, 1973), living on the periphery of society—in the provinces and in Siberia—a fact emphasized by the titles of Shukshin's anthologies: *Sel'skie zhiteli (Country Folk,* 1963), *Tam, vdali (There, in the Distance,* 1968), *Zemliaki (Fellow Countrymen,* 1970). Their difference and distance from urban society help make possible their discrowning of falseness and pretension.

Thus the Shukshin legend, like many legends, becomes a useful narrative for understanding the artist. Indeed, two of his works are even transparent retellings of it. When Ivan the Fool in *Till the Cock Crows Thrice* is sent on a quest not for wisdom but for a *certificate* attesting to his wisdom and then must undergo one trial after another in which his "folk origins" are put to the test before he finally outsmarts the Wise Man holding the key to his pursuit—the ubiquitous bureaucratic seal with which the certificate is to be validated—we sense a thinly veiled commentary on Shukshin's own journey from Siberia to Moscow for just such a "certificate of wisdom." Similarly, in *Pechki-lavochki,* when Ivan Rostorguev and his wife travel on vacation from Siberia to Moscow and then on to the Black Sea, we glimpse an account of Shukshin's own cultural (and geographical) trespassing in their story, for they are made to feel their country backwardness at almost every step of the journey in episodes that are as humorous as they are illustrative of the great cultural and social disparity between the provinces and the center. This conflict between the city and the country—whether in real life, hyperbolized legend, or fictional or filmic account—was the central drama in Shukshin's life and those of millions of transplanted rural dwellers, who came face to face with distrust, condescension, hostility, and prejudice in the big city. Thus the triumph of the "sly peasant" in Shukshin's legend and life (if nowhere else) was a victory for a whole new segment of "insulted and injured" little people in Russian society, an outcome that helps to explain Shukshin's status as a folk hero for some of his admirers.

The power of the Shukshin legend as a literary fact and heuristic construct is perhaps most evident in the reception of his last film. *Kalina krasnaia (Red Kalina Berry*, 1974) was the greatest popular success of Shukshin's career and one of the three all-time box-office hits of the Soviet film industry.[39] It is still recognized as the single work that permanently secured his reputation. Controversial in its themes and a near victim of censorship, the film created a sensation wherever it was shown throughout the nation. It relates the failed attempt of a repeat offender, the thief Egor Prokudin, to give up the fast life and loose morals of his former gang of urban criminals and to reclaim the folk heritage of his rural childhood. A bit of the folk buffoon, Egor is constantly changing masks and mischievously shamming even as he is engaged in a life-and-death search for his true identity. As he tries on one role after another—recidivist thief, village muzhik, man about town, sly rogue, comic clown—he also interrogates to humorous effect a whole host of social stereotypes, only to die a tragic death at the hands of his former gang members.

Shukshin's own sudden death of a heart attack just six months after the film's release only augmented the movie's already strong resonance with audiences. As a shocked nation mourned his unexpected passing, Egor Prokudin's death was reenacted each night on the movie screen. The temptation to view the fate of the film's hero as a foreshadowing of Shukshin's own was great; it even led to speculation that the artist, like his hero, had been similarly beholden to "unsavory types" who did him in. These villains, while not members of a criminal gang, were part of the "cultural mafia" of the capital, who meted out punishments and rewards for artistic orthodoxy and who eventually did away with the *skomorokh* from Siberia for his provincial independence. Here, the Shukshin legend comes full circle, only this time the sly peasant perishes in his clash with the urban guardians of culture.

As Grigori Svirski writes, "It was no accident that his Mafia killed off the leading character in the film he had made just before his death," for Shukshin "himself felt that the vodka-sodden literary Mafia would finish him off eventually."[40] The writer Viktor Nekrasov echoes these sentiments: "Egor Prokudin has left us, murdered by evil people. Vasilii Makarych—Vasia Shukshin to his friends—has left us, too. Who murdered him is not known, but he was murdered."[41] In each instance, the implication is clear: it was the constraints of the Soviet culture industry and the people in charge of it who were to blame for Shukshin's untimely death. Anatolii Gladilin writes that the "fuss and nervous strain, the terrible, intense work" of navigating those constraints and pleasing those people—especially in the movie industry— were more than enough to kill Shukshin.[42]

The murder theory has since grown in proportions. Shukshin's widow, the actress Lidiia Fedoseeva-Shukshina, turned to the tabloid *Ekspress gazeta* in 1996 to publicize her charge that her husband was murdered while acting in Sergei Bondarchuk's film *They Fought for Their Motherland* (*Oni srazhalis' za rodinu,* 1975). She expressed doubt that he really died from a heart attack and hinted at a conspiracy of silence among those who were on location with him. The correspondent for the paper supported the murder theory, couching his support, moreover, in terms of the Shukshin legend: "He had enough enemies. His peers in the art world couldn't forgive the Siberian muzhik in tarpaulin boots for crowding them out, all distinguished, bronzed, venerable laureates. They poisoned Shukshin down through the years."[43]

This part of Shukshin's legend cannot, of course, be proved. It is a fact, however, that *Kalina krasnaia,* more than any other work or event in the writer's life, shaped Shukshin's public biography, especially in the decade of the "Shukshin boom"[44] following his death. The tragic end of Egor Prokudin merged with that of Shukshin, who, like Egor, seemed doomed to die in that nether region between the city and his long-abandoned rural birthplace. The colorful, clowning ex-con, at home neither in the city nor in the countryside, seemed to capture both the rough charm and the ultimate tragedy of Shukshin's own position in Soviet culture. Here, however, we must leave legend behind and turn to the facts of his life.

LIFE

In life as in legend, Shukshin's position between Moscow and Siberia, between the center and the periphery, between the city and the countryside describes an important space for the artist, the space of interrogation, polemic, debate. Shukshin embodies that intersection in the provinces between the capital and the village where Anatolii Bocharov, in the epigraph to this chapter, says "stormy discharges" occur. It is a position at once liberating and frightening, as Shukshin acknowledges in an oft-cited passage from a 1967 essay: "And so it's turned out that, as I turn forty, I am neither entirely urban nor any longer rural. It's a terribly uncomfortable position. It's not even like trying to straddle a fence. It's more like having one foot on shore and the other in a boat. You can't avoid shoving off, but the thought's a little frightening."[45]

The perception of Shukshin torn between Moscow and Siberia was only strengthened by the posthumous publication of interviews done just prior to his death, in which the writer expressed his desire to give up the cinema and return to his home village of Srostki. Of his three muses, he vowed he was going to pick only one—literature—and dedicate himself to it when back in Siberia. "Srostki has long been luring me back. It's even

21

appeared to me in dreams. . . . A writer, in this I am convinced, can exist and move forward only thanks to the power of those life-giving juices with which his native surroundings nourish him."[46]

According to Bocharov,

Shukshin came to "conquer" Moscow and wrapped himself in her rhythm, in her dramas, in her tension. And he himself was torn between his passion for literature and his passion for directing and acting, which speeded up the tempo of his life even more and created psychologically stressful overloads. Thus biographically Shukshin turned out to be a "transitional" figure [*promezhutochnaia figura*].[47]

Or, to offer another translation of Bocharov's epithet, Shukshin was an *intermediary* figure, one who embodied mobility between a variety of realms: geographic (between Siberia and Moscow), political (between periphery and center), demographic (between country and city), social (between peasant and intellectual), artistic (between fiction and film), and cultural (between folk/popular culture and high culture). This mobility was not without its hazards. The move from country to city often resulted in what prominent Soviet demographer V. I. Perevedentsev called the "marginal personality," an individual who is unable to adapt from one environment to the next[48]—the enduring subject of Shukshin's art and a painful fact of his own life.

As we have seen in the writer's legend, many of the borders Shukshin sought to cross were, one might say, closely guarded. Indeed, it is the juxtaposition of these realms and the difficulty of moving between them that make up the living polemic implied in the artist's biographical legend, a polemic that, like the legend, has its origins in the writer's life. Thus the three thousand miles that separate the Altai from Moscow become much more than mere physical distance. It is the distance separating classes, cultures, and creeds as well.[49] If in the legend of his appearance before the exam board Shukshin exaggerated his simple origins, in his VGIK courses he rubbed elbows with "the progeny of highly placed bureaucrats and established cultural figures" who "represented the cream of Soviet society."[50] These were "children of filmmakers, of bureaucrats in the movie industry, of regional government officials and their prestigious higher-ups, of foreign correspondents and the like."[51] VGIK at that time was second only to the Gorky Institute of World Literature in its reputation as a center of the Soviet intellectual and social elite.[52] Shukshin, with his rural accent, spotty education, and Siberian peasant heritage, had to have felt woefully out of his element, even as he made light of his liabilities. In a 1954 letter home he writes:

We had a poll in class not long ago about who our parents were, i.e., the professions and education of the students' parents.

Almost everyone's are writers, actors, executives and so on. My turn comes. They ask: which of your parents is still alive?

I answer: my mother.

"What kind of education does she have?"

"Two grades," I answer. "But she understands no less than a government minister."

Laughter.[53]

Masked by this laughter and Shukshin's provocation of it is the writer's inferiority complex. Shukshin's very presence in VGIK spoke to the issue of access in Soviet society: access to power and the possibilities for success and social advancement. He stood as an embodiment of the backwardness and powerlessness of the provinces. At the age of twenty-five, he was not only older than his fellow classmates but was noticeably behind them in education. He lacked social grace and social connections. He also had to suffer the condescending attitude of many of his peers, who considered him no more than a "hick" with natural talent and by no means their equal. Aleksandr Sarantsev, Shukshin's friend from his VGIK days, offers the following insight:

[This] conflict with that kind of people, with everything they represented in life, came to light very early in his career, probably even before VGIK. It's absolutely clear that in VGIK, from his very first class, probably from the time he set foot on the stairways of this institute, the conflict became acute once and for all, became socially and ethically fully realized. There is no Shukshin—writer, actor, and director—outside this conflict.[54]

Exacerbating Shukshin's provincial complex was the fact that he was the son of "an enemy of the people." His father was executed during Stalin's rural purges in 1933, either for "sabotage in the kolkhoz" or for "inciting an uprising."[55] These facts changed Shukshin's life and engendered an identity crisis that the writer would never quite overcome, a crisis made all the more acute by his mother Maria Sergeevna's decision to renounce, for the sake of her family, her husband's name, taking her maiden name, Popova, after her husband's arrest. Thus, until he turned sixteen and applied for his internal passport, Shukshin was Vasilii Makarovich Popov. The name appears conspicuously in an autobiographical cycle of stories which the writer worked on from 1968 until his death six years later. In "From the Childhood Years of Ivan Popov," the first-person narrator refers to himself and his sister as *vrazheniata*, "children of the enemy." Thus, it is likely that the inferiority complex that marked Shukshin's entrance into the world of letters was not only a result of the physical, cultural, and social distance between Siberia and Moscow; it was also a corollary of the pall of "illegitimacy" under which Shukshin grew up and lived as a son of an "enemy of the people." Although Shukshin's father was posthumously rehabilitated in 1956, the marginalization the writer experienced during the first twenty-seven years of his life continued to find expression in his short stories and novels, where Makar Shukshin makes his shadowy appearance in fathers who rebel against the new Soviet order (in Book One of Shukshin's novel *The Liubavin Family*), fathers who leave for the camps and certain death (Book Two of *The Liu-bavin Family*), fathers who return from the camps (Shukshin's story "Priez-zhii" ["The New Arrival"]), and even in the seventeenth-century Cossack *bat'ka* (father) Stepan Razin (in the story "Sten'ka Razin" and the novel *I Have Come to Give You Freedom*). The father theme—part of the broader polemic between center and periphery that informs Shukshin's life and works—has yet to be seriously mined for its obvious contribution to the Shukshin legend.

Shukshin's realization of the great distance separating him from the other VGIK students can be detected in a paper he wrote as part of the entrance process.[56] The essay was supposed to describe the corridors of the institute during exam week. Shukshin chose instead to paint what one critic calls "a rather caustic portrait" of the elitist Muscovite kids who had an "insider's" familiarity with the world of cinema and of the institute.[57] In his essay, he addressed an issue that would resonate throughout his creative career, not only the genuine social dichotomy he observed at VGIK but also the subtler juxtaposition of cultural values he witnessed around him. What was born in the disparity between the heritage of Shukshin's *malaia rodina* (native region) and the background of his urban competitors was more than just a goading sense of inferiority and embarrassment. It gave birth to his unique artistic diction as well, which was markedly different from the smooth talk of his fellow VGIK applicants. This idiom had its roots in the folk dialects of the Altai and stood in stark contrast to the "cultured" but affected words that, according to Shukshin's essay, "sprinkled like peas" from the lips of his dormitory roommates. Shukshin's recognition of his native artistic diction, however, did not come quickly:

> I was ashamed of my rural dialect, the words I was used to but that no one spoke here. And, in order not to stick out, I even tried for a while to relearn how to speak and to express myself just like all the well-read, educated Moscow kids.
>
> I remember this agonizing period. My own self-ridicule, my own shame that I was mutilating, mangling my thought because I was mangling my words. And when I had gotten through this awful school of speaking in an alien tongue, I hated both myself and others who did the same thing. And for the rest of my life I hated any affected manner of expression.[58]

The differences between the substandard dialect and culture of his Siberian village and the language and culture of the Moscow intellectual and social elite forced upon Shukshin the status of the "other," the outsider, an identity Shukshin would make good use of as an artist but one that would also take its toll on the writer. Leonid Kuravlev described Shukshin's early years in the capital in the following way:

Not too long ago a critic wrote that at first Shukshin felt himself to be a pariah at VGIK, which was true.

It seemed to him that people here were from some other sphere than he, a native of the village of Srostki in the Altai. That his very appearance at VGIK had introduced a loud dissonance into some sort of long-established traditions. That he represented an outsider.

He clearly sensed all of this, without a doubt. Hence his shyness—to the point of sickness and tremors.[59]

This dissonance, however, was encouraged by Romm in his VGIK studio, whose star pupil was the future director Andrei Tarkovsky. Tarkovsky, born into an old intelligentsia family, was one of the bright and talented Moscow dandies who very likely set Shukshin's teeth on edge at their first meeting in Romm's studio.[60] According to Romm, Tarkovsky and Shukshin were "a direct antithesis to each other and didn't like each other very well," a situation, however, which was "very useful to the studio. . . . Many talented people grouped themselves around them. Not around them, I'll say, but thanks to their presence."[61] As Neia Zorkaia comments, Tarkovsky and Shukshin "presented two sides of the artistic Russian character, two poles of the national talent, one contributing sophisticated means of expression and the other a genuine folk spirit and close links to the people."[62]

Shukshin's rivalry with Tarkovsky confirms the polemical aspect of his development as an artist. The difference between Shukshin's "genuine folk spirit" and the sophisticated artistry of Tarkovsky and other VGIK students fanned the fire in which Shukshin forged his artistic identity. It was at VGIK that Shukshin understood and fully appreciated the folk culture he knew from his life in the village. His use of simple, dialectal turns of speech belonging to his own Siberian family and neighbors allowed him, in one critic's assessment, "to reintroduce into Russian letters a variety of style unknown since the formulation of the tenets of socialist realism in the early 1930s."[63] Linguistically, Shukshin and his texts remained in the provinces.

The feeling of provinciality, and the sense of inferiority and insecurity that accompanied it, haunted the writer throughout his brief career. In 1974, when Shukshin looked back on his years at VGIK, he admitted that he had come to the institute

a profoundly provincial person remote from art. It seemed to me that this was apparent to everyone. I had come too late to the institute—at twenty-five both my learning and my knowledge were relative. I had a hard time studying. Extremely hard. I accumulated knowledge in piecemeal fashion and with gaps. Besides that, I had to find out what everybody already knew and what I had passed over in life. And after a while I began to hide, I guess, my growing strength. And, strange as it may seem, in some twisted and unexpected way, I would arouse in others the certainty that, yes, they were the ones who should be artists, and not me. But I knew, knew beforehand, that I would lie in wait for the moment when . . . well, when I would turn out to be more solid, and they, with their endless pronouncements about art, would turn out to be less so. All the time I concealed within me from the eyes of others an unknown person, some sort of secret warrior, an undeciphered person.

"Just imagine," he concluded, "it's sort of a stupid thing, but it always seems to me that they should refuse me this—my right to be an artist."[64] To realize that Shukshin said this at the height of his popularity—after the spectacular success of *Kalina krasnaia*—tells us a great deal about the depth of his provincial complex.

According to Boris Pankin, "This is the complex of a first-generation intellectual who took off in one gigantic stride to the peaks of creativity, so that he can't quite believe, appearances to the contrary, that it is he."[65] Although the intellectual circles in which Shukshin moved in Moscow refined and educated him to a degree, we can see traces of this complex in the sometimes rough, self-conscious, aggressive tone of Shukshin's stories and essays. A certain rudeness, impertinence, and audacity seem to lurk just beneath the surface of the writer's personality, a desire to provoke others and to do away with polite fictions. The poet Bella Akhmadulina remembers how unsociable and quiet Shukshin was in the apartments of Moscow intellectuals in the mid-1960s. He would sit "somber and shy, not responding to polite inquiries . . . his untame, willful gaze flashing from time to time while dirty snow melted in puddles around his boots." These knee-high rural boots, Akhmadulina explains, were not the only footwear he happened to own but rather were "a sign, a confirmation of his moral and geographic allegiance, a declaration of his disdain for other customs and conventions."[66]

Akhmadulina exaggerates this disdain. What Shukshin and his rural boots advocate is difference, the right to be "other." Like so many of his characters and like the legend that developed about him, Shukshin was a bit of a village eccentric capable of odd actions and acts of rebellion. It is hardly surprising that the misadventures of the hero of Shukshin's story "Oddball" are based on episodes from his own life,[67] or that Shukshin should use his own birthday (July 25) as the date of Bronka Pupkov's incredible attempt on Hitler's life (in his story "Mille Pardons, Madame!") or of Venia Ziablitskii's "incarceration" of his mother-in-law in an outhouse ("My Son-in-Law Stole a Truckload of Wood!"). He clearly felt a strong kinship with the elemental village types who populate his stories, the folk artists and homespun philosophers who are, in Kathleen Parthé's succinct assessment, "peasants with the nervous systems of intellectuals."[68] Such was Shukshin himself, now brawling with the police,[69] now convincing an airport authority to let him and a reporter stand in for no-show flight attendants so that they could make their final connection on a trip back to Siberia.[70]

The Russian root *chud* (from *chudik*) in the title of Shukshin's story "Oddball" denotes both wonder and strangeness, and captures an important aspect of Shukshin's characters and the world they inhabit: they are quirky provincials who—to borrow from the French postmodernists—advocate "local, varied, heterogeneous 'difference' against the unifying, identity-obsessed practices of the massive states and bureaucracies."[71] While the center/periphery dynamic in this case is that of the political "distance" between Moscow and Siberia, in a more general sense this battle of difference is played out in smaller contexts, where the geographic and the demographic on the one hand and the social and cultural on the other often become conflated in Shukshin's art (and in the criticism surrounding it) with the urban/rural conflict. His heroes—like those of writer Mikhail Zoshchenko, to whom he is sometimes compared—are yesterday's peasants who are still learning to speak and act like people do in the newspapers, on the radio, and on television, in short, like city dwellers. His stories—like those of writer Andrei Platonov—chronicle how this linguistic and cultural transformation (engendered by political changes, urbanization, and the bureaucratization of all spheres of life) can distort human personalities and lead to bitter misunderstandings and explosive clashes.

In this context, the geography that informs Shukshin's life and art is not one tied to ethnically or ecologically specific features. As Anatolii Bocharov puts it, Shukshin "assimilated the provinces artistically."[72] Unlike the Village Prose writers, he did not counterpose Soviet Russia to Old Russia, but to Siberia, the provinces, the periphery. Moreover, the Siberian village of his stories—largely devoid of ethnographic description—is an oddly abstract place. Rather than being the preserve of rural traditions or the site of historical events, Shukshin's village represents the space of public spectacle, *skandal*, and debate on a host of issues, all safely distanced from the centers of power.

Most important, Shukshin returns this theater and this debate to the people, the common folk, both in his focus on the everyday—family squabbles, nasty store clerks, petty neighbors, eccentric dreamers—and through his thoroughly colloquial language. Dedkov writes that Shukshin's "authorial style is very often hardly distinct from the medium of the oral narrator, from the genuine intonations and lexicon of the third-class rail car, the *zavalinka*, or the front porch."[73] The effect is to restore the value of these places as the site of cultural debate, where the cultural and subcultural structures of control and resistance can evolve and be explored. Shukshin's media are perfectly suited for this task and for his popular audience: short stories ("probably the shortest in contemporary Soviet literature")[74] published not only in thick, literary monthlies but in daily and weekly newspapers as well, in addition to movies marked by straightforward narration and a simple cinematic language.

For Shukshin as an artist, the provinces had many attractions and many liabilities. His literal and literary movement between Moscow and Siberia testifies to the mobility the artist won for himself, yet in the end it also led to a certain feeling of homelessness and an abiding inferiority complex. Shukshin's negotiation of the distance separating himself from his peers in the world of art rightfully stands at the center of the writer's legend. It is also very likely a major source for the writer's talk about an "unknown, undeciphered" alter ego. This "other person" that Shukshin kept buried within appears to be a direct outcome of what one critic claims was Shukshin's desire "to preserve for himself the right to a certain amount of provincial 'autonomy.'"[75] As we have seen, it is this provincial autonomy—what Gerasimov called his "rural maximalism"—that emerges as the lesson of the Shukshin legend and suggests the important issues of his artistic program, his provincial polemic. The difficult task for Shukshin—one he would grapple with throughout his creative career—was preserving the provincial autonomy of his artistic program while still cultivating acceptance by the cultural establishment. How Shukshin navigated the difficult aesthetic path between rural maximalism and urban sophistication is the subject of the next chapter.

Chapter Two

The Actor and the Writer

> It's necessary that the person created in the end
> is both me and you. Get it? Then I'm an artist.
> —Vasilii Shukshin, "O See the Horses Gallop in
> the Fields"
>
> One person can never find complete fullness in
> himself alone.
> —Mikhail Bakhtin, *Problems of Dostoevsky's
> Poetics*

ONE OF THE FASCINATING ASPECTS about
Shukshin's aesthetic is that it managed to unite so successfully elements of
the oral folk culture of his childhood village with the art of the cinema. Indeed, as we have seen, even the notion of an artist who is writer, actor, and
director in one derives, ultimately, from those same oral traditions, dating
back to and including the time of the wandering folk performers known as
the *skomorokhi*. As it turns out, in his singular achievement as an artist in
three fields, Shukshin was but carrying on a tradition of popular synthesis
in the arts whose roots lie deep in the Russian folk imagination, a fact that
helps to explain part of the charm of the artist's creative persona.

For Shukshin, the benefits of a tripartite creative identity were immediate. The recognition he gained as an actor helped draw attention to the films
he directed and the stories he wrote; moreover, the films he directed enabled him to bring his own stories to the screen and thus to a larger audience.
It is even difficult to speak of Shukshin's cinematography outside of the world
of his fiction, an outcome that did not always bode well for his film career.
His first three movies, all based on his short stories, betray their literary origins and their director's relative indifference to matters of cinematic form.
Only in his last two movies can we discuss Shukshin first as a filmmaker and
second as a writer. Shukshin was aware of this fact, limiting his achievements in cinema to *Pechki-lavochki* and *Kalina krasnaia*, the only two films
originally conceived and written for the screen. "All the others," he noted
in 1974, "were just part of mastering the craft, were just part of surviving."[1]

But Shukshin's unique synthesis of fiction and film was a far greater
asset than liability and accounts for his legacy in both worlds. His movies

were popular because of their simple vernacular, with an emphasis on content over form,[2] and their lyrical realism.[3] His dynamic, dialogue-driven stories—with all of the movement of the cinema—helped to revitalize the Russian short story. Shukshin summarized this synthesis in 1973:

> I began to write under the influence of the cinema and to make films under the influence of literature. In my stories, novellas, and novels I almost never write: the hero thought this or that. I rarely lapse into description and make little use of authorial asides. More than anything else I rely on character action and dialogue. I don't like the verbose, weighty tomes we frequently feed readers.
>
> As for literature's influence on my films, it apparently has to do with how I rarely go the way of so-called pure cinematography. Long, endless takes, silent scenes which, for all their apparent significance, often lack any idea, the "penetrating," but unexpressive looks of mute heroes—all of this doesn't, as a rule, attract me.[4]

Shukshin discussed the link between his aesthetic synthesis of fiction and film and the village culture of his youth shortly before his death. In a posthumously published interview, he talked about the storytellers he remembered from his rural childhood, including his mother, who wove their stories and tall tales in their spare time or during breaks from work in the fields. Shukshin traced his own aesthetic to these *narodnye rasskazchiki* (folk or popular storytellers), whose art combines the same three facets of his own creative persona. According to Shukshin:

> The folk storyteller is *both a playwright and an actor, or, more likely, a whole theater in one person.* He composes the situation, plays the parts of all the characters, and comments on the action. Moreover, even if the narrator takes it into his head to lay out some concrete, real-life happening, then this real fact also is told in a very vivid, rich way, undergoing the most incredible coloring—to the point of hyperbolic acuteness and deft fibbing.[5]

In other words, for Shukshin the story is primarily an orally transmitted genre and involves a teller and a listener, a relationship in which the writer becomes not so much a *pisatel'* (one who writes) but a *rasskazchik* (one who tells). Storytelling in this context becomes performative, and the storyteller assumes the role of the orchestrator of the performance. Character dialogue occupies a central place in the story's poetics, and character type becomes the dominant factor of its plot, as Shukshin indicates in a working note. "Plot? Plot is character type. If you have the same situation but two different people in that situation, you'll get two different stories: one about one thing, another about something else entirely."[6]

Shukshin once explained his working definition of a short story with the following example:

A man was walking down the street, spied an acquaintance, and told him, for example, about how around the corner an old woman had crashed on the sidewalk and how some lanky fellow had howled in laughter. And then right away became ashamed of his foolish laugh, went up, and helped the old woman to her feet. And then looked around to see whether anyone had notice how he'd laughed. That's it.[7]

"[I]t is often not understood," he concluded, "that a writer (a storyteller) is an ordinary person, the same person who met a friend on the street and wanted to tell him some incident or other from his life."[8] It is here, in the notion of the story as an exchange between two people, that we can trace the persistent inclination in Shukshin's prose toward the speech of the other and its predisposition toward oral speech. Here also are where the informal qualities of Shukshin's dialogues originate, their "spontaneity" and "immediacy," all of which point to the "presence of the storyteller."[9] Shukshin's frequent "parceling" of his text and use of dialect also indicate his affinities with the oral tale.[10] As one critic asserts, "Shukshin addresses his reader, calling on him to take part in a dialogue."[11]

This need for dialogic contact with the "other"—the listener, reader, viewer—is an essential part of Shukshin's, and the folk storyteller's, art. "I personally see art not as an experiment," Shukshin stated in an interview, "but primarily as the opportunity for an essential conversation."[12] In speaking of his film *Strange People* as a failure, Shukshin twice lamented, "The conversation with the viewer did not take place."[13] Plot, too, is nothing more than "a reason for a profound conversation."[14] The value of art lies not merely in its formal qualities but chiefly in its ability to provide the artist and his audience with a pretext for dialogue. Successful works lead to essential conversations; unsuccessful works are dialogic dead ends. The frequency with which character speech comprises the titles of Shukshin's stories, projecting beyond the text proper,[15] underscores the urgency with which the writer initiates contact with his readers. It seems that he establishes his "conversation" even before the reader begins the story.

The emphasis Shukshin places on this contact helps to explain his laconic style, one aimed at reducing the distance between himself and his interlocutor in order to make as direct a connection as possible. Like the folk storyteller, Shukshin did not waste his breath or his listeners' time on superfluous details. His openings are as brief as they are evocative. "There was a fight in the village café. Here's how it was" (1:514). "Venia Ziablitskii, a small man, high-strung and rash, had a knock-down, drag-out fight at home with his wife and mother-in-law" (2:110). "The blacksmith Filipp Nasedkin—a calm man, well respected in the village, a no-questions-asked worker—suddenly took to drink" (1:477). "Pimokat Valikov took his new neighbors, the Grebenshikovs, to court. Here's how it was" (1:452). "Something like that meant you had to make up your mind once and for all. So he did" (1:395). "Everyone said that Serega Bezmenov had a nasty wife. Nasty, capricious, and foolish" (2:141). "It all began with Monia Kvasov's reading in some book that the perpetual-motion machine was an impossibility" (2:230). "This is the story of how gangly, intense, four-eyed Mikhail Aleksandrovich Egorov, Ph.D., almost got married" (2:398). "Ivan Petin's wife left him. And how she did it! Just like in one of those old-fashioned novels: she ran off with an officer" (1:334).

Conciseness, however, was never meant to substitute for a rich style, as Shukshin himself was quick to point out: "Simple and accessible form doesn't mean cheerless and gray."[16] The work of art, after all, had to be compelling enough to attract and keep an audience. The first criterion for any successful storyteller is, obviously, to be interesting. "I don't know what 'telegraphic style' is," Shukshin writes, "but I do know what a boring story is. You have to be interesting. That is everything."[17]

In his essay "How I Understand the Short Story," Shukshin states that the "laws by which good films and stories are made are the same." "The main thing," he writes, "is motion"; accordingly, a story is good if it "by some miracle has preserved this motion, has not destroyed life but somehow 'transplanted' it, unharmed, into the reader's consciousness."[18] Cinema, of course, is nothing if not motion. As a director, actor, and scenarist, Shukshin could not escape this truth, and it significantly influenced the way he wrote. Indeed, Shukshin's first apprenticeship as a writer took place at VGIK, in the context of his cinema training. In his first years in Romm's studio, Shukshin completed one writing assignment after another, assignments that eventually led to his first publications.[19] To capture motion in words, however, required a writing style that was dynamic and laconic. Shukshin's solution was to rely heavily on dialogue to propel his narratives. Indeed, no other Soviet writer comes close to using so much dialogue in his prose.

"The problem of economy—not only of time, but of energy (the reader's and the movie viewer's)—looms large before the artist," Shukshin told an interviewer. Romm, using Pushkin as an example, oriented his students toward such economy. "He taught us that being laconic is essential both in literature and film," Shukshin stated. He added: "Laconicism is dictated by life itself, which today is chock-full of knowledge, information, news."[20]

In the same interview, Shukshin confesses: "It seems to me that [today's] reader is just about to put down the book, because he's in such a hurry. . . . What a mad pace! The time of quiet evenings by the hearth has irretrievably passed. Nowadays you can't get away with weighty descriptions, there's no time to read them. You have to abridge yourself."[21] But, according to Shukshin, this does not mean the writer has to be less expressive. He points to Hemingway, Pil'niak, and Babel' as proof that fewer words can be more effective. "It seems to me," Shukshin states, "that our literature, in its tendency toward descriptiveness, has retreated from the positions it won in the 1920s and 1930s."[22]

Shukshin remembered how completely the storytellers of his childhood bewitched their audiences, creating the sensation that the teller—and the audience—took part in the tales themselves. Improvisation and a keen sense for the right word were paramount. "You could listen to them forever," Shukshin wrote. "It was like witchcraft. . . . Here is where the ardent, living, sensitive power of the word is." This power, though, lay not in complex literary (or cinematic) experimentation, but in "naked simplicity": "I don't think that any other 'systems of verbal art' except 'naked simplicity' could work that well," Shukshin declared.[23] The "rich speech, inventiveness, [and] unexpected narrative devices" of the folk storyteller "were not ends in themselves," he stated. "The folk master of the story never 'indulged' in an unexpected device or sharp word only to show off his own ability. And no matter how he adorned his story with verbal or thespian ornamentation, he would never go too far." The concerns of the folk storyteller were always channeled toward one goal: "to touch the reader to the quick as forcefully as possible."[24]

Many of Shukshin's protagonists suffer a similar need for dialogic contact. "Free spirits emoting without control, laughing with drink and weeping with strangers,"[25] they, too, seek out essential conversations with others. Nor is it surprising that a good number of them are likewise folk storytellers of a sort or folk artists whose art becomes their medium for communion with others. In this regard, Bron'ka Pupkov from "Mille Pardons, Madame!" ("Mil' pardon, madam!") is perhaps Shukshin's ultimate folk storyteller. The outlandish tale of his mission to assassinate Hitler is replete with unbelievable details (Hitler's close proximity to enemy lines, Bron'ka's "fluent" German, and the Browning with both poisonous and explosive bullets in it), yet it nevertheless touches and enthralls his listeners. In the film version from *Strange People,* Shukshin demonstratively emphasizes Bron'ka's role as a storyteller. In what has become a set study piece for Russian film students, Bron'ka tells his story by means of a long monologue, during which the camera—after scanning the listening faces of the assembled hunters—settles on Bron'ka alone. In rejecting an earlier idea to illustrate Bron'ka's story with actors (complete with dwarves playing the part of Hitler's generals),[26] Shukshin entrusts all of the scene's drama—and absurdity—to Bron'ka himself, who convinces the movie audience of his tall tale as much as he convinces the hunters. It is the film's most innovative moment.

Other master storytellers include San'ka Zhuravlev from "A Version" ("Versiia"), whose wild tale of three decadent nights in the city with a restaurant manager makes him a hero in the village, and Egor from "How the Bunny Went for a Balloon Ride" ("Kak zaika letal na vozdushnykh sharikakh"), who flies all the way from Siberia so he can tell a fairy tale to his sick niece. Grin'ka Maliugin, Van'ka Tepliashin, and Oddball from the stories that bear their names, Semen Malafeikin in "General Malafeikin," and Uncle Emel'ian in "Strangers" ("Chuzhie") all tell tall tales of one sort or another as well; they may do so to amuse or impress others, but they are always hoping to find in their interlocutors' response understanding and camaraderie.

Folk art has always fulfilled this kind of communal function. In "All by Themselves" ("Odni") Antip's balalaika playing inspires a heart-to-heart conversation between himself and his wife. Kol'ka's accordion playing in "Meditations" ("Dumy") not only helps him win his girl but sweetly torments kolkhoz chairman Matvei Riazantsev with memories of his youth and premonitions of his death. "Oddball" Vasilii Kniazev tries to make up with his sister-in-law by painting her baby carriage with folk motifs. Vaseka's need to do something for his fellow villagers in "Sten'ka Razin" finds release in his wood sculptures, including one depicting the betrayal of the famous rebel leader by his Cossack brethren. Arkashka Kebin from "Dancing Shiva" ("Tantsuiushchii Shiva") and Kol'ka Piratov in "A Wife Saw Her Husband Off to Paris" ("Zhena muzha v Parizh provozhala") use their consummate folk dancing to commune with others. Their dancing is at once entertainment for others and a personal symbol of some higher meaning in life. For Arkashka it represents a "free form of free existence in our material age" (1:518); Kol'ka, on the other hand, "works out, through dance, some personal, hidden, bitter pain" in his life (2:99). In both cases, dance promotes deeper contact between performer and audience.

Certainly, such communion with the audience was crucial to Shukshin himself, who did not stand on principle where those conversations took place. Rather than let a story rejected by major literary journals go unread, Shukshin would turn to provincial journals, newspapers, and literary weeklies as outlets. He was less concerned with the political allegiances of the venue in which his stories appeared than with getting his work out in a form true to his intent. His early publications in the conservative journal *Oktiabr'*, for instance, gave way to a long association with the liberal *Novyi mir,* mainly because *Novyi mir* was more prestigious and censored his works less stringently than *Oktiabr'*, and only partly because *Novyi mir* appealed to his own progressive side. But even *Novyi mir* limited the amount of dialectal and substandard elements in Shukshin's stories and refused to publish either of the writer's novels.[27]

For the same reasons, Shukshin switched from Gorky Film Studios to Mosfilm in 1973, because the former had failed to approve Shukshin's long-standing request to shoot a film on Stepan Razin, which Mosfilm promised to support. This switch was typical of the artist's restlessness, his impatience with the constraints of the culture industry in the USSR. His need "to get through" to his audience with as little delay (that is, as little editorial meddling) as possible even put some of the critics on their guard. As Igor' Dedkov remembers, "It began to seem that he was being published everywhere and far too often, and this was even troubling: wasn't he rushing things, being too generous, relaxing his own standards?"[28] In a similar way, Shukshin was criticized for his numerous interviews, criticism which he took to heart. After a review in the March 1974 issue of *Novyi mir* scolded him for giving too many interviews, he began categorically to refuse such requests from journalists.[29] These frequent interviews, however, serve as further confirmation of Shukshin's strong desire to engage the public in dialogue, and by an even more direct means than stories and films.

Whether we are discussing Shukshin as writer, actor, or director, his notion of the artist as interlocutor has important repercussions for his poetics, for it admits participation by the other party into the "conversation." For Shukshin, this participation goes beyond the mere aesthetic pleasure the reader or viewer derives from the text or film and takes place in the creative process itself. "The artist, when he creates, unconsciously tries to find among his viewers, readers, and listeners people like himself," he wrote, "and that is why, perhaps, any self-absorbed affectation or art for the sake of form is fruitless and artificial."[30] In Shukshin's view, the attempt to be artful often ends in artificiality; a work of art created outside of anticipated response or dialogue with another is in danger of being sterile, one-sided, monologic.

Here Shukshin's views of artistic creation distinctly intersect those of Mikhail Bakhtin, whose theoretical writings on dialogic art can help us understand Shukshin's approach. Indeed, Bakhtin's notion of art as dialogue and of the artist as interlocutor, and his insistence that this relationship between artist and audience begins as early as the creative act itself, are ideally suited to an investigation of Shukshin's own artistic approach in which a similar relationship between addressor and addressee is explored. What for Bakhtin is a core model for the interrelation between all artists and their audiences is for Shukshin a paradigm for his interaction with readers and viewers and an affirmation of the profoundly popular nature of his artistic program.

Bakhtin's theory of speech genres implicates speaker, utterance, and interlocutor in an important dialogic relationship that reveals the complex interaction among all three elements in the formation and development of style, genre, and canon. Ultimately, Bakhtin explores how "authoritative utterances" (in literature, journalism, and technical prose) arise, are perpetuated, reconstructed, and renewed through a process of reaccentuation carried on by speakers, writers, artists, and their interlocutors. In Shukshin's case, Bakhtin's ideas shed light on the artist's own dialogic relationship with his audience and suggest how this interaction conditioned his art and helped shape his influence in post-Stalinist film and literature.

For Bakhtin, every utterance—whether primary and simple (such as daily conversations, letters, greetings) or secondary and complex (such as fiction, scientific writing, poetry, reports)—is "shaped and developed in continuous and constant interaction with others' individual utterances. This experience can be characterized to some degree as the process of *assimilation*—more or less creative—of others' words."[31] Our speech—oral or written, pragmatic or artistic—is filled with varying degrees of our own and others' expressions. Among these expressions are authoritative utterances which "set the tone" "in each epoch, in each social circle," including those of the world of art. These utterances are the "artistic, scientific, and journalistic works on which one relies, to which one refers, which are cited, imitated, and followed."[32] According to Bakhtin, we assimilate, rework, and reaccentuate these utterances in our own way every time we speak, a process that takes place in the simplest of exchanges between individuals but which is particularly revealing and important when artists speak to their audience. Whether I am conversing with a neighbor or writing for a reader, I must always

> take into account the apperceptive background of the addressee's perception of my speech: the extent to which he is familiar with the situation, whether he has special knowledge of the given cultural area of communication, his views and convictions, his prejudices (from my viewpoint), his sympathies and antipathies—because all this will determine his active responsive understanding of my utterance. These considerations also determine my choice of a genre for my utterance, my choice of compositional devices, and, finally, my choice of language vehicles, that is, the *style* of my utterance.[33]

The interlocutor, the audience for whom a work is intended, can thus exert an enormous influence on the utterance. Depending on the intended result, a speaker can employ a style and genre that suit, are discordant to, polemicize with, mock, or even offend the expectations of his interlocutor. Indeed, Bakhtin argues, this choice is one way in which authoritative utterances are challenged and changed. Artists, in particular, define themselves and their work by how they assimilate or reaccentuate the dominant speech genres of their specific medium (literature, poetry, drama, film) or genre (novel, short story, elegy, epic, comedy, tragedy). This process determines how they distinguish themselves from the works of predecessors, from other works of the same school, or from the works of opposing schools.[34]

Shukshin had firsthand experience assimilating speech genres and reaccentuating authoritative utterances. His initial embarrassment at the film institute over his rural dialect and his shunning of village idiom when speaking to Moscow classmates taught him an important lesson about the relationship between the form of an utterance and its addressee. The clash of discourses that he felt the moment he crossed the threshold of the film institute became the crucible in which his own notions of language and style were formed. It comes as no surprise, then, that his aesthetic should be especially sensitive to this issue.

When Shukshin saturated his character dialogue with rural colloquialisms, dialectal elements, substandard forms, and vulgarisms, he was sending two messages: one to his popular readers and viewers and one to the cultural establishment. The first message signaled his trustworthiness to his audience, his knowledge of the worldview of his characters and their daily lives. It said, "I speak your language, I understand your lives. The style of my utterance vouches for its content." The second message marked his artistic innovation and linguistic "disobedience." On the one hand, it reintroduced "real speech" into post-Stalinist Russian literature, playing an "important role" in the "linguistic processes characteristic of fiction of the 1960s and 1970s in general and Village Prose in particular."[35] On the other hand, it polemicized with various clichés—bureaucratic, journalistic, belletristic— and opposed the "depersonalized, standardized language of the prose of the 1940s and 1950s, which was subject to harsh prohibitionary norms."[36]

The style and language of Shukshin's utterances were new to Russian readers of the 1960s. Unlike the slang and urban colloquialisms of the heroes of Youth Prose or the highly idiomatic folk language of the Village Prose protagonists with their regional dialects, Shukshin's characters' speech reflected the parlance of the lower and middle classes of Soviet society. It was a rural speech that was becoming urbanized. In this respect he resembles the Soviet writer Mikhail Zoshchenko, whose stories featured as characters and narrators peasants "in a state of transition toward urban mass culture" who spoke a hodgepodge of "newspaper jargon, foreign words, often distorted and imperfectly understood, and 'officialese'" and whose language thus also deviated from the literary norm.[37] Yet Shukshin differs from Zoshchenko in two important ways. First, while Shukshin's narrator (especially at the beginning of a story) may "speak" in his own voice ("There was a fight in the village café. Here's how it was" [1:514]), his is a much less chatty and intrusive narrator than Zoshchenko's, whose *skaz* technique exploited the indirect discourse (*erlebte Rede*) of a narrator distanced from the author and possessing a distinctive authorial voice. Shukshin's narrator was never as involved—or as outrageous—as Zoshchenko's. Second, and most important, Zoshchenko's character parlance is highly stylized. As Edward J. Brown argues, "No one has ever spoken the language of Zoshchenko's heroes. It is an invented speech made up of newspaper rhetoric, the pronouncements of Stalin and other heroes, misunderstood fragments of Marx or Engels, all mixed up in a weird linguistic brew and laced with the catchwords of popular prejudice." His narrator—neither the "Soviet man in the street" nor "a representative of the Soviet lower middle class or any other social group"—is a mere mask through which Zoshchenko speaks to the reader.[38]

Shukshin's peasants, on the contrary, spoke an authentic and believable idiom, whether in character speech or shared narrational discourse. One review likens its rhythm and intonation to the language of "a break room on some construction site or a truck-stop café."[39] It is conversational and earthy: as profane as Soviet censors would allow and more vulgar than some critics could tolerate, even in posthumous evaluations written under the influence of the Shukshin boom. One critic complained: "The language of his heroes is at times oversaturated with salty expressions, vulgarisms, and in places out-and-out naturalism. . . . [A]t times he overstepped the bounds of good taste."[40] Another lamented that Shukshin focused on the cruder aspects of his characters' speech to the exclusion of other, presumably "nicer," folk expressions.[41] Vladimir Korobov summarizes the main criticism as follows: "Shukshin's style is uneven in places, his heroes speak coarsely and use vulgar words, his editors should have corrected more."[42] This love-hate relationship with the language of Shukshin's characters emerged early and can be detected in the differing critical reactions to the writer's first two books, his collection of short stories *Country Folk* and his first novel, Book One of *The Liubavin Family*, published in 1965 but written at the same time as the stories.

    Country Folk attracted nearly universal praise for its author's command of authentic character speech. Its protagonists were admired for "speaking in their own language,"[43] one of "rich dialectisms and intricately individualized (but convincing) verbal forms."[44] These were no actor's lines assigned to stock characters, as Shukshin makes clear in "The Actor Fedor Grai" ("Artist Fedor Grai"), where an amateur village actor refuses to parrot the clichéd lines of a formula play. His heroes talked like real people: informally, not always correctly, expressively, laconically. Even in Shukshin's less successful works—such as his otherwise unremarkable debut in print, "Dvoe na telege" ("Two on a Cart") from 1958;[45] the O. Henry-esque "Doiar" ("The Milker");[46] or the highly schematic "Pravda" ("The Truth") and "Lelia Selezneva s fakul'teta zhurnalistiki" ("Lelia Selezneva from the Journalism Department")—the dialogues shine. Shukshin's ear for natural-sounding speech was his greatest asset, a fact he confirms in a working note: "I know when I'm writing well: when I write and it's as if the pen is extracting living human voices from the paper."[47]

    Shukshin's "living human voices" were among the greatest attractions of his prose and its chief stylistic innovation. Throughout his career, however, he was nevertheless subject to the puritanical standards of editors and censors still conditioned by the restrictions on literary parlance enforced during Stalin's reign. When he overstepped the bounds of linguistic propriety, he was asked to rewrite. But even when he managed to see the language deformations of his Siberian protagonists safely into print, he was still taken to task by critics who viewed deviation too far from the literary norm as a sign of bad form. Paradoxically, the same dialectal character speech praised in *Country Folk* was censured in *The Liubavin Family*. The eminent Soviet linguist V. V. Vinogradov scolded the aspiring novelist for the "dialectal-naturalistic style" of the speech of his Siberian characters,[48] implicating the novel and its style in an ongoing debate over language taking place on the pages of *Literaturnaia gazeta*.[49] The deviations from standard Russian, coming from the lips of the book's gloomy and harsh kulak heroes, were simply less charming than those same deformations in the speech of the rural characters in his short stories.[50]

Shukshin understood that his style and language would not suit all of his possible interlocutors. "There's this 'cultured' woman in my home village who's always so indignant: 'Nothing but swearing! And he calls himself a writer!' My mother doesn't know where to look out of shame."[51] But Shukshin's typical addressees were not these types of readers, and his contribution to Russian literature was not one of refinement and gracefulness. His was a different kind of utterance aimed at a different kind of interlocutor and with his own reaccentuation of authoritative forms in mind. As V. Serdiuchenko writes, the "Shukshin phenomenon" lay in his answering the reader's "deep need for extraliterary authenticity." Like Gogol' and Dostoevsky, Shukshin came to literature "from below," and that made it "easier for him to violate the canons and rules of the literary game." He "decisively democratized the language, hero, and genre. It is as if he removed from the literary superstructure elegant literariness." Indeed, Shukshin's success, according to Serdiuchenko, was "guaranteed" in a society where the "consumer of art" was not the "reading public" of the educated upper classes (as in the nineteenth century) but the "multi-million reading masses" of the Soviet period.[52]

Shukshin's unadorned, everyday vernacular was part of a larger polemic in Russian literature of the 1960s and 1970s between informal or familiar styles and the petrified, so-called neutral styles that had been canonized during the Stalin years. Indeed, this struggle against stylistic "normalization" makes up the dialogizing background against which almost all Soviet writing of this period must be viewed. For Bakhtin, the role of lower forms is particularly important in this process of developing new styles from the ashes of discredited ones. He writes, "[W]hen the task was to destroy traditional official styles and world views that had faded and become conventional, familiar styles became very significant in literature. Moreover, familiarization of styles opened literature up to layers of language that had previously been under speech constraint."[53] This is one reason why Shukshin's prose played such an important role in the development of Russian fiction after Stalin. Along with a handful of other writers, Shukshin sought a clear-cut renewal of the "correct" literary language of the 1940s and 1950s, which, "had entered too narrow a channel of stereotyped, popularized, middlebrow writing."[54]

Viktor Shklovskii, writing in 1923, speaks of a similar phenomenon, the "law of canonization of lower genres," in which popular or subliterary genres are assimilated into literature and gain "legitimacy" or are "canonized." Like Bakhtin, Shklovskii views literary evolution not in terms of the replacement of one style by another but of the "gradual canonization" of new, lower forms of popular art.[55] Galina Belaia, applying Bakhtin's ideas, credits Shukshin with a significant role in stimulating these changes in the post-Stalinist period.[56]

Shukshin valued popular diction not only for its innovativeness but because it best served "the simple and accessible form of the story," which should be told in such a way that the "reader absolutely understands everything."[57] "Real people" were always his most important judges. "Real people are intimidating critics because each of them filters art through his own, ever unique life experience, and in the collision with this real life experience, the clichéd thinking of the artist is laid bare. I don't fear professional critics—they have their own clichés."[58]

For Shukshin the influence of his addressees extended beyond that exerted by their anticipated response or actual reactions to his artistic utterances. His interlocutors also played a different kind of "co-authorship" role, a kind of joint creation that Shukshin learned as an actor and a director. Shukshin's aim was not so much to get the reader to "read between the lines" in a political sense but to spare the writer the need to indulge in empty verbiage:

> For some reason, when a writer-storyteller sits down to write about "an old lady," he will, as sure as rain, tell us who she was before she was seventeen years old. But it's clear to the reader without such digressions that she had been a girl or a young woman. Or he'll take two pages to tell us what a nice morning it was the day the old lady fell down. But if he simply said: "It was a fine morning, it was warm," the reader would probably remember a morning like that in his own life—warm, autumnal. After all, it's probably impossible to write if you don't keep in mind that the reader himself will "write in" a lot.[59]

Shukshin's frequent lack of description or authorial commentary allows the reader, in Wolfgang Iser's reader-response formula, to "fill up the blanks" of the text (and make value judgments about it) as his own life experience dictates.[60] Not only does this manner of writing allow Shukshin to be laconic, but it also invites the reader's participation in the text, albeit on a limited basis. Here, Shukshin is close in practice to the father of the Russian short story, Anton Chekhov, who admitted: "When I write, I rely fully on the reader, presuming that he himself will add the subjective elements missing in my story."[61] Like Chekhov, Shukshin eschewed authorial omnipotence and the kinds of background information about characters that would prejudice them in the mind of the reader. This principle of Chekhov's and Shukshin's art helps to democratize the text, so that no one voice—either the characters' or author's—dominates.

For Shukshin, a valuable exchange between author and reader takes place. The author presents his story to the reader; the reader, in turn, validates that story for his own life and the cultural life of his country. In such a relationship, the reception of art becomes every bit as important as its transmission, for it contributes to the broader transmission of that art and eventually can secure for it a place in posterity. Shukshin offers us an example from the cinema. The mark of a good film, he claims, is when the moviegoer "sits in the theater not simply as a viewer, but as a participant." This participation occurs when the viewer's "life experience" and memory of "people, personalities and events [. . .] begin to actively penetrate that other life, which is unfolding on screen," and the viewer measures its veracity against the reality of his own life.[62] The tension created by this constant dialectic between fiction and truth produces a synthesis in the minds of Shukshin's "interlocutors," an event in which the work of art becomes a part of an individual's life and fate and thereby enters into that of the country as well. As Shukshin says in a working note, "A work of art is when something *happens:* in a nation, to a person, in your fate."[63]

Shukshin applied his notion of the artist as interlocutor and the listener as co-author to his directing and acting as well. As a film director, he invited his actors to share the role of the storyteller, accepting them as co-authors and encouraging them to improvise, knowing they would not "distort the text."[64] For Shukshin, the movie scenario was just an "operations manual,"[65] a pretext for the improvisation of the actor and the director. He strongly believed, as did the folk storyteller,[66] that not only art but also truth is born in improvisation. And, as far as Shukshin was concerned, when it came to the truth, "any means are good"; therefore, he cried, "more improvisation!"[67] In the end, Shukshin concludes, "what in art isn't improvisation?"[68] The amount of improvisation in Shukshin's movies was sometimes so great that he confessed he had to rewrite scripts (to match the movies) before he published them in book form.[69]

"The art of directing," Shukshin states, "consists in how [the director] creates around the actor a micro-climate of respect so that the actor doesn't feel shyness, awkwardness, or the need to follow any formerly prescribed intonations."[70] These criteria also guided Shukshin's acting style. He once spoke of his special relationship with director Sergei Bondarchuk while shooting the film *They Fought for Their Motherland* (*Oni srazhalis' za rodinu*, 1975). Bondarchuk, according to Shukshin, was "tuned in" to his performance, provoking him toward greater "freedom, buffoonery, decisiveness, mischievousness, improvisation—any and everything. To put it simply," Shukshin concluded, "he liberated me."[71] Acting thus involves a dual synthesis: that of director and actor and that of actor and role. While a clear hierarchy is observed (director over actor and actor over role), the result is nevertheless synthetic. The aspiring actor in Shukshin's autobiographical story "O See the Horses Gallop in the Fields" ("I razygralis' zhe koni v pole") explains this relationship well: "It's necessary that the person created in the end is both me and you. Get it? Then I'm an artist" (1:188).

This synthesis between actor and role also helps to explain the important relationship between author and fictional persona. As in his acting roles, Shukshin often creates characters who are "both me and you," merging in varying degrees authorial and character discourse. Critics often complained that it is hard to tell the difference between the voice of Shukshin's heroes and that of the writer.[72] This fact is often attributed to Shukshin's work as an actor: "That the author seemingly 'hides behind' his heroes is linked to the fact that Shukshin's stories are by nature very theatrical and suitable for the stage."[73] At times this effect was a target for sharp criticism. In a 1969 review, Alla Marchenko dismissed Shukshin's "premature and overrated success" as a short-story writer as no more than thespian sleight of hand, claiming that the "colorful Siberian types" in his prose attract us only until we realize that what we are reading is "just the naturalness of a talented actor demonstrating his mastery of metamorphosis."[74] Two other critics sounded a similar cautionary note in a later review, pointing out how some of Shukshin's stories seem to be no more than improvisations on acting assignments.[75]

For most critics, the main difficulty associated with Shukshin's dialogue-driven stories was determining to what extent the author's voice orchestrated the whole chorus or sang along with the few or the select. As the author of a teacher's guide to Shukshin's works puts it, "It is necessary that the students sense where the author's voice is heard and where those of his heroes resound. Without this, it is difficult to understand the content of Shukshin's stories."[76] This is the crux of the matter for critics wishing to find the monologic, authoritative tone of the author. And yet, the beauty of Shukshin's prose is that the author's voice is not always the authoritative one. While his "actor's prose" might have lapsed at times into mere role-playing, it also allowed the author to play out a variety of positions, testing a multiplicity of truths. Moreover, the dominant voices and authoritative viewpoints of some of Shukshin's works were not always those of the author or even of characters that appealed to him. On the contrary, Shukshin often privileged the discourse of controversial if not altogether unattractive or "negative" characters. Yet even in these instances a subtle blending of authorial and character discourse is detectable. What the writer Iurii Olesha says is true of all writers is particularly pertinent to Shukshin: "It is impossible to describe a third person without becoming, if only for one minute, that third person. All the vices and all the virtues live in the artist."[77]

For Shukshin, becoming the other person as an actor or an author was one way to reveal "all the vices and all the virtues." He did so by merging with the part yet remaining in control of it. In a working note Shukshin

42

makes this point explicit for both actors and writers: "They praise an actor for living his part, for being 'completely in his role.' And yet this is bad! You have to be above the role. Like an author over his material."[78]

This essential truth about acting and writing, and the implied kinship between the two endeavors, bring us back to the figure of the folk storyteller. Actor and author in one person, the folk storyteller embodies the intersection of authorial and character speech and the complicated relationship between direct and indirect discourse. As author and director of the performance, he manipulates and controls character discourse, but as an actor, his voice joins that of the character, creating an unstable situation in which it is not always possible to determine when character and author are dialogic equals and when characters are simply playing predetermined roles. Here Shukshin's discourse types shift between represented discourse (what Bakhtin calls single-voiced words, where a character's speech is reported as if it were his own) and nonobjectified discourse (Bakhtin's double-voiced words, where the author's voice and that of the character coincide). In the latter instance, the character's voice either agrees with the author (so-called passive double-voicedness) or resists him (active double-voicedness).[79] All of these discourse types can be detected in Shukshin's works—indeed, they account for much of his attractive subtlety and ambiguity—but all of them originate and inhere in the theater of the folk storyteller and the oral tale. It is here, in the live interaction of teller, tale, and audience, that these relationships evolved and took shape in the first place.

In the end, Shukshin could hardly have picked a more apt representative of his tripartite creative identity than the folk storyteller, who personifies the dialogic nature of the artist's work, not only explaining the interaction among actor, writer, and director but also illuminating the essential relationship between artist and other, whether that other is an addressee or a character. Not only is his art driven by dialogue, but it is at its core dialogic, depending on response, affirmation, refutation, and comprehension. This is undoubtedly one reason why Shukshin's stories and films are so appealing, for they capture the unfinalizable nature of ordinary conversations and, like the best conversations, always seem open for further discussion.

Chapter Three

Shukshin's Bright Souls

> But I've got a soul, too. My soul also wants to
> kick up its heels and have a little fun.
> —Vasilii Shukshin, "All by Themselves"

VASILII SHUKSHIN ENTERED Russian culture as the creator—in word and film—of a character type who went by many names: *takoi paren'* (this guy), *chudik* (oddball), *khmyr'* (crank), *debil* (retard), *upornyi* (stubborn), *psikhopat* (psychopath), *suraz* (bastard), *zaletnyi* (transient), *shizia* (schizo), *priezzhii* (new arrival), *kharakter* (type). And with these provocative epithets, these *strannye liudi* (strange people) came to be recognized as "a sign of the times,"[1] the spokesmen for people displaced by history, social change, and their own restless natures. They occupy a unique chronotope in Russian literature and Soviet history: the *time* of dramatic demographic changes after World War II, when a large segment of the rural population began to migrate from the countryside to the urban centers and the face of the villages was being changed forever; and the *space* between the village and the city which these uprooted people sought in various ways to negotiate, in which they are figuratively or literally adrift.

It was at the intersection of these two axes that the drama of Shukshin's life took place and the central conflict of his art unfolded. Although the postwar years were marked by great demographic changes, this migration from village to city came at a time when, according to historian Zhores Medvedev, there existed "legal discrimination against the rural population which prevented *kolkhozniki* and *sovkhoz* workers from having internal passports, leaving the villages, or changing their jobs without the permission of the rural Soviets," due to a 1932 law intended to keep peasants in the village after collectivization. It was "fear of the irreversible loss of the right to an internal passport (which in legal terms meant the loss of freedom to travel within the Soviet Union)" that prompted many rural youths—including Shukshin himself in 1947—to leave the village when they finished school or reached the passport age of sixteen rather than to commit to a passportless life in the village, an outcome that "produced the very reverse of what had been intended" and that "militated against the rejuvenation of the rural working population."[2]

Thus Shukshin's chronotope reflects one of the most important problems of Soviet social history. In the chronotope, as Bakhtin notes, "space becomes charged and responsive to the movements of time, plot and history."[3] It takes on meaning and an importance that go beyond the mere notion of intervening expanses. For Shukshin and the characters he describes, the distance from the village to the city was a space highly charged by differences in class, culture, language, worldview, technology, standard of living, quality of life, and freedom of movement. As one of the writer's village innocents puts it during a visit to Leningrad: "The city's a helluva a lot closer to Communism than our mother, the village" (2:84).

These differences alienated Shukshin's heroes, turning them into oddballs and transients. This is why there were as many "strange people" who never left the village as there were those who did, and quite a few whose estrangement manifested itself when they traveled in the opposite direction, from city to village. Whether this distance is traversed by plane (as in the four-hour flight between Novosibirsk and Moscow in the story "Sel'skie zhiteli" ["Country Folk"]) or by bus (as in "Van'ka Tepliashin"), the gap between the city and the village cannot be crossed without weighty consequences. So remote and seemingly unattainable was life in the city—with the notoriously difficult-to-obtain *propiska*, or residency permit, guarding its sacred portals— that making the move was as improbable and extraordinary for most villagers as stepping through the looking glass. Indeed, in Shukshin's story "A Version," the villager San'ka Zhuravlev's incredible three days in the city begin only after he walks through, and breaks, a glass dividing wall in a restaurant. The allusion to Lewis Carroll is unmistakable—like Alice, San'ka experiences a fantastic world where all the norms of his life in the village no longer apply.

But Shukshin's hero was not always estranged, nor were his conflicts initially fraught with such drama. On the contrary, his appearance in the early 1960s was at first hailed as a welcome alternative to some of the less-than-positive heroes of post-Stalinist literature, such as Iurii Kazakov's meditative loners, the unheroic protagonists of the Thaw stories of Vladimir Tendriakov, Viktor Nekrasov, and Iurii Nagibin, or the iconoclasts of Youth Prose. Shukshin's characters seemed a happy amalgam of both the best and least controversial features of these new post-Stalinist heroes. They were the "bright souls" of the village (*svetlye dushi*, the title of one of Shukshin's earliest stories), provincial innocents who spoke a colorful country idiom and whose conflicts remained (for the time being, anyway) at the level of humorous rural anecdotes told concisely and skillfully. Among these early heroes we can read about the truck driver who returns home from a long haul but who cannot tear himself away from his vehicle, sneaking out to work under the hood on a bright moonlit night wearing nothing but his underwear ("Svetlye dushi"); or the village blacksmith who wins a prize for his performance in a local play after he substitutes his own words for the clichéd lines given to his "simple" village character ("Artist Fedor Grai"); or the driver who employs the traditional village matchmaking ritual in order to win the hand of a city girl ("Stepkina liubov'" ["Stepan in Love"]); or the driver who saves a gas station from a burning truck not out of heroism but out of "fool-hardiness" ("Grin'ka Maliugin"); or Granny Malania, who is afraid to fly to Moscow to visit her son after a local know-it-all scares her with tales of what can go wrong during the flight ("Sel'skie zhiteli").

Shukshin's vibrant and compelling early portraits shared a common origin with those of other Thaw writers: they were part of a larger reaction to the aesthetic and thematic straitjacket that had been imposed on writers and artists during the period of high Stalinism. After Stalin's death, the response in the world of art to the "cult of personality" led to the rediscovery, exploration, and relegitimization of personality in general—personality without quotation marks. Literature and cinema of this time were marked by a return to greater diversity in character types, psychological complexity, and the acknowledgment of a private life outside of the *kollektiv,* which had not been the case in much of Soviet fiction and film between 1934 and 1953, when the themes, heroes, and styles of literature and art were supposed to conform to the tenets of Socialist Realism. The overzealous application of these guidelines led to the creation of literature and cinema suffering from a variety of ailments, including the "varnishing of reality," in which life was painted in bright colors and given a glossy finish in order to accentuate the successes of Soviet rule; the depiction of reality to conform to current Soviet socialist policy; and "conflictlessness," in which a stigma was attached to portraying any negative aspects of Soviet actuality. Heroes were invariably positive and politically correct; enemies were clearly defined, condemned, and defeated. The literary language became highly standardized, so that by the 1950s the concept of "literariness" had narrowed to the point of bland "neutrality,"[4] with characters and authors speaking the language of journalists. Deviations from these perceived norms of artistic depiction—for example, showing an interest in problems of form or in moral and psychological issues—were denounced as "cosmopolitanism," a blanket term for cultural aberrations.

Shukshin's appearance on the cultural scene coincided with the discrediting of these Stalinist cultural policies, but this process of literary reform was neither fully embraced nor fully carried out by the cultural establishment. Different camps formed over the issue, and a struggle between conservative Stalinists and liberal revisionists ensued that spanned the decade of the Thaw (1953–63), with each side alternately gaining and giving ground, championing various artists, heroes, and movements, and debating the issues from the pages of partisan journals and newspapers. This debate—though in muted and more circumspect form—continued throughout the

Brezhnev period as well, and Shukshin's name was frequently dragged into the polemics. He had the dubious distinction of being at various times "everybody's favorite,"[5] a tribute to his wide appeal but an indication as well of his essential ideological and artistic autonomy.

This autonomy asserted itself as early in Shukshin's acting career as his first film, *The Two Fedors* (*Dva Fedora*, 1959, directed by Marlen Khutsiev). A typical Thaw-era film, *The Two Fedors* was controversial only in the way that other Thaw works were controversial: it showed a relatively undoctored reality. Based on a story by Sergei Antonov, *The Two Fedors* depicts the return from the front lines of a soldier who has lost his family in the war. He befriends an orphaned boy who turns out to have the same first name and eventually finds in him a substitute family. Although sentimental and predictable, the film's emphasis on the unremarkable, day-to-day aspects of postwar life and its neorealist cinematography struck many critics and viewers—who had been nurtured on more heroic depictions of war themes— as "impertinence and daring" on the part of the director, who was required to explain his naturalism.[6] Like Khutsiev, Shukshin challenged cinematic norms with what one critic calls "the unconventionality of his depiction of a positive hero," in this case, Big Fedor. According to L. Belova, "In Shukshin, everything—his physique, his gait, his manner of speaking—contradicted the sterility of cinema conditioning. He didn't have a 'neutral,' 'announcer's' voice, but his own particular voice, with a touch of a dialect, one you could not confuse with anyone else's."[7]

This unconventional depiction of a positive hero was the secret appeal of Shukshin's early protagonists as well. They were unconventional positive heroes; that is, they were colorful and diverting, but still optimistic and affirmative and hence noncontroversial. In short, they were "bright" (*svetlye*), an epithet that conjures up the promised *svetloe budushchee* (radiant future) of Communism. This clearly was not the intended effect, but it captures quite well part of the attraction of Shukshin's early heroes for conservative critics in particular. When Shukshin's stories started appearing on the pages of literary journals and newspapers (one in 1958, three more in 1961, eleven in 1962), these bright souls seemed to offer a promising variation on the positive hero in Soviet literature.

At a time when the heroes of Youth Prose were driving conservative critics to distraction, Shukshin appeared with modest sketches about a new and nonthreatening young hero whose unconventionality was (so far) limited to minor language deformation and an occasional independent streak. His heroes were working people, mainly young men, often uneducated, or students from the village living in the city for the first time, or perhaps small boys growing up in the countryside. These were not the self-assured smartalecks or ironic students so often met with on the pages of the influential journal *Iunost'*, around which a new generation of liberal writers rallied.

Indeed, Shukshin's heroes were often pointedly undereducated, somewhat coarse village jesters. But neither were they the more controversial type of rural rustic populating stories by the new Village Prose writers (Gavril' Troepolskii, Efim Dorosh, Vladimir Soloukhin, Fedor Abramov), who, in their tradition-based world outlook and skepticism about Soviet agricultural policy, implicitly challenged Soviet class mythology.

Shukshin's heroes, on the contrary, were generally truck drivers, engineers, mechanics, and tractor drivers, occupations relatively new to the village. They were mobile, technically inclined young men, in step with the newly mechanized collective farms and the rapidly modernizing villages. As one critic noted, in their hands "you'll sooner see a crankshaft than traditional oven prongs or a yoke for buckets."[8] They were direct, simple folk, capable of an almost maudlin sentimentality but just as likely to fly off the handle over a trifle. Though their restless impulses and elemental natures could lead to trouble (in later stories, even to prison), for the most part this emotional makeup reflected their rootless lives adrift between the village and the city. These are characters who are stuck between the hardworking, sacrificing generation of their rural parents and the new, better-off, acquisitive segment of the rapidly urbanizing postwar populace.

Shukshin's hero was innovative mainly in his unapologetic simplicity, ordinariness, and the almost provocative foregrounding of his lower-class origins. He was a product of the writer's own class consciousness—his desire to tweak the sensibilities of his urban rivals—and he exemplified what Anninskii describes as Shukshin's ability "to go against the grain." According to the critic, when irony was popular, Shukshin exhibited an artless simplicity. In contrast to the lyricism and introspection of the "confessional prose" of the Kazakov school of writing, Shukshin cultivated a "painstaking asceticism."[9] His "orientation on the everyday and on the emotional world of the typical rural laborer was polemical," A. Klitko writes, "because it promoted a different scale of values," one distinctly unlike that of the Youth or Village Prose writers.[10]

The hope among some critics was that Shukshin might prove to be a spokesman for a more conservative hero, one who would combine the lively presentation of Youth Prose and the rural setting of Village Prose with a more orthodox ideology. Vsevolod Kochetov, the editor of the conservative journal *Oktiabr'* from 1961 to 1973, particularly hoped to discover in Shukshin a champion for literary orthodoxy. He was responsible for publishing seven of Shukshin's earliest stories (all of which were included in the writer's first collection) and named him one of the journal's regular contributors in 1962,[11] adding the young writer to his arsenal of weapons in *Oktiabr'*'s unrelenting struggle against liberal tendencies in post-Stalin Soviet literature. But Kochetov's hopes turned out to be misplaced, for in 1963 the author "defected" to begin what would become a long association with *Oktiabr'*'s rival, *Novyi mir*, a relationship that ended only with the ouster of its editor, Aleksandr Tvardovskii, in February 1970. Shukshin's "betrayal" of the conservative literary camp, however, was not soon forgotten by its members, who were responsible for much of the criticism leveled at the artist and his heroes throughout the 1960s.[12]

Shukshin's first collection was well received by liberal and conservative journals alike, a testimony to the writer's ability to bridge literary camps and a sign of his charmed entrance into the world of letters. Although many of the stories from *Country Folk* (1963) were later dismissed as the imitative efforts of a still immature author,[13] the collection as a whole anticipates much of the artist's program, both its polemic and its future drama: a hero and a theme had been found. If these characters differ from the much-celebrated *chudik* or eccentric who was the writer's hallmark in the second half of the 1960s, there is still an innocence and idealism to them that would never quite disappear from even the harshest and most hardened of his later heroes (for example, the recidivist thief Egor Prokudin from *Kalina krasnaia*). While it is too soon to call the hero in his first anthology a "poet," as Petr Vail' would later do in describing Shukshin's protagonists,[14] there is nevertheless something distinctly poetic about their lives and their outlooks. The story "Bright Souls" is a case in point.

"Bright Souls" introduces one of Shukshin's favorite character types, the village truck driver. Mikhailo Bespalov has been on the road for a week and a half. Instead of immediately going in to see his wife, the first thing he does when he returns home is climb under his vehicle to have a look at the engine. His wife, Anna, takes offense. She spends the rest of the evening competing with the truck for her husband's affections, only to catch him twice sneaking away for a quick look at the carburetor. Anna's anger, though, is only halfhearted; she knows Mikhailo loves her, and indeed he is as affectionate as his nature allows. The story is permeated by the radiance of their simple love. Mikhailo himself is not without his own poetic sensibility. Twice in the middle of the night he makes exclamations of awe at the enormity of the summer night sky, likening it to a glittering fairy tale. The story closes on his second such whispered admiration.

For all of its saccharine qualities, the ending of "Bright Souls" illustrates a typical feature of Shukshin's hero: his ability to be amazed by creation, by the larger order around him. The hero of Shukshin's tale is capable of distinguishing between the material and the spiritual, hence the epithet Shukshin gives him. He is a soul (*dusha*) first and foremost. This feature of his personality explains his ability to elevate even an interest in carburetors to the level of the spiritual and marks Mikhailo's kinship with Shukshin's other soulful protagonists, those who carefully examine their lives and live for more than just their daily bread. While Anna frets over investing in a winter coat for herself, her husband responds abstractly, his mind drifting

49

back to his engine. Rubles and kopecks do not concern him, a sure sign in Shukshin's universe of the spiritual, of the poet within, for all of the writer's artistic types hold money in contempt. Indeed, protagonists who are overly concerned with money are invariably treated negatively. Wives and book-keepers in particular are especially charged symbols of a materialistic attitude toward life in Shukshin's universe, with all of the excesses of conspicuous consumption that such an outlook breeds.[15]

Mikhailo's "bright soul" is glimpsed in other characters from *Country Folk* as well, such as Vaseka from "Sten'ka Razin." Vaseka is a young man incapable of holding down a regular job who spends his free time making sculptures out of wood, including one of the legendary Cossack of the story's title. He despises money, stuffing what wages he earns carelessly into his pocket and turning them over to his mother upon arriving home. His mother, at a loss for what to do with him, at one point convinces him to train as a bookkeeper, a respectable profession in the village. But Vaseka lasts only four days; his artistic temperament will simply not allow him to spend all of his time counting money.

Shukshin goes to some length to emphasize the antimaterialistic na-ture of his characters' personalities, using bookkeeping and accountants as foils for his heroes in two other stories in the collection, "The Bookkeeper's Nephew" ("Plemiannik glavbukha") and "Stepan in Love." In the latter story, a bookkeeper competes with the story's hero for the affections of a visiting teacher. The hero, Stepan, is another "bright soul": like Mikhailo Bespalov, he is a simple truck driver who is as acutely sensitive to deep feeling as he is incapable of expressing it. In this instance, Stepan falls hopelessly in love with the village's new teacher, to whom he gave a lift in his truck and who impresses him with her performance in an amateur theatrical production. Although he has never spoken to her about his love, he naively relies on the village tradition of *svatovstvo,* or matchmaking, to make his feelings known. The bookkeeper, on the other hand, is smug and sure of himself, and even tells Stepan and his father that they are too late: although he has not pro-posed to the teacher yet, he is sure the outcome is a foregone conclusion. It is not. Here, again, the spiritual triumphs over the material, as the match-making ritual exposes the bookkeeper's calculating nature while revealing the earnestness of Stepan's love.[16] The bookkeeper retreats in disgrace.

Mikhailo is but the first of many characters in Shukshin's works who live for their souls. When Mikhailo's wife jokingly threatens to put a match to his beloved truck, she brings to mind a much more serious incident from "All by Themselves" in which another "bright soul" is contrasted to his more materialistic wife. There, during an argument with her husband, Antip, over his balalaika playing (which keeps him from his job making harnesses and thus from earning more money), penny-pinching Marfa throws Antip's bal-alaika in the fire.

Antip turned white as a ghost and stood and watched it burn. The balalaika burst right into flame, just like a piece of birch bark. It began to buckle. . . . Three times it let out an almost human moan—that was its strings snapping—and then died. Antip went outside to fetch an ax and then chopped all the half-finished horse collars, all the harnesses, saddles, and bridles, into bits. He chopped them up without saying a word, neatly. At his workbench. The terrified Marfa didn't make a peep. After that, Antip drank for a week, not once putting in a single appearance at home. Then he came home, hung a new balalaika on the wall, and sat down to work. (1:164)

Shukshin's point is clear: it is not important whether trucks or balalaikas are at the center of his character's world; what is important is that these objects stand for more than mere worldly possessions and speak to the spiritual sides of his heroes' personalities. As Antip says in "All by Themselves," "But I've got a soul, too. My soul also wants to kick up its heels and have a little fun" (1:163). This is Vaseka's quandary in "Sten'ka Razin": he cannot hold a regular job because "there is no soul" in that kind of work (1:32).

Thus "Bright Souls," "All by Themselves," and "Sten'ka Razin" are early treatments of important issues that recur throughout Shukshin's works. They also partly explain the writer's peculiar kind of misogyny. Since wives (or mothers) are often in charge of the household finances, they frequently are associated with the world of accounts and balances, of acquisitions and material well-being. They are thus antithetical to the intangible dreams and lyrical obsessions of their husbands, and indeed often stand in their way.[17] The consequence, as Lyndall Morgan points out, is that women—mainly wives—are frequently depicted in a way that emphasizes "the absence of non-temporal values" in them. "For them daily concerns are paramount and in fact are so vital that spiritual values and strivings are as interesting as last week's borshch."[18] Wives in Shukshin's prose are therefore invariably marked negatively and appear mainly in order to emphasize through contrast the bright souls and eccentricities of their husbands. Indeed, the theme of wives arguing with their husbands over money for coats recurs conspicuously in stories published long after "Bright Souls": "The Microscope" (1969), "My Son-in-Law Stole a Truckload of Wood!" (1971), and "Nighttime in the Boiler Room" (1974). In each instance, the conflict is the same, that of greedy wives opposing their dreamy husbands.

The conflicts in *Country Folk*, however, rarely rise to the level of the *skandaly* at the center of so many of Shukshin's mature works. By and large, the carpenters, mechanics, drivers, and collective farm chairmen of these stories confront the usual villains—dissembling or incompetent administrators, petty and insincere people—with predictable results. Indeed, at times the radiance of these bright souls takes on the shape of a halo, as in "The Truth," "Lelia Selezneva from the Journalism Department," and "The Sun, an Old Man, and a Girl." While Shukshin included very few of these early stories in later collections, *Country Folk* does establish several important themes. Besides showcasing the common spiritual makeup of his heroes, Shukshin also introduces other important future commonplaces of his prose: the estrangement between the city and the country, often expressed in the opposition of Moscow to Siberia; the search for a holiday in life; and the quest for some sort of liberation, understood both literally and metaphorically.

The opening lines of the initial story in the anthology, "Distant Winter Evenings" ("Dalekie zimnie vechera"), introduces the first theme: that of the juxtaposition—sometimes slight, sometimes pronounced—between Moscow and Siberia, which recurs in many of his literary works and films.

> February 1942.
> Just outside Moscow, heavy battles are being fought.
> But on the outskirts of a distant Siberian village, a rowdy band of kids has been playing *babki* since early morning. Their book bags lie in a heap off to the side. (1:57)

Here, our focus moves from the capital to the remote provinces and stays there for most of the remainder of the book. The expanse between Moscow and Siberia is emphasized—to humorous effect—two stories later in "Country Folk," where Granny Malania contemplates a terrifying four-hour flight to the capital to visit her son. Shukshin's first film, *There's This Guy*, based on two stories from the collection ("Klassnyi voditel'" ["A Classy Driver"] and "Grin'ka Maliugin"), underscores this distance in its opening shot of a map of the Chuiskii Trakt (the main road in the Altai region and former trade route to Mongolia), reminding its viewers of the film's "exotic" location.

This distance takes on a more polemical tenor in "Ignakha's Come Home" ("Ignakha priekhal"), in which a circus wrestler brings his wife from Moscow[19] to visit his parents in Siberia. It has been five years since he has been home, and the visit does not go well. Ignakha has changed; he refuses to get drunk with his father and has forgotten all of the old village songs. The holiday the old man had been expecting fails to materialize. The city has changed Ighnakha: he has abandoned his rural birthright. Although the depiction of the return of village sons and daughters corrupted by life in the city was not new to Soviet literature in 1963,[20] two themes important for understanding Shukshin's heroes are underscored. The first is that of the serious rift between the village and the city—once the gulf separating the two is successfully navigated (as in Ignakha's case), there is no turning back. The second theme is that of the need many of Shukshin's heroes feel for some sort of *prazdnik*, a holiday or celebration, a notion in Shukshin's stories that refers to both an earthly (often drunken) revelry and a higher metaphysical commemoration (what Egor Prokudin in *Kalina krasnaia* will call a "holiday of the soul"). The celebration Ignakha's father craves is not so much the drinking and singing of a welcome-home party, but the peace of mind and consolation of spirit that would have come had his son retained some sense of pride in his heritage. Both this search for a holiday and the estrangement between the city and the village grow in significance as themes in later works.

While some of Shukshin's heroes search for a holiday in life, others long for *volia*, the "sudden, total escape from intolerable reality."[21] *Volia* is a liberation from constraint and circumstance, the achieving of the age-old peasant dream of a life without obligations, a life lived for oneself. It is the joy of one's leisure hours, the indulging of one's fancies, reveling in one's freedom. The theme of *volia* is first articulated in the story "Sten'ka Razin" in a song the teacher Zakharych introduces to Vaseka:

> O-oh, freedom, oh my freedom!
> Oh, freedom, mine and free!
> Freedom is a falcon in the heavens.
> Freedom is my homeland, dear to me. (1:36)[22]

The song causes Vaseka to choke up "out of love and grief," instilling in him a sense of urgency and a need to act on it. Vaseka finds *volia* in carving; later heroes find it in a variety of ways, from homegrown science experiments to luxuriating in the bathhouse all day. This longing for *volia* is most prominently featured in *I Have Come to Give You Freedom,* Shukshin's novel about the rebel leader Sten'ka Razin, where *volia* is embodied in looting and banditry, anarchy and rebellion, disdain for the quiet, settled life, as well as the more serious battle for peasant and Cossack independence.

The concepts of *dusha, volia,* and *prazdnik*—already present in Shukshin's first anthology—endow his village and his hero with a subtle, but detectable, metaphysical quality, setting the stage for the appearance of the artist's later seekers of higher transcendence in life. They also distinguish Shukshin from his literary peers and establish him as an author with a unique hero and a distinct fictional universe, one with is own peculiar laws and properties. As early as his first anthology, Shukshin emerged as an author able to celebrate the extraordinary inner lives of very ordinary people.

Country Folk also contains an important early story on the *ars poetica* theme. "Sunday Boredom" ("Voskresnaia toska")—one of three stories in the anthology not set in the village and the only story Shukshin ever wrote in which he speaks at length about the writing craft—is a first-person account of a young writer's attempt to come to terms with his failed first novel. The writer-narrator, one of Shukshin's displaced village sons studying in the city, is an obvious reflection of Shukshin himself, who had just finished his own first novel at the time and was experiencing similar doubts about it. In the following passage, the writer-narrator ponders his calling as a writer:

So, I feel the urge to write. But what exactly do I know that other people don't know and what gives me the right *to tell stories?* I know how it is in the steppe on an early summer morning, the quiet green dawn. I know that in the hollows the fog is light as human breath and that it is quiet. You can lie face down in the fragrant, damp grass, embrace the earth, and hear her huge heart beating softly deep within her chest. So many things you understand at times like that; how much you want to live. This I know. (1:92)

Like Shukshin, the writer in "Sunday Boredom" is one of the many artists who have abandoned their native periphery for the city but who have not forgotten their roots. Shukshin makes it clear here, however, that although living in Moscow may stimulate a nostalgic love for the places a writer has left behind, he should not mistake nostalgia or homesickness for good writing. His writer-hero castigates himself for his plodding first novel and comes to the following conclusion:

I write poorly. . . . Endless "whimsical little breezes," tinny words about the sunset, about the rustle of leaves, 'about the honeylike smell coming off the fields. . . . Yet it was only yesterday that a gorgeous simile occurred to me. I even wrote it down: "You have to write so that the words explode like bullets tossed into a bonfire." What the devil kind of bullets do I have? More like buttons, not words. (1:83)

Here, in one brief passage, Shukshin encapsulates what would become the main point of distinction between his future anthologies and *Country Folk* as well as what would separate his mature village narratives from those of the Village Prose school: from now on his prose would contain less sentiment and more fireworks.

Originally appearing as "An Invitation for Two" ("Priglashenie na dva litsa") in the New Year's edition of *Komsomol'skaia pravda* for 1962, the story was radically rewritten for inclusion in *Country Folk*. Not only was the ending changed, but all of the passages on writing were added in the second redaction. Revised sometime in mid- to late 1962, "Sunday Boredom" helps to explain the distinct shift in style and substance of the four stories comprising his *Novyi mir* debut: "Grin'ka Maliugin," "A Classy Driver," "Ignakha's Come Home," and "All by Themselves," all of which were also written in 1962 and were the last stories to be included in *Country Folk*. Here a provocative edge appears in Shukshin's hero: he becomes more colorful and unpredictable in word and deed, less sentimental, a character capable of inexplicable actions and odd antics.

Perhaps in no other story is this new synthesis better expressed than in "A Classy Driver," whose hero, Pasha Kholmanskii, charmed movie audiences in Leonid Kuravlev's brilliant interpretation of the role in Shukshin's film *There's This Guy*.[23] Pasha was a new hero for Soviet cinema—a simple guy, but one unlike the other "simple" guys appearing on Soviet screens in the late 1950s, for whom simplicity was but a signal of an inner complexity.[24] Pasha was just simple: lowbrow, low culture, and on the "elemental" side,[25] qualities that led to accusations that Shukshin was promoting a "primitive" hero.[26] Pasha has no pretensions to self-improvement or refinement. On the contrary, he is quite happy as he is: a "prankster and a buffoon, an eccentric and a dreamer" whose dreams are "naive" and "banal."[27] He spices up his speech with terms misappropriated from the technical and medical sciences (*sfotografirovano, piramidon*—words he thinks make his speech sound sophisticated)[28] and expresses himself with a flair for the creative turn of phrase. The film, like the story, chronicles his search for his "ideal"—the perfect woman. What ensues is one comic episode after another as Pasha, in picaresque fashion, drives his truck along the Chuiskii Trakt, his antics alternating with good deeds and heroic feats.[29] *There's This Guy* was the sort of "feel good" movie that had instant appeal. Simple, almost crude, in its cinematography (it "possessed the naiveté and intimacy of an expanded home movie"),[30] the film revealed its director's great investment in accessible form. Although Shukshin swears that he did not intend to direct a comedy (he even felt compelled to write an "afterword" to the film to this effect),[31] audiences howled at Pasha's adventures, and the film was considered one of the best comedies of the year.

Pasha's appearance signals a further evolution of Shukshin's hero. The writer himself seemed to sense that he was on the verge of creating a new character, cautioning his audience that Pasha's adventures merely constituted his hero's "prehistory," that his "main story" still lay ahead.[32] Indeed, Pasha seems to retain some of the qualities of Shukshin's old hero while anticipating those of his new one. In his innocence and decency—Shukshin tells us he "'delivers' goodness to people in his truck"[33]—Pasha still belongs with the writer's "bright souls." However, with his irreverent pranks and stunts, he is quite unlike them, having more in common with the lively rogue of a picaresque novel, whose "contra-pathetic nature," according to Bakhtin, "is everywhere in evidence, beginning with his comic self-introduction and self-recommendation to the public providing the tone of the entire subsequent story and ending with the finale." Indeed, Pasha raises eyebrows and turns heads from the moment we meet him. As Bakhtin says about this character type, "A radically new tone is given here to discourse about human beings, a tone alien to any pathos-charged seriousness."[34]

Pasha's affected speech, outlandish manners, and flamboyant actions mock and make strange social convention and petrified discourse. Needless to say, Pasha steps on a few toes, as when he is surrounded at a village clubhouse by locals who think his activities have gone too far. But in these provocations, he renews—lightheartedly, parodically—the truth behind the worn concepts of love and goodness. In this way, he fulfills the function of the parodying rogue, who becomes an "agent of authenticity" and whose irresponsibility thus assumes a positive value,[35] which was Shukshin's hope for his character all along: "I wanted to make a film about the beauty of a pure human heart capable of goodness."[36] To make such a film and avoid the danger of bathos, Shukshin needed Pasha to be the way he appeared in the story: irreverent, light on his feet, ambiguous in his character and his appearance—"not so very bad, nor so very handsome" (1:137).

For these same reasons, Shukshin incorporated the story "Grin'ka Maliugin" into his film, assigning Grin'ka's actions to Pasha. The two complement each other well: Grin'ka is "arrested in his development, a bit of the fool," and is prone to eccentricity (*chudil*) (1:126). To Pasha's parodic antics he adds the "uncomprehending presence" of the fool, who also makes strange the familiar, stereotyped, and clichéd.[37] Grin'ka's rescue of a gas station from a burning truck is a case in point: he tells a journalist sent to write about the event that he acted not out of heroism but out of "foolhardiness"; he tells his roommates at the hospital that he broke his leg jumping out of a rocket. In mocking his heroic action, Grin'ka's jesting helps restore real meaning to a term every bit as clichéd and deadened by dogma as love and goodness. His foolishness constitutes a truer definition of heroism than the formulaic article written by the journalist in the story.

Pasha and Grin'ka anticipate the important role the rogue and fool will play in Shukshin's prose, just as the other *Novyi mir* stories anticipate new themes in the artist's works. "Ignakha's Come Home" hints at a deeper polemic developing over the relationship between the city and the country, while "All by Themselves" gives us our first glimpse of Shukshinian *skandal*—that deeply wounding conflict that disturbs the peace—in Marfa's burning of Antip's balalaika and his ax-wielding response.

Taken as a whole, *Country Folk* establishes an essential vocabulary for understanding Shukshin's universe: *dusha* (soul), *volia* (freedom from obligation, liberation), *prazdnik* (holiday, celebration), *chudit'* (to act eccentricly), and *skandal* (scandal). While this last term is the only one that does not actually appear in Shukshin's volume, the groundwork had clearly been laid for its introduction, and indeed Shukshin brings up the notion of *skandal* in his essay on the short story a year later.[38] For the time being, however, these issues lie just beneath the surface of the Shukshinian text. The critics saw what appeared to be innocent country folk, and to a certain extent they were right. At this point, the soul of Shukshin's hero is, indeed, bright; later, this will change. "True 'bright souls' can appear only when things depend solely on them."[39] When things do not go their way, these bright souls will begin to ache.

Chapter Four

Unforgettably Strange People

> The hero. The hero is, in my opinion, the artist
> himself, his work.
> —Vasilii Shukshin, "Kommentarii" to "Voprosy
> samomu sebe"

> [O]ne finally realizes that [Shukshin] continues
> to feel part of the mass of the people from whom
> he came, their ambassador in the city, one of
> those "oddballs" about whom he always wrote.
> —Boris Pankin, "Shukshin about Himself: Notes
> on the Collection *Morality Is Truth*"

FOOLS AND REBELS

One feature of Shukshin's characters that fascinated Soviet audiences was his heroes' propensity for acting on their impulses. As Geoffrey Hosking notes, "This is the stuff of Shukshin's human comedy: human feelings thrashing about, spilling out in all sorts of inappropriate, ridiculous and hurtful ways."[1] A few examples from his stories will illustrate. A village grandfather tosses a boot through his son's television screen because an actor in a TV movie portraying a village carpenter was holding an ax incorrectly ("Critics" ["Kritiki," 1964]). When a piece of shrapnel begins working its way out of a very tender spot on his derriere after years of lying dormant, an old war veteran is too embarrassed to have the local surgeon—a young woman—operate, so he tries to do the operation himself at home ("Efim P'ianykh's Operation" ["Operatsiia Efima P'ianykh," 1966]). A veterinarian is so thrilled over the first successful human heart transplant that he fires two shots from his rifle in the middle of the night, only to be hauled into the police station for disturbing the peace ("Let's Conquer the Heart!" ["Daesh' serdtse!" 1968]). A work-brigade foreman gets the sudden urge to demolish an old church and, despite the protestations and pleas of half the village, brings it crashing down ("Tough Guy" ["Krepkii muzhik," 1970]). A Siberian decides to demonstrate his superiority over a bunch of vacationing city types by unexpectedly throwing himself into the icy autumnal waters of

57

Lake Baikal, only to be rescued by them when his swim trunks become tangled around his feet ("The Strong Get Farther" ["Sil'nye idut dal'she," 1970]). A man is mistaken by a grocery-store cashier for last night's drunken troublemaker; when another customer waiting in line adds his own insults, the man is so mortally offended that he runs home to fetch a mallet to kill someone and has to be physically restrained by his wife ("The Insult" ["Obida," 1971]). A worker takes offense at a faceless bureaucrat and, in the heat of the moment, pours a bottle of ink over the bureaucrat's new white suit ("Rubles in Words, Kopecks in Figures" ["Nol'-nol' tselykh," 1971]). A muzhik who catches his wife fooling around with another man goes after her with an ax, but when he cannot catch her, he chops off two of his own fingers instead ("Fingerless" ["Bespalyi," 1972]). The list could easily be continued.

These protagonists reflect a change in Shukshin's hero. In the years following the appearance of *Country Folk,* Shukshin began to develop characters whose personalities and actions were noticeably more eccentric and contradictory. In 1967, this eccentricity and contrariness were explained in a word: *chudik* ("oddball," "quirky," "crank," "weirdo," "crackpot," and "nut" are all possible translations). With the publication of Shukshin's signature story "Oddball," a label would attach itself to Shukshin's protagonist that would outlive both hero and writer alike.

Chudik (stressed on the first syllable) is itself an odd word. It has a distinctly whimsical, folksy quality that sets it apart from its literary equivalent, *chudak* (stressed on the second syllable, "an eccentric"). The authoritative seventeen-volume Academy of Sciences Russian dictionary designates *chudik* as *prostorechie* (substandard colloquial), a fact that helps to explain Shukshin's choice. *Chudik* carries an informal, affectionate resonance, one that bespeaks the generally positive Russian attitude toward strangeness, be it the inexplicable behavior of holy fools or the antics of the village idiot. In fact, Shukshin's *chudik* has something in common with both of these fixtures of the Russian countryside. The word itself shares the same root as *chudo* (miracle) and the verb *chudit'* (to behave eccentrically, oddly; to clown, act the fool; to commit ridiculous, strange deeds).[2] Yet it is not so much the holy fool or village idiot but two different figures, the secular *chudak* and the *durak,* or "fool," from Russian folklore, who most closely resemble Shukshin's "oddball."

In favoring the term *chudik* over either *chudak* or *durak,* however, Shukshin makes a crucial distinction. He not only chooses the more stylistically expressive term; he also avoids the possible negative connotations of either of the other two words. This is an important point, for no matter what direction the nonconformity of Shukshin's "strange people" takes, it is vital that his hero gain the sympathy of the reader on some level. Later Shukshin himself will use much more negatively marked words for his hero—like *debil* (retard), *suraz* (bastard), and *psikhopat* (psychopath)—but even then he does so almost as a provocation, challenging us to feel compassion for heroes labeled at the outset as unsympathetic types.[3] Here we find one of the main differences between Shukshin's *chudik* and its folkloric counterpart. As Andrei Siniavskii explains in his study of the *durak,* the Russian fool usually "begins to enjoy sudden and incredible good fortune somewhere in the middle of the story and becomes an extraordinarily successful person," not because he grows any wiser but precisely because he continues to perform one absurd act after another.[4] Shukshin's fools are less fortunate. In describing the early Siberian heroes of Evgenii Popov (whom he introduced to the Russian reading public), Shukshin comes up with an appropriate epithet for his own characters. They are *neustroennye:* unlucky, unsuccessful, lacking something essential, characters with a difficult fate.[5] These are Shukshin's "strange people." Those who seek to fill this lack with material things become in Shukshin's prose *meshchane*—philistines and petty materialists—the artist's most frequent villains. Those for whom this deficiency is tied to spiritual matters occupy a privileged place among the writer's heroes.

The path to the figure of the *chudik* was not blazed by Shukshin alone but runs through the eccentric heroes of his predecessors. The potent figure of the *chudak,* or eccentric, as a symbol of nonconformity and autonomy became particularly prominent in the post-Stalinist period. This eccentric was not the safe, clownlike figure from approved works, such as old Shchukar from Sholokhov's *Podniataia tselina* (*Virgin Soil Upturned,* 1931–60). These new eccentrics were more profoundly at odds with their environment, and by their very existence they challenged the definition of what was an acceptable hero in post-Stalinist Soviet literature. They were strange, sometimes unattractive, and often antisocial types, people like Kazakov's wandering holy fool from his story "The Mendicant" ("Strannik," 1956); the alcoholic singer of folk songs in his "Trali-vali" (translated as "Silly Billy," 1959); the pathetic village inventor from Aksenov's "Strange One" ("Dikoi," 1964); or Bitov's dreamy hero in "Loafer" ("Bezdel'nik," 1962).

These curious heroes became so numerous by 1965 that, in a roundtable discussion on the pages of *Voprosy literatury,* Lev Anninskii—citing stories by Kazakov, Aksenov, Shukshin, Viktoriia Tokareva, and Fridrikh Gorenshtein, among others—declared the *chudak* and the *strannik* the new heroes of the contemporary short story.[6] Although Anninskii's thesis found little support, either from the other participants in the roundtable or from the editors, his comments coincided with the change taking place in Shukshin's hero. To the more "serious" questions concerning the positive hero, social purposefulness, and historicism, which the editors of *Voprosy literatury* lamented had not been broached in the discussion,[7] Shukshin responded with a character who looked less attractive, less positive, and altogether less socially acceptable, to say nothing of socially purposeful.

Like the eccentrics described by Kazakov, Aksenov, and Village Prose writers, Shukshin's *chudik* was a "reaction to 'uninteresting,' 'characterless' people, to human stereotypes, to the standardization of everyday forms."[8] His protagonist is as much a response to the one-dimensional positive heroes of Socialist Realism as it is a return to the tradition of eccentric rural characters begun by Ivan Turgenev in his *Hunter's Sketches* (*Zapiski okhotnika*, 1852) or a continuation of the colorful protagonists of Maxim Gorky, Isaak Babel', or Boris Pil'niak. As Shukshin himself said about his *chudiki*, "They make life brighter [*ukrashaiut zhizn'*], for no matter where they are, boredom flees when they appear on the scene. I wanted to tell about these 'strange people' because they teach us how to make life interesting."[9]

If we were to judge these strange people only by what Shukshin says about them, however, we might conclude that they hardly differ from the "bright souls" of his first anthology. After all, Shukshin describes his *chudiki* in the same terms he used to portray his earlier, more sentimental heroes. They are "talented" and "beautiful,"[10] "endlessly kind people" who do not hide behind "posturing," "demagoguery," or "the ability to conform."[11] They are "people with a kind and beautiful soul."[12] The difference is that where before these bright souls were the mark of pure country folk, by the writer's second anthology and second and third films they have become a sign of eccentricity. A shift has occurred in Shukshin's central conflict. It has intensified and broadened in scope. The soul has become an open battleground and the world a more hostile place. For Shukshin, the result of this collision between bright souls and grim reality is the strange person, the *chudik*.

The *chudik* was a more problematic resolution of the issue of the positive hero than the "bright soul" had been. Here was a character whose impulse to do good did not necessarily meet with success and who sometimes even ended up doing ill, a character whose strange behavior could hardly be deemed worthy of emulation. A good example is the hero of one of the first stories Shukshin would write after *Country Folk*. "Stepka" (1964) describes how its title character returns to his native village after serving a prison sentence in a labor camp for brawling. It is spring, the ice is melting on the river, and "the damp breeze whirls and makes you light-headed" (1:194). Stepka takes in all the familiar sights and sounds of his village and then puts in his appearance at his family's house. Joyous celebration follows, as they were expecting him months later. Neighbors start arriving, and Stepka—every bit as drunk with happiness as he is with the freely flowing vodka—tells his stories of life in the camp over and over again and then dances with his father to everyone's approval. When a policeman appears in the doorway, all of the revelers assume Stepka simply has paperwork to fill out. Only his deaf-mute sister senses trouble, and she is right. Stepka, apparently, had escaped with only three months of a five-year sentence to go. The policeman is amazed: "Now they'll tack on a couple of years." "It doesn't matter . . . ," Stepka responds. "I've charged up my batteries. Now I can do my time. Or else those dreams would've done me in—every night I dream of the village" (1:202).

But Stepka has forgotten about his sister, who has followed them to the village council building. When she understands what is happening, she is so overwhelmed with grief that she has to be forcibly separated from her brother. Stepka has also forgotten about his parents and neighbors who are still celebrating his homecoming but will soon learn the bad news. Indeed, the story ends on a sorrowful note, with his sister walking home, "stumbling along and weeping bitterly" (1:204).

Shukshin included "Stepka" as the first vignette in his second film, *Your Son and Brother* (1965), where it sparked a small controversy in the literary and cinematic press.[13] Stepka reflects the new complexity of Shukshin's hero. On the one hand, we read in Stepka's foolish act his service to a higher ideal, his willingness to trade two years of his life (his extended prison sentence) for the intangible but invaluable *prazdnik* his brief springtime return brings him and his family. On the other hand, we are also fully aware of the grief he has caused his loved ones by depriving them of his presence and, perhaps just as important, his labor in support of the household. "You all picked a fine time to fight," his father admonishes him shortly after his return. "We have enough trouble around here without that" (1:195).

Shukshin's originality consists in the fact that he took this character type and discovered in it a wholeness and depth lacking in the eccentrics of other writers and missing from his own early "bright souls." The eccentricity of Shukshin's *chudiki* was invariably symptomatic of a much more serious, often spiritual, striving and questioning. Whether their strangeness lay in their mildly annoying but harmless fixations or in their impulsive, elemental natures, these oddballs describe a hero in search of some higher meaning in life, be it personal fulfillment or general deliverance. "They are seeking to break out of the here and now, the immediate and empirical, the always imperfect, into some other, imagined world, of freedom and perfection."[14] For Stepka, this means the spiritual sustenance that only a walk in his home village in the springtime can bring him, a walk he had dreamed about in the camps. It is perhaps this quality of Shukshin's characters that prompted one reviewer of his second story collection to describe them as heroes "heretofore unknown" in Soviet fiction about the village.[15]

The reasons for the spiritual strivings of Shukshin's characters are varied, but in the broadest sense they can be traced to historical and social change. Revolution, war, collectivization, and urbanization sundered many of the ties to traditional life and traditional belief systems. The Russian Orthodox Church, long the spiritual sustainer of the peasant, suffered the closure and destruction of thousands of churches and monasteries during the

1920s and 1930s[16] and no longer played a significant role in daily village life in the Soviet period. At least part of the spiritual longing of Shukshin's heroes can undoubtedly be traced to the consequences of state-sponsored atheism, a fact the artist alludes to in stories where characters attempt to tear churches down ("Tough Guy"), preserve them ("The Master"), or interrogate the meaning of religious belief ("I Believe!" ["Veruiu!"], "Gena Proidisvet"). In these and in other works, Shukshin's protagonists "feel a pain in the place where man used to have a soul."[17] Hence their attempts to fill that place with other things: quirky obsessions, song, dance, artistic creativity, sometimes vodka, anything but religious belief. For Shukshin, his characters, and the majority of Soviet citizens, religion remained a remote realm.[18]

Thus even the priest in "I Believe!" freely admits his doubt in "an eternal Higher power" and likens man's attempt to find meaning in life to trying to bail the ocean with a cup. Instead of affirming belief in God, he chants a strange profession of faith "in aviation, in the mechanization of agriculture, in the scientific revolution" (1:541). It is here—in the components of a liturgy for the scientific age—that Shukshin identifies much more specifically the locus of his heroes' sense of physical and metaphysical displacement.

The postwar, newly mechanized countryside transformed the peasant's life. His roots were no longer in the soil, and, given the chance, he was more likely to leave for the city than to stay in the village. New opportunities for education and technical training lured the younger generation away and bled the villages dry of new farmers. The peasant's eternal worry about his daily bread was no longer the driving force of his life. Indeed, unlike their parents and grandparents, the younger generation of villagers was no longer satisfied with living "just for their stomachs." Shukshin's new protagonists reflected this change. Ivan, a truck driver from "In Profile and En Face" ("V profil' i anfas," 1967), complains: "I don't know what I'm working for. [. . .] Is it really just so I can stuff my face? Well, I've stuffed it. Now what? [. . .] All the same, my soul's all limp." His interlocutor, an old man who has lived through collectivization and the war, does not understand him. "When I was your age, I didn't think like that," he says. "You're from the stone age," Ivan responds. "I can't live like you lived" (1:320).

Ivan's problem is that his boss caught him drinking while on a haul and had his license suspended for a year. The only job left in the village is cleaning out the stables, something Ivan, with his three specializations and a high school diploma, is unwilling to do. Ivan is one of Shukshin's "unlucky" heroes. His wife took their daughter and disappeared, and now he must say good-bye to his mother to seek his fortune working in the coal mines. While his most immediate problems are of a material nature—finding a job, rebuilding his home life—his true quandary is spiritual: "I really don't know what I'm living for" (1:321). As is often the case with Shukshin's soul-searching heroes, Ivan is also an artist: he plays the accordion and improvises folk ditties. His departure from the village is colored by an almost existentialist anxiety. "No, you have to live alone in this world," he thinks to himself. "Then it will be easy" (1:325). Like many of Shukshin's protagonists, Ivan is physically and spiritually adrift, and the traditional attitudes or answers to everyday questions are no longer adequate.

Sensing the importance of social change for understanding his characters, Shukshin turned—uncharacteristically and unsuccessfully, his critics would say—to historical themes in his three novels. While his book about Sten'ka Razin treated the Cossack leader's 1670 peasant rebellion, Books One and Two of *The Liubavin Family* looked to more recent events in Soviet history. As many of the Village Prose writers would do after him, Shukshin sought in the upheavals of the Soviet century the root cause of his and his heroes' lack of moorage.

Book One of *The Liubavin Family* deals with the arrival of Soviet power in the 1920s to the remote Siberian village of Baklan'. The Liubavins are among a handful of prosperous and powerful peasants in the village. They are kulaks, the class enemy of Party activists sent from Moscow to collectivize agriculture. A violent clash of ideology, politics, and tradition ensues as the Liubavin family attempts to preserve its relative wealth and autonomy in the face of change introduced by outsiders. The novel develops two main plotlines: the trials and tribulations of the Liubavins and the mission of two Party activists, Vasilii Rodionov and his nephew Kuz'ma, agents of the GPU (a forerunner of the KGB), who are to exterminate a local band of outlaws containing remnants of White Army officers and appropriate local grain harvests for redistribution.

A complication arises when Egor, the youngest son of the Liubavins, and Kuz'ma Rodionov both fall in love with the same girl, Mar'ia, the beautiful daughter of the poorest peasant in town. The Liubavin patriarch, Emel'ian, opposes the marriage, and Mar'ia herself is unresolved, but Egor kidnaps her anyway and a wedding follows. Meanwhile, Kuz'ma is seduced by a woman from the family with whom he is living and eventually settles into a loveless marriage with her. Between battling the band of outlaws, coercing grain from Emel'ian Liubavin, and succumbing to his ongoing attraction to Egor's wife, Kuz'ma loses sight of his ideological commitments, a mistake compounded by the death of his uncle Vasilii. Kuz'ma's continued attention to Mar'ia eventually leads to a violent confrontation in which Egor accidently kills his wife and must flee into the mountains to join the outlaws, leaving behind a newborn son (who reappears in Book Two) and a father eventually broken by the new order. Kuz'ma is replaced by new and tougher outsiders, and the novel ends ostensibly in the middle of the NEP period, but on a note whose tone is more suitable to the eve of collectivization.

Book One of *The Liubavin Family* is evidence that Shukshin long had another conception of his hero in mind. While Pasha Kholmanskii was the first incarnation of a new eccentricity, Egor Liubavin appeared, almost startlingly so, as a more desperate and controversial figure, the first of the writer's more serious rebels. The novel, however, was not a success. Its plot twists and episodic nature betrayed too plainly its writer's cinematic training. It lacked philosophical and historical depth and offered, on the whole, mainly a series of lively character sketches. If Shukshin began writing the novel with the goal of understanding the effects on the inhabitants of a Siberian village of the arrival of Soviet power, he ended up instead with a novel that focused more on the conflicted relationships of a relatively small cast of characters.

In genre and character type, *The Liubavin Family* marked a sharp departure. Its violent kulak protagonists stood out in particularly stark relief from the heroes of Shukshin's short stories and of his second film, *Your Son and Brother*, released the same year the novel was published. Based on the stories "Ignakha's Come Home," "Stepka," and "Snake Poison" ("Zmeinyi iad," 1964), the film is centered around another peasant patriarch, old man Voevodin, and his four sons—Stepka, Maksim, Ignakha, and Vas'ka—who match in number those of the Liubavin family. While both works are treatments of a dying rural way of life, the differences between the novel's portrayal of the violent fate of a kulak peasant clan and the film's depiction of the problems of the Voevodin family are dramatic. Stepka's prison sentence and Ignakha's and Maksim's "betrayal" of the village by moving to the city are minor conflicts indeed in comparison to the great force bent on destroying the Liubavin way of life.

This sharp contrast between the families from the novel and the film and the conflicts they represent, however, is more than just a product of the differences between two historical periods. It also illustrates a strategy Shukshin employed throughout his career, that of dividing his heroes into two broad categories: rebels and fools. The former—Egor Liubavin, Ivan Liubavin (from Book Two), and Sten'ka Razin—are part of a more serious polemic concerning autobiographical, political, and historical issues. These are the more controversial protagonists of the novels, whose rebellion signifies more than mere *skandal*. The latter—the oddballs and rugged individualists of the short stories and films—reflect smaller, more localized conflicts, which rarely exceed the confines of the family, workplace, or village, and only sometimes cross the boundaries of the law. This distinction helps to explain the otherwise inexplicable appearance within the same year of works as different as *The Liubavin Family* and *Your Son and Brother*, or the paradoxical fact that the novel filled with rapes, murders, arson, fistfights, and

64

shoot-outs was written at the same time as *Country Folk* with its idealists and innocents.

There are, however, curious connections between *The Liubavin Family* and the "country folk" and "simple guys" of Shukshin's first anthology and films, connections having to do with his repetition of character names. Indeed, the "Hero of the Soviet Union" from the story "Country Folk" is none other than a Liubavin, while Grin'ka Maliugin, a carefree truck driver in the short story that bears his name, is in the novel a scarred and murderous thief. Furthermore, in Book Two of *The Liubavin Family*, Shukshin appropriates Pasha Kholmanskii's storyline and assigns it to Pasha Liubavin, who is a darker, more brooding incarnation of the simple guy from his first film. Shukshin's point seems to be that there is a kinship between his fools and rebels, indeed that the line between foolish eccentricity and more serious rebellion is a thin one. In the stories, of course, that line is never crossed. The problem is partly one of genre: serious rebellion is hard to realize within the limits of the short story. But its very possibility accounts for the feeling in Shukshin's stories that he was sometimes writing just on the edge of what was allowed.

Thus, in lieu of open rebellion, Shukshin indulges in open buffoonery in his short stories and films. In place of dissidence, he celebrates eccentricity. Instead of protest, he offers the seemingly foolish deed. And moral indignation is expressed in an elemental lashing out invariably concluding in *skandal*. There is no opposition per se to the repressive powers that be— only all of those strange people and *chudiki*. Here we have reached a critical moment in Shukshin's art, for while strangeness (difference, eccentricity) is by its nature rebellious, and strangeness made theatrical (buffoonery, carnivalesque inversion of hierarchy) is itself an act verging on rebellion, there is, ultimately, no revolt. Shukshin's foolishness "was always acceptable fun, and he never pushed far beyond what authorities would tolerate from a Party member."[19]

This outcome, however, is in keeping with the nature of the fool and of folk buffoonery and carnival in general.

> The Fool does not lead a revolt against the Law, he lures us into a region of the spirit where . . . the writ does not run. . . . There is nothing essentially immoral or blasphemous or rebellious about clownage. On the contrary, it may easily act as a social preservative by providing a corrective to the pretentious vanity of officialdom, a safety-valve for unruliness, a wholesome nourishment to the sense of secret spiritual independence of that which would otherwise be the intolerable tyranny of circumstance.[20]

As for carnival, Bakhtin describes it as the "*temporary* liberation from the prevailing truth and the established order."[21] Carnival was never meant to be equated with revolution. The point is that Shukshin's *chudiki* speak to the spiritual freedom embodied by the fool, to the liberating qualities of laughter and the joyful relativity of carnivalized celebration, precious qualities indeed during a time of political reaction in the second half of the 1960s.

Much the same can be said of what is now considered the quintessential incident of Shukshin's stories, the *skandal.* One critic claims that Shukshin introduced the "grievance, slander, and insult" into Soviet literature,[22] and, indeed, there is hardly a story without harsh words or heavy blows being exchanged between characters. Far from promoting anarchic impulses, however, the domestic squabbles and public disturbances of Shukshin's stories are cathartic in the Aristotelian sense: they give form to emotions (the pent-up frustrations and aggravations of everyday life) and thus control them, thereby relieving the pressure of social restraints (and there were many in Soviet society) and channeling otherwise destructive action into textual enjoyment.

These qualities of Shukshin's prose struck a distinct chord with readers and moviegoers in the mid-1960s, a time when Shukshin wrote a number of stories that made him very popular. After the Stalinist period and during Brezhnev's decade-long return to neo-Stalinist policies (1964–74), there was a need for this kind of fool and eccentric in Soviet Russian culture, someone who could suspend the normal laws by which the universe, or a country, is governed. Shukshin understood this. The folk buffoonery and *skandaly* of his heroes were sanctioned unruliness and allowable nonconformity at a time of increasing regimentation in Soviet life and culture. In print and on screen, they raised larger issues of Soviet reality and the spiritual health of the so-called new Soviet man that were nevertheless safely couched in localized conflicts. "A lot is understood through humor," Shukshin once asserted, "a lot gets through. If we shift the conversation from the rationalizing, level plane in the direction of the grotesque, the game, there is the chance to have your say, to attract attention to yourself."[23]

In a 1968 essay Shukshin writes: "The hero of our time has always been the fool, in whom the times, the truth of the times, lives in the most expressive way."[24] Part of the fool's attraction for the writer is his ambivalence. Polemicizing with the idea of the positive hero, Shukshin argues for a hero who is not "made up," who is neither positive nor negative, neither moral nor immoral. The hero must instead express the "bitter truth" of his time, like Pechorin in Lermontov's *Hero of Our Time* and the eponymous hero of Goncharov's *Oblomov.* In fact, Shukshin describes these latter heroes in terms suitable for his own protagonists: they are *iarkii* (colorful), *neprikaiannyi* (restless, lost souls; people without a definite occupation or place to stay), *neputevyi* (good for nothing, unlucky, unsuccessful).[25]

In his essay, Shukshin mentions the long tradition in Russian culture of truth-telling fools, from holy fools and mendicants to Ivan the Fool from

Russian folklore and fairy tales.[26] His *chudiki*, he implies, belong on this list. Indeed, Dmitrii Likhachev's summation of the essential nature of the Russian fool seems ideally suited to Shukshin's well-intentioned but strange heroes.

> The Russian people have always loved fools, not because they are stupid but because they are wise: wise with a higher wisdom that lies not in cunning or in deceiving others, not in jesting or the successful pursuit of their own narrow advantage, but in a wisdom that knows the true value of any falseness, ostentatious beauty, and miserliness, that sees the value of doing good unto others and therefore unto themselves as individuals.[27]

Likhachev's description does not fit all fools, of course, and it is important to stress that Shukshin's *chudiki* represent their own special category. It is also clear that Shukshin took delight in describing their antics and did not always or immediately seem concerned that some sort of moral or higher truth be attached to their adventures. Oftentimes, it seems to be enough that they simply affirm their right to be different, independent, unique, other. Indeed, herein lies one function of eccentricity in general, which, according to Bakhtin, helps reveal the "'internal man,'" "his 'free and self-sufficient subjectivity.'"[28] Here, we are reminded of the Shukshin legend and its similar privileging of the eccentric act over the sensible answer, the foolish deed over the serious response, all in the service of an individual's right to express his difference and "to make life more interesting." But, as in the legend, the buffoonery in Shukshin's stories has a polemical edge, a hint of protest: do not underestimate or prejudge those of us from the provinces or from the margins of society. We, too, know the truth. We, too, have the right to our quirks. We, too, have souls. This polemic is implied in the very notion of "strange people." After all, individualists in the age of the *kollektiv* must, by definition, be oddballs.

Shukshin's third film is prototypical in this regard. Its title, *Strange People* (1969), emphasized the writer's new hero. The film brought to the screen the recently published stories "Oddball," "Mille Pardons, Madame!" and "Meditations," as well as one story written earlier, "Sten'ka Razin." Although it fared poorly with audiences—its three separate vignettes failed to coalesce into a meaningful whole for many viewers—it is an important film for understanding Shukshin's strange people and their quests, not so much for its formal qualities but for its content. It conveniently brings together stories that address specific themes and aspects of Shukshin's *chudik,* elements that recur and are developed elsewhere in the writer's works. The film's separate vignettes will thus serve as a way of organizing my discussion of three important aspects of Shukshin's *chudiki.* "Oddball" and "Meditations" highlight the spiritual qualities of the *chudik* and how those qualities come into conflict with the material world; "Mille Pardons,

Madame!" celebrates eccentricity and its challenging of hierarchy and conformity; "Sten'ka Razin" underscores the creative and redemptive potential
of the fool as artist. By examining these features of the *chudik*, we can arrive at the essence of Shukshin's most enduring literary type.

LIVING FOR THE SOUL: THE ODDBALL
IN THE MATERIAL WORLD

"Oddball" describes a frequent collision in Shukshin's prose: that between
the soul—the province of kindness, beauty, individuality, freedom, idealism—and the hostile world, which seeks to constrain it. Both the story and
its greatly altered movie version relate their hero's journey from the village
to the distant city to see his brother. Oddball got his nickname because
"things were always happening to him" (1:340). He is one of Shukshin's uncomprehending fools who wind up in minor but vexing scrapes that illumi-
nate their guileless, spiritual nature. In the story, these scrapes occur during
Oddball's journey. Curiously, two of these episodes are taken from Shukshin's own life;[29] the author also gives his protagonist his own first name
(Vasilii). But what in real life are simply foolish episodes become in the
story indicators of a special kind of innocence, one linked to a world outlook that came to occupy a privileged place in Shukshin's art.

The story's first autobiographical incident occurs in a store while Oddball is waiting for the train that will take him on the first leg of his trip. After making some purchases, Oddball notices a fifty-ruble bill lying on the
ground by the line of people waiting to pay. Not wishing to be forestalled,
he merrily informs the line that, where he's from, they "don't just toss bills
like that around" (1:341). Pleased with the impression he has made, Oddball leaves the store, only to realize that he was the one who had dropped
it. Too embarrassed and ashamed to claim it, he goes back home, confesses
everything to his wife, and takes another fifty rubles out of their savings account. For Oddball, it is not worth getting too upset over money. Shukshin
felt the same way about his own experience, consoling himself that "people
lose arms and legs, and here it was just a lousy bill."[30]

Another incident occurs during a rough airplane landing, when Oddball's hostile neighbor—who had refused to fasten his seat belt—loses his
dentures, then throws a fit when Oddball finds them and picks them up. Attempts by Oddball to tell stories (on the train) or to send a poetic telegram
to his wife are similarly met with hostility: in the first case, no one believes
him; in the second, he is forbidden to send a poem over the wires. At every
step, his open, creative nature is opposed by narrow-minded, scornful people lacking the spiritual freedom latent in all of Shukshin's *chudiki*. These
adventures prepare us for the conflict between Oddball and his sister-in-
law, another belligerent and materialist Shukshinian wife. It turns out that

she is ashamed of her own country roots and angry that her backward husband is not a successful executive. She takes an instant dislike to her bumpkin brother-in-law. Oddball's attempt to make up with her by painting her baby carriage with folk motifs is the last straw. Ranting and raving, she throws him out.

Hiding in the shed until the storm blows over, Oddball "began to hurt. When people hated him, he felt very hurt. And scared. It seemed like this: well, it's all over now, so why go on living? And he'd want to go somewhere far, far away from the people who hated him or were laughing at him. 'Why, oh why am I like this?' he whispered bitterly" (1:344–45). This is the threshold moment in many of Shukshin's stories and, as in "Oddball," it is often reached through *skandal:* arguments, insults, ugly scenes, shouting, even physical blows. The moment arrives when the souls of all participants are laid bare and their essence revealed. In this case, Oddball's brother's wife is exposed as the nasty village émigré in the city who has acquired all of the negative traits of urban life, including an obsession with material goods and career success. She is but another in Shukshin's line of consumerist wives who oppose and constrain the impractical world of the spirit, which here consists of song (the brothers' singing of village songs), childhood memories (the brothers' nostalgic talk of the good old days), and folk art (Oddball's embellishing of the carriage with flowers, roosters, and chicks). For his part, Oddball returns home not so much the bumpkin or fool but an unlikely hero, an outcome produced by the story's concluding paragraph, where we learn Oddball's real name and biography, information usually given at the beginning of stories: "His name was Vasilii Egorych Kniazev. He was thirty-nine years of age. He worked as a projectionist in the village. He adored detectives and dogs. As a child he dreamed of becoming a spy" (1:347). The effect is to turn Oddball into a sort of Everyman, a human being with all the dignity and importance implied by the appellation. Clearly, this is what is at stake in the story's climactic moment: recognition of Oddball's right to his name and his quirks. While the crisis in this story is resolved peacefully (Oddball goes home), in other stories this crisis moment has far greater consequences and is sometimes resolved more tragically, in suicide.

Such is the case in the stories "The Bastard" ("Suraz," 1970) and "A Wife Saw Her Husband Off to Paris" (1971). Spir'ka Rostorguev from "The Bastard" is a hell-raiser and a womanizer. He meets his match in an encounter with the new village teacher, who beats Spir'ka mercilessly for kissing his wife. Although he is more elemental than innocent, Spir'ka is another Shukshinian fool who lives for his soul. He cares as little for his own good looks as he does about which women he sleeps with, and he is as likely to help out the old folks in the village as to go on a drinking spree, such as the one that landed him in the camps for five years. That time he had stolen a case of vodka and held off the police for two days while holed up in his bathhouse with a gun. For Spir'ka, it is not the physical beating at the hands of the teacher that hurts so much as the blow it inflicts on his soul. His soul has been violated, and he will never be able to live in his accustomed easy and carefree manner. So he takes his own life.

Kol'ka Piratov from "A Wife Saw Her Husband Off to Paris" is a "jester" (2:99) and "clown" (2:102) of a different order. A Siberian transplanted to Moscow, he likes to give "concerts" in the courtyard of his apartment complex in which he plays the accordion, sings folk ditties, and dances folk dances. This only irritates and exasperates his wife, who is mortified at his country backwardness and his melancholic longing for his Siberian village. One fine evening her insults lead to a true spiritual crisis for Kol'ka. After a particularly vicious exchange between the two of them, Kol'ka grabs an ax, intent on killing his wife. She flees, so instead of killing her he turns on the gas in the oven and kills himself. As with Spir'ka, Kol'ka's reasons have to do with the soul. His life had become "absurd, shameful, disgusting"; his "soul was drying up" and being "poisoned" (2:102).

In a similar situation involving a quarrel with a wife, Alesha's brother from "Alesha at Large" ("Alesha beskonvoinyi," 1973) also chooses suicide. Alesha himself is spared this fate, but he must still defend the province of his soul—his Saturday bathhouse ritual—from both his wife and the local kolkhoz. His wife wants him to do chores instead of devoting a whole day to the bathhouse; the kolkhoz wants him to work. While Alesha successfully holds out against the kolkhoz, his wife takes more convincing. "What am I supposed to do," Alesha "shriek[s] wildly" when they argue about it, "cut my soul up into little pieces?" (2:248). Afraid Alesha might follow in his brother's footsteps, his wife gives in; on Saturday Alesha steams himself to his heart's content in his bathhouse. Hence his nickname in the village: "Alesha at large" (literally, "without escort"). For one day a week, Alesha is "at large," living for his soul. "That is why Alesha loved Saturdays. On Saturday he would meditate, reminisce, and ponder, as he could on no other day" (2:252).

Spir'ka, Kol'ka, and Alesha are all misfits to be sure, and Spir'ka is even a lawbreaker, but they are all nevertheless privileged by Shukshin for their soulful outlooks. Indeed, what is at stake in each of their confrontations with the outside world is precisely that most vague, poetic, and famous entity of all: the Russian soul itself. Shukshin's oddballs are all knights-errant of one sort or another, pledged to defend the soul as the site of everything that is good, creative, free, and unrestrained, be it Spir'ka's free and easy lifestyle, Kol'ka's folk heritage, or Alesha's bathhouse ritual.

Alesha is one of the lucky few. For many of Shukshin's protagonists, if the soul does not perish in its collision with the hostile world, there is still the sense that the end is very near. Shukshin describes this feeling best in his autobiographical story "A Slander" ("Kliauza," 1974), an instance where the author himself steps into the pages of his fiction as one of his own "offended and humiliated," large-souled heroes. For all of its factual basis, however, "A Slander" is perhaps the writer's most interesting treatment of his *chudik* theme. This "attempt at a documentary story" (the story's subtitle) supposedly depicts Shukshin's real-life confrontation with a hospital orderly over the latter's refusal to let Shukshin's wife bring their children into the ward to see him. Children were not allowed, although other patients had circumvented this rule by giving the orderly a fifty-kopeck bribe. Shukshin did not have any money on him and, he claims, was not able to give bribes anyway. A *skandal* ensues, during which the orderly shouts at Shukshin—in front of a room full of people, including Shukshin's children—to return to his room. Meanwhile, his wife goes to fetch the doctor, who lets the children in. The whole incident is ugly and petty, but Shukshin is most amazed at the "profound" and "sincere malice" with which the orderly vows her revenge (2:348).

> I don't know what happened to me there, but I suddenly felt that that was it—the end. What kind of an end, an end to what, I can't say, I don't know even now, but the premonition of some sort of very simple, meaningless end was distinct. It wasn't death I felt, or its approach, but some sort of END. (2:348)

The worst came later when the orderly followed through on her threat not to allow Shukshin to have any more visitors. That same day after visiting hours, the writer Vasilii Belov and the secretary of the Vologda Writers' Association came by with an after-hours visiting permit to discuss business with Shukshin. The orderly refused them entrance. Another *skandal* followed, this one ending with Shukshin—acting every bit like one of his own heroes—storming out of the hospital into the raw December evening to catch a taxi in nothing but his hospital gown and slippers, knowing full well he could exacerbate his chronic pneumonia.

One critic calls "A Slander" a key to understanding Shukshin's hero because it highlights the latter's "acute sense of fairness," "emotional sensitivity," "abruptness, impulsiveness, and explosiveness."[31] "A Slander," however, essentially repeats the central features of a fictional incident Shukshin related in the story "Van'ka Tepliashin" a year and a half earlier.[32] The similarities between the two accounts are striking and raise questions as to Shukshin's motivations for "rewriting" "Van'ka Tepliashin" as "A Slander" and for casting himself in the role of the hapless *chudik*.

In "Van'ka Tepliashin" the hero, a country Ivan the Fool, also has a run-in with a city hospital orderly, who, like the nameless orderly from "A Slander," is also a depersonified figure, here referred to only as "Red Eyes." The conflict starts when Red Eyes refuses to admit Van'ka's mother after she arrives from the village on a day visitors are not normally admitted. On this occasion, more than mere words are exchanged. When Red Eyes fails to relent, Van'ka sends him and another orderly flying and a scuffle breaks out, after which he checks himself out of the hospital without having completed his treatment, just as Shukshin would later do. Furthermore, Van'ka's explanation as to why he did not simply offer the usual fifty-kopeck bribe— "You have to be human" (2:206)—is almost the same as the accusation Shukshin flings at the orderly after he also failed to proffer the usual offering: "You're not a human being!" (2:348). Both Shukshin's and Van'ka's victories are Pyrrhic—they each go home unwell—and Van'ka's noble words of protest, like Shukshin's, are also rendered ridiculous when he repeats them to the attendant returning his clothes: "'You gotta be human and not try to squeeze fifty-kopeck coins outta people,' Van'ka said again with an air of importance. But there, in the basement, in the midst of all the clothes hangers, in the close-smelling clouds of mothball fumes, these words didn't sound so solemn" (2:207).

In "A Slander," however, Shukshin seems to be up to something else. Unlike "Van'ka Tepliashin," it is a very self-conscious story, with its narrating persona commenting throughout on his own theatrical behavior. For instance, when other patients begin to protest on his behalf, the narrator's eyes fill "with tears out of love and gratitude": "'Well, well!' I thought, but you can be assured that I held back from any insults or loud indignation. I'm an actor, I understand these things . . . On the contrary, I even assumed 'a posture of complete helplessness' and made an expression of profound sorrow on my face" (2:347). Later, when the orderly refuses to let his friends come in—an incident which he describes in suitably thespian terms as a "spectacle"—Shukshin wants to rend his hospital pajamas and then storms out of the hospital "like [Gogol's Cossack patriarch] Taras Bul'ba" (2:349). The effect is very Dostoevskian, recalling as it does the theatrical self-consciousness of the Underground Man.

Like the Underground Man, the narrator continually weighs his words and assesses his discourse. He takes particular pride in his use of the words "humanly" and "incident," the latter a "harsh, zinc-coated" foreign borrowing which will "speak highly of itself and of me: that I know such words" (2:346). These words, the narrator feels, will distinguish his letter of complaint from the one the orderly has already written about the event. Elsewhere, the narrator makes a point of not capitalizing the possessive pronoun in the phrase "your hospital" when addressing the director, so as not to look as if he is resorting to flattery (2:346). Other instances of the narrator's acute self-consciousness include his repeated amazement that he cannot remember the orderly's face (2:345, 348, twice on 349), and his bizarre interest in whether her face has a wart on it (a detail, he admits, he might have added himself "out of nastiness" [2:345]).

In the final analysis, Shukshin transforms himself into a hyperbolized version of Van'ka, a grotesque Dostoevskian variant of the *chudik*. In so doing, he heightens the central conflict of the story and raises it to a level it failed to achieve in "Van'ka Tepliashin," that of a universal accusation hurled not only at life's petty tyrants but also at their victims who respond in kind and thus sink to their level. Here the polemical function of the writer's strange heroes in exposing falseness, folly, and vice is turned against the writer. Through his self-conscious appropriation of his hero's behavior, Shukshin unmasks himself and his own petty nature, coming to the realization that his written complaint is no nobler than that of the orderly: "I've just read all of this . . . And I'm thinking: 'What is happening to us?'" (2:351). Hence the title of the story, "A Slander," which is both an accusation and a self-indictment.[33]

In these stories and in many others, Shukshin's hero (and by self-implication, perhaps Shukshin as well) suffers from what one reviewer of *Strange People* called "a unique hypertrophy of conscience."[34] This hypertrophied conscience—another way of describing the enlarged souls of Shukshin's *chudiki*—often expresses itself in inappropriate ways, as in the story "Friends for Fun and Games" ("Drugi igrishch i zabav," 1974), whose hero flies like an avenging angel to punish the guy who got his sister pregnant, only to wind up taking his vengeance out on the wrong party. The problem is essentially the same for all of these oddballs: a wronged soul. Only the degree of seriousness of the collision between soul and world changes from story to story, along with the consequences, which range from suicide and prison sentences in the worst-case scenarios to alarmed and aching souls in the best.

In Shukshin's fiction, to live for your soul is to cast off, firmly and festively, that which compromises you and ties you to the here and now, be it a steady job, an antagonistic wife, adherence to bureaucratic procedures, consumerism, or a prosaic approach to life. This is the first step toward overcoming the aching in your soul. As the priest tells Maksim in "I Believe!": "Your soul aches? Good. Good! You've at least begun to stir, damn you! Or else it'd be impossible to drag you with all of your spiritual inertia off your berth on the stove" (2:539). In turn, these heroes, with their strange, aching souls, point the way for others to rid themselves of their own "spiritual inertia." Shukshin writes: "It's necessary to bring out their beauty in such a way that the satisfied philistine won't want to scoff at their 'strangeness.' On the contrary, so that he will bitterly feel his own good-for-nothingness and at least for a little while be alarmed."[35] Here Shukshin is speaking to the ability of his strange heroes to *make strange* the crass materialism of everyday life, thus revealing the bankruptcy of an outlook tied too strongly to the temporal and worldly.

This estrangement was clearly Shukshin's intent in the movie version of "Oddball," where Oddball leaves his brother after only two nights due to his intense sense of shame over his brother's materialistic behavior. Mired down in *byt,* life's petty concerns, the brother spends all of his time trying to increase his living space by marrying advantageously (a second time). He has turned into the cynical, materialistic antithesis of Oddball, a fact emphasized by the actor Evgenii Evstigneev's interpretation of the role. He turns the brother into a grotesque parody of the petty bourgeois. The spiritual crisis that sends Oddball home early is meant to highlight his brother's own "good-for-nothingness," which is why the vignette in the movie is called "Bratka" ("Brother") and not "Oddball." That the episode was filmed on the Black Sea and included a scene in front of Chekhov's Yalta residence only underscores Shukshin's theme. His hero's proximity to the master unmasker of spiritual emptiness, Pharisaism, and parvenu vulgarity acknowledges both an important debt and Shukshin's affinity with Chekhov's artistic program.

Shukshin accomplishes a similar estrangement through characters whose oddness is connected to the contemplation of death, the ultimate leveler of the material world and the point of final reckoning for the soul. "Meditations" ("Dumy," 1967), which together with "Sten'ka Razin" comprises the third part of *Strange People,* describes how kolkhoz chairman Matvei Riazantsev is kept awake each night by the accordion playing of Kol'ka Malashkin, who is courting his girlfriend. The music evokes various scenes from Matvei's own life and thoughts of his own death. As Kol'ka passes by the house and the music recedes into the distance, Matvei examines his life, waking up his wife with various questions and going out frequently onto the porch for a smoke. His wife thinks he is losing his mind, and Matvei himself cannot explain what is happening to him. His life has suddenly been thrown out of its normal routine and has become suffused with an elusive, higher meaning. He even begins to anticipate Kol'ka's late-night playing and the aching it causes in his soul, "a strange kind of ache—one he longed for. Something was missing without it" (1:315).

Matvei is also one of Shukshin's strange people, and indeed his existential pondering bears little resemblance to the portrayals of stoic peasants calmly accepting death that were made famous first in the works of Tolstoy and other nineteenth-century writers and later in Village Prose. Unlike those depictions, "Meditations" and stories like "Passing Through" ("Zaletnyi," 1970), "Uncle Ermolai" ("Diadia Ermolai," 1971), and "There Lived a Man" ("Zhil chelovek," 1974) are angst-driven interrogations of the meaning of death by heroes who force us to reassess our own lives.

Though there seems to be no belief in the afterlife connected to Shukshin's heroes' spiritual quests, the contemplation of death often has a life-affirming and transcendent effect. As Sania Neverov states in "Passing Through," "If we aren't in the position to comprehend it, then to make up for it, death at least allows us to understand that life is wonderful" (1:481–82). Sania is an alcoholic and intellectual who has moved to the village to live out his days. The blacksmith Filipp Nasedkin and other village men get in the habit of going to Sania's to drink and talk about life, because in his company "everything would become fine and clear in your soul, as if suddenly—for just a moment—you had become immense and free and could touch with your hands the beginning and end of your life, as if you had measured something valuable and understood everything" (1:478). The village council warns Filipp and the others not to go to Sania's—the womenfolk are afraid their men will become alcoholics like him—but they go anyway. With Sania, their lives acquire some sort of deeper significance. Although Sania dies lamenting the meaninglessness of death, which he likens to an execution, and although his name (Neverov, or "nonbeliever") suggests an absence of faith in an afterlife, he gives Filipp and the others a deeper understanding and love of life as well as hope to go on living. After all, as Sania tells them, "There are lots of us eccentrics and strange people in this world!" (1:481), that is, people capable of imparting—as Sania does to Filipp—the "fervent belief that life is indeed wonderful" (1:482), even when life or the cosmos (through the specter of death) wrongs you. The human spirit, Shukshin says through his oddballs, can overcome even death, if only through its ability to acknowledge the end that awaits all living things and still not give in to pessimism, cynicism, indifference, or the other faces of despair. Such are the rewards of Shukshinian eccentricity, and they are great indeed in an otherwise hostile and indifferent world.

THE ODDBALL AND CARNIVAL

There is another side to Shukshin's strange heroes, one visible in the mock funeral scene from the film version of "Meditations." In a fantasy sequence Matvei Riazantsev witnesses his own burial and even answers a reporter's questions about what it feels like to be dead. Vladimir Solov'ev calls the scene "carnivalesque stage-buffoonery," where "thoughts of death are brought down from a high register to the lowest, from tragedy to farce," an instance "when laughter allows what thought will not."[36] This moment when eccentricity intersects with buffoonery is most apparent in the middle vignette from the film, "The Fatal Shot" ("Rokovoi vystrel"), based on the story "Mille Pardons, Madame!" This side speaks to the compulsive and eccentric aspects of the *chudik*, his need to assert his unique and unfinalizable essence, to participate in his own coronation or public confession, his own comic crowning and discrowning, his confrontation and communion with other people in the public square.

Like Oddball, Bron'ka Pupkov from "Mille Pardons, Madame!" is another one of Shukshin's carefree village fools. His strangeness consists in his inexplicable need to tell the bizarre story of his alleged attempt on Hitler's life to groups of hunters whom he serves as a guide. Although his wife gives him hell for it and the village council threatens to take measures against him for distorting history, Bron'ka cannot resist. He can no longer live without his tale, and he awaits "like a holiday" (1:348) the opportunity to tell it once again. The tale is certainly fantastic: an orderly in the army, Bron'ka is spotted by a general who sees in him the spitting image of a recently captured German spy. Since the spy was personally to give Hitler (present incognito on the frontlines) important stolen documents, the opportunity arose to send Bron'ka instead, who could then carry out the assassination. Bron'ka vows after undergoing "special training": "Either . . . they'll have to lay me out dead next to Hitler, or you'll have to send out a team to rescue Hero of the Soviet Union Pupkov, Bronislav Ivanovich" (1:352). The problem is, neither outcome is obtained. Neither Bron'ka nor Hitler perishes, this despite the fact that Bron'ka, "a rare shot, indeed" (1:354), was supposedly within a few paces of Hitler when he fired. Moreover, no explanation is given of how Bron'ka escapes or even of how he crossed enemy lines in the first place.

All of this might incline Bron'ka's listeners to ridicule him were it not for two facts: Bron'ka's consummate storytelling skills, which enthrall his listeners, and the fact that the story itself is his own self-reproach. After all, what larger accusation could you throw at yourself than that you failed to kill one of the worst monsters the world has ever known? At the same time, the story is very funny for the reader, and for the viewer, who can recognize Bron'ka's *vran'e* (tall tale) in all of the suspicious details or lack thereof, such as Bron'ka's fluent German despite his never having studied it, the absence of specifics in his description of his special training, and Hitler's presence on the frontlines. What is obtained in the final analysis is Bron'ka's crowning (as a secret agent on one of the world's most important missions), his discrowning (he missed, and readily confesses it publicly and dramatically), and their comic consequence (the laughter "offstage" of the reader and author, for whom the ridiculous figure of Bron'ka Pupkov—like his ridiculous name—is a source of amusement). All told, the effect is restorative: hierarchy is relativized (Bron'ka is put on the same level as Hitler, the charged notion "Hero of the Soviet Union" comes to naught, the rare shot misses, and so on), while the leveling laughter associated with folk humor provides reader and author with the vicarious suspension of prevailing historical truth and of the commonsense rules of everyday life.

This strange combination of self-crowning and discrowning in the name of one's right to one's quirks is rehearsed in several other narratives. In each instance, Shukshin's heroes astound and annoy their neighbors and relatives with their flamboyant gestures of self-aggrandizement and their equally spectacular acts of self-effacement. A good example is "Let's Conquer the Heart!" written the same year as "Mille Pardons, Madame!" Having heard late one night on the radio of the first successful human heart transplant, veterinarian Aleksandr Kozulin fires two rifle shots into the air to mark the occasion. The problem is, he does so at three in the morning. What to him is a salute to a breakthrough in medicine is seen by the police as a "violation of public law and order" (1:386). Kozulin is hauled in to answer questions but is unable to explain his action satisfactorily. They warn him against future "nighttime salutes": "Who knows what sort of achievements the future may bring us! You'll make psychopaths out of all us citizens" (1:388). When he realizes that no one can understand his triumphant gesture, Kozulin "slanders" himself: he suddenly confesses to the police that he is a "schizo." "Forgive me, I wasn't thinking at that moment . . . I'm a schizo. [. . .] it just comes over me, I lose all self-control" (1:388). Indeed, as he leaves the station, he has another "attack": "At the threshold he stopped . . . and turned. And suddenly he made a wry face, closed his eyes and surprisingly loudly— just as if he were standing before a battalion—he drawled out the commands: 'R-r-right dress! 'Ten-tion!'" (1:389).

The village chairman is at a loss, but the policeman is sure Kozulin is faking it, "slandering himself" just "to be on the safe side. In case something comes up, he'll say, 'I'm a schizo.' We're on to all those little tricks" (1:389). The officer is partly right: Kozulin, like Bron'ka, provides a "loophole" for himself, "the retention for oneself of the possibility of altering ultimate, final meaning of one's words."[37] Whereas Bron'ka's "distortion of history" is not a crime because it is "not a printed work" (1:354) and therefore never assumes a finalized (and prosecutable) form, Kozulin also evades ultimate responsibility for his acts by pleading schizophrenia. In this way Kozulin protects what Galina Belaia, in her commentary on the story, calls "the world of the pure heart, the sincere outburst" against the world where "bureaucratized and formalized thinking reigns."[38] This, of course, is one of the main functions of Shukshinian eccentricity and buffoonery, which provide an outlet for nonconformity while masking it as a harmless kind of deviation. The provincial location of most of Shukshin's stories also helps to mask the challenge implied in the iconoclastic ideas and deeds of his strange characters: these are backwater freaks who behave the way they do out of a lack of culture, education, information, or sophistication.

In Bakhtinian carnival, where authority is always ambivalent and all structure and order is made joyfully relative, a "decrowning always glimmers through the crowning."[39] This is particularly true when Shukshin's *chudiki* take on the world of science. Andrei Erin from "The Microscope" ("Mikroskop," 1969) is a vivid example. He shows up at home one day with the news that he has somehow lost his month's salary. His wife at first refuses to believe him, but when she finally does, she goes straight for her frying pan. When things calm down, they decide that he will work one and a half shifts until the money is made up. In reality, Andrei has blown his salary on a microscope and is only waiting for the opportunity to bring it home.

When he does, he is "quietly radiant" (1:397). Explaining that he had been rewarded for his "shock labor," Andrei unpacks it and places it on the table.

Like a king's scepter, the microscope confers power and authority and brings with it a magical transformation: Andrei suddenly becomes "the loud domineering master of the house" (1:399). Thus crowned king of his castle, Andrei bosses his wife around, earns the respect of his neighbors (the villagers all start calling him a scientist), and even forgets about his usual drinking sprees. He is obsessed with his new mission: to kill all the microbes so that man can live to be a hundred and fifty, as he is "supposed to" (1:400). For a week, Andrei lives "as in a dream" (1:400). Then his holiday comes "crashing down." In a scene of classic comic reversal, a tipsy coworker on a binge shows up and lets Andrei's secret out of the bag. The microscope disappears (his wife takes it to the consignment shop), and, without his "scepter," Andrei is transformed back into his former self, drowning his decrowning in vodka. As in all carnival celebrations, the established order prevails. But some renewal is achieved, along with hope for better times: Andrei now encourages his son to become a scientist.

With similar gusto and to comparable humorous effect, Monia Kvasov from "Stubborn" throws himself into inventing a perpetual-motion machine "such as the world had never seen" (2:230). He simply cannot believe that perpetual motion is an impossibility. Like Andrei Erin, Monia is not very well educated—only eight and a half years of schooling—so the principles of "friction and the laws of mechanics" (2:230) do not overly concern him. Consequently, it does not take him long to find his solution, which he discovers one night and then announces the next day to a village engineer. The engineer responds with an angry lecture. Mortified, Monia runs with his plans to the village physics teacher, who confirms the worst: his design will not work. Undaunted, Monia spends the rest of the day and all night building his *perpetuum mobile,* only to discover that the engineer and physics teacher are right: friction and the law of mechanics cannot be overcome. In one moment, Monia goes from genius inventor to village idiot, as predicted by the engineer: "You're making a laughingstock out of yourself" (2:236). But as Monia later muses: "People have to have their laugh. They work hard, there's not much to entertain them around here—let them have their laugh" (2:241). Indeed, Monia even feels a special love and pity for his neighbors that night.

The laughter Monia anticipates from his fellow villagers actually becomes a life-affirming force for him, a weapon that helps people "bear their cross" (2:241), their knowledge of the inevitability of death. In fact, the story is a submerged treatment of this larger issue: the meaning of life, mortality, and death, a theme connected most directly to the character of Monia's grandmother. First, we learn how she "sidestepped death" (2:233) during the war by stealing grain. Then, in a conversation with Monia, she herself brings up her impending death, a habit which displeases her grandson. Later, she tells the engineer enigmatically, "[W]e'll all sleep someday" (2:243). Her consistent association with this theme in the story lends Monia's attempt to build his perpetual-motion machine a deeper significance. After his failure, Monia is suddenly inspired to get married and have children, to join the cycle of life that is the closest thing to perpetual motion attainable. Images of the ever-flowing river near his home, the daily morning sounds in the village, and the endless rising and setting of the sun confirm Monia's discovery of life's true perpetual motion, a discovery made possible only by his foolish venture. In giving up on his plans to build a *perpetuum mobile* and giving in to the life-affirming nature of folk laughter, Monia accepts the finite nature of his own life and gains a deeper appreciation and understanding of it.

"Cutting Them Down to Size" ("Srezal," 1970) is probably Shukshin's most controversial instance of carnivalesque inversion and attracted considerable critical debate. It is the story of Gleb Kapustin, a "fat-lipped, towheaded muzhik, about forty years old, well read and venomous" (2:7), who has one distinct talent: his ability to cut people down to size. In this sense, he is the quintessential discrowner in Shukshin's fiction. Whenever any notable visits the village of Novaia, the village men gather on Gleb's porch and lead him to the guest themselves, "just as if they were going to a performance" or "escorting an experienced village fistfighter when folks find out that a new tough guy has appeared in a rival neighborhood" (2:8). The semantics here are important—Gleb is a performer and a fighter, and he rarely disappoints.[40] On this occasion, the visiting notable is Konstantin Zhuravlev, a local boy who has made it big in the city, having just become a *kandidat filologicheskikh nauk* (comparable to the American Ph.D.). Moreover, he's married to another *kandidat*, has a daughter, and has enough wealth to come rolling into the village in a taxi with too many suitcases in the trunk. Word spreads throughout the whole village: Agaf'ia's son has come, "the rich one, the scholar" (2:7). So the village men turn to Gleb to pass judgment on this upwardly mobile success story and cut him down to size, if need be.

At first, Gleb is almost forgotten by the men in all of their childhood reminiscing with Zhuravlev. Then he takes center stage. He proceeds to ask Zhuravlev a series of "philosophical" questions, which, however, are posed in such a way that the *kandidat* is at a loss for what to reply: what does the *kandidat* make of the primacy of matter over spirit in light of the "recently discovered" phenomenon of weightlessness? What is the *kandidat*'s opinion of the problem of shamanism in the autonomous regions of the north? What does he think about the fact that the moon may be a man-made object? Although several critics have argued that these questions actually speak to substantive issues of Marxism-Leninism, Soviet policy on nationalities and local religion, and the uneasy relationship between Soviet science and ideology and are only camouflaged by Shukshin to look ridiculous,[41] the point is actually not *what* Gleb asks but *how* the *kandidat* answers him. His consternation and irritation reflect his unwillingness to meet Gleb halfway, to set his degree aside and converse with Gleb not as Konstantin Ivanovich, Ph.D., but as Kostia, come back to the village for a spell. Gleb gives him this chance at the beginning of their conversation, when he asks his first question about primacy: "Gleb threw down the gauntlet. Gleb affected a casual pose and waited for the gauntlet to be taken up. The *kandidat* took the gauntlet up" (2:9). Konstantin could have chosen not to answer a question so inappropriate for a *zastol'e,* or bout of friendly drinking. Instead, he attempts to answer Gleb's question seriously, as a scholar, refusing to let his guard down. Here the duel terminology is appropriate, for Konstantin is signaling his readiness to engage in a battle of wits.

But those who live by the (s)word die by the (s)word, and Gleb soon delivers his knockout blow. At a crucial moment in the debate, when Gleb likens himself to an earthling trying to communicate with possible lunar inhabitants, the *kandidat* exchanges a meaningful look with his wife. Their condescension is caught by Gleb, who swoops down on them like a bird of prey. What follows is a lengthy invective on the evils of judging people by their appearances, after which Gleb exits dramatically to the wonder of the peasant men assembled, who are amazed by Gleb's performance but pity Zhuravlev. It turns out Zhuravlev is neither very "smart" nor very "witty"— the key qualities of contestants in a game show Gleb mentions, *Klub veselykh i nakhodchivykh* (*The Club of the Smart and Witty*). He understands neither Gleb's game nor Gleb's cosmic analogy on Zhuravlev's own arrival in the village when Gleb asks in the context of a hypothetical meeting on the moon with extraterrestrials, "Are we ready to understand each other?" (2:11). The question, of course, is aimed at Konstantin, who, with his degree, educated wife, and taxi full of suitcases and gifts, is as alien in the village as Gleb's hypothetical lunar beings.

Gleb emphasizes the intellectual isolation of the village ("Even if a person in these parts wants to have a good chat, it's impossible to round somebody up" [2:9]) and his own provinciality ("I can share with you in what direction our thoughts are leading us provincials" [2:11]), giving the *kandidat* clear opportunities to "come down to earth" (2:12) and behave more modestly. But Konstantin is either incapable of understanding or unwilling to understand, just as he fails to realize that his arrival in the village and ostentatious display of wealth and success have made the wrong impression. He is therefore cut down to size.

The image of a village demagogue reducing intellectuals to stammering rage through "verbal buffoonery"[42] was not popular with the critics, who immediately attacked Gleb and made Zhuravlev out to be an innocent victim.[43] Shukshin's position, however, is ambivalent. Although in an interview he calls Gleb's performance "revenge in the purest sense of the word, not in the least embellished,"[44] and although the narrator remarks that Gleb is "cruel, and nobody anywhere has ever yet loved cruelty" (2:13), Shukshin also indicates in a working note that Gleb "isn't, by the way, such an idiot" (2:573). Indeed, we can detect a trace of Shukshin's own provincial complex in this story of the villager who cuts the rich, famous, urban careerist down to size. The lesson here for the reader—and the author—is to avoid Zhuravlev's mistakes while not mistaking Gleb's demagoguery for anything but what it really is: vengeance. In Zhuravlev's discrowning there is the potential for renewal, but as in all carnival it is connected to a recognition of the relativity of status, rank, and privilege.

Shukshin is consistently suspicious of self-promotion and rank, and much of his humor is connected with debunking those who hunger after titles and recognition. A few examples will suffice. In "General Malafeikin" (1972) the title character, a housepainter and pensioner, passes himself off as a big shot to his fellow travelers on an overnight train trip, unaware that the person asleep on the bunk above him is none other than his sometime co-worker and apartment neighbor Misha Tolstykh, who wakes up and overhears the incredible story Malafeikin is telling. In the morning, as they pull into the Moscow train station, Malafeikin realizes Misha has heard everything; frightened and humiliated, he flees in a panic. In another story, Anatolii Iakovlev tries to shake his foolish nickname—"The Retard" (*debil*, the 1971 story's title)—by buying a hat, which he thinks will make him look intelligent. It fails. His wife explains: "It's as if they put a chamber pot on a pumpkin" (2:93). Here the quite literal crowning of the hero has just the opposite effect. The hero of my final example, "How Andrei Ivanovich Kurinkov, Jeweler, Got a Fifteen-Day Sentence" ("Kak Andrei Ivanovich Kurinkov, iuvelir, poluchil 15 sutok," 1974), attempts something similar. In order to frighten a noisy neighbor, a tailor by trade, with whom he has been feuding for years, Kurinkov shows up in a military coat and cap (his substitute for a robe and crown) and places the tailor under arrest. The tailor, with his trained eye, however, can see immediately that the coat was not made for him; Kurinkov's self-crowning collapses, and he gets a two-week sentence for impersonating an officer.

In all of these instances, Shukshin employs the eccentric antics of his heroes in the service of humorous discrowning not only to reveal but also to revel in human foibles, including his own. This point cannot be overemphasized, for while Shukshin exposes vice and folly through eccentricity and buffoonery, he also acknowledges that he is as flawed as those he humbles, which is what carnival and the leveling effects of folk laughter are all about. There is no self-righteousness, only self-deprecation. Moreover, in the midst of all this buffoonery, Shukshin also flings a challenge down before the petrified forms of daily living and of the stagnation of the human personality. Shukshin's strange people, after all, are first and foremost nonconformists, and while their *skandaly* at times may seem a pale substitute for true conflict or their search for *volia* over *svoboda* (personal freedom over civic freedom) an avoidance of "the larger question of liberty . . . in the USSR,"[45] they nevertheless affirm another precious right: the right to be themselves, to be different, to be individuals.[46]

THE ODDBALL AS ARTIST

Shukshin's most conspicuous soul-searching protagonists are his artist-heroes, who mediate between the world of the spirit and that of everyday reality and thus most personify the quest for the transcendent in Shukshin's universe. These heroes confirm Thomas Moore's assertion that the "soul lies midway between understanding and unconscious, and that its instrument is neither the mind nor the body, but the imagination."[47] Vaseka in "Sten'ka Razin" is an important early incarnation, and his reappearance in *Strange People* heightens the significance of the artist-hero in Shukshin's fiction. In both story and film, Shukshin draws a parallel between the mission of the artist and the figure of Stepan Razin, a connection that illuminates the artist's special role. The artist, like the ataman, seeks *volia,* but what the rebel Cossack achieved with his saber, Vaseka accomplishes with his carving tools. In both instances, the service of a higher ideal is emphasized. The freedom from obligation and servitude that Razin seeks is the artist's search for liberation as well: from the daily drudgery of a mundane job, from artistic and domestic convention, from any constraints on one's creativity.

When Vaseka finally unveils his sculpture of Razin, it is not a statue we see before us, but a whole story of how Razin's traitorous fellow Cossacks burst in upon him in the middle of the night to arrest him and hand him over to the tsar. It is a narrative fraught with drama and tension in which we can hear the thud of blows and the dreadful swearing of the combatants. As Ignashev points out, Vaseka's sculpture is not static—it "sings"; through it, both Vaseka and Shukshin sing as well, achieving their own *volia* through the medium of art.[48] Razin—bound and betrayed by his men and, at least in the story, dressed only in his undergarments—is at once a blasphemy of Soviet historical hagiography and a distinct allusion to Christ's crucifixion. Indeed, the cock crows thrice after Vaseka unveils his statue for the village teacher Zakharych, and a "radiant morning" begins to break to the muffled sobs of Razin's distant "disciples," Zakharych and Vaseka (1:38). The implication—that the trials and tribulations of the true artist rival those of Razin or even Christ—is an important one. It points to the potential redemptive qualities of creative expression, bought sometimes at a high price, that are inherent in Shukshin's fiction and underscores the special nature of his artist-oddballs.

For Shukshin's oddballs, art is the truest way to achieve on earth a higher realm of freedom and truth. Arkashka's unrivaled dancing in "Shiva Dancing" (1972), for instance, is described as "the free form of free existence in our material age" (1:518). As in Shukshin's own stories and the traditions of folk art in general, Arkashka's dancing both parodies and celebrates, and thus revives. His masterful spoof on one of the village carpenters—Arkashka calls its "How Van'ka Seleznev Pulls Nails Out with His Rear" (1:518)—entertains his fellow workers and yet also leads to a brawl when Van'ka, who does not share everyone else's enjoyment of the dance, tries to take his revenge. He is stopped by an out-of-town brigade leader, who fells Van'ka by "fighting dirty" (1:520). Everyone is repulsed and another fight erupts. Even Arkashka rushes to Van'ka's aid. But between Arkashka's dance and the melee that follows, equilibrium is restored and human relationships renewed. Here, the creative potential inherent in the wounding upheaval of Shukshinian *skandal* for this and other stories is affirmed. Like his namesake, Shiva, the Lord of the Cosmic Dance (an Indian deity),[49] Arkashka, through his dance and the free-for-all it inspires, speaks to the dynamic interrelatedness of creation and destruction, the joyful relativity of life which is constantly building up and tearing down.

The artist, Shukshin implies, is at the center of this process of creation and destruction in which existence and the world—as in the ancient Greek understanding—are justified only as an aesthetic phenomenon. This would explain the depth of the aesthetic sensibilities of some of his village protagonists and homespun artists, who see in beauty an answer to the riddle of life. Such an artist is Semka Rys' from "The Craftsman" ("Master," 1971), a master carpenter who becomes captivated by a church he discovers in a nearby village. Semka's thoughts, however, proceed with an almost chilling inevitability from contemplation of the church as a confirmation of man's aspiration for beauty and harmony to a philosophical acceptance of another person's right to reject and destroy that same beauty:

What did that unknown master think about when he left behind him this bright fairy tale in stone? Was he praising God or showing off? But people who want to show off don't go very far away, they stick close to the beaten track or go straight to the crowded town square, where people'll notice. This one was concerned about something else: beauty, maybe? As if a man sang his song, and sang it well. And then went his way. Why did he do it? He didn't know himself. His soul moved him to. [. . .] And what could you say anyway? Sure, it's good, it's beautiful, it moves you, it makes you happy . . . Is that what really counts? He also was happy, he also was moved, he also understood that it was beautiful. What of it? It doesn't matter. If you know how to be happy, be happy, if you know how to make others happy, make them happy . . . If not, make war, give orders, or do something like that—you can even destroy this fairy tale: put a couple of kilograms of dynamite under it and blow it sky high. To each his own. (1:497)

In this latter remark we see, of course, a reference to Stalin's antireligious campaign in the 1930s as well as veiled criticism of the indifference shown by the Soviet government toward preserving what churches remained. Here, as in much of Shukshin's prose, the transcendent (the church itself and Semka's desire to restore it) and the empirical (the authorities' refusal to approve funds for Semka's project because specialists in Moscow have determined it is only a copy of an older Vladimir church) are juxtaposed and come into conflict.

The outcome in this story is bleak. After his meeting with the authorities, Semka thenceforth avoids passing the church whenever he can. It is unclear whether his bitterness stems from his having been deceived by this secondhand copy or from the inability of the authorities to see the beauty of the church, a beauty independent of documents, specialists, and historical or religious assessments. The greatest tragedy is that Semka's artistic impulse has been frustrated at the hands of politicians and bureaucrats, a danger oft-repeated in Shukshin's stories about artists: that of the vulnerability of their songs, tales, sculptures, or dances in the face of opposition from hostile or uncomprehending sources.

Gena Proidisvet, from the story of the same name (1973), marks the last of Shukshin's carefree artists and the end of his engagement with the oddball as a central hero. Gena's surname, with its implied command to "walk through the world," suggests the cultural and physical mobility central to all of Shukshin's fools, especially his artist-oddballs. "We artists," boasts Gena, "are a special kind of people"; to learn a profession, he says, is a "mortal sin. My occupation is people" (2:210). Gena is a *massovik-zateinik,* an organizer of recreational activities at a sanitorium. But, as his Russian epithet implies, he is also a practical joker. "Everyone was amazed at Genka's songs and his tomfoolery. The songs he composed himself and played on the guitar. As for his tomfoolery . . . It wasn't really tomfoolery, but his complete—and demonstrative—freedom and lack of restraint" (2:208). In the story, Gena tries unsuccessfully to talk his uncle out of his recent religious conversion. For Gena, his uncle's sudden interest in the Church is a lie; he cannot imagine his fun-loving uncle—who used to drink, sing obscene limericks, and "wallow in life like a satiated stallion in ripe oats" (2:212)— suddenly leading a monastic life. Organized religion has little in common with the true world of the spirit, which for Gena is tied to a pantheistic celebration of the spiritual in life here and now, in living life fully and joyfully and in making others happy as well.

In Gena, Shukshin unites and summarizes the main features of the *chudik* discussed in this chapter: he is a fun-loving jester (*zateinik*) and fool (his uncle twice calls him a *durak* [2:214–15]) who brings joy to others and who opposes anything that constrains the soul, be it the professional grind or religious dogma. His antics—such as jumping into a pool with his guitar while singing at the top of his lungs—militate against the routine and the ossified in life and make possible carnivalesque inversions of life's categories and hierarchies, including those having to do with religious belief. (His uncle even calls him the Antichrist 666 [2:219].) As a poet and a performer, he speaks to the importance of creativity and the need to transcend prosaic reality. But Gena also marks the late appearance of a character type from which Shukshin had already begun to turn at the time he published the story. The frequent appearance and predictable behavior of his favored oddball characters at this point in Shukshin's career actually began to make commonplace and redundant what was formerly eccentric and unique, and with deadly consequences. By 1974, with critics charging that his stories were starting to repeat themselves, Shukshin realized that his odd heroes were becoming anachronisms. The times—and the artist—were changing, and so his hero also changed. The eccentric and the elemental in Shukshin's hero became increasingly more grotesque and satiric. *Chudiki* were giving way to *kharaktery*, types.

Shukshin's oddball was a response to the transient state of the modern Soviet peasant, now more educated and more divorced from the land than ever before. He represents the estranged generations caught in the midst of the transformation from a rural to an industrial economy and from country to urban living, hence his eccentric blend of naïveté and knowledge, superstition and science, art and homespun philosophy, hooliganism and respect for the law. For other transplanted country folk, this shift led to a different kind of deformation. They became complacent and condescending urban dwellers, conspicuous consumers, arrogant Ph.D.'s, petty black marketeers, and recidivist thieves. This latter development led Shukshin away from his beloved *chudik* toward a character type who evoked a harsher response from the writer, one of biting satire and grotesque mockery.

Still, the *chudik* is Shukshin's most famous character and his lasting contribution to the evolution of the fool in Russian literature, who, thanks to Shukshin, was alive and well even during the Brezhnev "period of stagnation." Indeed, the *chudik* testifies to the physical, moral, and spiritual resilience of the masses from which he comes. As one critic asserts, Shukshin succeeded in "elevating the personality from the masses," allowing for his "spiritual requirements" and the "realization of his human self." He "was able to capture the historical shift in the spiritual world of his hero, the man off the street, the carrier of mass consciousness."[50] Shukshin "paid attention to what was 'private' in [his heroes], to the torturously complicated problems of their inner lives, their spiritual disarray."[51]

These are important insights into the great attraction of this character for Shukshin's audience, both the *intelligentsiia* and the mass reader. His hero is a representative of the common folk, but one devoid of the ideological generalizations previously plaguing this character type in Soviet film and fiction. Shukshin's protagonist from the masses has been highly individualized; he has been given a soul and the right to manifest his quirks. Hence the sometimes controversial reception of Shukshin's hero, whose novelty, as one critic argues, was also his "literary 'illegality,'" one that "evoked a storm of differences" among critics, all a testament to "Shukshin's creative daring."[52]

Chapter Five

Grotesque Characters

> What is comedy? It's when the intention, the
> means, and the end are all distorted! When
> there's a deviation from the norm!
> —Vasilii Shukshin, *Till the Cock Crows Thrice*

> But what is comedy without truth and malice!
> —Nikolai Gogol', letter to Mikhail Pogodin, 20
> February 1833

THE TITLE OF SHUKSHIN'S 1973 collection of short stories, his fourth and the last to be published during his lifetime, underscores an important feature of the mature writer's presentation of his hero. *Kharaktery* (characters, types) marks, in name and content, the writer's more demonstrative turn to typification in the last five years of his life, a change most pronounced in his experimental works. These works—the fairy tale *Till the Cock Crows Thrice* and "theater novellas" *Energetic People (Energichnye liudi)* and the unfinished *And They Woke Up in the Morning (A poutru oni prosnulis')*—foreground and expand Shukshin's dependence on types, but do so toward openly satiric ends. Here, as in the "fairy-tale novella" (*povest'-skazka*) *Point of View (Tochka zreniia)* and the cycle "Unexpected Stories" ("Vnezapnye rasskazy") written prior to them, character names give way almost entirely to labels. In the case of *Till the Cock Crows Thrice*, Shukshin even uses stock types from Russian folklore and stereotyped caricatures of well-known heroes from nineteenth-century Russian literature. What previously in his short stories had been a more subtle delineation of characters into a recognizable gallery of contemporary types[1] becomes in his later prose an open reliance on grotesque labels in the service of satire.

Shukshin's move toward satire both reflected and contributed to a growing culture of irony in the Soviet Union, which was partly due to a collapse of hopes and a loss of faith in the face of political reaction at the end of the 1960s[2] and partly due to the rising popularity of comedy in general. The 1970s was a time of satire, popularized on television by the long-running programs *Tavern of the Thirteen Chairs (Kabachok 13 stul'ev)* and *The World*

87

of Laughter (*Vokrug smekha*), featured in newspaper humor columns such as the "Twelve Chairs Club" ("Klub 12 stul'ev") in *Literaturnaia gazeta,* and marked by the growing popularity of the humor journal *Krokodil* (*Crocodile*).[3] Shukshin's own turn toward satire is both an outgrowth of the lightly ironic and humorous nature of many of his stories and films and an indication of a change in the writer's attitude toward his themes and Soviet society in general. As his attitude changed, so did his methods. Satire's caustic blend of truth and malice replaced the light humor and carnival laughter that had heretofore surrounded the artist's bright souls and oddballs. The folk storyteller was returning to the irreverent traditions of the *skomorokhi* with their set casts of satiric types. Folk buffoonery was giving way to grotesque mockery.

Shukshin's satirical works—routinely overlooked by critics and an undervalued part of the artist's oeuvre as a whole—occupy an important place in post-Stalin Soviet literature, for in them, particularly in his novellas, Shukshin lampoons the mores and institutions of Soviet society in a way that would not be repeated in print and published in the Soviet Union until after the ascent of Mikhail Gorbachev and his policies of glasnost. In the best of his satirical works, Shukshin accomplished under censorship what Sergei Dovlatov, Evgenii Popov, Viacheslav P'etsukh, Vladimir Sorokin, and others would achieve only when there was almost no more censorship at all. This fact has still not been acknowledged in studies of the late and post-Soviet period. Indeed, it seems as if Shukshin has suffered the fate of the American writer Sherwood Anderson, whose influence on American authors of the 1920s (especially Hemingway and Faulkner) was significant but not always properly acknowledged. As Anderson did in American literature, Shukshin prepared the thematic and stylistic ground in Soviet literature that others would later work to greater success.[4] In his late prose, Shukshin proposed a new and unattractive hero: the grotesque *Homo sovieticus* of the Soviet 1970s as seen through the distorting lens of satire and in a variety of highly suggestive and often debased settings, from communal apartments to city drunk tanks. This grotesque hero can now be identified as the important forerunner of the nasty heroes whose appearance marked the end of Soviet fiction and the rebirth of Russian literature.

SHUKSHIN'S *KHARAKTERY*

Kharaktery was the most critically acclaimed of all of Shukshin's anthologies published during his lifetime. Its twenty stories were hailed as a major event in fiction and were the object of sharp critical discussions.[5] The collection also marks a departure for Shukshin. As one reviewer notes: "Shukshin is distancing himself more and more from his 'strange' heroes, acknowledging that there is a lot of posing in their nobility. [. . .] The writer is more inclined toward irony, often crossing over into open mockery verging on the style of the feuilleton. His pen is becoming more and more caustic, more cruel."[6] I. Solov'eva and V. Shitova conclude their review of the book by comparing it to the French satirist Jean de La Bruyère's *Les Caractères, ou Les Moeurs de ce Siècle* (1688).[7] Although they do not elaborate, the analogy is appropriate. Like *Les Caractères, Kharaktery* is composed of character sketches of recognizable types with the goal of painting the manners and customs of the times. A satirist of social evils who sought "the general and universal in the local and temporary," La Bruyère also influenced French literary language, introducing new words from the everyday vocabulary of trade, the army, and agriculture.[8] Shukshin performed a similar service in Russian literature almost three centuries later, democratizing Soviet literary parlance and addressing universal themes through localized conflicts. Like La Bruyère's, Shukshin's later stories reveal society's ills and expose human defects. Even Voltaire's assessment of La Bruyère's style—"rapid, concise, and nervous"[9]—could accurately be applied to Shukshin.

Although it is not known whether Shukshin was aware of La Bruyère's book, the stories comprising his *Kharaktery,* like those of *Les Caractères,* can be summarized according to the social malady each tale illustrates. One review of the collection begins this task, mentioning "bureaucratic boorishness" ("Rubles in Words, Kopecks in Figures"), "arbitrariness and willfulness" ("Tough Guy"), "empty posing" ("Step Out, Maestro!" ["Shire shag, maestro!"]), and "sanctimoniousness and hard-heartedness" ("Shameless Ones" ["Bessovestnye"]).[10] To this we could add hypocrisy and vindictiveness ("My Son-in-Law Stole a Truckload of Wood!"), vengeance ("Cutting Them Down to Size"), selfishness ("A Ticket to the Second Showing" ["Biletik na vtoroi seans"]), covetousness ("The Bastard"), self-righteousness ("The Nonresistor Makar Zherebtsov" ["Neprotivlenets Makar Zherebtsov"]), falsehood ("Uncle Ermolai"), puerility ("A Roof over Your Head" ["Krysha nad golovoi"]), pride ("The Retard"), self-indulgence ("Petia"), obsequiousness and petty tyranny ("The Insult"), and crass materialism ("The Brother-in-Law" ["Svoiak Sergei Sergeevich"]).

In these stories Shukshin has begun "to undress" his heroes, using typification to turn characters into "representatives of certain intellectual attitudes, the social consequences of which are ridiculed by their sponsorship of them."[11] The quirks and eccentricities previously celebrated in his famous character types have become the aberrations and fixations now condemned in many of the stories in this collection. Here Shukshin is moving away from the stance of the comic writer, who "delights in the vagaries of his creatures and even admires them for their successful evasion of the moral issue," and is assuming the position of the social critic, who "notes that [people] ought to be different and consequently writes satire."[12] The transition was not a complete one, for it is not always clear in *Kharaktery* whether

Shukshin's comic effects are for the sake of satire or vice versa. Overall, however, the dominant mood is that of satire.

Kharaktery opens and closes with distinct instances of satiric abasement, beginning with Gleb Kapustin's "cutting down to size" of a couple of freshly-minted Ph.D.'s and ending with Sergei Sergeevich forcing his brother-in-law Andrei Kochuganov to give him a piggyback ride to show his gratitude for an expensive gift ("The Brother-in-Law"). Throughout the collection, similar satiric portraits are painted, as Shukshin holds up for censure and/or ridicule self-righteous activists ("My Son-in-Law Stole a Truck Load of Wood!" and "A Roof over Your Head"), boorish saleswomen ("Boots" ["Sapozhki"], "The Retard," and "The Insult"), shallow glory-seekers ("Step Out, Maestro!" and "Tough Guy"), and colorless bureaucrats ("Rubles in Words, Kopecks in Figures"). Shukshin is like Roman Zviagin from "Stuck in the Mud" ("Zabuksoval," also in the collection), who realizes that Gogol's symbolic *troika-Rus'* in *Dead Souls* is carrying none other than a scoundrel and a swindler: he wants to expose the scoundrels for everyone to see. At times in *Kharaktery* this kind of exposure leads to the farcical and absurd, such as when Venia Ziablitskii in "My Son-in-Law Stole a Truckload of Wood!" locks his tyrannical mother-in-law in an outhouse and is subjected to a show trial over it, or in "A Ticket to the Second Showing" when a drunken muzhik mistakes his visiting father-in-law for St. Nicholas (patron saint of peasants) and starts confessing to him all sorts of abominable things—including his true opinion about his wife and in-laws. Here as elsewhere in *Kharaktery,* Shukshin points an accusing finger at all parties, including at times the author-narrator himself.

This aspect of Shukshin's late fiction is particularly interesting and marks an intensification of the artist's ongoing polemic with himself over issues of Soviet society and his identity, heritage, and artistic calling. In "Uncle Ermolai" this self-accusation is innocently couched in a first-person childhood account of a lie the narrator tells the foreman of his work brigade, which later inspires in the narrator a reverie at the man's grave on the meaning of life and the nature of truth. In the collection's only other first-person narrative, "Petia," Shukshin's self-accusation—expressed this time in biting satire—is more pronounced. "Petia" is the clearest indicator in *Kharaktery* of the more caustic turn Shukshin's writing and thinking would take in the last years of his life.

Stuck in a provincial hotel with nothing else to do, the narrator spends two days spying on the people in the building across the street: Petia and his wife, Lial'ka. In this activity he is joined by an old woman who is a neighbor of the couple. Unlike the old woman, however, who mutters her approval of the couple's devotion to each other, the narrator takes great pleasure in exposing their character defects.

The narrator first seizes upon the pair's physical appearance as a sign of their flawed spiritual makeup, describing the odd couple at great length and in grotesque detail. Petia—"small, plump, barrel-chested, ears that stick out like axe-blades, jutting lower jaw"[13]—is a manager in a housing-goods warehouse. Lial'ka, skinny as a rail, works at a snack bar. Together, they are perfect types for satiric and comic exploitation. In the opening paragraphs, the narrator's eye dwells on Petia's fat body in order to ridicule its owner's apparent pride in its musculature as he washes himself in the yard:

> Somewhere in the back of his mind, perhaps, Petia thinks that when he is standing like that, leaning forward with his legs apart and twisting his fingers in his ears, his back presents a picture of rippling, resilient muscles. In fact, there are no rippling muscles. There is a fair layer of premature fat and it quivers a little. Petia is fond of his freckled body; on Saturday and Sunday before dinner he walks about the yard stripped to the waist and all the time he keeps stroking himself and giving himself little slaps to catch gnats or mosquitoes, which he afterwards examines at great length. Or sometimes, all of a sudden he will for no apparent reason smack his chest quite hard and then rub it for a long time. (2:32/103)[14]

The narrator next turns his attention to Lial'ka, who is described in similarly derisive terms. She laughs, we are told, "like a bag of dry beans scattered over the floor—in shallow, staccato, humorless fashion" (2:34/105). When the couple goes out for the evening, she "clings to Petia like a withered branch caught in an oak, a branch from some other tree. The wind tugs at her but she won't let go. She hangs there stubbornly, leaves fluttering" (2:36/107). At one point she dances for her husband, shaking her shoulders "Gypsy fashion" in front of him, "her emaciated breasts shaking from side to side," which the narrator calls "not a pleasant sight" (2:34/106).

Besides turning them into caricatures, the narrator also makes unflattering assumptions about them and is particularly suspicious of the sincerity of Lial'ka's affections. He calls her "a real pretender," somebody who has "been around the block." "The only thing I can't understand," the narrator confides,

> is why she has to let everyone know how much she respects and treasures her husband. Petia, I can see, is just a warehouse manager. What's behind it—concealment of some past sin? Or is she trying to pull the wool over his eyes? I don't know. Anyhow she makes such a display of her wifely respect that it nearly knocks you over. (2:33/104)

At the base of the narrator's satiric undressing of his heroes, however, there is a deeper anger, which we learn about toward the end of the story. Petia and Lial'ka, we discover, are former villagers who have "sold out" to urban temptations. The narrator states: "This couple from the country has long since ceased to feel out of place here in town, in this great ant-hill; they have made themselves at home. But what they have brought with them is not their best, no. I feel insulted. Ashamed. And angry" (2:36/106). The story, it turns out, is an accusation and a condemnation of the ease with which "bright souls" become tarnished in the city and former country folk become urban philistines.

And yet the story does not end on this note. On the contrary, the narrator turns the tables on himself in the final paragraphs. As he watches Lial'ka guiding a tipsy and protesting Petia back home after their night out, it suddenly strikes him that he has been wrong all along: what seemed false and affected, repulsive and grotesque in Lial'ka's relationship with her husband is actually genuine and sincere. "That's how it is: she's been around the block and loves him anyway. That's the reason for her boasting and showing off—it's all because she loves him" (2:36/108). The accusation is turned back on the accuser, as Shukshin makes clear in a later addition to the ending: "What the hell have I been doing sitting here speculating! [. . .] She's proud and boastful because she loves him. Well, let her. And what's wrong with that?" (2:36). The narrator thus concludes on a self-effacing note, raising the possibility that perhaps he—by implication also a villager moved to the city—has not "brought his best" with him from the village either.

This self-denunciation becomes a consistent feature of Shukshin's late satire, whose ridiculing laughter proves to be a double-edged weapon. In a story written a year after "Petia," "The Three Graces" ("Tri gratsii"), Shukshin makes this explicit. "The Three Graces" is another first-person account, with a narrator who also likes to spy on the outside world. This one does his spying from the balcony of his new apartment, and in this he is joined not by one old woman, as in "Petia," but by three women in their thirties and forties, who sit on a park bench in front of his balcony and gleefully and maliciously criticize all passersby. The women are never given names, only labels: "The Quiet One" (Tikhushnitsa), "The Activist" (Deiatel'), and "Redhead" (Ryzhevolosaia). The story—in later publications subtitled "A Joke"—is one of Shukshin's harshest satires.

Every Sunday the narrator awaits the arrival of his three graces with impatience, relishing in advance how he will "spend the whole day hating" with them (2:125). And, indeed, that is how it turns out. On this occasion, the targets of their ire include a young man suffering from a hangover, accused of being a drunk; a balding "four-eyes" writing a dissertation, branded a teetotaler and an idler; a girl in a miniskirt, condemned for her loose morals; an old man visiting from the village, reproached as a kulak and counterrevolutionary; and his motorcycle-riding son, denounced as mentally ill. The narrator, who drinks a toast each time these three graces cut someone down, silently cheers his secret allies on. The drunker he becomes, however, the more he is taken with an idea that occurs to him: why not saw through the supports on one of the park benches and invite his three graces up to his balcony to watch what happens when people try sitting down? Here he makes a fatal mistake: he comes down from his balcony to visit his graces and share his plan with them, explaining to them that "every idea should be embodied in an image" and that "there should be a spectacle, a performance" (2:131). In other words, his dirty trick will be the perfect visual embodiment of their vicious slandering. They promptly turn him over to the police, and the narrator lands in the drunk tank for three days. The joke is on the narrator, who is punished for quite literally "descending to their level" in word and deed. As in "Petia," Shukshin's satire is both inwardly and outwardly directed, aimed at the malicious women and at the narrator himself, who admits his desire to turn his three graces into a perverse ideal of Perfection, Wholeness, and Beauty (2:131).

The three graces are obviously grotesques whom only the equally deformed and hyperbolic narrator could love (in fact, he declares his love to them as he is being hauled away by the police [2:131]). Unlike Petia and Lial'ka, they have no redeeming qualities. They are nasty, ugly, even dangerous, the markers not of Perfection, Wholeness, and Beauty—which, as any satirist knows, do not exist in the real world—but of their absence. As such, they become the presiding muses of Shukshin's satiric works and a measure of the writer's own growing pessimism over his society and human nature. His "bright souls" and oddballs, he implies, are no longer adequate to his task.

"The Three Graces," like "Petia" before it, originally appeared in the literary weekly *Literaturnaia Rossiia* in the newspaper's humor department, "Laughter through Prose."[15] Shukshin, who had published in *Literaturnaia Rossiia* only twice before during the 1960s,[16] turned to the paper in the 1970s as an outlet when Tvardovskii was ousted as editor of *Novyi mir,* Shukshin's preferred venue. From late 1970 until his death four years later, Shukshin placed a dozen works with *Literaturnaia Rossiia*. Besides "Petia" and "The Three Graces," the other satiric pieces published there include "The Insult" (whose subtitle, "A Satiric Story," appears only in its newspaper variant), "Stubborn," "Vladimir Semenych from the Upholstered Furniture Department" ("Vladimir Semenich iz miagkoi sektsii"), "The Psychopath" ("Psikhopat"), two stories published under the rubric "Two Absolutely Ridiculous Stories"—"How Andrei Ivanovich Kurinkov, Jeweler, Got a Fifteen-Day Sentence" and "Nighttime in the Boiler Room"—and his satiric play, *Energetic People,* published in three installments.

With the exception of "The Insult," these works have generated little critical commentary, either during Shukshin's lifetime or afterward. Part of the problem has to do with Shukshin's choice of venue. *Literaturnaia Rossiia,* founded in 1963, was the poorer cousin to the more venerable *Literaturnaia gazeta,* established in 1929. Whereas *Literaturnaia gazeta* boasted a circulation of over 1.5 million in 1973, *Literaturnaia Rossiia* had a total circulation of only 100,000 the same year.[17] *Literaturnaia gazeta* was clearly the more prestigious, more widely read weekly newspaper. Thus Shukshin's stories may have languished on the pages of the lesser of the two major literary weeklies. Appearing on the humor pages of *Literaturnaia Rossiia,* these works simply did not look like serious literature but rather popular anecdotes told to a mass audience.

Anatoly Vishevsky addresses this topic in his analysis of Soviet literature of the 1970s, where he discusses Shukshin's works in the context of ironic prose. In particular, Vishevsky investigates an ironic "subgenre of the humorous short story that began appearing at the end of the 1960s and enjoyed unparalleled popularity" in the Soviet Union. He argues that since most of these kinds of ironic stories were "buried in the humor pages at the end of periodicals" and were "bound to be thrown out with the newspaper in which they appeared," they were often viewed as "trifles" by the literary-political establishment. Readers, however, viewed them very differently, and they became "both an attribute and an expressive medium for intellectuals in Soviet society of the 1970s," true examples of "the ironic world-view in its pure form."[18]

Although Vishevsky refrains from including Shukshin's stories in his larger discussion of periodical humor-page fiction, it is clear that Shukshin's satirical *Literaturnaia Rossiia* works fit in this category. Indeed, the brevity and satiric humor of many of his short stories are strong recommendations for their classification as just this kind of ironic prose, as some reviews of the collection *Kharaktery* indicate. Paradoxically, it would not be until the publication of his four long satiric novellas shortly before and after his death that critics would finally recognize the extent to which Shukshin had become a full-fledged satirist in his own right. I will conclude with an extended look at these underanalyzed novellas, for in them we can trace the final stages of the evolution of the writer's hero, an evolution that anticipates developments in Soviet prose of the 1980s and 1990s.

SHUKSHIN'S GROTESQUES

Satire is marked by its aggressive spirit of irreconcilability (which, to a large extent, distinguishes it as a literary method from irony, humor, and comedy). The satirist attempts to transfer this aggressive spirit to his or her audience, whose members thus participate in the author's moral ridicule. And yet this aggression is rarely nihilistic, for it is ultimately driven by the hope of the amendability of that which it attacks. To criticize is always to hope and, therefore, in the end, to affirm (as Plato declared, you cannot escape affirming what you negate). Shukshin's satire was driven by the hope for change in Soviet society, even as he himself became more and more pessimistic about its likelihood.

For Shukshin as for satirists in general, satire is a way to demytholo-gize, to deconstruct the present state of affairs in the search for authentic-ity. Consequently, in his novellas, Shukshin refracts his satire through a number of highly symbolic Soviet settings, the better to strip from them the veneer of Soviet social, political, and ideological accretions. Thus we en-counter the communal apartment of *Point of View;* the cooperative apart-ment of a band of black marketeers in *Energetic People;* a Soviet library full of beloved Russian literary and folkloric characters in *Till the Cock Crows Thrice;* and the drunk tank of *And They Woke Up in the Morning.* Each set-ting is evocative of particular Soviet worldviews and attitudes and functions as a microcosm of Soviet society as a whole, in this way serving as an effec-tive platform for Shukshin's social critique.

Shukshin's method of composition in these works, which he alludes to in a 1974 interview, is eminently suitable to the conventions of the stage for which three of the four works were written: to gather characters together in one place and put them into a situation where they must resolve some cen-tral conflict.[19] This reliance on a "chamber" method of exposition maximizes the possibility of playing types off of one another and heightens the inten-sity of the satire and the comedy. It also augments the symbolic value of the distinctive settings of each work.

Despite the number of satiric short stories Shukshin wrote during the last five years of his life, the publication in June 1974 of his "satirical novella for the theater" *Energetic People* and of his "fairy-tale novella" *Point of View* a month later was seen by many commentators as the announcement of a dramatic new direction for the writer. *Energetic People* not only re-vealed to the public Shukshin's new interest in the theater and confirmed his status as a satirist, but it also put his new hero, the grotesque, in the spotlight before a broad audience. *Point of View* seemed to reaffirm and con-tinue this development. Appearances in this instance, however, were slightly deceiving, for a draft of *Point of View* had first been finished as early as 1966, when Shukshin mentioned the work as the possible script for his third film, thus giving us an indication of Shukshin's initial interest in satire. The work was subsequently revised as a novella for a reading in the Central House of Writers in February 1967.[20] These experiments in mixed genre, with their roots in the cinema and theater, are the natural outcome of Shukshin's own mixed aesthetic and are evidence that the artist never ceased trying to find the ultimate artistic form most suitable to his tripartite creative persona.

Point of View, like Shukshin's other theater novellas, marks a depar-ture from his favorite setting of the village in favor of the communal apart-ment, the ultimate "metaphor of the distinctive Soviet mentality."[21] It is the home of the Bride, the Mother of the Bride, the Father of the Bride, Grandfather, a Neighbor Girl, a Neighbor, and a Humble Citizen, all of whom are referred to almost exclusively by these labels. An obvious satiric device that heightens the allegorical resonance of the story, the labels also perform an important function: they transform the "living human voices" Shukshin sought to capture in his short stories into the hollow and detached mouthpieces for grossly clichéd social attitudes. Thus made grotesque, these characters are distanced from the reader and elicit not sympathetic response but impartial judgment.

A brief prologue establishes the premise: a Magician agrees to settle a dispute between an Optimist and a Pessimist as to whose outlook is more accurate by using his magical powers to conduct an experiment in which both will be allowed to present a matchmaking as they see it. The Magician will then judge whose version is closer to the truth.

The subtitles Shukshin considered for the story include "An Attempt at a Contemporary Fairy Tale," "A Farcical Presentation in Four Scenes," and "A Fairy Tale for Children Past School Age" (2:587). The latter subtitle, with its implied warning of adult content, is particularly apropos, for, as Northrop Frye writes, "Satire is usually what is called obscene—that is, openly scatological—because under the hypocrisy of dressing up there is a democracy of the body usually concealed in public."[22] *Point of View* is a quite literal realization of this principle.

The novella is divided into four parts, the first of which is comprised of just such an "obscene" undressing of the body public (the Pessimist's point of view). Part Two relates the attempt to dress the body back up (the Optimist's point of view). Part Three represents an interrogation (in both senses) of each position, as both the Optimist and the Pessimist are called in for questioning by a Certain Somebody. In Part Four, an attempt is made to combine both outlooks. Shukshin's satire in *Point of View* is particularly charged, since the body he is "undressing" is that of the Soviet public and the points of view he is lampooning are the black-and-white perspectives most often encountered in the rhetoric of Soviet social propaganda. We are given the Pessimist's version first.

The opening scene reveals a dirty common room where the family of the Bride is at the dinner table. Into this setting arrives the family of the Groom, including the Mother and Father of the Groom and someone referred to only as It's Unclear Who. While It's Unclear Who starts to measure the room's size and make inquiries about the furniture, the two families begin the matchmaking. The conversation, though, never rises above the crude and vulgar, reflecting the coarse and unattractive natures of the families themselves. Sexual and scatological references—surprisingly racy by Soviet standards—abound, stripping the matchmaking ritual of the polite decorum hiding its essential carnal and procreative goals while unmasking the ritual's participants at the same time. Here, as he does in many other works, Shukshin avails himself of the liberating low humor of the common folk.

An example is when the Groom warns how watching television or going to the movies can lead to marital infidelity. He explains: "My friend had a TV. The neighbors came over to watch some love story. The lights, of course, were turned out. Well, the neighbor starts groping his friend's wife. [. . .] She says: 'Is that you, Vasia?' Vasia's her husband's name. But Vasia's clueless. 'Huh?' he says. 'Nothing,' she says. 'I thought it was you.'" The Father of the Bride can only exclaim "in admiration": "That's slick!" The Mother of the Bride, however, takes up his warning: "'Come over, we'll at least have a laugh,' they say! [. . .] Before you know it, they've groped you all over" (2:422–23).

The Pessimist's version is low, dirty, and at times juvenile, but by its conclusion each family has been duly divested of all pretense of dignity and sincerity. The Groom is exposed as an impudent poser, the Bride as a capricious coquette. Both fathers admit to drinking so much they either black out or crawl home on all fours, although this is not considered wrong or abnormal. "Who doesn't drink these days?" the Mother of the Bride asks (2:424). She herself is revealed to be a coarse and vindictive tyrant. As other residents of the apartment come by to watch the spectacle or to complain about the noise, the matchmaking falls apart. The Father of the Bride chases the family of the Groom out with his rifle, and the Bride is betrothed to It's Unclear Who, who has waited quietly in the wings for his opportunity, not to declare his love but to improve his housing allotment.

The Optimist's version attempts to rectify the situation. If the first version is filled with low diction and vulgar content, the second is saturated with political rhetoric and journalistic clichés, all in the service of lacquering reality. The apartment is scrubbed and clean. When the family of the Groom arrives, the matchmaking proceeds in an atmosphere of mutual respect and courtesy. Neighbors drop by with gifts and congratulations, the Bride and Groom debate the four components of a successful marriage (listed edifyingly in a popular youth magazine), and everything points to a happy conclusion until the Groom boasts that his father has promised him a car. His misplaced proprietorial pride and the revelation that he keeps company with actors prove his undoing. Again It's Unclear Who winds up with the Bride, who confesses her love in a succinct and politically correct declaration: "I always voted for you!" (2:439).

Shukshin's order of presentation is crucial to his overall purposes. In beginning with the Pessimist's "undressing" of his heroes, he dooms to certain failure the Optimist's subsequent attempt to "hide" the defects of the human personality thus mercilessly exposed under the clothing of Soviet propriety and socialist decency. Indeed, Shukshin's sympathies, as one critic points out, clearly lie with the Pessimist, in whose unmasking of human vice he takes obvious delight.[23] Like the satiric author-narrators of "Petia" and "The Three Graces," the Pessimist is a Peeping Tom, spying on people's lives and feeding his own malice. "My favorite occupation," he confides, "is to look into other people's windows. And what do I see there?! Nothing but swinish vileness" (2:442). In these sentiments, the Pessimist expresses the credo of Shukshin himself as a satirist.

At this point, both the Optimist and the Pessimist are hauled off for interrogation by a Certain Somebody, who looks like a secret policeman to the Pessimist but to the Optimist is a kindly old man. A parody of a typical literary censor, the Certain Somebody seeks to channel the philosophies of each party into rhetoric acceptable to Soviet ideology. We learn, for instance, that the Optimist is someone who, "in an Einsteinian universe," can move forward while lying still, a position from which he can best point the direction to the radiant future (2:447), thus transforming him into the perfect embodiment of the double-talk and empty rhetoric of Soviet propaganda promoted by just such "certain somebodies" in the censorship.

In the novella's conclusion, the Magician combines both worldviews, and the matchmaking is played out once more, this time with grotesque results. The Groom knocks the Father of the Bride out and then picks a fight with the Grandfather. The Grandfather starts singing a popular song about going to Siberia ("Ia edu za tumanom"). The Bride revives her father and implores him to shoot the Groom. Someone steals the Magician's watch. The Groom tells everyone to "watch his footwork" as he gets ready to knock Grandfather out. The Mother of the Groom tells him to hit Grandfather in the liver. The Father of the Groom advises him to aim for the groin. And the Optimist and the Pessimist join hands and dance in circles, singing "In this world, tra-la-la, life's not worth a thing!" (2:452–54). The whole play deteriorates into an absurd farce, the inevitable consequence, Shukshin implies, of trying to impose any single point of view on society.

Had Shukshin ended his "fairy-tale novella" on this note, we could consider *Point of View* a daring, if uneven, work. The progression in the novella from low satire to mocking burlesque is as inevitable as it is imperfectly executed, and both pessimism and optimism are duly exposed as bankrupt philosophical positions, the signs of decay and superficiality respectively. Although its schematic framework often makes itself felt, in its best moments *Point of View* evokes the Theater of the Absurd in its ridicule of Soviet middle-class values and the political ideology that promotes them. There was very little of this sort of thing being published in 1974, and the play exudes an irreverence refreshing for its times.[24] However, whether by choice or due to editorial demand, Shukshin added an epilogue in which a Neighbor throws out all but the family members, who then sit down to the matchmaking "the way it really happens—from the point of view of normal people" (2:454). This "happy ending"—certainly a disappointment—considerably blunts both Shukshin's satire and his innovative achievement. It also contradicts the story's central effect. If, as Deming Brown notes, the function of the story "is not to find a 'correct' view, but rather to expose the unreliable eye of the indoctrinated and biased beholder,"[25] then we should be suspicious of anyone's claim—especially the author's—that there is such a thing as a "normal" point of view.

Shukshin's next satiric work avoids such implied judgments. Indeed, in *Energetic People* Shukshin approximates a twentieth-century Soviet equivalent of Gogol's play *The Inspector General*, both in its structure and in its ruthless satire. There is the same parade of unsympathetic characters whose desperate situation is at once a source of comic tension and farcical hilarity. There is the same admirably caught dialogue, in which, as has been said of Gogol's play, "there is not a wrong word or intonation from beginning to end."[26] There is the same tight, circular plot, concluding in a mute scene that anticipates the speedy punishment of the principal players. There is the same authorial laughter, at once parodic and despairing.

If *Point of View* is, in part, "an indictment of the distortions which writers have imposed on society,"[27] then *Energetic People* is an indictment of the distortions Soviet society has created in its citizens. In many ways it is an elaboration on a statement uttered by the Pessimist from *Point of View:* "There are no good people. Writers make them up in order to earn good money. There aren't any honest people either. Everyone thieves, lies, and insults each other" (2:442). To make this point loud and clear, Shukshin focuses on a fateful night in the lives of a group of black marketeers, whose imminent undoing stems from an affair the group's leader, Aristarkh Petrovich Kuz'kin, is having with a woman named Sonia. When his wife, Vera Sergeevna, finds out, she threatens to expose the whole operation in retribution. The drama unfolds over a period of twenty-four hours, during which time the drunken antics of Aristarkh and his cohorts turn into a series of desperate attempts to convince, cajole, and threaten Vera into giving up her plan.

As in the former play, the central premise of *Energetic People*—one just on the ragged edge of what the censorship would allow—is rife with possibilities for satiric exploitation. It created a minor sensation when it premiered under Georgii Tovstonogov's direction at the Leningrad Gorky Drama Theater (Bol'shoi dramaticheskii teatr imeni Gor'kogo) in the summer of 1974 and has been restaged several times since. Also like *Point of View, Energetic People* opens with a standard fairy-tale device, akin to the English "once upon a time." The fairy-tale beginning adds a sense of timelessness and universality to both works and conditions our response to the stories' contemporary setting and themes, preparing us for a modern allegory, complete in both instances with a reliance on overt typification. In *Energetic People,* all but the three protagonists already mentioned are referred to strictly by labels. As the narrator declares in the opening pages of the novella:

From now on that's how we'll refer to them: the raven-haired one will be called Raven, the paunchy one—Paunchy, the one with the snub nose will be Snub Nose, the bald guy singing all the songs will be called Baldy, and the man with the simple face will be called, for the sake of brevity, the Simple Man. (2:458)

Thus deindividualized, the characters become easy-to-manipulate types, the better for Shukshin to effect his satire.

Throughout the play, Shukshin preserves comic tension and pace through his observance of the classical unities of time (in this case, twenty-four hours), place (the apartment of the Kuz'kins), and action (all plot development occurs onstage).[28] As in *Point of View*, he also relies on lowering elements—scatological references (2:461, 474), two strip scenes (2:464, 466), mention of erection anxiety (2:481), and a bizarre remark about static electricity and women's synthetic underwear (2:490)—to help achieve his satire.

The play is divided into four scenes. The first, "The Evening Which Imperceptibly Turned into Night," introduces us to a favorite occupation of Aristarkh and his accomplices, that of drinking cognac by the glassful and pretending to take trips. In this instance, they "fly" to "tropical locales" by waving their arms like cranes and moving to another room, from there returning "by train" to their original destination by forming a line and hooting like a train whistle. On both trips they cross through Vera's room, flying through it on their way "south" and "changing trains" there on their way back. Hardly amused by this, Vera hints at trouble ahead for these "passengers," and by the end of the scene she is already writing a letter to the local district attorney about five hubcaps her husband has just appropriated for sale on the black market.

Aristarkh learns of her intentions in the next scene ("Morning"), where she confronts him over a note from Sonia she found in his jacket. The first of six attempts to talk her out of her plan ensues. After failing to explain away the note, Aristarkh makes Vera take off all of the fancy clothes he bought her with his illegally gotten profits and gives her a lecture on the economics of "energetic people," on whose initiative "every developed society thrives" in order to avoid "stagnation" (*zastoi*, probably one of the earliest such instances of the application of this term to the Brezhnev period to appear in Soviet fiction). In particular, he draws her attention to the "economic phenomenon" of the five hubcaps, which, although they are piled on top of each other in the corridor, do not really exist, since they are not accounted for in any official inventory or production plan (2:465). This "phenomenon," of course, is the key to the play itself, revealing as it does the artifice and illusion of the Soviet command economy as well as those of this contemporary fairy tale, whose subjects (like the five hubcaps, which match in number the principal players in the gang) also exist on the basis of very unstable laws of physics. This point is brought home forcefully at the play's conclusion when the expanding edifice of guile and wish fulfillment that procured these hubcaps and supports the lives and livelihoods of our heroes comes crashing down in spectacular fashion, and all members, with the exception of the Simple Man, are frozen in place like Lot's wife witnessing the destruction of Sodom and Gomorrah. When Aristarkh's speech fails to change his wife's mind, however, he locks her in the apartment and awaits the arrival of reinforcements.

The story of the sinking ship and its doomed passengers continues in the final two scenes ("Two Hours Later" and "The Evening Which Failed to Turn into Night"), as the previous night's company reassembles. One by one, they go into Vera's room with different ploys and arguments, and each time they are sent packing, but only after revealing to comic effect their own particular character defects. Hope is restored only when Raven disappears and returns with Sonia herself, who has agreed—in exchange for an imported bookshelf—to tell Vera that she had wanted to become Aristarkh's lover but, in fact, was really carrying on an affair with Raven. The scheme works so well that Vera and Sonia become friends "the way a proper woman will sometimes befriend an infamous harlot" (2:487). Aristarkh is forced onto his knees to beg forgiveness, and the two make peace with the help of a children's game. As the company sits down to dinner together, however, the police come bursting in looking for the hubcaps. Everyone freezes, turning into the gravestones to which they had twice previously been likened, and the Simple Man turns to the audience and asks "with genuine interest": "So who was it, citizens? Huh? Who squealed?" (2:495).

Shukshin's concluding mute scene, although less theatrical than Gogol''s, has an advantage over the latter's in that the Simple Man's question directly involves the audience in the mute scene itself: its members sit as frozen and surprised as the "energetic people" onstage. Here, as in his film *Pechki-lavochki,* Shukshin concludes with a direct appeal to the audience, whose "co-authorship" in this case includes answering the final question on which the curtain descends. The question, in reality, is a rhetorical one, for the whole play has been driven by the tension surrounding the inevitability of the catastrophe that ultimately befalls the gang of black marketeers, an inevitability constantly delayed, detoured, and stretched to the breaking point throughout the play. Indeed, much of the humor in *Energetic People,* as in *The Inspector General,* derives from this tension and how the author visits doom on the heads of his scheming protagonists only at the very moment when that inevitability seems finally defeated, when their maneuvering has seemingly snatched victory from the jaws of defeat. Herein lies Shukshin's achievement in *Energetic People*—not in punishing wrongdoing per se, but in creating and suspending to the last moment the unsustainablility of his characters' positions.

While greed, arrogance, dishonesty, depravity, and other human failings are held up for ridicule and eventually punished, the rather perfunctory appearance of the police at the end undercuts the impact of the impending arrests. Shukshin's goal in *Energetic People* has not been to vanquish evil but to partake in what the narrator calls the "nasty laughter, the unhealthy laughter, the morbid laughter" (2:482) of the characters themselves. In this approach, Shukshin directly anticipates the methods of the late and post-Soviet writers of "dark" and "cruel" prose (*chernukha, zhestokaia proza*), who similarly revel in a morose laughter. It is a laughter born of the distortion of intention, means, and end that drives the lives of these black marketeers and from which the comedy of Shukshin's play itself derives. This is no longer the restorative carnival laughter of folk buffoonery, just as Shukshin's characters are no longer *chudiki* and simple country folk. This is the caustic laughter of the hateful narrator of "The Three Graces," and the characters themselves are hardly better than that story's slandering protagonists.

The notion of unhealthy laughter is a key to understanding Shukshin's turn to satire and his interest in obviously unattractive characters. In these late works Shukshin projects this unhealthy laughter against a society that, as Hosking argues, has either "lost its ideals or distorted them beyond recognition."[29] Shukshin fills the moral vacuum that ensues with grotesques and a sense of helpless cynicism that calls into question everything from the failures of the Soviet command economy to the bankruptcy of socialist values. His task in these satiric works is to provoke his readers and expose through morose laughter the vices ailing society. As critics have pointed out, Shukshin's late fairy tales are all bitter ones. The most bitter of all, perhaps, is *Till the Cock Crows Thrice*, where, according to Leonid Ershov, Shukshin "not only unmasks, he laments."[30]

Till the Cock Crows Thrice was completed a day after Shukshin's forty-fifth (and final) birthday but published only posthumously. In it, Shukshin makes literal the notion first raised in *Point of View* about turning Soviet society into a fairy tale, where "representatives of dark powers" like the witch Baba Yaga and the three-headed snake Gorynych appear (2:442). The twist is that these fairy-tale antagonists are nevertheless only the transparent masks of very recognizable modern villains. The plot is telling: Ivan the Fool is sent on a quest for a "certificate of wisdom" by the characters from Russian folklore and literature with whom he lives in a library or else face expulsion from his place in Russian literature. The question is purely bureaucratic and thoroughly Soviet: it is not important whether he is truly wise, only that he have the proper document. Ivan's quandary takes on a very contemporary tenor, as he battles on his journey not the supernatural villains from Russian fairy tales but the petty tyrants of modern Soviet society.

Thus Baba Yaga is a typical materialistic Shukshinian wife: she is trying to build herself a summer cottage with illegally attained building materials and marry off her daughter to whomever will help her. When Ivan refuses to come to her aid, she tries to roast him alive. Gorynych the snake is an embodiment of the censorial Soviet cultural establishment: he makes Ivan sing folk songs but then expunges all "vulgar" references and changes their endings to make them uplifting. Misha the bear, the beloved figure from Russian folklore, has taken to drink, abandoned his family, and is contemplating going to the city to join the circus. The devils who force Ivan to help them break into a monastery are caricatures of Western-minded Russian intellectuals. The Wise Man from whom Ivan is to obtain his certificate is a time-serving bureaucrat whose wisdom consists in his mastery of bureaucratic language and his possession of the all-important official rubber stamp. He tries to make a laughingstock out of Ivan in order to impress Queen Nesmeyana. She and her nihilistic friends are members of the disaffected and disillusioned Soviet youth, who are indifferent to Ivan and to the fate of Russian folk culture. For his part, Ivan the Fool bears little resemblance to his folkloric counterpart, playing instead the role of the common man who is neither foolish nor stupid but rather the hapless pawn of powers beyond his control.

Shukshin's fairy tale is one in which the normal conventions are inverted: the folk hero does not understand the reason for the quest he is being sent on and nothing in the end is resolved. Baba Yaga's cottage remains unbuilt and her daughter unmarried. Gorynych is killed deus ex machina by an unnamed Cossack ataman from Russian literature (probably Razin himself), but his death does not bring any closure. Misha the bear wanders off into the unknown, despondent and resigned. The monastery remains in the hands of the devils. And Ivan has a rubber stamp but no certificate of wisdom. His quest has turned into a pointless and harmful exercise in futility.

Ivan returns from his perilous trip angry and dissatisfied. His dissatisfaction is taken up by the ataman, who proposes an act of elemental rebellion: a Cossack campaign of plunder. Ivan seems on the verge of agreeing when the third cock crows and the story ends. Shukshin thus stops short of implicating Ivan in any sort of peasant revolt. (The ataman's call for a Cossack campaign on the Volga is not the same thing as a march on Moscow anyway.) The only victory Ivan wins is over bureaucracy, which is quite literally stripped of its power and prestige in the episode with Nesmeyana when the company of bored youths—at Ivan's suggestion—tries to find the Wise Man's "extra rib." During a vigorous and ticklish search, the Wise Man is not only undressed, he is also brought down to earth when, struggling against his tormentors and laughing against his will, he farts, "quietly, the way old men do" (2:531). In the ensuing hysterics, Ivan steals his stamp and leaves.

The Wise Man himself speaks of the power of "the people's laughter," which has beat the enemy back throughout history (2:528), but little does he suspect it will be turned on him. This earthy humor permeates the story, from Ivan's facial-hair remedy for Baba Yaga's daughter made of chicken droppings and manure (2:506), to a discussion with the Wise Man about flatulence (a discussion that anticipates the Wise Man's own downfall) (2:525), to Ivan's "messy diapers" in the last episode with Baba Yaga's daughter and Gorynych (2:539). The effect is to restore the coarse traditions of folk humor at a time of official prudery in the arts, thus resurrecting "another world, where everything is comical, lighthearted, absurd, but healthy. Life outside of rank, outside of certificates, outside of bureaucracy."[31] This humor becomes an important "zone of contact" between Shukshin and his audience.[32] And yet in the end Shukshin's humor is not so much disparaging as despairing, for the fairy-tale world of *Till the Cock Crows Thrice* remains in disorder at tale's end, reflecting the distorted real world of Soviet society. The people's laughter is no longer enough to carry the day. It has assumed a bitter and hopeless tone. Moreover, folk culture itself has been betrayed, and by none other than Ivan himself, all in his pursuit of the certificate.

Three times Ivan is asked—by Gorynych, the devils, and the Wise Man—to "sell his soul": to sing folk songs and perform folk dances for the express purpose of receiving his certificate of wisdom. Three times he complies. Each time the experience is a humiliation and a betrayal of his cultural heritage, for he allows Gorynych to bowdlerize a folk song, teaches the devils how to use a folk song to sneak into the monastery, and lets the Wise Man make a mockery of both his folk origins and his folk culture as a way to amuse Queen Nesmeyana. The magnitude of this betrayal is hinted at in the title of the story itself, which evokes the disciple Peter's three denials of Christ on the night of his arrest. By the time he returns to the library, Ivan is as sick at heart as Peter, for each has denied a sacred part of himself.[33]

In depicting Ivan's betrayal of his origins, Shukshin also hints at his own possible disloyalty to his folk lineage. Like Ivan, Shukshin sacrificed his folk heritage for his own "certificate of wisdom" and used his folk culture as a way to build a career in fiction and film.[34] Indeed, Shukshin fits the description of the unnamed "writer from the village with the four-bedroom apartment in Moscow" who is scorned by Paunchy in *Energetic People* for praising the countryside but living in the city (2:457).[35] Snub Nose's response—"He's being paid good money to praise the countryside" (2:457)—reflects Shukshin's realization of his own compromised position as an artist who profits from writing on country themes but who chooses not to live in the village. Yet Shukshin makes no excuses for Ivan's, or his own, compromises. On the contrary, in these late works the author holds up his heroes—and, in a sense, himself—in the grotesque mirror of satire for ultimate judgment by his reading public. It is clear what was at stake for Shukshin:

loyalty to his origins and to the village son he always kept within him, a question which in *Till the Cock Crows Thrice* is bound up with the constraints and compromises of Soviet reality as they are refracted in the collision between Ivan's folk heritage and Baba Yaga's materialism, Gorynych's despotism, the devils' profaning of Russian Orthodoxy, and the Wise Man's arbitrary bureaucracy. It is unclear, however, what Shukshin was ultimately planning to do in order to resolve his inner conflicts. While Ivan left his demons behind him in the monastery at the end of the story, Shukshin was still confronting his own.

The unfinished "novella for the theater" *And They Woke Up in the Morning* is an indication of the direction Shukshin was moving in when he died. Set in a Moscow drunk tank, the novella continues Shukshin's interest in dubious heroes. It is his own *Lower Depths,* although unlike Gorky's depiction of the inmates of a flophouse, *And They Woke Up in the Morning* is devoid of moralizing. Indeed, when a sociologist visits the hungover residents in order to ascertain the reason why people drink, he is told in no uncertain terms that people do not drink "for a reason." "What if there are no reasons," one of the inmates seethes. "Why go looking for them if there aren't any?" (2:556).

The eight inmates of the drunk tank—several of them veterans of the place—include a gloomy crane operator, a rumpled electrician, a nervous man with a snub nose and a high womanly voice, an ex-convict, a village tractor driver, and a bespectacled intellectual. They are all referred to by labels—Gloomy, Electrician, Con, Four-Eyes—and, as we hear the stories of how they wound up there, we learn several of their names, including that of the intellectual Grishakov, whose tale is based in part on Shukshin's "A Slander" and who shares the theatricality of the autobiographical narrator of that story.

The ironically named Bright Hills (Svetlye gory) sobering hole is Shukshin's most degraded setting yet in which to reflect the outside world of Soviet society, whose citizens, we learn in the course of the play, are no better—and certain instances much worse—than the hapless inmates awaiting their sentences. As if to hint at the larger scope of its satire, the play opens with a farcical cry of existential angst in the darkness.

Early in the morning, in the darkness, someone cried out in desperation:
   "Hey! Where am I?! Is there anybody there?! Where am I?"
   And in that very darkness, nearby, several displeased voices rang out at once.
   "You're in the other world. What're you screamin' at?"
   "Where am I? Where are we?"
   "We're in the other world. What're you screamin' at?"
   "What's the use of scarin' the man? We're not in the other world, we're still at the morgue. I've got a tag on my toe. I can feel it, danglin' there. Wonder what number I am?" (2:544)

After some delay, the question is finally answered:

> ". . . We're in a medical sobering-up station . . . what part of town, I couldn't tell you. Anyone know what part of town we're in?"
> "What part of town!" replied a gloomy man. "I don't even know what town!" (2:545)

In moving from the other world to the morgue to a drunk tank, Shukshin comically emphasizes the lowliness of his protagonists and their situation yet also introduces the larger scale by which their predicament must be measured. Although the effect is one of satiric exaggeration, Shukshin also augments the importance of the ultimate target of that satire—the decayed state of Soviet society, where the only honest people to be found are in sobering-up stations.

It is fitting that the judges before whom each of the inmates must ultimately appear are "three stern women" (2:567), for they mark the late reappearance in Shukshin's last satiric work of his "Three Graces." It is they, appropriately enough, who are to decide the fates of the Bright Hills residents. Self-righteous and officious, they have little sympathy for the hungover inmates, including Grishakov, whose plea for understanding falls on deaf ears—just as the narrator's would in "The Three Graces"—at which point the unfinished play breaks off.

Shukshin's vision of Soviet society as a drunk tank is powerful testimony to the writer's growing sense of disillusionment, as he turns to satire and farce and focuses increasingly on negative characters in his prose. With few exceptions, the stories and novellas Shukshin wrote in 1973 and 1974 all feature unattractive or spiteful heroes, who invariably end up instigating bizarre *skandaly* or wind up at the police station. With these characters, Shukshin paves the way for the appearance of a different kind of *chudak*, one—as the Russian euphemism goes—that begins with the letter "m" (*mudak,* or "prick").

According to Mikhail Epstein, these *mudaki* would become the new heroes of Russian prose in the 1980s,[36] a time when what Viktor Erofeev calls Russia's *fleurs du mal* began to bloom.[37] The heroes of this prose were negative and its themes dark. Epstein, however, names not Shukshin but his heir apparent, the Siberian writer Evgenii Popov, as the transitional figure in this evolution.[38] Like many commentators, Epstein sees in Shukshin only the creator of harmless eccentrics, ignoring the nasty characters of Shukshin's late prose. This is an unfortunate oversight, for these protagonists, appearing in print some ten to fifteen years before the glasnost-inspired publication of the controversial works described by Epstein, are clearly the forerunners of the cruder, darker heroes and antiheroes of Evgenii Popov, Viktor Erofeev, Viacheslav P'etsukh, Tatiana Tolstaia, and Liudmila Petrushevskaia. Indeed, part of the achievement of Shukshin's late interest in satire is that it marks the first decisive stages in this transformation of "hicks" into "pricks," one that occurred on the pages of Soviet periodicals and under conditions of censorship.

In the unattractive characters of Shukshin's satiric novellas and the heroes of his late short stories, we can detect distinct traits of the *mudak* in whom, as Epstein asserts, "foolishness degenerates from [a] charming bit of cleverness to [a] joke on the clever one himself."[39] Such are the rancorous heroes of "Nighttime in the Boiler Room" and "How Andrei Ivanovich Kurinkov, Jeweler, Got a Fifteen-Day Sentence," whose own clever jokes— their disguised confrontations with a professor's wife and an upstairs neighbor, respectively—actually land them in jail. Moreover, the *mudak* as "an erased image of societal madness"[40] can be discerned in Sergei Ivanovich Kudriashov from Shukshin's 1973 story "Psychopath." An obsessive whose idée fixe—collecting books for libraries—has taken the place of contact with human beings, Kudriashov is a hostile idealist who writes political proclamations to the newspaper and denounces people to the police. He is someone whose eccentricity verges on mental illness (hence the story's title).

Another critic, Georgii Tsvetov, traces the literary fate of Shukshin's *chudiki* to the protagonists of Vladimir Krupin and Viacheslav P'etsukh, in the latter of whose characters he sees the *chudik*'s demise. Yet, like Epstein, Tsvetov fails to account for the change in Shukshin's late heroes, who are clearly no longer *chudiki*.[41] Had he done so, he would have seen that the "coarseness, lack of principles, amorality, calculating natures, mercantile qualities, egoism, and passion for acquisition"[42] he finds in P'etsukh's heroes are directly anticipated by the protagonists of the collection *Kharaktery;* the novellas *Point of View, Energetic People,* and *And They Woke Up in the Morning;* and the stories "Vladimir Semenych from the Upholstered Furniture Department" and "Iakovlev the Eternal Malcontent" ("Vechno nedovol'nyi Iakovlev"). In these two stories, the negative qualities are hinted at in the titles themselves. The alcoholic Vladimir Semenych, for example, is Shukshin's worst philistine yet. A bribe taker and speculator whose wife has left him, Vladimir Semenych invests all of his self-esteem in the imported furnishings of his apartment, which he uses to attract women. His attempts to impress a lady friend, however, fail dramatically at a banquet marking a relative's successful defense of his *kandidatskaia* degree, where Vladimir Semenych gets drunk and causes a scandalous row straight out of Dostoevsky, then goes home and chops up an expensive china hutch in anger and despair—but also with an eye toward how a furniture restorer can put it all back together. The "eternal malcontent" Boris Iakovlev, on the other hand, visits his native village on vacation with the sole purpose of bragging about his one-bedroom apartment in a high-rise, his large salary, and the expensive suit he is wearing. He then proceeds to pick a fight with an old childhood friend out of sheer spite and a sense of his own superiority.

Prodigal Son

Diane Nemec Ignashev argues in her analysis of "Cutting Them Down to Size" that Shukshin "establishes the anti-hero as an aspect of himself," achieving in "the potentially destructive act of accusation" an "act of creation."[43] Although she is speaking specifically about one character (Gleb Kapustin) and one story, the same could be said of much of Shukshin's late prose. But more than that, in his self-deprecating allegiance with his anti-heroes, Shukshin also reveals the depths of his despair and disenchantment with Soviet society. The grotesque protagonists of Shukshin's mature prose are the distorted portraits of the dissembling bureaucrats, acquisitive consumers, spiritually bankrupt husbands and wives, and indifferent and anesthetized youth of contemporary Soviet life. They are also an indictment of his own compromises as a village émigré come to the city for urban conveniences. The shallowness, materialism, careerism, cynicism, and hypocrisy of these characters are but the surface symptoms of a deeper social malaise which Shukshin was just beginning to explore at the end of his life and which other writers—most notably Iurii Trifonov—would diagnose in greater detail throughout the 1970s. Indeed, Shukshin's cri de coeur from "A Slander"—"What is happening to us?"—resounds through the last two decades of Soviet literature and is eventually answered by the writers and heroes of *chernukha* and *zhestokaia proza,* whose appearance marked the fitting end of Soviet literature.

These themes converge in a final and important satiric self-portrait, titled, appropriately enough, "Lines for a Portrait" ("Shtrikhi k portretu," 1973). Its hero, Nikolai Nikolaevich Kniazev, shares the same last name as Chudik from "Oddball," a coincidence that serves as a symbolic measure of how far Shukshin had distanced himself from his former hero. Whereas Kniazev-*chudak* suffers from an excess of *dusha* (kindness, innocence, goodness), Kniazev-*mudak* suffers from an excess of *duma* (thought, ideas, philosophizing). As in Epstein's characterization of one variety of the *mudak,* this Kniazev is "meditative to the point of an ache in the brain."[44] A television repairman stuck in a provincial backwater, he is a compulsive writer (a *grafoman*) who fills notebook after notebook—the same *obshchie tetradi* in which Shukshin himself wrote—with his philosophical thoughts about the government, the meaning of life, and the problem of free time. These three topics form the titles and the subjects of three of the four subsections of the story.

Kniazev, who likens himself to Spinoza (2:269), is unpleasant and disliked, a provocateur who himself is to blame for much of the scorn and abuse hurled at him. Wherever he goes, Kniazev constantly plagues new victims with his ideas, often in an irksome manner. These ideas revolve around one topic: organizing society in such a way that everyone will give their maximum effort to the government in order to achieve great projects, such as

digging a subway from Moscow to Vladivostok or asphalting the entire surface of the planet. His attempts to communicate his ideas invariably lead to
misunderstandings, ridicule, and even fistfights. Twice he winds up at the
police station.

The worst happens in the final section, titled "An End to Thoughts"
("Konets mysliam"), when Kniazev attempts to mail his treatise to "the
center"—to Moscow. A girlfriend of his wife's, knowing the contents of the
package, refuses to accept it at the post office, either out of sympathy for
his wife—who disapproves of his obsession—or out of fear of the possible
consequences. Kniazev kicks up a row, becomes abusive, and has to be sub-
dued, bound, and led to a nearby police division. There he is interrogated,
given a psychological examination, is found to be normal, and is released.
The police, however, keep his manuscript under arrest for the time being.

The story ends with an excerpt from the introduction to Kniazev's first
notebook. A glimpse into the mind of an obsessive compulsive, Kniazev's introduction also contains the essential facts of Shukshin's own biography:

> I was born into a poor peasant family . . . It goes without saying that there
> wasn't much talk about education, nor a proper upbringing. We were brought
> up by work as well as the street and nature. And if I nevertheless broke
> through the barriers hanging over me, then I did it on my own . . . When I
> had learned to read, I read voraciously, although I suffered much unpleas-
> antness for it. My father, who did not approve of my passion, gave me more
> chores to do. But I eked out the time and read anyway. I read everything I
> could get a hold of and the more I read, the more doors were opened to me,
> and the stronger I was seized by a sense of unease . . . And so I, of course,
> began to write. I can't get by without it. Without it, my head will burst from
> the strain, if I don't give my thoughts an outlet. (2:289)

Though in a muted fashion, this narrative essentially retells Shukshin's
own story, related in his autobiographical cycle "From the Childhood Years
of Ivan Popov" ("Iz detskikh let Ivana Popova"), including Shukshin's battles with his mother over his obsessive reading habits, his spotty education,
and, of course, his need to write. Kniazev is thus an unlikely alter ego, a
Shukshin who left the village but never made it to the center. But toward
what end does the writer leave us with these lines for a satiric self-portrait?
One clue comes in a change Shukshin would make in the story shortly before he died.

In the first publications of the story, Kniazev screams, "They've arrested Spinoza!" as he is being led to the police station. In a revision first appearing in the three-volume collected works (*Sobranie sochinenii*, 1984–85),
Shukshin substitutes the name of the famous leader of the 1773–74 peasant
insurrection, Emel'ian Pugachev, for Spinoza, thereby introducing the
specter of rebellion into the drama of his hero (2:287). The substitution is

an important indicator of Shukshin's ultimate attitude toward Soviet society. Spinoza

> taught that if you could understand the patterns of the universe . . . you would cease to kick against the pricks, for you would realize that whatever was real was necessarily what and when and where it was, part of the rational order of the harmony of the cosmos. And if you saw this you became reconciled and achieved inner peace for you could no longer, as a rational human being, rebel in an arbitrary and capricious fashion against a logically necessary order.[45]

Pugachev obviously stands for just such "arbitrary and capricious" rebellion. By substituting his name for Spinoza's, Shukshin also signals which side of the philosophical argument he himself is on.

Like Kniazev, Shukshin tried to understand and accept the patterns and limits of his times as something "real and necessary," even if this included a government responsible for killing his father and oppressing its citizens. After all, we should remember that Shukshin was a member of the Communist Party in good standing. Indeed, at times—whether by choice or necessity—Shukshin sounds like his idealistic protagonist in his own essays and interviews, exhorting his fellow citizens to build a better, more ideal Communist society. In a 1966 interview about his plans to make a film based on his first version of *Point of View*, for instance, Shukshin exclaims: "My future film should ring as an ardent appeal for active participation in the construction of our new life."[46] In an unpublished letter to a critic a year earlier, Shukshin declares: "Give me today the person who is sincerely building Communism and I'll tell you who the hero is and who he isn't."[47] Portraits of flawed but decent Communists are featured prominently in his *Liubavin Family* novels as well.

In the end, though, it seems that Shukshin could no longer be reconciled to or achieve inner peace with the "logically necessary order" so praised by his *grafoman* hero in his notebooks. He wanted to "kick against the pricks." Hence his own interest in disagreeable characters and his turn to caustic satire. Hence also the transformation of his *chudak* into a *mudak*. In saying good-bye to his *chudiki*, however, it is clear that Shukshin was also acknowledging the loss of his own naïveté and innocence.

So where did this leave Shukshin? On the verge of a new stage in his career, one much more openly oppositionist in theme and character type? Or would his efforts to film his long-planned movie on Stepan Razin have given preeminence to his cinema career? These are good questions, indeed, but impossible ones to answer. The grotesque character type was doubtless not the final destination for his hero's journey, but it and the ubiquitous figure of Stepan Razin are the ones Shukshin would leave us with when he died.

Kniazev's notebooks never made it to "the center." Shukshin's did. And while the outcome was not rebellion, "Lines for a Portrait," with its confiscated manuscript and writer-hero by turns interrogated and given a psychiatric examination, nevertheless presents a disturbing and dissonant, if not dissident, picture. Indeed, "Lines for a Portrait" is another example of just how far Shukshin managed to push the boundaries of what was allowed to appear in print under Soviet censorship. It is a portrait of the writer and of his times, one left tantalizingly unfinished at the writer's premature death. The trajectory of Shukshin's critique is clear, however: one leading away from the celebration of country folk and eccentrics to a parade of grotesque types and eventually ending in despair and protest. Like Kniazev's, this protest was also to be personified by a famous Cossack rebel, whose revolt in the name of *volia* came ultimately to embody Shukshin's response to the constraints and compromises of life in Brezhnev's Soviet Union.

Chapter Six

The Author and His Critics

> The literary critics behave in an especially base
> way. Their kind doesn't waste time with formali-
> ties. All they need to know is "Who do we get
> next?"
> —Vasilii Shukshin, from a working note

BEGINNING WITH VISSARION BELINSKII in
the nineteenth century, literary critics have long made Russian literature a
distinctly extraliterary phenomenon. As in tsarist times, so in the Soviet period, they have acted as social (and socialist) commentators and watchdogs
whose reactions to a writer's work could play a major role in determining
the shape of his or her career. Shukshin, as both a writer and a filmmaker,
was no exception. Frequently the object of comment and controversy in the
critical press, Shukshin found himself implicated in one extraliterary debate
after another, his name flying, in Anninskii's apt assessment, "like a car-
tridge clip" from one warring camp to the next.[1] As N. A. Bilichenko notes,
in Shukshin's case there was often "a lack of unanimity in evaluation that
went to extremes. The divergence between the writer's intent and what the
critics read in him sometimes lent a sense of drama to the history of [his]
literary recognition."[2]

This drama was only augmented by the potent mixture of the public
and private aspects of Shukshin's own life that were implicated in the arguments surrounding his works. Here features of the artist's life and legend
became part of the debate in the 1960s over the polarization between the
city and the countryside caused by the mass migration from rural to urban
areas and the idealization of the countryside in the works of the Village
Prose writers, among whose ranks Shukshin was often listed. This polemic,
in turn, raised questions about Soviet history, agricultural policy, and national identity. The result was a debate charged with personal and professional consequences for Shukshin.

These questions were first raised in the 1950s, when writers like Valentin Ovechkin and Efim Dorosh wrote and published the first honest assessments of conditions in the countryside to appear in Soviet literature. The

investigation of the state of rural Russia undertaken in Ovechkin's *District Routine* (*Raionnye budni*, 1952) and Dorosh's *Village Diary* (*Derevenskii dnevnik*, 1956–70) marked the end of the unchallenged varnished rural portraits typical of Stalin-era Kolkhoz Literature. At the same time it ushered in the beginning of Village Prose, which was conceived during the reform years of the Thaw and which preserved the spirit of the Thaw's critical legacy over the next two decades of political reaction. This is an important aspect of the achievement and the reputation of Village Prose in the Brezhnev era. As Kathleen Parthé argues, Village Prose provided a politicized and, at times, highly charged literary context in which not only literature but the most important contemporary problems were debated.[3]

Shukshin's appearance on the cultural scene—indeed, his entire six years at the cinematography institute—coincided with the Thaw and its heady atmosphere of liberalization. However, as we have seen, his first published stories are not exceptionally bold for the times, particularly given his personal history (his father had just been posthumously rehabilitated in 1956 under Khrushchev). On the contrary, the style and thematics of these stories were sufficiently traditional, even orthodox, to appear on the pages of Kochetov's *Oktiabr'*, Mikhail Alekseev's *Moskva*, as well as *Molodaia gvardiia*, all bastions of political and cultural conservatism headed in the first two instances by well-known—and in the case of Vsevolod Kochetov, even notorious—neo-Stalinists. Shukshin could not have picked venues for his works more opposed to the spirit of the Thaw than these journals. In fact, some critics see in this early association the signs of a submerged conservatism that runs the length of Shukshin's career. The writer Vladimir Maksimov argues that, despite his "enormous talent," Shukshin, "in his psychological makeup and his civil and social disposition," was a "typical conformist" who spoke "Soviet and Party banalities at meetings."[4] Others insist that in the difficult and repressive years that followed the Khrushchev era—a decade of political and literary trials—Shukshin published stories and made films that, however rich and colorful, were nevertheless also cautious. His critics claimed that he skirted dangerous themes and avoided anything that could be construed as open opposition. However dissonant his language, theme, or reputation, he was never fully a dissident, a distinction some see as tainting Shukshin's legacy.

To a certain extent, this interpretation is correct. Shukshin never felt the need to wave the banner of protest, neither as a student in the exciting and unsettling days following Khrushchev's secret speech exposing the ills of Stalin's "cult of personality" nor as an established artist. A fellow student from Romm's studio, Aleksandr Gordon, paints a picture of a wary and reluctant young Vasilii Shukshin during the days of heated student debates at the institute in the spring of 1956:

Khrushchev's speech at the Twentieth Party Congress shook the whole country, but many people did not like the exposé of Stalin's cult. Soon the situation was further complicated by the Hungarian events of 1956. Spontaneous
rallies were held in many colleges. For two days our fellow students debated
the subject in the auditorium; the administration got scared. People did not
know how to react to such major political events. The students began de-
manding changes, changes in everything. But no one was ready for such
changes. The administration wanted to keep everything as it was, at least
outwardly. . . .

What about [Andrei] Tarkovsky and Shukshin? Were they manning the
barricades? No, they weren't. But this does not mean they were not interested in what was happening. It's just that nothing could get Shukshin up on
the speaker's platform, and although Tarkovsky was ready to put his support
behind reforms, the whole situation was so chaotic and feeble that he cooled
off quickly.[5]

Gordon's account elucidates important truths about Shukshin and
Tarkovsky, both of whom were hesitant to engage politics head on. As Vida
Johnson and Graham Petrie note, "Although Tarkovsky over the years complained frequently about his treatment by Goskino and its chairman, he,
too, exercised a form of 'self-censorship' by never pointing a finger at the
power which stood over Goskino—the Communist Party itself."[6] Both filmmakers had a great stake in reaching their audience, and each was therefore
careful not to overstep the bounds of what was allowable. "[N]o artist would
work to fulfill his personal spiritual mission," Tarkovsky writes, "if he knew
that no one was ever going to see his work."[7] Shukshin in particular had to
be careful that an imprudent step in one of his professions did not have an
untoward effect on the other. Thus, for both Tarkovsky and Shukshin, dissidence was out of the question. Even when Tarkovsky defected to the West
while abroad in 1984, he refused to call himself a dissident.[8]

Later in life, Shukshin keenly felt the sting of criticism that implied
he was not sufficiently bold in his themes. He wrote in a working note: "Opposition is fine. But let there be more to opposition than mere posing."[9]
Like many artists in the Soviet period, Shukshin took a different tack, writing in the space that lies somewhere between dissent and conformity. He
cultivated that middle ground that provided the fertile soil of a number of
talented writers who published through official channels. Although this was
scornfully referred to as an apolitical "intermediate literature" (*promezhutochnaia literatura*) whose writers, while not obedient hacks, enjoyed analo-
gous privilege and status,[10] the works of Shukshin, Trifonov, Rasputin, Bitov,
Iskander, and Aitmatov played an important role in examining "the moral
imperatives created by Soviet history and the ethical dilemmas of Soviet society" in prose whose impact on Soviet readers was actually enhanced for being published against a "landscape of largely banal and predictable fiction."[11]

These writers managed to say a great deal about their society while circumventing stifling stylistic and thematic prohibitions. They did this in a variety of ways. "Generally speaking," Shukshin writes, "one might say a whole theory is taking shape, that of 'blurred emphasis.' Don't emphasize the main thing (the main idea, one's joy, pain, compassion), impart it alongside that which is secondary. But impart it skillfully. Play dumb."[12] In this way Shukshin and others learned how to negotiate successfully the "interlocking of culture and politics" that was "the context of officially published literature" in the Soviet period,[13] gaining the respect of dissidents of no less stature than Solzhenitsyn himself. By including Shukshin among the dozen or so representatives of the "core of contemporary Russian prose" in a 1973 interview, Solzhenitsyn echoes the writer's own theory of creativity in a totalitarian regime: "if you take into consideration the incredible mincing machine of censorship through which writers have to pass their works, then you cannot but marvel at their growing skill in preserving and passing on to us by means of minute artistic details an enormous area of life that it is forbidden to portray."[14] The minutiae of everyday life in the Soviet Union, communicated in just such "minute artistic details," was, of course, the very stuff of Shukshin's prose.

But this recognition—and this refinement of his artistic method— came much later, well after Shukshin was an established artist. In 1961, having just graduated from the director's faculty of the cinematography institute, Shukshin was faced with a different and more immediate problem: the sudden prospect of having to leave Moscow. Without a steady position at one of the Moscow film studios, Shukshin could not obtain the necessary residence permit to allow him to continue living in the capital. Still lugging the heavy baggage of his Siberian peasant origins and his perennial sense of being undereducated, Shukshin correctly sensed that he could make his way in the world of art only by remaining in the capital, where his development as an artist would best be served. Acting roles in some four movies kept him occupied for much of 1961 and the beginning of 1962 and temporarily alleviated the situation,[15] but the problem remained. A solution would present itself in the person of Vsevolod Kochetov, an instance when Shukshin's personal need would intersect with political expediency.

Shukshin's association with Kochetov and the journal *Oktiabr'* arose out of pressing personal and professional considerations: the desire to remain in Moscow and the need to establish himself in a career. Permanent status at one of the Moscow film studios or, at the very least, affiliation with one of the capital's prestigious literary journals was an integral part of attaining these goals. Shukshin's initial submission of stories to these periodicals followed a strategy the writer learned from his mentor, Mikhail Romm. Taking Romm's advice in 1958, Shukshin submitted his works to a variety of journals and newspapers in the hope that one would respond. Rejected stories from one venue were then sent to another (Shukshin even made up a graph to keep track of which periodicals had seen which stories).[16] Like all beginning writers, Shukshin was anxious to see his work in print, especially in one of the thick literary monthlies. After his 1958 debut in *Smena,* however, the aspiring writer went through a two-year drought during which he did not place a single story. When *Znamia* turned down three of his stories in May 1960,[17] Shukshin, though perhaps not yet desperate, must have been concerned about when he would be published again.

By the fall of 1960, he either decided to try the conservative *Oktiabr'* in his next round of submissions or was brought there by a well-wisher, depending on which version of Shukshin's first appearance at the magazine's editorial offices you believe. In the first version—from the editor's introduction to *Country Folk*—Shukshin stormed into the editorial office, an impatient young man in a coarse beaver coat, huge red cap, and rural boots. Handing over his stories, he asked the editorial staff to render an instant judgment, as he was hurrying to what must have been his final exams at the film institute.[18] According to the second account—from the reminiscences of Ol'ga Rumiantseva (another editor at *Oktiabr'*)—a student from the Gorky Literary Institute, L. Korniushin, brought Shukshin to the office. Shy and sullen, the young Shukshin supposedly muttered a pessimistic opinion on the likely outcome of the venture and left to await the journal's decision.[19] In any case, all the stories except for "Sten'ka Razin" were accepted, but with changes suggested by the editorial board.[20] What followed was a rather brief association—seven stories in three issues in 1961 and 1962— that ended when Shukshin began publishing in *Novyi mir* in 1963.

This brief association, however, constituted Shukshin's initiation into the literary politics of the day. His decision to publish in *Oktiabr'* could not have been taken lightly, for it coincided almost exactly with the circulation in samizdat at that time of Mikhail Romm's comments (from a closed discussion) in which he criticized the appointment of "the obscurantist" Kochetov as editor of *Oktiabr'* (in late 1960) and went as far as to explain "the fascist import of the literary pogroms" taking place in various cultural quarters in Russia.[21] If Shukshin was aware of his former teacher's comments, as is likely the case because they circulated widely in Moscow, why did he cast his lot with Kochetov anyway?

Political conservatism seems unlikely, especially in light of Shukshin's long association with *Novyi mir* throughout the 1960s. The answer seems to have more to do with short-term practical solutions. Clearly Shukshin was in a difficult situation with few options. Romm, who found jobs at Mosfilm Studios for Tarkovsky and two others from his class, passed over Shukshin, supposedly on the basis of Shukshin's weak final film project.[22] Ironically, the director credited with securing Shukshin's legendary admission to the film institute was almost responsible for his disappearance from the film world altogether.[23] With his future as a director uncertain and his acting career just beginning, literature must have seemed an increasingly viable career alternative. Kochetov's support represented his first big break as a writer. Eager to secure his new recruit—the most promising young talent yet to come his way in his turf war with the liberal *Iunost'* and *Novyi mir*—Kochetov even offered to help the writer obtain a Moscow residence permit. The price was loyalty to the conservative journal. Desperate for the permit and eager to be published, Shukshin agreed.[24]

Thus began another identity crisis, one as serious as that surrounding the question of Shukshin's rural or urban allegiances and which, like it, would also plague the writer throughout his career. As Grigori Svirski puts it, in allowing himself to be taken in by the conservatives, Shukshin had fallen into "a fatal trap." Svirski views this predicament as the defining conflict of Shukshin's career:

> Various unsavory types quickly made it their business to assure him that he was really one of them, a real Russian from the timeless depths of the Russian countryside, and to marry him off to Anatoly Sofronov's daughter. He was also quickly introduced to Sholokhov. This honest, vulnerable man found himself caught between publishing with Tvardovsky in *Novyi mir* on the one hand and being associated with Sofronov in his domestic life on the other. . . . With whom was he to side? Life itself, which as everyone knows is controlled by the Cultural Section of the Central Committee of the CPSU, nudged him in the direction of the Sholokhovs and Sofronovs, yet his heart strained towards the truth. Not surprisingly, by the time he was a little over forty he had developed heart disease and suddenly died.[25]

Although his account is factually inaccurate, Svirski still captures the essence of Shukshin's quandary. While Shukshin would break with Kochetov before his relationship with Viktoriia Sofronova began and first met Mikhail Sholokhov not in the early 1960s but in 1974, the question facing Shukshin was the same one facing all artists in the Soviet period. What compromises—personal, artistic, political—was he willing to make in order to see his prose in print or his films on the big screen? And where would the compromising end? The dangers were great, as Anatoly Gladilin points out: "[C]ompromise thinking led the writer to gradually retreat step by step. Thus arose a habit, which as we all know, is second nature—the habit of self-censorship. And suddenly, one fine day, it's clear that a supposedly 'leftish' and honest author is a cosy literato tamed by the authorities."[26]

The aspiring author was saved from Kochetov by the novelist Viktor Nekrasov, who met Shukshin through the director Marlen Khutsiev during the filming of *The Two Fedors*. When Shukshin showed Nekrasov the manuscript for *The Liubavin Family* in late 1962 and mentioned he was publishing it in *Oktiabr'*, Nekrasov refused to return it and instead took it to *Novyi mir*. Though not interested in the novel, the journal's prose editor, Asia

Samoilovna Berzer, was impressed enough to ask Shukshin to bring some of his short stories, which became his *Novyi mir* debut in the February 1963 issue. "And that," Nekrasov concludes, "is how the writer Shukshin was born."[27] Shukshin would never publish in *Oktiabr'* again. Kochetov, who had just secured Shukshin's residence permit,[28] was furious but helpless: he could do nothing about the writer's "defection." His revenge would come two years later, in an article by one of the journal's critics which almost single-handedly set the tenor of the debate over Shukshin's works for the rest of the decade.

Shukshin was no sooner safely outside the reach of the conservative Kochetov, however, when he met the daughter of Anatolii Sofronov, the establishment playwright and winner of two Stalin prizes, whom Svirski sarcastically dubs one of "the old draft horses of the 'hangmen's guild.'"[29] A reviewer of Shukshin's first collection,[30] Sofronova became acquainted with the writer while he was finishing his first film. A short-lived romance followed; it produced one child but never led to marriage.[31] Contrary to Svirski's speculations, Shukshin had little to do with Sofronov himself, but apparently got into arguments with Sofronova's mother, who liked to sing pro-Soviet songs around the dinner table. Shukshin would object, wanting nothing to do with her "lousy Soviet power" and "lousy Lenin."[32] Although he broke off the relationship with Sofronova, by all accounts he did his best to live up to his responsibilities as a father, mindful, according to Sofronova, of his own "fatherlessness" as a child.[33]

By this time, Shukshin was well aware of the danger that conservative alliances posed to artistic independence, as we can see in the text of his first proposal for his second film, *Your Son and Brother,* written shortly after his liaison with Sofronova. Originally titled *Fools Go Rushing In (Durakam zakon ne pisan)*, the film was to follow its hero beyond the events depicted in the short story "Stepka" to include an episode about his involvement with a group of black marketeers (a plot later developed in the novella *There, in the Distance* and Book Two of *The Liubavin Family*) and another scene about his involvement with the "world of the creative intelligentsia." Here, Stepka meets "Vika, Vika's father, her friends, mother, acquaintances," a transparent allusion to Viktoriia Sofronova and her family. In Stepka's story, we read Shukshin's own:

> Again it was something akin to love, but this time on the part of the girl [Vika]. She tries to understand Stepan, to help him (but only in the way she thinks he needs helping). Stepan's strong nature attracts her, she sincerely tries to help him but, as it turns out later, she only wants to make him into a mediocre, "second-rate" intellectual, slicked down and convenient. Nothing turns out. Again the question is begged: maybe Stepan foolishly passed up a splendid opportunity to "get ahead in the world" (she had everything to help him make his way, including the means). And let the viewer decide whether he's a fool or not.[34]

Shukshin never made *Fools Go Rushing In;* by the end of the year the script was reconfigured as *Your Son and Brother,* which was released late in 1965. And yet, if Shukshin really feared turning into a "second-rate," "slicked down," "convenient" intellectual, the unanswered question is one Nekrasov asks in his memoirs: why did he seek to please all those establishment artists, like state-sanctioned directors Sergei Bondarchuk of Mosfilm and Sergei Gerasimov of Gorky Film Studio? Why the politically correct roles in state-funded patriotic blockbusters, like that of Marshal Konev in Iurii Ozerov's *Liberation* (*Osvobozhdenie,* 1972) or Lopakhin in Bondarchuk's film of Sholokhov's *They Fought for Their Motherland?* As Nekrasov asks, "Why did he need all of those Konevs, Bondarchuks, Gerasimovs, and Sholokhovs?"[35]

The answer is simple: in order to obtain permission to shoot his next movie (and eventually win support for his two-part epic film on Razin). As Gladilin notes: "Look what a solid reputation Vasilii Shukshin seemed to have! However, he was allowed to do his own work 'every other time'—one film, so to speak, on special order, the next one for himself. How he toiled over his *Sten'ka Razin!*" Gladilin links Shukshin's appearance in Bondarchuk's film to a deal he cut with Mosfilm to win approval for his Razin film.[36] Even Shukshin's own last two films—*Pechki-lavochki* and *Kalina krasnaia*—were apparently done in exchange for permission to continue preparations for the filming of the Razin movie, in the first instance at Gorky Studio, in the second at Mosfilm.[37]

Yet, even outside his pursuit of the Razin project, Shukshin still seems uncomfortably beholden to the patriarchs of Soviet culture, praising Sholokhov in on-set interviews during the shooting of *They Fought for the Motherland* and corresponding with Konstantin Fedin at the height of the latter's campaign to sabotage the possible publication of Solzhenitsyn's *Cancer Ward* in *Novyi mir.* Fedin wrote a letter praising some of Shukshin's stories just three days after a meeting of the Secretariat of the Soviet Writers' Union on September 22, 1967, in which Fedin led an attack on Solzhenitsyn that eventually resulted in the suppression of the writer's novel and contributed to a twenty-year break in Solzhenitsyn's publishing career in the Soviet Union. Shukshin's reply to Fedin, dated September 30, was grateful and effusive.[38] While Shukshin may well not have know about Fedin's role in the battle over Solzhenitsyn's book, the exchange suggests a conservatism that Shukshin did not appear to possess, especially with regard to Solzhenitsyn, whom he praises elsewhere in a working note.[39]

Here we come up against a side of the writer's character that leaves him vulnerable to criticism that he was too cozy with the Soviet cultural establishment, too ready to say and do the right thing. Shukshin's behavior suggests that the inferiority complex he brought with him from the provinces expressed itself in contradictory ways: as a son of an enemy of the peo-

ple, he lashed out against Soviet power at Sofronova's dinner table; but as
an insecure, undereducated latecomer to cultural circles, he heaped praise
on two of the worst hatchet men of the Soviet cultural establishment. Such
was Shukshin's psychology, and he paid dearly for it. At times, this side of his
personality expressed itself in an odd inversion of scale: having compromised
himself in a large way (through his membership in the Communist Party),
for example, he makes an elaborate point of taking the moral high ground
in a small thing (his inability to give a fifty-kopeck bribe in "A Slander").
The effect is jarring.[40] It is as if Shukshin tried to maintain the untenable
position of a writer who, in A. Marchenko's disparaging 1969 assessment,
"wants to be accepted by all sides."[41] At the very least, such a position leads
to a certain degree of schizophrenia; at the worst, it leads to hypocrisy.[42]

If Shukshin did try to be liked by all, it did not work. His great public visibility following the success of *There's This Guy* only invited greater
scrutiny of his hero and his themes by a wider public. Popular culture of the
kind exemplified by Shukshin's movies proved to be the battleground on
which critics would wage very serious wars of words. As L. Belova points
out, it was often the case that the stories on which Shukshin's movies were
based—published separately ahead of the films themselves—failed to attract any controversy at all, while on screen "they appeared provocatively
aberrant." As movies, their plots seemed more contentious, their heroes'
judgments (often mistaken for Shukshin's own) more controversial, and
their lack of a clearly spelled-out conclusion more obvious on-screen than
in print.[43] The popular artist became a polemical lightning rod. Beginning
in 1965 and for the next five years, Shukshin's name and his works were
dragged into one debate after another. The loudest and most important
round fired in these battles came from the journal *Oktiabr'*.

Although Shukshin's film *There's This Guy* enjoyed huge success with
audiences and critics alike when it was released in June 1964, winning prizes
at home and abroad—including the Golden Lion Award that year at the
Vienna Film Festival[44]—a backlash followed in early 1965 that picked up on
one of the few criticisms expressed in otherwise glowing early reviews: that
of the "intentional emphasis of the hero's 'simplicity,' his insufficient intel-
lectuality."[45] In March of that year, within weeks of each other, letters critical of Pasha Kolokol'nikov's behavior and lack of social-mindedness appeared
in the movie-industry journal *Sovetskii ekran*,[46] a parody of the movie titled
"There's This Girl" came out in *Voprosy literatury*,[47] and articles were published in *Sovetskaia kul'tura* and *Oktiabr'* condemning Shukshin's hero.[48]
This initiated a reappraisal of Shukshin's first movie that would also condition the response to his second, *Your Son and Brother*.[49]

Bilichenko summarizes this change in attitude: "The critics of the
1960s upbraided Shukshin for a narrowness that allegedly did not permit
him to link the fate of his character to that of social progress. Moreover, his

hero was sometimes perceived as an inconspicuous, 'uncultured' antipode of the hero of our time, by which was meant the intellectual." Shukshin was accused of "denying the ideological, the intellectual premises of life, of upholding an abstract humanism that lacked social content, of preaching an 'elemental goodness.'"[50] Larissa Kriachko's article in *Oktiabr'* was both the most damning and the most influential in this regard, for she established the terms in which the Shukshin debate would be framed for years to come. Moreover, her article represents a very personal settling of scores with the artist. Speaking, as it were, directly for Kochetov, the editor of *Oktiabr'*, Kriachko inveighs at one point: "And I want to tell V. Shukshin about this precisely on the pages of *Oktiabr'*, where he began his path in art."[51]

In essence, her critical rereading resurrects the central issue of the Shukshin legend itself, that of the clash between "elemental" provincial truth and progressive, centralized Soviet truth. At issue were Pasha Kolokol'nikov and the heroes of Shukshin's latest stories in *Novyi mir*, all of whom were found to be ideologically deficient. "In an age when everyone is educating themselves, it is unprogressive to sing the praises of the hero's ignorance, to profess in an age of great social revolutions some kind of 'homespun truth,'" she argues,[52] referring to the rural, lower-class origins of Shukshin's undereducated protagonists. This argument was taken up by others. "A hero capable of great generalizations, of strong civic passions, of a holistic worldview is needed. A contemporary hero is needed."[53] Pasha was "out of step with his time," as was Shukshin's art, which was not deemed "up to the challenge of the ideas of Communism."[54] Maksim from "Snake Poison" was coarse, while Stepka from the story of that name was deemed capable of "sticking someone with a knife." Both heroes reflected their creator's romanticization of simple, elemental characters who were literally and figuratively dangerous to society[55]—the dimly perceivable portent of the "terror of the underclasses" (*terror nizov*).[56]

These were issues that would resurface a year later, shortly after the December 1965 release of *Your Son and Brother*, which was based in part on the writer's new works. The film is comprised of three linked stories, two of which, "Stepka" and "Ignakha's Come Home," are set in a Siberian village in the Altai. It opens with an extended sequence of undoctored scenes of village life during a spring thaw. We see the ice breaking on the River Katun', kids playing on the riverbanks, young women strolling the still muddy streets, rugs being beaten, boats being repaired, farm animals being fed, a tipsy muzhik staggering home, and a village barber trimming his client's hair right outside his house. Throughout the sequence, we hear the lyrical melody of the film's soundtrack and the lilting strains of a Russian folk song. It is to this setting, filled with the much-longed-for sights and sounds of the village in springtime, that the hero of the first segment "Stepka" returns. As unadorned and simple as it is effective, this opening sequence establishes

Prodigal Son

the lyrical tone of the movie. It shows us why Stepka escaped three months before his prison sentence was up and why Stepka's brother Maksim in the next segment (based on the story "Snake Poison") is so homesick in Moscow when he receives news of his mother's illness. The abrupt transition from Siberia to Moscow between the two segments, figured by a shot of a train moving thunderously across the steppe, prepares us for the many sequences of crowded city streets filled with harried, care-worn Muscovites, a vivid contrast to the movie's opening scenes. Maksim's impatience and frustration over his inability to find any snake poison with which to cure his mother leads him to lash out at the indifference of the big city, insulting the one kindly pharmacist who tries to help him. Eventually Maksim's brother Ignakha, who also lives in Moscow, uses his contacts to secure the prescription. It is Ignakha who takes the medicine back home in the movie's concluding segment, which returns the action to Siberia. There the implied contrast between Siberia and Moscow, the country and the city, is made literal when Ignakha's father tries to goad Vas'ka—the fourth son, who, like Stepka, remained in the village—into wrestling Ignakha in order to prove his physical (and, presumably, moral) superiority.

Kriachko again took the lead in the attack on Shukshin, publishing in the February 1966 issue of *Oktiabr'* a reprise of her former comments on the stories, this time in response to the release of *Your Son and Brother* and in defense of her previous comments on Shukshin. As before, her criticism of Shukshin's hero is essentially class-oriented. In vehemently defending her views, Kriachko expressed her solidarity with "the victims . . . terrorized by drunkards and hooligans" like Stepka, about whom his sympathizers "don't like to think."[57] She also finds the stories lacking a proper social orientation. Early reviews of the film in *Literaturnaia gazeta* and *Sovetskii ekran* followed suit, accusing Shukshin of cultivating a "primitive, malicious individualism"[58] and faulting him for promoting a "village idyll."[59] This last point in particular was controversial. There were howls of protest among certain critics over Shukshin's apparent juxtaposition of urban Moscow and rural Siberia in which the capital appears as an uncaring human anthill and Siberia a rural Arcadia. In fact, early criticism of the film became so intense that a roundtable discussion was called for by the Union of Cinematographers on April 8, 1966. According to Vladimir Korobov, the film's very distribution prospects hung in the balance.[60]

Shukshin spoke at the meeting. The criticisms of his film had hit him in his vulnerable spot, his provincial complex. His comments at the roundtable were a first public attempt to come to terms with his own departure from the village, his attitude toward Moscow and the *intelligentsiia*, and his own conflicted identity. "I am indebted to the *intelligentsiia* for everything," Shukshin declared, "and there is no basis for somehow seeing in the *intelligentsiia* some bad aspect of our modern life which needs to be examined.

122

. . . I love the village, but I think you can leave it." He added, no doubt slyly commenting on his own biography: "Lomonosov, too, left the village, and the Russian people haven't lost anything because of it, but the question is: where do they arrive?"[61] Shukshin's comments focused on what happens to the villager when he or she reaches the city. Speaking of his own experience, he complained of the "masses of half-baked intellectuals" who try to mold the new arrivals "in their own image and likeness" only to produce "braggarts" who hold their village roots in contempt.[62] While the city is certainly at fault in this process, Shukshin argued that these transplanted rural folk are every bit as much to blame for this outcome. In other words, the city in and of itself is not the enemy. Shukshin's speech had the desired effect: the film was approved for wide release.

The controversy surrounding *Your Son and Brother* continued throughout the year. The journal *Iskusstvo kino* published opposing views on the movie in its July issue. Lev Anninskii defended the film, arguing that Shukshin's point was not *where* people lived but *how*.[63] N. Klado, on the other hand, accused Shukshin of endorsing the village patriarchy over the "constancy of revolutionary transformations" and went as far as charging Shukshin with advocating a return to the principles of the *Domostroi*, the sixteenth-century guide to running a patriarchal household. He also leveled a charge at Shukshin that would reemerge with his fourth film, *Pechki-lavochki:* that the director had not noticed the changes taking place in his own village.[64]

The debate over the changing village and the place of rural patriarchy in the age of the "scientific technical revolution" was "a polemic in which Shukshin's name rang out particularly loudly and which in many respects defined the attitude toward his work taken during those years."[65] These were the opening salvos in the debate over Village Prose, at that time just recognizable as a cohesive literary development distinct from the rural sketches of writers like Ovechkin or Dorosh; Shukshin had stumbled right into the line of fire. From 1966 until 1973, when *Kharaktery* was published, Shukshin was continually implicated in these polemics and was often associated with the Village Prose movement, although his attitude toward the relationship between the village and the city differed somewhat from that of the most prominent Village Prose writers.

Shukshin tried to stake out his positions in a series of essays, the first of which responded to the clamor that had arisen over *Your Son and Brother.* "Questions to Myself" was published in late 1966. Together with "Monologue on a Staircase" and an unfinished article commissioned by the newspaper *Pravda* written a year later, it represents the writer's first musings in print on the controversy over his second film and his reflections on the changing countryside and his own departure from the village. Shukshin's questions are very personal and reveal his pain over the fate of the village and his deep sense of guilt over having left it. Perhaps under the influence of this potent combination of culpability and regret, Shukshin at times is almost indistinguishable from the village apologist he was accused of being.

In the first essay, Shukshin asserts that he is not favoring the village over the city in his prose or films but only trying to understand the reasons for the mass exodus of the village youth to the cities. In depicting the village in the context of this exodus, he admits trying to emphasize "everything that is beautiful" about it, but he justifies his decision by addressing himself directly to others who have left, advising them to "at least remember what remains behind!"[66]

In the second essay, Shukshin vigorously defends aspects of traditional rural society, calling the village a "sanctuary" from the noise and crime of contemporary urban life. According to Shukshin, the twentieth century, with "its fast pace and [modern] burdens," oppresses people: they "are tired, nervous, have forgotten what peace and quiet is, have forgotten how to smile at life, at beauty; they don't see the sun rise or set for years, and are so used to noise, they can't tell if you've yelled 'Hello!' or 'Help!'" He declares the need "to preserve the ill-fated 'patriarchal structure'" of village life while acknowledging that this sentiment is likely to provoke "either a condescending smile or a wrathful rebuke." But by patriarchy (and he warns us not to be frightened by the word) Shukshin means nothing "new, out of the ordinary, artificial," but "the customs, rituals, and respect for the testaments of ancient times which have accumulated through the centuries."[67] He even agitates for the observance of Easter, Christmas, and Maslenitsa (Shrove Tuesday) in the countryside, since they "have nothing to do with God. These are Spring holidays, the marking of Winter, the leavetaking of Winter. They are ways of expressing our joy at our close, somewhat dependent kinship with Nature." He adds, "you can't make up rituals," citing the failure of public bathhouses and marriage palaces in the village setting. He reminds us that the reasons for these customs are still valid: "It was not for nothing that when people wanted to say 'I'm not your enemy' they would say 'I danced at your wedding.'"[68] According to Shukshin, "the border between the city and the village should never be fully erased"; furthermore, "the peasantry should be hereditary," and, so long as it offers physical and spiritual freshness, the patriarchal character of the village should likewise be preserved.[69]

As conservative and antiurban as these comments sometimes are, Shukshin also exhibits a "progressive" side that seems to contradict many of his more traditionalist sentiments. As a man who had profited from the blessings of urban culture—namely, education and the conveniences of city life—Shukshin had a deep belief in the benefits of progress. In his essay "Questions to Myself," he calls the village "a yawning hole" in desperate need of "a cultured person" and those urban amenities—mainly stores stocked with food and other necessities—that can lighten the daily workload.[70] There-

fore, it is not surprising that, while extolling various aspects of the patriarchal village, Shukshin also admits that there is no stopping the exodus of
youth from the countryside; nor is there any way of preserving the village
and protecting it from change, and he does not see any real reason for doing
so. "What's bad about electricity, televisions, motorcycles, a good movie theater, a big library, school, and hospital?" he asks.[71] He offers a compromise:

I understand that the nature of the peasant's labor will change with time . . .
(that's good! that's necessary!), but give him the chance to build himself his
own home. Let him unburden his heart—carve designs on the cornice, dec-
orate the shutters, plant a birch tree under the window, slap something on
the roof that'll make everyone gasp. And then he'll be satisfied.[72]

In this way, Shukshin parts company with those Village Prose writers
who make an issue of preserving Siberian forests, lakes, and rivers and saving the traditional lifestyles of the inhabitants of Siberian villages. Shukshin's concerns about the village seem to operate exclusively on the moral
plane. What is bad in Shukshin's eyes is not scientific progress and its destruction of nature, but rather scientific progress when it destroys *human*
nature. What is wrong is not the exodus of the youth from the villages, but
the fact that in the city these youths become indifferent, corrupt, and
petty—that by leaving the village they "lose themselves . . . their personality, their character."[73]

In Shukshin's works, therefore, the quintessential themes and concerns
of Village Prose—the village and its natural surroundings, the *izba* (peasant
hut) and its contents, the writer's native region and its dialect, and the narrative's backward-looking, nostalgic point of reference[74]—are put to different uses, if they are present at all. So, while in theory Shukshin's artistic and
philosophical program had much in common with the Village Prose writers,
in practice his stories and films are often quite different. The uprooted
peasant, the village in transition, the moral and ethical consequences of the
"scientific technical revolution"—all favorite subjects of Village Prose—appear in Shukshin's stories not in order to celebrate what was and to lament
its passing, but to analyze what is happening now. Moreover, these themes
are treated in a vibrant narrative style that was more akin to Youth Prose.
Shukshin's works, as Deming Brown points out, are "fast moving, with dynamic plots and, not infrequently, surprise endings. The narration is taut
and racy, so economical that it often seems impressionistic, even glibly cinematic."[75] As Geoffrey Hosking aptly puts it, Shukshin "stands rather to one
side of the 'village prose' school."[76]

The more we read, the clearer it becomes that Shukshin's "village
complex" stems not from a desire to preserve the traditional state of the village but from a sense that he—and others like him who had left for a better life in the city—had somehow sold out. The resultant sense of alienation

is Shukshin's real theme, while his hero is the "village youth who is wounded by the great temptation of the twentieth century—the city."[77] Shukshin admits as much in the opening paragraphs of "Monologue on a Staircase," in which he describes a meeting with a group of scientists after a showing of *Your Son and Brother.*

> A note was passed up: "And how would you like to take your place behind the plow?" I was thrown for a loss. I blurted out something about how they also wouldn't like to exchange their atomic reactors for the smithy. But they weren't fighting for that. Just the opposite. As for me, it turned out that I wanted to preserve that "patriarchal life" in the village for others, while I myself was settling into life in the capital with a clean conscience.[78]

Shukshin returns to this question in an unfinished article for *Pravda,* where he chides himself about the reasons for his departure:

> So why did I leave the village? Maybe, if I didn't want to be too sly about it, I could just up and say: it was like this—when the time came, I picked myself up and set off to look for a better lot in life. I forgot the peasant's "eternal" love of the land, magnificently overcame the "urge to till the earth," and shuffled down the street in my dress shoes, dreaming of getting an "apartment with its own john." At least that would be honest.

But he refutes this a few sentences later: "But then I came to my senses and thought: hold on, what time are we talking about? That was 1946! Those times were nothing like today. There was famine, they didn't give you anything for your work; whoever could leave left *involuntarily.*"[79]

In a technique characteristic of his short stories, Shukshin raises a number of different possibilities in the minds of his readers about what motivates the narrative. Is this a confession? A justification? A self-accusation? Did Shukshin use the harsh circumstances of the postwar village to conceal his own ambitions for a better life in the city? Or was he really forced into "exile" from his *malaia rodin*a by policies emanating from the capital? The writer's sister Natal'ia hints that her brother left primarily for material reasons.

> [H]e came home to Srostki from his third year at the vocational school and said: "Mom, I'm going to Moscow." Mama was very upset. Why? What for? We don't know anyone or have any kinfolk there. And it was such a difficult time—the postwar years. . . . How he convinced Mother, I'll never know, he probably didn't—she was impossible when it came to this, but she understood, she felt it in her heart: you can't keep a young man at home.[80]

As it turns out, the antiurban theme to which so many critics objected was to a large extent Shukshin working out his feelings of betrayal about leaving the village. This was lost on most critics of Shukshin's prose in the late 1960s. When his collection of stories *There, in the Distance* came out in 1968, Shukshin was still, in Anninskii's words, "an 'argument' in the battle between the Village Prose writers and the anti–Village Prose writers."[81]

The year 1968 was, of course, a fateful one in Soviet culture. The Soviet invasion of Czechoslovakia in August to quash the "Prague Spring" sent a clear message to artists back home. Galina Belaia writes: "The recoil from the truth which had been revealed at the XXth congress, followed by the reanimation of ideas that in the light of that truth had seemed obsolete, the falsification of our country's history which again took hold from the end of the 1960s—all this had a profound effect upon the psychology of writers."[82] For Shukshin, May and June of 1968 saw the publication of his screenplay about Sten'ka Razin in the journal Iskusstvo kino. The appearance of this narrative of a popular uprising on the eve of the events that August was a case of fateful timing. Shukshin's script, which cast Razin's rebellion not so much in terms of a peasant uprising as a revolt against government, governmental decrees, and all that sought to constrain freedom (in this instance, Cossack volia), suddenly acquired a heightened contemporary relevance. While Shukshin's Razin marched on Moscow, killing government officials and burning government documents, the Soviet government made it very clear that no opposition of any kind would be tolerated. As Belaia explains, the "question of the nature of power" raised in I Have Come to Give You Freedom was "seditious" and therefore partly responsible for the difficulty Shukshin faced in winning final approval to shoot the film in the years of increasing social and cultural prohibitions that followed.[83] Although the movie could not be shot, the script was a critical success and was named best screenplay of the year at the Second All-Union Competition of movie scripts.[84]

Besides illustrating the paradoxical workings of culture in the Brezhnev period, these events remind us that Shukshin's interests as an artist went far beyond the city/country debate. Shukshin was "not only partly villager, partly city dweller, but also partly a man of the sixties and partly a man of the seventies."[85] He shared the same concerns as the other writers of his generation—Trifonov, Aitmatov, Iskander, Okudzhava, and others—namely, the spiritual bankruptcy of society, the devaluation of personality, the falsification of the past, the deformation of the present, and "despair at the sight of indifference and evil triumphant."[86] Like them, he also tread the fine line between conformity and dissonance, compromise and independence "in conditions when social life was falling apart and becoming distorted and the discord between word and deed had attained official government direction."[87]

Over the next two years, the cultural situation worsened. In November 1969, Solzhenitsyn was expelled from the Writers' Union; partly as a consequence of his defense of Solzhenitsyn, Tvardovskii was removed as editor of Novyi mir three months later, after which the journal's editorial staff was reorganized. As Lenin's centenary was celebrated across the country, a bust was placed on Stalin's grave, symbolically marking the high point of Brezhnev's re-Stalinization.

Shukshin's work appeared in the reorganized *Novyi mir* only once, in the July 1970 issue, and then the journal turned him away.[88] Within a year, he joined a group of other writers of rural prose—such as Vasilii Belov, Vladimir Soloukhin, Viktor Astaf'ev, and Valentin Rasputin—rallying around the journal *Nash sovremennik,* which had already proved controversial in the late 1960s for its increasingly nationalist bias. *Nash sovremennik* was becoming the home of Village Prose authors who deserted both *Novyi mir* and the orthodox journal *Molodaia gvardiia* in the early 1970s. It also routinely published works by other major authors, including Iurii Nagibin, Iurii Kazakov, Evgenii Evtushenko, Vasil' Bykau (Bykov), and Fazil' Iskander. In this way, *Nash sovremennik* essentially took the place of *Novyi mir* in the 1970s as the preferred venue for the most talented authors of the day.[89] Over the next four years, Shukshin appeared in five issues, with seventeen stories and the novella *Kalina krasnaia,* and in 1973 he even joined the journal's editorial board.

But even as a member of the editorial board, Shukshin did not always have an easy time publishing in *Nash sovremennik.* In a letter to Vasilii Belov from early 1974 he complains: "*Sovremennik* returned what in my view was a harmless novella. They said: 'We're not going to publish anything provocative this year.' The journal has been swamped. I'm not even going to try them anymore. Whoever will publish me right away, without a lot of talk, is where I'll go."[90] This approach was nothing new. Shukshin had been doing precisely that since 1970, trying venues as varied as *Sel'skaia molodezh'* (a magazine for rural youth), the Leningrad journals *Zvezda* and *Avrora,* the provincial *Sever* and *Sibirskie ogni,* the newspaper *Sovetskaia Rossiia,* the Sunday newspaper supplement *Nedelia,* and the literary weeklies *Literaturnaia Rossiia* and *Literaturnaia gazeta.* Perhaps as a result of his frequent and varied publications, by 1974 he was known as "the most professional, that is, the most regularly appearing 'storyteller' in Soviet literature."[91]

All of this kept Shukshin in the critical spotlight. While his third collection of stories, *Fellow Countrymen* (*Zemliaki,* 1970), passed without much comment (only half of its contents were new), his publications between 1971 and 1974 stimulated lively critical debate. The 1973 publication of *Kharaktery* and the spring 1974 release of *Kalina krasnaia* were the main catalysts. Some seven reviews of the collection appeared in major journals, including a point/counterpoint analysis in *Literaturnoe obozrenie* featuring the liberal Lev Anninskii debating the conservative Vladimir Gusev.[92]

The most controversial evaluation came out in *Novyi mir.* Titled "Settling Accounts among Ourselves" ("Svoi liudi—sochtemsia"), the article goes well beyond the stories of *Kharaktery* to propose a rereading of Shukshin's works as a whole. As the title suggests, the article is also a settling of accounts on the part of the new *Novyi mir* with its former contributor. To blame was Shukshin's affiliation with *Novyi mir*'s chief rival, *Nash sovremennik*. In fact, the editors and writers of *Nash sovremennik* were the first to protest *Novyi mir*'s treatment of Shukshin, a sure sign of the competition between the two journals. The nationalist critic Viktor Chalmaev, a *Nash sovremennik* editor since 1968, called the article "a belittling" of Shukshin in which "under the guise of praise" the writer was "oversimplified to the level of a master of the anecdotal story."[93] Vsevolod Sakharov notes the "practiced irony" thrown Shukshin's way in the review,[94] while Aleksandr Ovcharenko reproaches the article's authors for seeing nothing in Shukshin's prose except "approximation, sketchiness, imitation, and anecdotes."[95]

Although certainly not as vicious as Larissa Kriachko's avenging of Shukshin's defection from *Oktiabr'*, the *Novyi mir* review does make its share of digs at the artist, some of them personal. Besides taking the writer to task for the frequency with which his "legendary" lower-class, Siberian origins are mentioned and for his numerous interviews in the press, Shukshin is also criticized for the recurrence in his early stories of heroes who, like himself, have "exchanged the 'blossoming steppe' for the 'bonds of high society and the tiresome brilliance of the ballroom.'" Furthermore, Shukshin is cast as an uneven writer whose stories are sometimes "in bad taste" and who is "well known for not being up to large prose genres."[96] The reviewers equate his stories with anecdotal oral tales, at times no better than improvisational acting assignments.[97] Still, although clearly a pretext for delivering some pretty damning criticisms, the reviewers' remarks are far from being exclusively negative. On the contrary, the review ends with a clear endorsement of Shukshin's works, although it is an endorsement with a polemical twist to it: Shukshin is declared to be philosophically opposed to the village themes of many of his fellow *Nash sovremennik* writers. "His stories are anti-idyllic, they can offhandedly irritate and upset those who believe in the safe-keeping of a golden fund of psychological gene types in distant log-hut preserves. But Shukshin doesn't polemicize. He simply knows that there aren't any such preserves, that life to which everyone belongs goes on."[98] Here the rivalry between the journals is most keenly felt. One last time Shukshin would be implicated in the Village Prose debate, one last time used as a weapon in someone else's argument.

In the end, Shukshin's relationship with the critics can be summarized by his movement among three journals (from *Oktiabr'* to *Novyi mir* to *Nash sovremennik*) and by the ideological reading each move provoked. But, as we see from his letter to Belov, by 1974 Shukshin still felt "homeless" when it came to a reliable venue for his stories or a reliable studio for his Razin film, just as he felt rootless in real life, at home neither in Moscow nor in Siberia. Indeed, Shukshin's relationship with the critics is ultimately conditioned by this tenuous state of being between movements, between journals, between literature and cinema, between Moscow and Siberia, as well as by the provincial complex that must be factored in at every stage of the writer's development.

This complex—both a sore spot and a weapon—is singled out by Boris Pankin as the defining element in the artist's interaction with the critical establishment. Particularly in his publicistic writing and in interviews, Pankin argues, Shukshin's provincial complex became part of a duel between the artist and his interlocutors over loaded questions about "modern acting," the "cultural plasticity" of his films, and the "linguistic constructs" of his stories.

> Inevitably I wondered, What prompted my colleagues to ask questions of precisely this kind, in this form? Aesthetic deafness, loss of hearing? Or a sincere, albeit naive, desire to help an artist "from the people" to interpret his own work in terms of contemporary scholarship? Was this a debate between "eggheads" and a "man of intuition," a primitive artist? . . .
>
> Sometimes it seems as though . . . a duel of sorts has started or is in progress between Shukshin and his interlocutors—journalists, art experts, and critics. "To tell you the truth, I don't quite understand what is meant by stylistics," says Shukshin in response to one of the questions. But God help you if you take that "to tell the truth" at face value. Shukshin is skillfully and mischievously shamming here. . . .
>
> And one finds this over and over again: the interviewers with their knives at his throat, "in the language characteristic of them" . . . and Shukshin answering in his own way.[99]

Unwittingly or not, Pankin is taking his cue directly from the pages of the Shukshin legend, that encounter between the sly peasant and the city know-it-alls. And yet he has not strayed too far from the truth. Anninskii also notes Shukshin's ability to disarm his critics with admissions of his doubts, ignorance, or inexperience.[100] These statements are sprinkled throughout his essays and interviews: "Others have put it better than I can . . ." "I'm no politician, I can easily get lost in complicated questions . . ." "I don't quite understand the question . . ."[101] While these statements might not really constitute "mischievous shamming," they originate in the same sense of inferiority that informs both the genuine provincial complex and the biographical legend. Indeed, it is a tribute to the value of the legend for understanding Shukshin that its traces can be found in so many aspects of the artist's life and works. For his part, Pankin sees "this game, this duel" as the key to understanding Shukshin's publicistic writing and the "deep sources, the springs of his work."[102]

Shukshin's final answer to the critics—and the final word on his legend—is undoubtedly *Pechki-lavochki*. It relates the story of how the tractor driver Ivan Rostorguev travels with his wife, Niura, from Siberia to Moscow and then on to the Black Sea on a trip Ivan has earned through his exemplary labor. In the "half-anecdotal plot about how Vania the Siberian went to the ocean and along the way had his fill of the wonders of the seven seas,"[103] Shukshin lays bare and gently ridicules his provincial insecurities while at the same time condemning urban condescension and intellectual pretension. Everyone in the film is held up to laughter: the arrogant city slicker who lectures Ivan and Niura about how to behave outside of the village; the thief who takes advantage of their country trustfulness to sneak on board their train to Moscow; the professor who collects substandard village words and phrases as if they were archaeological artifacts and then marches Ivan before his students as a "real-life" representative of a lost civilization; the professor's Moscow colleagues, whose discussions about the fate of the village read like the transcript of the city/country debates surrounding Shukshin's works; and, perhaps most of all, Ivan and Niura themselves, whose hilarious "odyssey" is more like a "flight to the moon,"[104] so fantastic and otherworldly do Moscow and the southern beaches of the Crimea seem to these residents of a distant Siberian village.

Two rejected earlier titles—*Ekhal Van'ka* and *Istoriia odnoi poezdki* (*Vanka Went for a Ride* and *The Story of One Journey*)—reveal the film's emphasis on journey, travel, life on the road, life in between realms and destinations. Following in the tradition of John Ford's *Stagecoach* and Frederico Fellini's *La Strada*, and cognizant of his experience as an actor in Boris Barnet's road picture *Alenka* (1962) and of his own directorial debut, the mini-picaresque *Zhivet takoi paren'* (1964), Shukshin exploits the great opportunities the road picture gives "to use the novella principle in his narrative, and thus to combine the most varied scenes and episodes into a single compositional whole."[105] The physical movement through space and time of the road picture emphasized an important theme at the center of many of his works, that of the human being in transition, while also allowing him to treat the central chronotope of his life and art: that of the space between the village and the city during the Soviet 1960s and 1970s.

This travel theme reveals the serious side to Shukshin's comedy. The movie, which celebrates the journey of two *kolkhozniki*—one of them (Niura) traveling illegally without a *putevka* (official invitation) and neither of them possessing an internal passport—also celebrates a larger freedom normally denied rural dwellers: freedom of movement in their own country. This aspect of Shukshin's movie cannot be ignored or discounted, for in 1972, when the movie was released, the introduction of internal passports for the rural population was still four years away. Phased in between 1976 (two years after Shukshin's death) and 1980, legislation guaranteeing internal passports for village dwellers was, according to historian Zhores Medvedev, "the single most important social reform during Brezhnev's tenure of office."[106]

No one mentions the right to cultural mobility when they talk about *Pechki-lavochki*, yet this aspect of life in the countryside under the Soviets lies at the heart not only of Shukshin's movie but of his life and art as well. When viewed in light of the humiliating stigma attached to the Soviet government's refusal to issue collective farmers the internal passports possessed by urban citizens, *Pechki-lavochki* becomes a much more serious treatment of freedom and constraint in Soviet society and culture, albeit one cast as a comedy. As Shukshin commented in his proposal to Gorky Film Studio: "If I had to determine the genre of the subject, I would have to call it a comedy. But, I repeat, the discussion will be a very serious one."[107] The attitudes and obstacles Ivan and Niura encounter on their journey are thus the products not only of urban condescension and prejudice but of official government policy as well. As it turns out, not only were *kolkhozniki* expected to know their place in society—that is, on its lowest cultural and social rung—but they were legally kept there by laws forcing them to give up their right to an internal passport upon joining the collective farm. It is here we can locate the very real malice with which the city slicker warns Ivan: "You need to leave your country ways at home [. . .] and learn how to behave properly. You're not in the village anymore. [. . .] Or I'll see to it that you get off this train as easily as you got on" (4:111–12).

Certainly, any serious treatment of the issue of internal passports would not have passed the censors. As it was, *Pechki-lavochki* was severely cut and censored at every step of the production process and shot with such substandard equipment that the crew left a crane behind in Siberia as scrap metal when they finished shooting.[108] After viewing Shukshin's first edited version, Gorky Film Studio demanded cuts that amounted to almost two-thirds of the material.[109] The film was eventually released in the next-to-lowest distribution category. It was given a "three" rating ("four" is the worst);[110] between one hundred and two hundred copies were released to theaters in limited distribution.[111]

The movie was Shukshin's first with cameraman Anatolii Zabolotskii, whose influence is felt in the many almost-documentary scenes of real Russian villages, train stations, and city streets. The interlacing of these scenes with the decidedly theatrical, almost vaudevillian adventures of the movie's country innocents made for an interesting effect. The resulting contrast between real and make-believe, serious and comic, modern and folk becomes the dialectic in which the film's larger issues are played out. Serious debate of social questions is both muted by farcical comedy—thus making it safer and more palatable for the censors—and enabled by it. This paradox helps to explain why *Pechki-lavochki* at times feels like one of the first honest depictions in Soviet cinema of the bleak conditions of the Soviet countryside—something akin to Andrei Konchalovsky's *The Story of Asia Kliachina Who Loved but Did Not Get Married* (*Istoriia Asi Kliachinoi, kotoraia liubila, da ne vyshla zamuzh;* 1967, released 1987), whose documentary style was a direct influence on Shukshin and Zabolotskii[112]—while at other times it evokes the slapstick comedies of Grigorii Aleksandrov from the 1930s and 1940s.

For example, the opening sequence of the peasant *zastol'e* celebrating Ivan and Niura's departure is filled with shot after shot of undoctored rural reality. We see real villagers, not actors, wearing their own modest clothing and singing real Russian folk songs and *chastushki* (folk limericks), not bowdlerized Soviet versions. Their dancing is likewise simple and clumsy but genuine, and they all look a little self-conscious on camera. The interior and exterior of the peasant *izba* are spare if not dilapidated. An old man, frail and pathetic, sits off by himself and later sleeps on a simple, high, raised bed (called a *polati*). In the picturesque and lovingly filmed landscape, the camera picks up a rusting drum, rutted dirt roads, and a primitive wooden bridge. These are not the sort of images you would see in such politically correct rural depictions as Yuly Raizman's film version of Semen Babaevskii's *Kavaler zolotoi zvezdy* (*Knight of the Golden Star,* 1950).

These shots of authentic realia, however, stand out in stark relief to the deliberately contrived and burlesque sequences on the train that follow, such as when Ivan makes a misalliance with the thief who has snuck on board the train. The thief, aware that Ivan is away from his home village for the first time in his life, passes himself off as a railroad engineer and tells Ivan a fantastic story about his invention (which he calls *sistema igrek*) that allows trains to fly over rivers without bridges. He gives Niura an expensive stolen blouse and then disappears when police board the train. When Ivan is told who his neighbor was, he runs all over the train car in a panic trying to get rid of the blouse, eventually flushing it down the toilet and explaining to the investigator that his wet sleeve and prolonged stay in the bathroom were due to diarrhea.

The very real backwardness of country life glimpsed in the documentary village scenes is thus supplanted by the comic country backwardness of Ivan's behavior on the train and made "safe" or rendered "harmless." But "real" life is never forgotten entirely, as Shukshin continually intersperses other documentary shots of actual life at provincial train stations and on Moscow streets between scenes from his unfolding comic folk tale, which itself is punctuated by "serious" conversations, both on the train and later in Moscow, between Ivan and the professor about life and living conditions in the countryside. Eventually, we come to realize that the folk tale and "real life" are meant to be read as an essential commentary on each other, that the whole story of Ivan and Niura's vacation is, as Eduard Yefimov puts it, the kind of "inspired 'blarney' . . . necessary for the artistic effect and emotional and moral impact of the story."[113]

Thus, when in the final scene Ivan—now safely back home and sitting barefoot on a hill above his native village—looks the camera in the eye and, without a trace of irony, pronounces, "That's it, folks, the end," the effect is not comic at all. On the contrary, it is not only a declaration—made not so much by Ivan Rostorguev as by Shukshin himself—that the slapstick folk tale is over, but a hint at the quite serious social issues raised by this modern-day journey of Ivan the Fool. In Shukshin's own words: "'Comedy' here can be understood as the obvious disparity between true significance and the borrowed complexity and self-importance that empty people love to put on." This disparity is played out in the collision between the trusting villager and the "shady operators" who mock and prey on them,[114] a collision that reveals, according to one reviewer, the hero's almost Dostoevskian "wounded pride" and "pathological sensitivity."[115] Here, of course, is where the artist's own provincial complex peeks through, where he seems to be conducting "an unfinished debate with himself" over the city/country dichotomy in his life and art.[116] Indeed, the fact that Shukshin steps out of character and addresses the audience directly hints broadly at the personal significance of the movie for the actor and director himself. To understand the leap that Shukshin made in his own lifetime, we need only contemplate the distance—geographical, cultural, and social—that separates the scene where Ivan and Niura are sitting in the professor's elegant dining room, sipping coffee and discussing the "village question," from the noisy and humble Siberian *zastol'e* at the beginning of the film. *Pechki-lavochki*—as well as Shukshin's life and art—is built on that kind of contrast, a clash of discourses as much as it is a clash of cultures.

Despite cuts and a limited theater run, the film was received positively by critics, one of whom even ends his review with a plea to the powers that be to allow Shukshin to move on to his much-anticipated film on Razin.[117] There was one important exception, and it came from an unexpected source: Shukshin's fellow Altaians, a development that would have a pronounced effect on the artist. The newspaper *Altaiskaia pravda* accused the director of portraying his Altaian countrymen as simplistic hicks and, most important, faulted him for not noticing the changes that had taken place in his own home village.[118] Other bad reviews from the Altai and an anonymous letter followed: "Don't pass yourself off as one of us, don't disgrace your homeland and us."[119] Letters were even written to the Supreme Soviet.[120] Shukshin was cut to the quick. His response was the essay "The Place Where I Was Born" ("Slovo o maloi rodine"), the third time in his career that he appeared in print to explain his films. On this occasion, Shukshin talked about *Pechki-lavochki* in terms of his own departure from the village.

The essay is, as the original title suggests, "A Declaration of Love" ("Priznanie v liubvi").[121] In it, Shukshin confronts his conflicted identity with an honest confession of guilt over having left the Altai, and then lovingly and nostalgically revisits the sights and smells of the land of his childhood. He writes:

For people who had to leave home (whatever the reasons), and there are very many such people, there is always an involuntary residue of loss, a feeling of guilt and sadness. With the years, the sadness grows less, but it doesn't pass altogether. . . . I would like to get to the bottom of all this. Is it mine—the place where I was born and grew up?[122]

Shukshin answers his own question with a confident "yes," but concludes his essay ambiguously several pages later: "Why is it that the thought still lives on in my heart that someday I shall go back and remain there for ever? When? Life doesn't seem to be turning out that way . . . And why?"[123] That question—why you cannot go home again—would be answered in Book Two of *The Liubavin Family* and, most famously, in his next film, *Kalina krasnaia.*

The incredible success of *Kalina krasnaia,* released only two years after *Pechki-lavochki,* overshadowed the significance of the earlier film. This is unfortunate, for *Pechki-lavochki* is clearly one of Shukshin's most important movies,[124] expressing as it does its maker's very public and private pain over the village, Siberia, the city, the *intelligentsiia,* and the critical debate that had enveloped all of these questions. As he does so often elsewhere in his late works, in *Pechki-lavochki* Shukshin strikes out with one hand and beats himself with the other. He castigates the government for its legal constraints on rural dwellers, rebukes the city for its higher standard of living, accuses city dwellers of condescension and conspicuous consumerism, and criticizes the intelligentsia for its perennial inability to understand the peasant. Yet he also mocks his country bumpkin heroes, whose misadventures are largely brought on by their own provincial backwardness.

Kalina krasnaia deepened Shukshin's provincial polemic in dramatic fashion, turning the artist himself into a cult hero. In the tale of the prodigal son and recidivist thief Egor Prokudin, Shukshin would become not merely the object of critical discussion, he would make cultural history. It is to *Kalina krasnaia* that we turn next.

Chapter Seven

Return of the Prodigal Son

> Very few events have taken place in recent times
> in our art that have so shaken the social and aes-
> thetic self-consciousness of the viewer.
> —B. Runin on *Kalina krasnaia*

SHUKSHIN'S *KALINA KRASNAIA* ranks among
the most sensational Soviet movies of the 1970s. Not only did the tragic and
controversial story of recidivist-thief Egor Prokudin's attempt to "go
straight" and return to the rural home of his childhood draw over sixty million people to movie theaters across the country—and many of these viewers saw the movie more than once—but it generated public debate over the
film's themes on a scale virtually unprecedented in Soviet film history.
Thousands of letters poured into the editorial offices of newspapers and
magazines with viewers' reactions and questions.[1] The journals *Sovetskii
ekran* and *Voprosy literatury* organized roundtables to discuss the film and
the cine-novella on which it was based.[2] The magazine *Iskusstvo kino* published a lengthy article on the making of the movie in direct response to
public demand.[3] Readers of *Sovetskii ekran* voted the movie the best Soviet
film of 1974 and Shukshin the best actor in the magazine's annual contest.[4]
In April 1974, shortly after its premiere, the film won best picture at the
Seventh Annual All-Union Film Festival in Baku.[5] Shukshin was even posthumously awarded a Lenin Prize for the film in 1976.

The controversial content of the film no doubt accounted for much of
its popularity. As Hedrick Smith states, "[T]he film's whole thrust—crime
growing in the supposedly pure soil of Communist society, the hero's tragic
ending, doubts about the perfectibility of man, and the clear implication
that it was the depravity of modern city life which had made a good country boy go bad, all ran counter to the canons of Soviet Socialist Realism."[6]
Kalina krasnaia was forbidden fruit, and viewers flocked to the theaters for
a taste. Indeed, the release of *Kalina krasnaia* marks the second time in
post-Stalinist Soviet society that political intervention at the highest level—
by the general secretary of the CPSU (Communist Party of the Soviet

Union)—produced a cultural act.[7] Just as Nikita Khrushchev intervened to obtain the publication in 1962 of Aleksandr Solzhenitsyn's *One Day in the Life of Ivan Denisovich*, so did Leonid Brezhnev reportedly rescue *Kalina krasnaia* from the censors in 1974, approving the movie for wide distribution after a private screening at which he was "moved to tears."[8] Though the first intervention was for a work of "high" culture, a book, and the second was for a work of "low" culture, a popular film, in both cases camp-life ethos, convict culture, and a peasant hero are central.

To date, most commentators, East and West, have focused on the social dimensions of the film: Egor's tragic end was predetermined by his "childhood of deprivation and early exposure to the underworld," both traceable to sociohistorical conditions in the village after World War II.[9] A different view was offered by Donald Fiene, who rejected the argument that Egor Prokudin is the "victim of Soviet social forces," asserting instead that his story "makes sense psychologically and literarily only if we see it as a modern hagiography modeled on the ancient Russian saints' lives."[10] Taking his cue from Fiene, Robert Mann identified St. George as Egor Prokudin's "clearest prototype" and saw in the story many allusions to folk tales and Christian lore about the saint.[11]

These are all valid and productive ways in which to understand *Kalina krasnaia*, yet the movie as a filmic and verbal text has largely been ignored. For the first time in his film career, Shukshin had found the magic cinematic formula for telling his story of marginalization and transition. His embrace of the conventions and traditions of popular cinema in *Kalina krasnaia* greatly heightened the accessibility and emotional impact of the movie and merits special attention. After all, Soviet moviegoers responded not only to the story unfolding on the screen, but also to the way Shukshin the writer, director, and actor told Egor Prokudin's tale, that is, to the acting, editing, use of symbols, foreshadowing, music, lighting, and other cinematic effects employed in the making of the movie. Shukshin's popular aesthetic—his great investment in most effectively reaching cinema's "audience of millions" (*mnogomillionaia auditoriia*)[12]—had more to do with *Kalina krasnaia*'s success than has been generally acknowledged. Commentators on the film, especially Fiene and Mann, have routinely relied heavily on Shukshin's cine-novella in their analyses, referring to the film sometimes only in passing. But, as Shukshin himself points out, "the cinema is a special form of art and for that reason demands its own judgment," especially since in the case of *Kalina krasnaia* "the cine-novella didn't evoke any controversy, the film evoked controversy, so it makes sense to dwell on it."[13]

Shukshin's distinction is an important one. The greatest film triumph of the actor and the director, *Kalina krasnaia* had gone virtually unnoticed by critics when published as a novella a year prior to the film's release.[14] It was the movie that sent readers to libraries in search of the issue of *Nash sovremennik* in which the novella appeared and that won for Shukshin's prose, already popular at that time, an even wider audience.[15] Of all of Shukshin's films, *Kalina krasnaia* most resoundingly rewarded its creator's faith in the power of the cinema to advance his artistic program. Moreover, *Kalina krasnaia*, more than any of his previous four films, testified to the interrelatedness of all three aspects of Shukshin's artistic identity. From its creation to its reception, the movie was a product of the synthetic nature of Shukshin's art, his ability to blend literature and cinema, to mix high and low elements, and to marry folk, popular, and high culture. As Eduard Yefimov reminds us:

> Shukshin was not just a film-maker and a man of letters, he was also a vivid exponent of the syncretic element in folk art: there was much in his work that was pre-literary, folklore, fantastic and bound up with the ancient tradition of song and dance. Story-telling, parable, folk-tale, the comic song or the lament, dances and flamboyant folk-dancing are all important elements in both the context and form of his works, whether written or intended for the cinema. His gift for synthetic thinking, when words and sounds, visual images and musical melodies all exist as a single whole, is the main feature of Shukshin as a creative personality and of his artistic method—in literature as in films.[16]

Kalina krasnaia was a showcase for Shukshin's "synthetic thinking." At once a "high tragedy" and a "cruel romance," a "melodrama" and an "oral tall tale" (*ustnaia baika*), a "lyrical confession" and a "provincial low farce" (*provintsial'nyi balagan*),[17] the movie defies definition in much the same way its creator does. Although critics complained about the film's eclecticism, Soviet audiences were enthralled. What made the film so appealing to the Soviet public? What was its importance for Shukshin?

KALINA KRASNAIA AND THE "AUDIENCE OF MILLIONS"

In his book on Soviet popular culture, Richard Stites states an obvious but important truth: "mass audiences—in Russia as elsewhere—have always preferred 'simple' emotional subjects and a display of familiar feelings—even to the point of sentimentalism." He adds, "Audiences did not flock to heavily socialist realist potboilers or to masterpieces of cinema art. Surveys revealed that audiences were drawn by contemporary themes, fast tempo, spectacle, and simple editing."[18] These qualities—a simple, emotional theme, quick pace, spectacle, straightforward editing, and a topical subject—are the same ingredients that led to the success of Shukshin's *Kalina krasnaia*. In responding to critics who objected to the film's "banal characters," "unrealistic plot," and "sentimentality," Shukshin stated, "All the same, I was mentally addressing myself to different people,"[19] meaning, in this instance, the broad, popular audience.

On the one hand, Shukshin's movie told the kind of story everyone can understand and relate to: the return of the prodigal son to his native home.[20] It did so in a brisk, straightforward manner, using obvious symbolism, melodramatic effect, and openly sentimental scenes (in particular, Egor's notorious birch-petting scenes, which were attacked by critics but defended by moviegoers). The film's protagonists are likewise simply delineated. The main character is colorful, sympathetic, and unpredictable, while secondary characters include the stock protagonists from any mass-audience movie: impossibly decent and likable good guys (Egor's love interest, Liubov' Baikalova, her steadfast brother Petro, and their kind, trusting parents) opposed to formula villains (Egor's former gang members). Character names are intentionally transparent. Egor's nickname is Gore—"sorrow, woe, trouble." Liubov' means "love" and "charity," while Baikalova calls to mind the largest freshwater lake in the world, Lake Baikal, located in Siberia—an obvious sign of Liuba's purity and virtue. For their part, the bad guys have appropriately grotesque appellations. The gang leader is Guboshlep, or "Fat Lip," while one of his lowbrow thugs is Bul'dia, or "Bulldog." All told, in direction, cinematography, plot, and characterization, Shukshin availed himself of all of the makings of "a typical melodrama, a mass-market movie, a tearjerker, a middle-class smash hit," a fact one critic claims helps to explain "the extraordinary popularity of *Kalina krasnaia* with the 'average viewer.'"[21]

On the other hand, *Kalina krasnaia,* for all of its film stereotypes, also struck Soviet audiences as an honest, truthful depiction of a very recognizable contemporary reality. Egor's rootlessness, his transient position between the city and the countryside, his various comical encounters in town, the provincial city streets lined with Soviet placards, the village amateur talent show (*samodeiatel'nost'*) with its cloying performances of folk songs (echoing the seemingly endless number of such programs on Soviet television), even the snatches of radio overheard in the Baikalovs' *izba* all lent the picture a compelling sense of authenticity. This, too, was an important part of the movie's appeal. Indeed, Shukshin's candid depiction of undoctored aspects of modern-day Soviet reality was actually made possible precisely because it was done in the background of an otherwise contrived and sentimental melodrama where its implied social critique was far less obvious or threatening. The film's submerged indictment of Stalin's social and agricultural policies (policies that uprooted thousands of Soviets like Egor) and embedded critique of aspects of Soviet "socialist reality" were safely camouflaged by their close proximity to cinematic cliché. The best way, then, to understand why the movie was such a sensation is to investigate both the film's popular poetics and its depiction of "socialist reality."

Compared by some critics in style and theme to the traditional folk song and folk story,[22] *Kalina krasnaia* is the ultimate embodiment of Shukshin's popular art. One of the earliest reviews of the film likened its style to

that of the penny prints known as *lubki,* which began appearing in the six-
teenth century and were popular up to the revolution.[23] Like the *lubki,* the
film was "bright, without halftones" and "captivated you through its naive
freshness and primitive symbolism."[24] Like the *lubki* artists, Shukshin made
playful use of contrasts between colors, scenes, and characters. "If the
scenes at the thieves' 'hideout' are resolved intentionally in dark, muted colors, the village scenes simply explode in a fireworks of color," explains M.
Kuznetsov in his review. In a similar way, the film alternates between the
utterly realistic depiction of life in the village and the simplistic, farcical
portrayal of Egor's city debauch.[25] In this latter aspect, Shukshin continues
the same method he employed in *Pechki-lavochki.*

While Kuznetsov saw in the movie's reliance on popular style and accessible form a distinct advantage, several critics in the *Voprosy literatury*
roundtable discussion saw in it only cliché and a lowering of cinematic standards. Whole episodes were singled out for criticism: the scene in the *bania*
where Egor scalds Petro by throwing hot water on him instead of on the
stove; Egor's attempt to organize a debauch in town; the scene in which
Egor weeps and tears at the grass after visiting his mother in disguise; the
poorly motivated murder of Egor by the gang (described as "lightweight
and artistically primitive");[26] the Hollywood-style car stunt at the end of the
movie when Petro rams the thieves' vehicle into the water; and, perhaps most
frequently of all, the scenes in which Egor strokes and talks to his beloved
birch trees. Shukshin was reproached for his stereotypical characters and
his dependence on a formulaic plot, along with other "miscalculations"
(*proschety*).[27] But were these aspects of Shukshin's movie really "miscalculations"? Lev Anninskii—alone among the roundtable's participants—
correctly sensed that Shukshin's reliance on cinematic cliché and story
conventions was not a "miscalculation" at all but an intentional strategy.[28] In
telling "the Soviet version of the John Garfield good-looking trying-to-
reform tough whose past determines his tragic end," Shukshin is openly relying on the conventions of the popular melodrama, creating in the final
analysis "one of the most effective Soviet tear-jerkers ever made."[29] Toward
that end, he uses a wide range of tools to condition viewer response.

As in many tearjerkers, music—the movie score, various popular and
folk songs in instrumental or sung renditions—plays an important role.
From the opening shot of the film in which real inmates of a penal colony
are shown singing the "pensive song" "Vechernii zvon" ("Those Evening
Bells") to the concluding scene in which we hear Egor reading one of his
letters to the accompaniment of an angelic-sounding choir, *Kalina krasnaia*
is not so much a movie as it is a melody. Indeed, the title itself derives from
a popular folk stylization that was a hit in the early 1960s.[30] The fact that this
song, which gives the movie its title, is not a "real" folk song but a modern
stylization is particularly significant as it underscores the artifice of the

movie's subject and the popular nature of the genre in which the director cast his film. As Shukshin himself admitted in an interview, it is hardly likely that a village woman would correspond with a repeat offender whom she had never met and then invite him home to live with her extended family. The plotline, he confessed, "is extremely hypothetical, or as the reviewers like to say, far-fetched [*nadumannaia*]."[31] This is, of course, perfectly in keeping with melodramas, those "feasts of feeling" designed to "provide audiences with vicarious emotional experiences" or the "shape and occasion for fantasy enactment of real but repressed inner turmoil."[32] It is not essential that such movies be plausible or adhere strictly to the rules of common sense, especially when they are telling a love story, which is the case with both the movie and the song "Kalina krasnaia."

The song, whose first two verses appear in the novella, is about an unhappy love affair told from the woman's point of view. When she does not give in to the sexual advances of her lover, he leaves her, an outcome reflected in one episode from the movie in which Egor propositions Liuba—on his first night in the Baikalov home—and is rebuffed. The next day he leaves for town, uncertain whether he will come back. Only one line, the first, is actually sung in the movie (Shukshin was apparently unaware that he would have to pay its composer royalties to use the song in his film).[33] Instead, he relied on his viewers—most of whom were quite familiar with the popular tune—to "fill in" the melody themselves. In its absence, other songs take on significance, both in terms of creating the appropriately heightened emotional resonance of the film and in communicating its themes. Here Shukshin's "synthetic thinking" is foregrounded, his ability to weave seamlessly various media—words, sounds, images, and music—into one meaningful whole.

"Vechernii zvon," sung to such heartfelt effect by the prison chorus at the beginning of the movie, helps to condition the audience for the film's elevated emotional register while establishing a crucial theme, that of the singer's longing to return to the land of his childhood and the impossibility of doing so. A free translation by the Russian poet Ivan Kozlov (1779–1840) of "Those Evening Bells" by the Irish poet Thomas Moore (1779–1852), this song belongs to the category of so-called literary folk songs. Like "Kalina krasnaia," it is not an actual village folk song, even though it has become part of the Russian folk repertoire.[34] Such is the case with two other famous songs taken from Russian poetry featured prominently in the film: Nikolai Nekrasov's poem "Shkol'nik" ("The School Boy," 1856) in praise of Mikhail Lomonosov's journey from the village to become Russia's first great scholar and scientist, and Sergei Esenin's "Pis'mo materi" ("Letter to My Mother," 1924) about a ne'er-do-well son's promise to visit his mother once more before he dies.

Shukshin relies on these literary and pseudo–folk songs to achieve several important goals. First, all three songs are well-known, sentimental favorites guaranteed to elicit a familiar and sympathetic response from an audience that grew up listening to them. Second, the songs function as significant thematic and plot markers in the movie. The Kozlov and Esenin poems provide an important frame for the film. While the prison chorus performs "Vechernii zvon" to open the movie (in anticipation of Egor's journey back to the place of his birth), a lone prisoner sings "Pis'mo materi" in a dramatic black-and-white sequence—in front of the same audience of assembled convicts as in the opening scene—shortly after Egor visits his own mother and just before he is murdered by Guboshlep in one of the film's last episodes. Each comments on an important theme: Egor's return home and his betrayal of his mother, respectively. The Nekrasov song, occurring near the middle of the movie, addresses the choices facing Egor: can he reform his ways and make a new start (the way the schoolboy in Nekrasov's poem is about to embark on a new journey)?

Third, the folk associations of all three songs lend *Kalina krasnaia* the emotional resonance of a folk ballad appropriate for the movie's melodramatic content. Finally, these folk songs help to establish in an acoustic way the visual and thematic opposition between the city and country in the movie.[35] The country is signified musically by these literary and folk stylizations as well as by the Russian folk songs sung in sanitized, pro-Soviet renditions at the village talent show. These songs sentimentalize the village and denote its privileged status as a sacred space. The city, on the other hand, is signified by orchestral variety melodies, such as the lively band music that Egor plays on his tape player. This music is associated with Egor's roguish, fast-and-loose mannerisms. It accompanies the scene in which Egor leads the police away from his gang associates as well as his antics in the city when he tries to organize a debauch, in each instance inclining the viewer toward farce and buffoonery. *Blatyne pesni* (criminal songs), rendered in instrumental versions and submerged in the movie's soundtrack, are also linked ostensibly to city culture, marking the city negatively as a profane place where loose morals and crime dominate.[36]

Shukshin was well aware of the connection among subject matter, music, and his audience's emotional investment in his film. V. Fomin, who witnessed much of the shooting and technical work on the movie, reports that Shukshin requested his sound technician to heighten the already dramatic orchestral score that accompanies the scene in which Egor weeps inconsolably after visiting his mother. The intent was to augment the emotional impact of the film where possible at the expense of its analytical aspects, particularly after the decision was made to limit the film's length.[37] Music would obviously carry a good deal of the burden of communicating that emotion. The lyrical strains first heard in another Shukshin movie about an ex-convict, *Your Son and Brother,* play in scenes where Egor is contemplating his fate. This music and the angelic choir heard in the final episodes of the movie are predictable but effective ways of creating a sympathetic response on the part of the audience to the movie's criminal protagonist—an important task, given Shukshin's decision to focus on a nonpositive central hero.[38]

Shukshin employs his musical score in a variety of ways. In some instances, music is limited to performative moments recorded in the film, as when the Baikalovs' neighbor sings "Shkol'nik" or Egor sings "Kalina krasnaia." At other times a song or melody that begins as a performance in a scene is used nondiegetically, that is, outside the frame or strict narrative sequence, as with "Vechernii zvon," sung in the opening scene but linked seamlessly to the opening credits as well. Another example is the lively march which in some scenes Egor plays on his tape recorder where it is heard by all, characters and viewers alike, while in other scenes the march is heard only by viewers as part of the soundtrack. In this latter practice, Shukshin not only provides many of the film's transitional links but also reveals one way in which he directly engages—and manipulates—his audience emotionally through music. This is especially true of the song "Pis'mo materi," sung outside of linear narrative time in a black-and-white sequence inserted between shots of Egor plowing, shortly before he is killed by his former gang members. Although the prison singer is actually singing the song at the same show with which the movie opens, we see and hear him only at the end of the movie, both within the black-and-white sequence as well as outside of it, where it becomes part of the soundtrack accompanying Egor's plowing. Its sentimental strains and sorrowful themes greatly heighten our emotional response to the film's tragic denouement.

The abrupt shifts in emotional register and style that Shukshin's use of music helped to underscore were a source of contention for some critics. Even those who defended the film from criticism on this count nevertheless acknowledged that it shifts abruptly in register from "cruelty" to "sentimentality," from "coarseness" to "romance," and that the movie almost willfully juxtaposes such disparate images as birch trees, blood, radiant love, and criminal physiognomy.[39] The film's "strong emotional effect" was also blamed for "muting" critical debate of the film.[40] For Shukshin, however, running the viewer through a wide range of emotions was crucial to the movie's success. His far-fetched plot and antihero could not have succeeded in capturing the interest and sympathy of the viewer on any level but the emotional one, hence the theatricality of Shukshin's interpretation of the role of Egor and the movie's dependence on musical motifs designed to produce emotional reactions in the audience.

Shukshin's performance in the role of Egor Prokudin was perhaps the paramount factor in the film's success. Regardless of their other objections, critics saw in the role the actor's greatest triumph. Soviet director Sergei Gerasimov's comments summarize most critics' assessments: "I imagined for a moment this role in the hands of some other performer and instantly the picture fades, falls apart, simply disappears. It is difficult to say what attracts the viewer more in this picture: its subject—dramatic, touching, stirring—or Shukshin's own personality."[41] Gerasimov's point is well taken. We are as captivated by the performance of the actor as by the story the actor tells. One review notes the challenges presented by the role, which "first borders on the edge of melodrama, then comes dangerously close to farce, and occasionally soars towards tragedy. In none of these twists and turns does one detect a single false note."[42]

But in Shukshin's tour de force as an actor there is much that strains the audience's credulity, just as the premise of the film itself does. Indeed, it often seems that Egor is not so much a seven-time-convicted felon as an actor himself. In Galina Belaia's assessment, Egor plays no fewer than four roles—that of a bookkeeper, thief, investigator, and commissar—in his first encounter with Liuba's parents, changing "verbal masks" as he spars with old man Baikalov in a brilliant demonstration of his command of the various layers of "social language" typical of each profession. As Belaia points out, though, the "ease of this transformation arises not from the fact that Egor Prokudin really just got out of prison, but from [Shukshin's] dazzling mastery of the discourse of the other [*chuzhoe slovo*]."[43] In these moments Shukshin's recidivist-thief looks more like his actor-creator. As Diane Nemec Ignashev notes, "Egor is a criminal only in the figurative sense. Above all, he is an actor, a singer, a poet, an artist."[44] Even Liuba does not seem to take his criminal side seriously. To his proud declaration that he can "only be a thief in this world," she responds sarcastically: "Oi-ei-ei! How scary we are! Only no one's afraid."[45]

Throughout the movie, Egor assumes various identities, from that of ex-con to honest Joe, sincere philanthropist to insincere philanderer, city *fraer* (chump) to village muzhik. He changes costume and changes his name. Now he is Gore the gang member in his black leather jacket and flaming red shirt, now the "poor relative" Zhora in Liuba's husband's old underwear and shirts. On his visit to the city he is Georgii in his newly acquired loud tie, tweed jacket, beret, and suede shoes. Plowing in the fields in his quilted peasant's jacket he is simply Egor. At each stage, his attire determines his performance. Gore is the desperate ex-con, and Shukshin plays him with an intensity that at times is almost diabolical (especially in the nighttime scenes, low-key or "hard" lighting picks up a demonic gleam in his eyes that bores into the audience from the black screen). Zhora is the comically awkward new arrival, who accidentally scalds Petro in the bathhouse and is chased back into his bed by Liuba's mother after she overhears him proposition her daughter. Georgii is the rogue-buffoon, who tosses around thick wads of bills at a restaurant, follows women around on the street, flirts with a postal worker, and then organizes a debauch that falls through for lack of nice-looking single women. Finally, Egor is the prodigal son, come back to make an attempt at an honest life.

While this all makes for entertaining cinema, it is not by any stretch of the imagination "realistic." Egor is obviously a hyperbolic, theatrical character (in the novella, he even quotes from Georg Christoph Lichtenberg's *Aphorisms*—hardly a believable portrait of an ex-con who has spent half his life in Siberian corrective labor camps). But Shukshin is clearly more concerned with creating an interesting and, most important, an entertaining character than in being true to life. Thus, instead of a realistic portrait of a thief, Shukshin gives his audience a colorful and charismatic hero perfect for the cinema.

Analogously, Shukshin's use of symbolism and foreshadowing never strays far from cinematic conventions or from what is sure to satisfy popular expectations. Scenes are linked and become overtly symbolic, such as the three episodes in which Egor addresses his beloved birch trees. Twice he calls them his "brides" and later refers to one as a pregnant Vasilisa (a maiden from Russian folklore). The fourth time we see them—when Egor, shot by Guboshlep, has smeared his blood on them in his final, dying moments—the emotional impact is that much more intensified for our having been witness to his special relationship with them earlier in the film. His blood on them—a symbolic deflowering of his brides—is itself a sign of his unrealized desire to begin a new life with Liuba.

Similarly, the shots of flooded churches at the beginning and end of the movie and, most significantly, in the background when Egor repents of abandoning his mother reflect the hero's sinful state (Shukshin calls his story that of a *grekhopadenie,* or "fall from grace"),[46] even as they remind us of the fallen state of the Orthodox church in the former Soviet Union. Further, Shukshin employs an obvious bit of light symbolism when the dark, nighttime scenes at the gang's hideout and during the police chase afterward give way slowly and meaningfully to dawn as Egor decides to visit Liuba. In one scene, Egor paces on a children's carousel, then sits down and spins round and round on it, literally and figuratively going in circles till he makes his decision to return to his birthplace where Liuba lives, again a plain but effective way of communicating Egor's state of uncertainty. By the time he arrives at Liuba's village, it is broad daylight and a bright new life beckons.

Other symbolic motifs include Shukshin's use of Ivan Kramskoi's portrait *The Stranger* (*Neznakomka,* 1883). The reproduction appears in a medallion that Liuba wears when she meets Egor for the first time. Twice during their visit at the village café the camera focuses on the medallion. Later, at Egor's failed debauch in the city, the reproduction hangs prominently on the wall just behind him, where it appears to be looking over his shoulder. For those viewers unfamiliar with the portrait, it serves simply as

Prodigal Son

a reminder of Liuba, who is waiting for Egor in the village. For those who
know the portrait and its title, it is also a sign of Egor's own status as a
stranger in his native parts.[47] The fleeting shot of a little boy throwing red
kalina berries into a stream is also significant. Not only does it support the
otherwise weak motif of the kalina berry itself in the film, but it is also possibly a passing flashback to Egor himself as an innocent child, before his
"fall." The wrench that he slips into his pocket before he walks out to meet
the gang at the end of the film is likewise unmistakably symbolic (a close-
up shot makes it impossible not to notice). Like Dmitrii Karamazov, who
snatches up a brass pestle with the intent of assaulting his father but refrains
from following through, Egor never uses his weapon in his confrontation
with Guboshlep.[48] The wrench instead becomes a symbol to the audience
of Egor's conflicted state, a sign of what Shukshin later would call Egor's
suicide wish.[49]

Scenes of cawing crows at the beginning and end of the movie—during
Egor's first meeting with his birch trees and just before the gang comes
back to kill him—are obvious portents of his doomed fate. Moreover, the
long shot of Egor walking out of the prison to his freedom early in the
movie is reflected in a similar long shot of him walking across a freshly plowed
field to his fateful meeting with Guboshlep late in the film.[50] When shortly
thereafter Liuba runs to bring a dying Egor water, she stumbles in the same
place where Egor had stumbled moments before, as if to emphasize their
linked fates. These connected scenes, recurring motifs, and conspicuously
symbolic elements are all important contributing factors to *Kalina krasnaia*'s overall emotional impact on viewers. Together with the movie's simple plot, clear-cut characters, sentimental songs, movie score, and theatrical
central hero, they help to explain why the movie was so appealing to Soviet
audiences. It fulfilled all of the expectations associated with popular cinema: it told a simple story well and won audience sympathy by its skillful
use of all of the cinematic tricks of the trade.

KALINA KRASNAIA AND "SOCIALIST REALITY"

Good movies are more than the successful negotiation of the dictates of
popular taste. They also speak to their audience's own experience and society. Indeed, despite *Kalina krasnaia*'s various concessions to cinematic convention and its thoroughly hypothetical plot, many reviewers praised the
film's truthful depiction (Gerasimov's review is called "The Truth of Life"
["Pravda zhizni"]). This seeming contradiction is less puzzling when we realize that the larger story Shukshin is telling is one to which many Soviets
could relate. Egor's uprooted past and unsettled present reflect a contemporary reality familiar to many in Shukshin's wide audience. The social relevance of his story is pronounced and, as the artist himself noted, has little

146

to do with Egor's life of crime. "Strange as it may seem," he stated, "the crime story interests me least of all. I'm more interested in the story of the peasant. Of the peasant who left the village."[51]

Far more than in the novella, Shukshin conducts a subtle social critique in his movie, where Egor's fate is viewed and weighed against the conspicuous backdrop of Soviet socialist reality. From the film's opening shot, his story tests and probes the myths and promises of Soviet socialism, but it does so in a subtle, often ambiguous way.[52] The movie opens with a prolonged shot of a banner draped across the stage where the prison chorus will sing. On the banner we read: "In conditions of socialism, any person who has gone off the track of labor can return to useful activity." Just beneath the banner is a poster depicting people from the various republics in their native dress and framed by the ubiquitous slogans "Peace to the World" and "Peace, Friendship, Equality, Fraternity." Other posters on either side of the stage show birch trees, a Russian maiden in folk attire, and a Russian lad with a balalaika, while a pan of the room full of convicts reveals another banner running the length of one wall with figures depicting scenes from the revolution and civil war. Everything here—the labor colony's main credo, the endorsement of Soviet internationalism, the appropriation of sanitized folk culture, the dominant position occupied by the Russian folk figures, and the heroic battle scenes—is as much a fixture of daily Soviet life as it is an encapsulation of Soviet social and historical propaganda. Here, as throughout the movie, these images and slogans provide the background against which we must understand and judge Egor's lot in life.

While Shukshin is being ironic in his use of some of these images and phrases of Soviet socialist propaganda, he also needs them to form a truthful social backdrop. Indeed, some of the scenes in the movie have an almost documentary quality to them, as commentators have noticed.[53] The most famous of these documentary-like scenes is the one in which Liuba talks to Egor's mother while he waits in the next room. The part of the mother is not played by an actress but by an old woman whom Shukshin filmed simply telling her own life story—a decision necessitated by the last-minute withdrawal of the actress who was to play the part. While, as one critic put it, the scene "sanctified the film,"[54] the old woman's truthful tale of her son who abandoned her and his home village also speaks to a burning issue in the Soviet Union at that time: the depopulation of the countryside by young people attracted to urban life.

Elsewhere, Shukshin documents Soviet reality in an ironic light. The character of Egor Prokudin (whose surname alludes to his roguish, mischievous personality)[55] allowed Shukshin considerable freedom to parody the clichés of Soviet rhetoric and to interrogate the myths of Soviet society from the point of view of someone outside that society's mainstream. Filtered through the perspective of a repeat offender and muted by its proximity to melodrama, the movie's ironic look at Soviet life could be safely distanced from Shukshin himself.

Egor's use of Soviet-speak is a good example of Shukshin's irony. Egor's mastery of the slippery qualities of Soviet political jargon and the language of interrogations and denunciations—as in his wild accusations that old man Baikalov served in General Kolchak's counterrevolutionary forces and stole grain from the fields during collectivization—struck a chord with viewers all too familiar with the dangerous uses to which Soviet rhetoric could be put. At the same time, Egor's bombastic speeches, and Shukshin's inimitable delivery of them, make for hilarious cinema. As Elizabeth Pond notes, "Egor [. . .] has the most glorious non sequitur arguments in contemporary Soviet cinema."[56] Egor's pronouncements—like those of Soviet propaganda—do not correspond to reality, but rather re-create the skewed visions of Soviet mythology. This, for example, is how Egor concludes his "interrogation" of Liuba's father:

> See how cozy we've learned to live! The country is producing electricity, steamships, millions of tons of cast iron. People strain with all of their might. People are literally falling from the exertion. People are even beginning to stammer from the strain. In the Far North people are getting old before their time and have to go out and have gold teeth put in. And what do you expect? It's necessary! But at the same time there are people who of all of mankind's achievements have chosen for themselves only a warm stove. Think of it! Really cozy! They'd rather prop their feet up on the hearth than work in harmony with all those others who are killing themselves![57]

The effect is dual. On the one hand, Soviet rhetoric is parodied and the audience has a good laugh. On the other, Egor's speech reveals the bankruptcy of the very rhetoric on which Soviet society is built.

Shukshin makes use of this kind of irony throughout the movie, as in the scenes in town where Egor is shown following women up and down a street lined with billboards of all of the emblems of the various republics of the Soviet Union. The incongruity of his skirt-chasing against the background of these symbols of state makes for a rather irreverent—and humorous— overall picture. The socialist paradise whose advent these placards proclaim is cheapened by their use as mere stage decoration for Egor's amorous plays. At the same time, these signs were such a ubiquitous part of Soviet life that Shukshin could hardly be accused of trying to ridicule government propaganda.

A less ambiguous instance of this sort of ironic juxtaposition occurs when Egor stops in front of a poster warning of the dangers of alcoholism. As the camera pans down the poster's text—which reads, in part, "if you've been drinking, partying, and working poorly, you've only yourself to blame"— Egor suddenly reaches out and strokes a woman's legs on the other side of the sign, then beats a hasty retreat to her indignant cry of "Hooligan!" The strident moral tone of the poster is mocked by Egor's not-so-moral behavior and by a restaurant director's report in a following scene of a drunken brawl between two members of the collective farm New Life. The implication—that the "New Life" has not been changed by the empty rhetoric of propaganda posters—is subtle but clear.

Other snippets of Soviet reality lend the movie a contemporary and realistic texture while at the same time serving as indirect commentary on Egor's situation. If we listen closely to the radio at the Baikalov house, for example, in the scene just before Egor goes to visit his mother, we hear the announcer—speaking softly but distinctly in between character dialogue—introducing a guest who "considers feeling oneself to be a citizen of one's homeland the highest satisfaction in life." This bland pronouncement—so typical of the style and themes of Soviet radio programs as to seem little worthy of note—is in this case an obvious reference to Egor's quandary and thus an important statement of theme.

Another instance of Shukshin's use of background detail to elucidate larger themes involves a village talent show which Egor sees while working as a driver for the local chairman. There, an announcer introduces a performance with the usual trite formulas: "Much has changed since the Russian muzhik in union with the workers overthrew the tsar. The life of the people has changed, and their songs have changed, too. The people have begun to make new songs." These words—as hollow and empty as the Soviet emblems lining the streets in the city—and the performance that follows, complete with "authentic" folk costumes, also serve as a reminder of the Sovietization of village culture, where true folk culture has been replaced by the affected folk stylizations of Soviet literary parlance.

Shukshin once complained: "The contemporary Russian folk song! Underlined: contemporary. Folk. 'The little kolkhoz field, my dearie on a tractor, and I on my motorcycle after him . . .' Give it up! A typical, bad stylization!"[58] Stylization, of course, meant capitulation before the neutralizing and standardizing discourse of the Soviet cultural establishment. Shukshin, a country boy from the provinces where folk culture still thrived, knew the real thing. His own mother, who in many ways played the role in his life that Aleksandr Pushkin's nanny, Arina Rodionovna, played in Pushkin's, told Shukshin stories and folk tales, related dreams and village superstition to him, and sang him folk songs.[59] It is to his mother that Shukshin credited his artistic success: "I learned how to write stories from her."[60]

In *Kalina krasnaia*, the sanitized folk performances of the village talent show only augment Egor's estranged position between the city and the village, between his gang and Liuba, for to return to an honest life in the country requires that Egor live in accordance with the myths of Soviet life that those songs and performances support. As Egor later tells his birch trees, "I've got to plow now . . . You keep standing here, but I've got to become a Stakhanovite." At the talent show, he is unable to take that step, quitting his cushy job as a driver for the chairman on the first day because he feels like he's compromised himself.

These instances create a believable background for Shukshin's film and deepen the social relevance of the movie. Even the disagreement between Shura and Bul'dia from Egor's gang about whether Egor had become a "proletarian" or "peasant" now that he had begun an honest life in the village reminds the viewer of the larger social questions at stake here concerning the fate of peasant culture, the fate of the peasant who has left the village, the interrelationship among the city and the proletariat and the village and the peasant, and so on. As one assessment of the movie concludes, "We only need imagine this hero [Egor] outside the social categories so completely conveyed by Shukshin and his image is deprived of its foundations, falls apart, and becomes that of a hero from a mediocre detective movie."[61]

Shukshin's ability to marry serious social issues to entertaining, popular cinema marks the film's achievement and explains its huge success at the Soviet box office. In a movie in which episodes with operettalike villains exist side by side with documentaryesque scenes featuring a real village *starukha* (old woman) talking about her life, Shukshin somehow remained utterly believable, utterly honest, and, more important, utterly entertaining.

KALINA KRASNAIA AND SHUKSHIN

Shukshin's investment in *Kalina krasnaia* was enormous. As the film's scriptwriter, director, and leading actor—and there is hardly a scene without Egor—Shukshin rarely had a moment's rest during the mere nine months he was given to shoot. Work on the film seriously undermined his health and landed him in the hospital both during and after production.[62] But Shukshin's great personal stake in the film goes well beyond his intense physical toil, for the movie also represents his most famous treatment of the central chronotope of his life and art. Egor, caught between his urban gang and life with Liuba in the village, is the most well known of Shukshin's restless, rootless heroes who are at home neither in the city nor in the country. Indeed, in Egor's story Shukshin was, to a certain extent, addressing certain issues of his own fate.

In a preface to a 1973 excerpt from the novella, Shukshin talks about how Egor—like Shukshin himself—left his native village in the "difficult years after the war."[63] Elsewhere, Shukshin fixes the date of Egor's departure as 1947—the year he, too, left the village.[64] "I also was forced to leave my home and I saw my fill of what would happen to country folk away from their home villages. I even met people like my Egor," he says.[65] By all appearances, *Kalina krasnaia* is an attempt to understand this departure, Egor's as well as his own.

Shukshin discussed his own guilt over leaving the village in an essay he wrote shortly before beginning *Kalina krasnaia:*

> I don't know how it is with other people, but for some reason I feel awkward and over-eager to please. I see that the people from home are a bit irritated and displeased by something—possibly by the fact that I left in the first place and now look, I've come back. . . . [E]very time I go back I stumble into some awkwardness, and even sometimes feel ashamed that here I am and that once long ago I'd taken it into my head to leave for somewhere else. And it is as though everything around were no longer my own, my birthright, as though I'd lost the right to call it my own.[66]

Although his awkwardness has a different origin, Egor, too, feels out of place returning to the village, and he, too, feels guilty over it.

Egor seeks to assuage his feelings of guilt by searching for a "holiday of the soul" (*prazdnik dushi*), a vague concept at best, but one that Shukshin insists signifies more than "women, an easy life, or drunken oblivion."[67] Perhaps this *prazdnik* must be understood in a more religious sense as a spiritual feast day, a day of atonement for past sins, an interpretation to which Shukshin alludes in an interview about the movie: "You have to pay for everything in this world. . . . For the good and the bad. For lies, dishonesty, being a burden on society, time-serving, cowardice, and betrayal."[68] This latter sin—Egor's betrayal of his mother and his village roots, the dominant factors that constitute his *grekhopadenie*—is the biggest one in this tale of a prodigal son. Unlike the biblical parable, however, there is no fatted cow killed by a grateful father to celebrate his lost son's return, no earthly *prazdnik* in Egor's story. Instead, in *Kalina krasnaia* it is Egor himself who perishes, a suicide/sacrifice in the name of past sins.

Just as Egor's encounter with Liuba is an encounter with the part of himself that never left the village,[69] Shukshin's engagement with Egor as a writer and actor was a way for the artist to confront his unresolved feelings over his own choices in life. Yet, aside from the link between Egor's departure from the village and Shukshin's own and an episode Shukshin shares with his protagonist about how the family cow was killed by a neighbor,[70] Egor is an autobiographical alter ego—and *Kalina krasnaia* an autobiographical movie—only in the broadest sense. Its importance for Shukshin seems to lie elsewhere: in the larger stories being told about leaving the village, betraying one's roots, and the impossibility of going home again. It was these stories that struck such a powerful chord in Soviet audiences, together with Shukshin's singular investment in his film of his varied talents and magnetic personality. The movie's powerful resonance long after the Soviet period is a testament to its harmonious marriage of popular aesthetics, a universal storyline, and strong social critique.

As such, *Kalina krasnaia* remains Shukshin's greatest triumph, for it catapulted the artist to superstar status in the Soviet Union and placed him in a category by himself. The film earned Shukshin the kind of critical acclaim that had previously eluded him in his separate acting, directing, and writing careers. Most important, it gave the artist the crucial clout he needed to renew his ten-year bid to film his movie on Sten'ka Razin, a project mired in controversy over Shukshin's unorthodox depiction of the Cossack rebel. The filming was granted qualified approval in the wake of *Kalina krasnaia*'s sensational success.[71] Tragically, Shukshin died within a month of receiving the news, while on location acting in Sergei Bondarchuk's film *They Fought for the Motherland*. *Kalina krasnaia*—the film which had seemed to herald the most mature and fruitful phase in Shukshin's tripartite career—turned out to be his swan song.

Chapter Eight

Telling His Own Story

> Every real writer, of course, is a psychologist, but
> he himself is the patient.
> —Vasilii Shukshin, from a working note

EGOR PROKUDIN from *Kalina krasnaia* and Vasilii
Kniazev from "Oddball"—to choose two characters who could not be more
different from each other—are alike in two important ways. Like their creator, they both navigate in various ways and with different consequences the
hazardous distance between the village and the city. In addition, they share
episodes from Shukshin's life and aspects of his personality. Yet, strictly
speaking, these characters cannot be considered autobiographical, for in
both instances Shukshin seems to have attributed to them events that happened in his own life simply for the convenience of plot, and perhaps out
of a sense of affinity with them. Still, there is a fine line between "the autobiography invaded by fiction" and "fiction involving the autobiography of the
author,"[1] and in a number of other works—most important, his *Liubavin
Family* novels—a submerged autobiographical discourse emerges that is as
distinct as it is important for understanding Shukshin.

The distance between Shukshin's home village and Moscow, and the
disparity between his private history and his public biography, created a painful duality in the artist. Like many of his characters, Shukshin was stuck,
spiritually and psychologically, between two realms: the rural landscape of
his childhood, innocent but unattainable, and the city of his adult years,
where he achieved success but felt he had compromised his identity. This
duality is reflected in stories that span Shukshin's career. The successful
urban hero of Shukshin's story "Two Letters" ("Dva pis'ma," 1967) calls the
sudden, intense longing to revisit his home village—a yearning tinged by
feelings that he had betrayed his childhood dreams—the onset of "a mild
schizophrenia" (1:331). In so doing, he gives a name to the artist's own malady.

Initially, the artist treated his "split personality" in third-person nar-
ratives whose plots are only indirectly autobiographical. In stories such as
"Ignakha's Come Home," "O See the Horses Gallop in the Fields," "Two
Letters," "How the Bunny Went for a Balloon Ride," and the screenplay *My
Brother,* Shukshin invests the different sides of his conflicted identity in

separate characters—typically older and younger brothers, former village classmates, or fathers and sons—who confront each other and themselves over the choices they have made either to leave or remain in the village. Later, in the cycle "From the Childhood Years of Ivan Popov," Shukshin resorts to a more openly autobiographical first-person narrative in order to address these issues. His most important autobiographical treatment, however, emerges in Book Two of *The Liubavin Family,* which represents a combination of both approaches.

SHUKSHIN AND THE BROTHER COMPLEX

Diane Nemec Ignashev was the first critic to identify the importance of "the schizophrenic/brother complex" in Shukshin's fiction.[2] One brother has left the village, usually for a successful but somehow compromised life in the city; the other has stayed home in the village and leads a quieter, less conspicuous life. In playing these two characters off each other, Shukshin is also examining two sides of his own personality. While this does not strictly constitute autobiography, Shukshin had a decidedly personal stake in the outcome of this kind of artistic investigation.

In "Ignakha's Come Home," the first of his stories about brothers, Shukshin's wrestling with the problem of a split identity is glimpsed in the wrestling match that never takes place between the Baikalov brothers, Ignakha, visiting from the city, and Vasia, who has remained in the village. As we have seen earlier, their father disapproves of Ignakha's life and is especially dismissive of Ignakha's job as a circus wrestler. We learn in the film version of the story in *Your Son and Brother* that he considers Ignakha's circus work a waste of the strength given him by his Siberian homeland, strength that should be given back through honest labor. He is confident that Vasia's brawn will triumph over his older brother's circus training. Vasia refuses to wrestle, however, and the story ends with this central conflict unresolved.

Shukshin's own quandary is easy to discern here. Shukshin "wasted" his strength not in the circus but in another urban form of diversionary entertainment—the cinema. In "O See the Horses Gallop in the Fields," written shortly after "Ignakha's Come Home," this analogy is made explicit in the story of a visit by kolkhoz chairman Kondrat Liutaev from the Altai to his son Min'ka, studying to be an actor in Moscow. The implication is the same: Min'ka is wasting his time and talents pursuing acting; he should be home working at the collective farm. This point is underscored when the two visit the Exhibition of the Achievements of the People's Economy (VDNKh) to view a prize stallion. Kondrat sees immediately that the stallion is nothing but a pretty showpiece, a far cry from his own workhorse back home.[3] After a row at the exhibition with the horse's keeper, the older Liutaev boards his train and departs for home. Min'ka is left vaguely apprehensive. The danger is clear: Min'ka's fate is prefigured in that of the prize stallion. As an actor, he will be no better than the worthless show horse. That night he dreams of his father's stallion running free over the Siberian steppe at the head of a herd of horses.

In these stories we can clearly glimpse early and thinly veiled third-person accounts of Shukshin's ambiguous feelings about leaving his Siberian home and the consequences at stake in such a departure. He is like Ignakha and Min'ka, someone who has forsaken his heritage for an easier lot in the city and, like the latter, unsure whether he has done the right thing. Shukshin passes no ultimate judgment here, but he returns to this issue repeatedly in other works, such as the screenplay *My Brother*, originally written in 1968, but revised and published only in 1974.

When the Gromov patriarch dies, the elder son, Ivan, who now works in the city as a foreman, returns to his native village, too late for the funeral. Senia, left alone in the village, takes advantage of his brother's return to enlist his aid in winning the hand of a local beauty, Valia Kovaleva. The problem is that Senia is small, skinny, and slightly lame, unlike Ivan, who is handsome and well built. As in the story "An Accidental Shot" ("Nechaiannyi vystrel," 1966), whose hero's withered leg is "a metaphor for the handicap all rural-based youth inherit at birth,"[4] Senia's lameness symbolizes the disadvantages of remaining in the village. Senia wants Ivan to convince Valia that what counts is not outward appearances but "inner content." Instead, the inevitable happens and Valia falls for Ivan. Ivan leaves the village not only feeling guilty for missing his father's funeral and ruining his brother's prospects for marriage, but also feeling somehow responsible for the village's decline through his own choice to live in the city.

In *My Brother*, however, Shukshin seems to imply that the departure from the village, while painful, is an inevitable occurrence. The village is dying, and only the old and unlucky remain there. It is not Ivan's fault that his life has turned out better than his brother's. He is not to blame for the fading fortunes of life in the countryside. This, of course, does not make his departure, now or in retrospect, any easier. The scars inflicted by his leaving the village are very real for both Ivan and Senia, as the original title of the script, *My Enemy*, attests.[5] This rejected title underscores the seriousness of the rift not only between the brothers in the movie but between the warring sides of Shukshin's personality.

In other "brother" stories, this discord develops into a full-fledged spiritual crisis. In "Two Letters" Nikolai Ivanych has a disturbing dream of his abandoned native village, a dream in which part of the poetic epigraph about frolicking horses from "O See the Horses Gallop in the Fields" is excerpted. He gets up in the middle of the night and writes a letter to an old village buddy who went to college with him and who has also made a name for himself. In his letter, he recalls their last visit home after graduation and how they drank themselves senseless, while the rest of the village worked round the clock to bring in the grain harvest. Years later, from his perspective as a successful boss, Nikolai Ivanych is filled with regrets and feelings of guilt. He likens the betrayal of his village to "a sin on my soul" and proposes a trip home (1:332).

After a day at the office, however, his mood changes, and he drafts a second letter, abandoning his confessional tone in favor of a clever, irreverent style and suggesting a camping trip, but not necessarily to their native region. Even this version is ultimately rejected, and, upon reflection, Nikolai Ivanych gives up altogether on his plans, putting his crisis behind him and returning to his daily routine of work and the evening paper. It is enough to have assuaged his own feelings of alarm by writing about them, a fictional resolution that curiously mirrors real life, where Shukshin turned his own bouts of guilt into the stuff of his fiction while never making the permanent move back to the village.

"How the Bunny Went for a Balloon Ride" is Shukshin's most autobiographical brother story. Here, it is the country brother who comes to the city to see his successful sibling, initially in order to tell his sick niece fairy tales while she recovers from a serious illness. As the two brothers talk into the night, the conversation turns into a discussion of the choices each has made. The more successful older brother's situation suggests Shukshin's own life story. Fedor, who has made a successful career for himself in the city, complains to his younger brother about the pressures and constraints of his life and, as Shukshin often did, confesses feeling insufficiently educated. He bitterly remembers the war he waged with his grandmother as a child over his voracious reading habits and ridicules village wariness of book knowledge. (In Shukshin's own childhood, it was his mother who objected to his interest in books, believing, like her village neighbors, that reading too much drove people crazy.) Like Shukshin, Fedor suffers from a distinct provincial inferiority complex, complaining how he has been told that "a peasant emigrant isn't capable of grasping the prospects of the country's development" (2:192). He confesses that he dreams more and more often of their father, of mowing and threshing with him, and of horses.

Horses become a leitmotif in these stories, the symbol of freedom and the Siberian steppe as well as of the innocence Shukshin's protagonists have left behind them in the village. Distant and elusive, they reflect the elusiveness of the ultimate cure for "the tortured dividedness" that John Dunlop speaks of with regard to so many of Shukshin's characters, an inner division stemming from "the schism within Shukshin himself."[6] If there is often no resolution to Shukshin's "brother" stories, it is because the author himself could not mend his split personality. As Dunlop notes, Shukshin "has been wounded by the city,"[7] one might say even cleaved in two. Much of his art, in one way or another, seeks to probe that wound, inflicted by the social upheaval that uprooted millions of Russians and, in the case of Shuk-shin and many others, took away fathers and stigmatized entire families.

Shukshin's most sustained autobiographical attempt to deal with his split identity was the story cycle "From the Childhood Years of Ivan Popov," which he began in 1968 and worked on until his death. These stories— straightforward first-person accounts of episodes from his life in Siberia up to the age of sixteen—are marked by Shukshin's decision to borrow family names for his narrating protagonist. Although his readers could not have known it, Shukshin's choice of his mother's maiden name and his cousin's first name for that of his narrating hero was significant. The son of an "en-emy of the people," Shukshin, as we noted in Chapter One, went by "Popov" until he applied for his internal passport, presumably to avoid the stigma attached to his father's name. Thus the protagonist of the autobiographical cycle speaks to an important issue of the writer's childhood and his early psychological (and political) makeup, a fact which, ironically, does not fig-ure at all in the cycle itself. With the exception of a reference in the first journal edition of the stories to being one of the *vrazheniata* (children of an enemy of the people)—a reference missing in all subsequent republications— no other mention is made in the cycle of this aspect of Shukshin's biogra-phy.[8] The stories, therefore, enabled Shukshin to revisit the landscape of his youth but did not allow him to confront the complexes that arose over the fate of his father and his own decision to leave Siberia at a young age.

The resentment Shukshin felt toward the Soviet state over his father's fate is an important but submerged feature of the writer's psychological makeup and his artistic program. This aspect of the writer's creativity was discussed for the first time only during the second half of the 1980s. One critic states outright that the arrest and execution of Makar Leont'evich Shukshin was "a circumstance that foreordained Shukshin's special role" in Russian literature.[9] Another claims that the year Makar was purged "played a profound role in Shukshin's fate, leaving a lasting wound which festered all of his life. This year, 1933, pulses subtly throughout Shukshin's books, arising or showing itself in a variety of ways."[10] This tragedy, however, did not prevent Shukshin from becoming a member of the Communist Party himself in 1955, two years after Stalin's death. Although it is likely that he joined as part of a postwar campaign to repopulate the decimated ranks of younger Party members,[11] such membership was also critical to future ca-reer advancement. Shukshin knew this even as he strove to understand his Party membership in the light of subsequent revelations about the Party's culpability in carrying out Stalin's policies. Thus to his already complicated attitude toward the history of his family and his country was added the am-bivalence of his status as a Communist.

This tension between an "inner" autobiography hinted at in "From the Childhood Years of Ivan Popov," which only Shukshin can recognize, and an "outer" autobiography, which he relates in the text of the cycle, resurfaces in the sequel to the writer's first novel. *The Liubavin Family: Book Two,* discovered and published posthumously in 1987, was one of the earliest examples of so-called delayed prose: previously unpublishable fiction which saw the light of day only under Gorbachev's policies of openness. In this, the only work he wrote "for the drawer," Shukshin confronts his past and focuses on the place where the child "Popov" meets the adult "Shukshin," where the "illegitimate" son of the fatherland and innocent victim of the consequences of Stalin's rural purges in Siberia cohabits with the successful careerist and Party member in Moscow. He does so, however, through a submerged discourse by investing these two conflicting tensions in his own life in two equal, interactive fictional alter egos: the characters Ivan Liubavin and Petr Ivlev. Unlike his use of this technique in his short stories, where the autobiographical elements were for the most part so muted or generalized that the accounts in which they appear can scarcely qualify as autobiography, in this novel Shukshin consciously draws a self-portrait, albeit a fractured one. Moreover, this self-portrait raises issues about his past—the fate of his father, his feelings about Soviet power and the Communist Party—that were either too complicated or too politically delicate to treat in his short stories.[12] For the first time, Shukshin deals extensively and dispassionately with facts of his life and features of his personality that had previously been taboo.

In essence, Book Two of *The Liubavin Family* combines the technique from the short stories we have been discussing of using dual—and dueling—protagonists with the more openly autobiographical approach of his first-person story cycle, "From the Childhood Years of Ivan Popov." In this way, Shukshin preserves the sense of objectivity of his third-person stories while reaping the confessional benefits of his autobiographical accounts. In so doing, he is also following in a distinct autobiographical tradition: that of the "autobiographical novel of co-consciousness."

Writers have often divided their personalities among the characters they create, "fictionaliz[ing] what appear to be equally *conscious* sides of their personalities" in order to secure "a stronger buffer of detachment between the writers and the immediacy of the autobiographical materials they choose to incorporate into their novels."[13] Tolstoy is an obvious example from Russian literature. In *War and Peace* he divided the negative and positive aspects of his own personality among various characters.[14] Galya Diment calls this technique that of co-consciousness, "a special way of projecting inner conflicts onto multiple fictional selves" as "a very powerful and conscious artistic tool" with which to impersonalize the personal.[15] For Shukshin, such an "extrapersonal" literary device was essential, as it allowed him to treat the most private, painful, and hidden aspects of his own life while avoiding the "dangers of self-centered and self-expository presentation,"[16]

especially when such exposition could run the risk of very real public sanc-
tion from the Brezhnev-era, neo-Stalinist Soviet literary establishment.

By investigating how Shukshin, through an artistic use of co-consciousness, neatly splits the conflicting aspects of his biography between the uncompromised, "true" village son Ivan Liubavin and the compromised Party
member Petr Ivlev, we can discover the "fictive action" Shukshin employs
in order to be "reconciled in complete being."[17] As we will see in the following analysis, the use of co-conscious protagonists[18] offered Shukshin the
great advantages of detachment and impersonalization at a time when those
qualities were much to be desired, not only for artistic ends but for political
ones as well. This is an important consideration, for in addressing the issues
of the artist's duality, Book Two of *The Liubavin Family* also raises questions of the grim legacy of Stalinism and exposes the hypocrisy, cynicism,
and corruption of the Party. When Shukshin wrote the novel—between
1968 and 1970,[19] at the height of Brezhnev's re-Stalinization—these topics
were obviously off limits. As Josephine Woll points out, "Explicit systemic
criticism of contemporary Soviet society was not tolerated in the Brezhnev
years; neither was explicit examination of the Stalin era and its consequences
in modern Soviet society."[20]

SHUKSHIN'S AUTOBIOGRAPHICAL NOVEL
OF CO-CONSCIOUSNESS

Both of Shukshin's Liubavin family novels draw on the history of his home
village, Srostki. Lev Anninskii reports that the genesis for Book One came
from conversations Shukshin had with village elders about the civil war and
collectivization.[21] Anninskii further asserts that features of Shukshin's father
are discernible in several characters in Book One, though he does not go
into more detail.[22] I have argued elsewhere that in the first book Egor Liubavin most closely resembles what Shukshin remembers of his father, not
only because he is described in like terms but because both marry girls with
the same name: Mar'ia Sergeevna Popova in the case of Egor; *Mariia
Sergeevna Popova* in the case of Shukshin's father.[23] But Book One, which
describes the arrival of Soviet power to a remote village in the Altai, can be
called autobiographical only in a limited sense. Although Shukshin described
its contents as "that which I lived through, that which I heard, listened to,
absorbed,"[24] the novel is more accurately a depiction of his prehistory rather
than an attempt at autobiography.

By linking his own parents with the lot of the fictional Liubavin family, however, Shukshin provides an important insight into how he understood his heritage. In spite of a Soviet writer's ideological duty to paint a
damning portrait of kulaks, Shukshin portrayed the Liubavins objectively,
even sympathetically. Indeed, at least four reviewers professed admiration

for the retrograde kulaks as they are presented in the novel.[25] In particular, Egor Liubavin and his brother Makar (who bears the name of Shukshin's father) emerge as significant fictional reflections of the "inner autobiography" Shukshin was weaving into his Liubavin novels. Unrepentant sons of proud kulaks who take up arms against Soviet authority, Egor and Makar speak to a different side of the writer's personality, one having to do with his legacy as the son of an enemy of the people. This side eluded contemporary reviewers and later commentators, who actually praised Shukshin's first novel for its ideological correctness because it depicted how the kulak Liubavins are dealt a serious blow by progressive villagers and Communist agitators.[26] Only one contemporary reviewer comments on the fact that the novel's central conflict—that between the kulaks and the new Soviet order—remains unresolved.[27] While Makar perishes in a shootout with Soviet forces and his father is arrested, Egor flees into the mountains, undefeated and bent on revenge.

Egor's flight, which Shukshin originally placed in the novel's final chapter, is symbolically weighted, both for the novel and for Shukshin's hidden autobiography. As Evgenii Vertlib puts it, by the end of the novel, Egor becomes "an avenger of the destroyers of his native home."[28] Perhaps sensing this outcome, the editorial board of the journal *Sibirskie ogni*, which first published Shukshin's novel, asked Shukshin to add another chapter that would hint at the bright new era dawning on the village of Baklan'. According to one of the editors, "It seemed to us that [Shukshin's original] ending was fraught with the possibility of the shift of important psychological accents."[29] In other words, the novel's original ending would give the last word to Egor, an unrepentant rebel and potential peasant avenger, and thus potentially send the wrong ideological message to Shukshin's readers.

Egor's significance for Shukshin grows when we consider that the writer planned to focus Book Two on his protagonist's fate as an outcast. In an interview published on New Year's Day 1967, Shukshin states:

> I'm thinking of getting down in a couple of years to the writing of the second part of the novel *The Liubavin Family*, in which I would like to tell about the tragic fate of its *main hero*—Egor Liubavin, my fellow Altaian. The novel's main idea has to do with where fate might take this strong and free muzhik, driven from a society to which he has no return. . . . This, the tragedy of the Russian man caught on the border of two different epochs, is what will make up the basis of my future novel.[30]

Shukshin's intimate epithet ("my fellow Altaian") and his reference to Egor as the novel's main hero significantly elevate Egor's importance. Not only does Shukshin endow Egor with his father's features, but, through Egor, the fate of the Russian peasant forcibly torn from his roots and his livelihood asserts itself as an important Shukshinian theme.

Shukshin, however, never finished Egor's story. While mixed reviews of Book One might have discouraged him, the writer never revealed the reasons for dropping his plans. Perhaps the tale of a rootless rebel became too problematic or was no longer of great importance to him. Having established the context of his story in Book One, Shukshin could now shift the focus to his own generation, the sons and daughters of purged and collectivized Siberian peasants. Subsequently, Book Two of *The Liubavin Family* deals not with Egor but with Egor's son, whom he left behind as an infant and whose mother he had killed in a jealous fit. This infant son, Ivan Liubavin, reappears in Book Two as a young man returning permanently to his homeland in the Altai.

Perhaps because it was left unfinished at his death or perhaps because he had no intention of publishing it, Book Two of *The Liubavin Family* reveals much more clearly the lines of the inner autobiography Shukshin was writing. Unlike Book One, where biographical references are few and deeply embedded in the text, Book Two is rich in autobiographical details, making it clear that the writer had undertaken a serious evaluation of his own life and, through it, of painful aspects of Soviet history. It is equally clear, however, that Shukshin had no intention of making his sequel openly autobiographical. This was not to be the sort of first-person account that characterizes his cycle of nostalgic short stories, whose other-named narrator relates events from Shukshin's life in essentially undisguised form. A sophisticated discourse was required, one in which the writer could work through his personal complexes in an impersonal way. Shukshin's solution was as simple as it was effective. He would project the conflicting sides of his own personality and the essential dualities of his own biography onto equally conscious, interacting fictional characters.

Ivan Liubavin from Book Two functions as one of Shukshin's alter egos. Not only is he the progeny of characters from Book One who resemble Shukshin's own parents, but other facts from his biography overlap with those of his creator. Like Shukshin, Ivan lived in dormitories, barracks, and dugouts (3:397) while working as a laborer in Vladimir and Kaluga (3:296), facts Shukshin mentions in a 1966 autobiographical statement.[31] Also like Shukshin, Ivan had been arrested for fighting and was divorced at a young age (3:296).[32] Most important, however, Ivan Liubavin reflects the side of the writer's personality that sought to reject the compromises and constraints of life in Moscow and return home to the Altai, and, by such a return, to alleviate the guilt he felt over having abandoned his home in the first place. In light of the writer's strong feelings on this subject, Ivan Liubavin's permanent return to Siberia takes on a heightened significance.[33]

Book Two opens with Ivan's arrival in Baklan' from Moscow and his meeting with the local kolkhoz chairman, Kuz'ma Rodionovich, one of the Party activists from Book One. Ivan's initial hostility to Kuz'ma clearly derives from the latter's symbolic link to the centralized authorities in Moscow. Shukshin uses the character of Ivan to quickly establish an opposition between the *rodina* (homeland; in this sense, the USSR) and the *malaia rodina* (little homeland or native region; in Shukshin's case, the Altai) within the opening pages of the novel. Throughout his conversation with Kuz'ma, Ivan is reticent, even rude. He not only tells the Party chairman that he has done time in prison but tries to provoke him with comments critical of the Soviet system: "I'm unsociable, don't go to meetings, don't tolerate people who talk a lot . . . In general, I don't like our [Soviet] life a whole heckuva lot" (3:296). When pressed by Kuz'ma, he enumerates his dislikes: "[I don't like] empty talk. There's a lot of thievery and plenty of boorishness . . . and greed. But we say that all's well" (3:297). Ivan adds insult to injury when he declines Kuz'ma's offer to "be a driver for the bosses" (3:297).[34] He is an important conduit for Shukshin's criticism of collectivization, dekulakization, the reorganization of collective farms into wage-based Soviet farms, and the corruption and hypocrisy of Soviet bureaucratic practices. This is not an unexpected outcome, however; Ivan's return home itself justifies a good deal of the political commentary, for his reappearance prompts a reappraisal of Baklan''s past, a time filled with massive social change.

In stark contrast to Ivan's cold, essentially hostile meeting with Kuz'ma, his reunion with his Uncle Efim and his reception by the Liubavin household is warm and genuinely affectionate. Efim is moved to tears; his daughter-in-law Niura is overjoyed. As word spreads, neighbors and other relatives appear to welcome Ivan home, for, though no one in the village may have even known Ivan existed, he is a Liubavin and a native son, and thus one of theirs—*svoi*. This crucial epithet—which denotes one's inherent quality of kinship with a group or a place—emphasizes, as it did in Book One, the sense of distance and foreignness of people or places that are not *svoi* but *chuzhoi* (alien). Ivan is immediately included as *svoi liudi* ("one of us," 3:304). His time away from Baklan' is seen as a time of tribulation: "V chuzhikh-to kraiakh ne sladko" ("It isn't easy to be far from home" [literally, "in alien parts," 3:310]). Moscow is *chuzhoi;* Siberia is *svoi*.

From the moment Ivan appears before Efim, the reader is introduced to aspects of traditional peasant life that have survived collectivization and Soviet rule. Accordingly, one of the first things Efim does is to prepare the bathhouse. The *bania,* as the place where not only dirt but the *nechistaia sila* (unclean spirit) is beaten out of the body, is of particular significance in this early scene in Book Two. In Book One, the bathhouse was a weekly observance that marked the end of the work week and the blessings of domestic comfort. In Book Two, however, it takes on a deeper meaning. Returning from years in "alien parts," Ivan must be purified in a ritualistic as well as a physical sense in order genuinely to come home again.

While he waits for the bathhouse to be prepared, Ivan is left alone in his Uncle Efim's house. As he looks around its interior, he is suddenly flooded by primal memories of his childhood.

> Efim's house was large and light. The rooms—the entrance and the main room—weren't smartly done up, but they were clean. In the city, when it would happen that Ivan was seized by an inexplicable, hollow melancholy, when he would sleeplessly toss and turn on his narrow cot in the dormitory, he would fancy he saw just such a house—spacious, cozy, with painted floors. Perhaps his tenacious childhood memory had seized permanently upon this image of home, perhaps he had thought it up, but the house was exactly like this one, his Homeland [*Rodina*] . . . Something like that from our homeland remains with us, lives within us all of our lives, at times gladdening, at times tormenting us, and it always seems that we'll see it again someday, our homeland. Be it some sort of hill, or house, or a moldy log by the porch where we sat one deep spring night and listened to the dark, there will live in us something from our homeland. (3:300)

Even though Ivan had earlier been in Kuz'ma's home, which was "festively decorated" and "very cozy" (3:295), only his uncle's house triggers memories of hearth, kin, and country. Kuz'ma, after all, represents Moscow, while Efim and his house are symbols of Ivan's homeland. Therefore, the "homeland" (the capitalized *Rodina* in the text) to which Ivan refers is none other than his *malaia rodina* (little homeland), the place where he was born. Shukshin himself reminded his readers of this distinction in an essay that provides an important commentary on *The Liubavin Family: Book Two*, "Slovo o 'maloi rodine'" ("The Place Where I Was Born").

In the first three references to *rodina* in the opening paragraph of this essay, Shukshin adds the phrase "the Altai" (his native Siberian region). The fourth time he uses *rodina*, he finally adds parenthetically "it's understood that I have in mind the so-called *malaia rodina*."[35] This essay, written after Book Two (1973), is filled with lyrical childhood memories of much the same tenor as Ivan's. Indeed, Ivan's memories in the passage quoted earlier seamlessly blend into Shukshin's own in the narrative (the part beginning "something like that from our homeland" is preceded by a significant ellipsis), and it becomes impossible to distinguish between the two. Nor should we feel compelled to, since Ivan seems to fulfill the role of Shukshin's co-conscious alter ego. In his essay and in Book Two, Shukshin, like Ivan, is following the distant call of his childhood and the remote lure of his homeland.

In "Slovo o 'maloi rodine,'" Shukshin introduces the same juxtaposition that drives both books of *The Liubavin Family*, indeed, that haunts his biography—the opposition of Moscow and the Altai, "the center" and "the provinces." Elements of Shukshin's *malaia rodina*—the *polati* (sleeping benches) of his childhood; the language spoken and routines observed in his grandfather's house; the sense of ease and lack of affectation or pretension of village life; the legacy won by his ancestors who came from the North, the Volga, and the Don; and so on—create a picture of the Altai (and Siberia) as a place superior to Moscow on the social, moral, and historical levels.

> I have had time and opportunity to see beautiful buildings, smart drawing-rooms, well-educated, highly-cultured people, who feel at home in such drawing-rooms, walk in easily, sit down, chat, smoke, drink coffee . . . Always as I watched them I thought: "Well now, is that what life is about? Is that how we should all be living?" But something in me resisted this beauty and this ease; perhaps I felt that it was not ease but a demonstration of ease, which in itself is a kind of constraint. In my grandfather's house everyone was genuinely at ease, completely free. I struggle with these thoughts, I try them out, of course, and am aware how hard it is to defend them, particularly against irony . . . But at the same time I want to be totally honest with myself, and for this reason I say it again: nowhere have I seen such clear, simple, perfect functionalism as in my grandfather's house, or such natural, true, and essentially kindly relationships between people.[36]

Shukshin, through his hero Ivan, is attempting a return to that life he remembered so well. He is putting his notions about his Siberian homeland to the test, seeing whether it is really possible to return to the past.

In this regard, the identical depiction in the novel and the essay of the native region as a refuge is conspicuous. As Ivan sits in his uncle's house, he thinks: "All the same, it is terribly pleasant to have a little corner somewhere on earth where you can go, sit, and listen to the ticking of the clock, and think about nothing. 'I've become tired in these cities, tuckered myself out'" (3:301). For Shukshin, the Altai and the village were a "reserve," a "homefront,"[37] a place where he could "get his breath back and refuel his courage" and "recover the vital circulation of blood that seemed exhausted."[38] Having returned to his homeland, Ivan wants to "drink in the free air" of Siberia and "fall into the steppe, into the grass, into a reverie" (3:311).

Ivan's desire "to live right" (3:402) in Siberia is reflected in his plan to build a house, specifically a *krestovyi dom,* or large peasant house in the form of a cross.[39] The house symbolizes Ivan's need to "begin living" (3:403) and represents the central question Shukshin poses through his alter ego: can one really go home again? In order to economize on effort and expense, Ivan decides to build the house with his cousin, Pavel Liubavin. The house is to be shared by their future families. While the process of selecting, cutting, and floating the timber downstream on rafts and then raising the house itself reflect village traditions, it becomes an empty exercise for Ivan, who afterward spends evenings alone in his new home or with Pavel. Further compounding Ivan's failure to turn his house into a home is his sudden, paradoxical, and unrequited love for Kuz'ma Rodionov's daughter, Mariia.

As the daughter of a Party leader, Mariia stands in symbolic opposition to Ivan, the son of the kulak rebel Egor. Her extreme cynicism and indifference toward the Soviet system, however, contradict the beliefs of her father and are particularly damning indictments of the failures of Communism to build a new and optimistic society. In her first meeting with Ivan, Mariia identifies her generation as "passive, lacking initiative, and apathetic" (3:322). She admits her lack of interest in the Siberian virgin lands projects ("they'll plow it all up without me"), her apathy toward "government questions," and her indifference toward Soviet films ("I already know how everything will end in them") (3:322). She also flirts with Ivan and sings old Russian folk songs so well that Ivan imagines he hears "above the steppe the dear music of his childhood" (3:326). Indeed, we learn that her father forgives her much for her singing (3:325).

The fact that this jaded representative of the next generation—and not some "purer" or "truer" Russian woman (such as Niura Liubavina)—should be the one to sing these folk songs with such feeling is an intended irony. From bathhouse rituals and folk songs to Ivan's desire to build his own *krestovyi dom*, Shukshin is attempting to discover whether the traditional folk aspects of village life he remembered so well have survived Sovietization, whether form still corresponds to content. Although Ivan's fatal attraction to Mariia is perhaps one of the least successful plot lines of the novel, their relationship underscores the mutual incompatibility of the legacies they have inherited from their fathers. The failure of their love, which might have healed the rift between the kulak Liubavins and the activist Rodionovs, casts a pall over Ivan's attempt to come home again.

Their unsuccessful romance essentially repeats the story of Mariia and Petr Ivlev. Ivlev, like Ivan, shares significant aspects of Shukshin's biography. Indeed, in his problematic relationship with Mariia, to whom he was once married, Ivlev's character at times almost blends with Ivan's, an expected outcome when we realize that he embodies Shukshin's other co-conscious alter ego in this autobiographical novel.

If Ivan Liubavin represents the innocent and "true" village son come back home to reclaim his peasant heritage, Petr Ivlev represents a different side of Shukshin's personality, that of the compromised careerist who persists doggedly in his belief that "Communism with a human face" may yet be possible. Of the two, Ivlev's character is more complicated and has a longer history. He first figured in Shukshin's final film project for the cinematography institute, *Report from Lebyzhe* (*Iz Leb"iazhego soobshchaint*, 1960), where Shukshin played Ivlev's role himself, an interesting and significant coincidence in light of the autobiographical aspects of the character that would later appear in the writer's novel. Ivlev next figured as the main protagonist of Shukshin's 1966 novella *Tam, vdali* (*There, in the Distance*). Only in Book Two of *The Liubavin Family*, however, does Shukshin invest in the character important aspects of one side of his own dual personality.

Like Shukshin, Ivlev hides the fact that his father is an enemy of the people and alters personal documents accordingly. Also like Shukshin, Ivlev is a writer, albeit an unpublished one. Moreover, the poems that Ivlev writes and later reads to Mariia and Ivan are poems Shukshin himself wrote early in his career. One of them is the poem that figures as the epigraph to "O See the Horses Gallop in the Fields," an appropriate coincidence, since the hero of that story is also an autobiographical surrogate of sorts for Shukshin. The second, "Tary-bary-rastabary . . ." (3:419), appeared in slightly different and abbreviated form in the novella (but not the film) *Kalina krasnaia* (4:173). The last poem, "Ei, stikhi moi—gol' neumytaia" ("Hey, my poems, unwashed beggars"), is published in the novel for the first time (3:473–74) and is a thinly veiled verse about Stepan Razin's peasant revolt that seems to match the poem Ol'ga Rumiantseva reports having heard Shukshin recite in 1961.[40] This writerly aspect of Ivlev's personality was added only in *The Liubavin Family* sequel; as far as the novel's plot is concerned, it is a curious but clearly superfluous feature of the character. Ivlev's interest in poetry, however, has enormous importance metatextually, where it speaks volumes about his function as Shukshin's fictional alter ego.

Other facts of Ivlev's biography confirm his kinship with the writer. The year his mother and father were arrested and shot as enemies of the people, 1933, is the same year Shukshin's father was purged (3:363). Ivlev's name, like Shukshin's, is changed to avoid the stigma of being the child of state enemies. Ivlev is the name of his aunt, who raises him in a village near Barnaul (in the Altai). His father's name was Dokuchaev. When his aunt finally tells him about his parents, he walks around in shock for three days, "not knowing what to think about his aunt, Soviet power, life in general" (3:364). Eventually he decides to continue living his secret life, hoping, as his aunt had assured him, that his documents had all been "fixed" so that no one would ever find out. (As one character says elsewhere in the novel, "one's biography in our day, in our country, has serious significance" [3:467]). When he enters the army (and there applies for admission to the Party), he lies about his family on the "personnel résumé sheet" (3:363),[41] the only time Shukshin alludes in his fiction or essays to the white lies in the autobiographical statements in his own official résumé papers.[42]

No one discovers Ivlev's secret, and he becomes a successful officer. Life seems to offer him everything he could want. Then, during a summer visit to his village, Ivlev's aunt gives him a letter his father had written for him before he was executed. The letter, which Shukshin reproduces in its entirety in the text, is a deeply moving personal message, the more remarkble for the fact that Shukshin himself obviously invested in it the painful, ambiguous emotions he himself experienced in contemplating the fate of his own father. What is significant about the letter, however, is that although Ivlev's parents are charged with crimes similar to those of which Shukshin's father was accused ("harming Soviet power" and "disrupting collectivization" [3:366]), they are both squarely on the side of Soviet reform in the village, something that could hardly have been said of Makar Shukshin. Ivlev's father claims that the charges against him were brought by a "parasite" who "doesn't know anything about the peasant's cause" (3:366). Thus Ivlev's parents, unlike Ivan's, are not rebellious kulaks but Soviet martyrs. Indeed, Ivlev's father blames their predicament on their "naïveté and lack of experience" and is confident that "things will be set right" in the future (3:366), imbuing the letter with a certain faith in the eventual triumph of the Soviet cause in the countryside. This marks an important difference between the two characters and the two sides of Shukshin's duality. Ivlev's grudge, as it turns out, is not against Communism as such but against those who have sabotaged it.

Changed by the letter, Ivlev informs his army unit of his true biography. As a child of an enemy of the people, he is forced to resign his commission (this part of the story takes place during Stalin's reign). From then on, Ivlev dedicates himself to living an honest life, refusing only to change his name from the one he had grown up with. When Ivlev subsequently meets Mariia, falls in love, marries her, and moves to the city, he discovers that her friends are all dissolute black marketeers. After finding stolen goods in his home, he goes to the police, not suspecting that his own wife will be arrested. He meets Kuz'ma in connection with Mariia's arrest and, after a stint training as a policeman himself, joins Kuz'ma in Baklan'.

Ivlev's idealism gets him into trouble in his dealings within the Communist Party as well (he reestablished membership during his police career). He has little tolerance for the many empty, bureaucratic aspects of the Party. Elsewhere, he denounces the "young careerists and muslin princesses" flooding the Party's ranks (3:454). In one instance, Kuz'ma and Ivlev break up a smuggling and prostitution operation run by a local Party leader (3:431–33). Later, they are opposed in their efforts to confirm a colleague as Komsomol secretary by self-seeking party hacks, one of whom, we find out, had once informed on his own brother (3:464). In these episodes, Shukshin emphasizes the treacherous hypocrisy rampant at all levels of Party organization, but does so always from the point of view of "good" Communists like Ivlev. Even Ivan— who, unlike Ivlev, is openly hostile to Party representatives—is chided into admitting to Kuz'ma that it takes a "good man" to make a "good Communist" (3:451). Ivan is quick to point out, however, that it is not always easy to tell which Communist is a "good man":

> [F]or you it's only important that a person's biography be clean, that he knows what to say, that he looks solid. [. . .] We had one such type in our trucking headquarters in Moscow. He was the first to howl "Communism! Commu-

nism!" at meetings. Then he gets caught hauling containers of government goods from the warehouse on fake documents. That's Communism for you! (3:452)

While this kind of exposé of the Communist Party was, as Viktor Gorn points out, "clearly 'not in fashion'" at the time of the novel's composition,[43] Ivlev and, to a certain degree, Kuz'ma stand out as conspicuous symbols of what is right about the Party. Even so, we learn that it was Kuz'ma who arrested the Liubavin patriarch, Emel'ian, and Efim's older brother, Kondrat, in 1933, at the height of the rural purges (3:303); Efim saved himself by entering the kolkhoz. We also learn that Kuz'ma himself disappeared in 1937, spent two years in Siberian labor camps, and narrowly avoided being arrested a second time (and likely shot) only through the help of a friend in Moscow, who himself was later arrested and executed. When Kuz'ma tells Ivlev that "there are things more terrifying than prison," he does not mean the firing squad. He is referring to his own sense of guilt and helplessness over his friend's fate and his fear that his friend might have thought, at the last moment, that it was Kuz'ma who had informed on him (3:411). Ivlev's callous reaction to Kuz'ma's story ("my father didn't sit it out"), on the other hand, is a chilling confirmation of the horrible nature of the time to which Shukshin alludes: even fellow victims do not sympathize with each other.

The portrait of the "good Communist" that Shukshin nevertheless attempts to paint in Ivlev is an important reflection of the writer's complex feelings about the Communist Party. When Shukshin wrote in a 1965 essay, "I do not picture Communism without decent people,"[44] he appears to be affirming his optimism about the Communist Party. His use of Party rhetoric is ambiguous, however, and masks his ultimate meaning: is he really praising Communism by implying that decent people will bring it into being or is he actually damning it by implying that decent people do not make up its ranks? Shukshin availed himself of this sort of political double entendre on other occasions, such as when he defended the heroes of his short stories from criticism that they were not positive role models for Soviet readers:

[A]s a rank-and-file member of the Communist Party of the USSR, I believe that I belong to an active and fair party. But as an artist I cannot deceive my people by showing them, for example, that life is only happy. The truth can also be bitter. If I hide the truth, if I affirm that everything is good, that everything is wonderful, then I will in the long run actually let down my Party. . . . I'd like to help the Party. I'd like to show the truth.[45]

Shukshin was well aware that few "decent" people populated the ranks of the Party. Indeed, his Ivlev is clearly an idealist fighting a losing battle. The extent of the corruption, treachery, and hypocrisy in the Communist Party, openly documented in *The Liubavin Family: Book Two,* is one indication that "decency" and "Communism" may coexist only theoretically, or in very few individuals. Through Ivlev, though, Shukshin is able to couch his criticism of the Party by presenting the point of view of one of those few, someone whose biography, like his own, was compromised by "bad" Communists but who nevertheless had not given up on the idea that "decent people" may yet triumph. This is an important aspect of Ivlev's character, for it speaks to Shukshin's own condition. As a successful writer, actor, and director who benefited from his good political standing in the Party that executed his father, Shukshin, it seems, needed to believe that one could be a Communist and still be a decent person. This accounts for Ivlev's return to the Party as well as Shukshin's portrait of Kuz'ma Rodionov, who in both books of *The Liubavin Family* is a flawed but decent Communist.

When Mariia asks Ivlev whether he considers himself a cultured person, Ivlev's answer addresses the heart of his own philosophy and that of Ivan Liubavin: "In any case, I can tell black from white, what's genuine and what's a surrogate, a fake, an affectation" (3:430). In a world full of inauthenticity and dissimulation, both characters—and Shukshin through them—are engaged in a search for the truth. In their individual quests, each character employs a different approach. Ivan chooses to reject his "Soviet" life in Moscow in order to return to his homeland and find authenticity in traditional Russian village life. Ivlev chooses to work within the system to achieve authenticity through the Party. Ultimately, both characters fail: Ivan because his house is not a home and the village and its traditions have changed; Ivlev because the Party, in which he has invested his future, is too corrupt. Moreover, in their respective failures, the characters seem to merge into one by the end of the novel. With one entangled in the loveless embraces of Mariia and the other poisoned by her self-serving, dark cynicism, Ivan and Ivlev become almost indistinguishable. When Kuz'ma Rodionov dies of a heart attack during a confrontation with his daughter, Ivan and Ivlev carry his coffin to the cemetery in a symbolically charged scene shortly before the conclusion of the novel.

By ending his novel with Kuz'ma's death, Shukshin seems also to be emphasizing the dead end that each of his co-conscious protagonists has reached in his quest, the dead end Shukshin also sensed himself to have reached. Unlike Book One, Book Two has no optimistic ending tacked on. Indeed, the sense of failure and pessimism with which Book Two closes stands as an indictment of the obligatory optimism of Soviet society, with its emphasis on progress and historical development. Ivan's return has not righted the wrong that sent his father, Egor, into self-imposed exile; Ivlev's faith in Communism with a human face dies with Kuz'ma. Both of these "sons of an enemy of the people" fail to find authenticity in their lives. For both protagonists, the form (village tradition, Communist ideology) does not match the content and the result is paralysis. Such was their creator's own sense of stasis. Caught between Moscow and Siberia, between his life as a successful artist in the capital and that of his country childhood, Shukshin could not clarify his own situation, although clarification was obviously one of his goals in writing his autobiographical sequel to *The Liubavin Family*.

The failed journeys of Ivan Liubavin and Petr Ivlev in the second book reflect their creator's failure to resolve the conflict between the two complex, vying sides of his personality and biography. The way Shukshin neatly splits the conflicting aspects of his biography does not result in reconciliation. And yet, some closure is achieved. If nothing else, Shukshin's manipulation of his fictional pair allowed him to isolate the opposing sides of his duality and play them off against each other, thus achieving some small therapeutic benefit. Moreover, it is possible that the mere act of assigning his inner conflicts to two protagonists was a clarifying moment for the writer, a moment whose ultimate value only he could know or appreciate. In any case, by investing equal parts of his own biography in each character, Shukshin also managed to achieve the control over his material that he so valued (a writer must remain above his material, he writes in a marginal note).[46] Maintaining a saving distance from his emerging self-portrait while effectively obscuring his autobiographical interrogation from others would have enabled Shukshin to gain the benefits of confession while avoiding the dangers of self-exposure, had the novel ever been published. Clearly, this was Shukshin's goal.

The question of whether or not the novel could have been published in Brezhnev's time, is, of course, anyone's guess. It is doubtful that the work would have avoided controversy because of the scenes exposing corruption and careerism within the Communist Party and its criticism of Soviet agricultural policy. Furthermore, we do not know whether Shukshin even considered the novel to be finished (the manuscript shows no enumeration of chapter breaks). Whether he would have eventually tried to submit it for publication or had already decided against submitting it are also unknown.

While these issues prevent us from making a definitive assessment about Shukshin's autobiographical novel, some conclusions can be drawn. First, the fact that Shukshin should so carefully split himself between two interactive protagonists heightens the importance of the issues they represent for understanding the writer and his works. Second, Shukshin's desire to remain safely hidden behind these alter egos gives us an important clue to the workings of his art. We should be on the lookout for evidence of a submerged confessional discourse in his other works, something Shukshin himself alludes to in another marginal note.[47] Finally, Shukshin's use of fictional alter egos underscores the writer's (and the director's and the actor's) need to remain essentially detached and impersonal in the presentation of his subject matter, regardless of how personally invested he might be in the process of creating it. In this context, Shukshin's autobiographical novel of co-consciousness emerges as an important but overlooked chapter of the writer's life in art.

Chapter Nine

The Search for Freedom

Shukshin and Sten'ka Razin

There is the passion of every poet for a rebellion
personified by one individual. . . . Without
passion for the transgressor, there is no poet.
—Marina Tsvetaeva, "Pushkin i Pugachev"

FOR ALL OF HIS CREATIVE LIFE, Shukshin was
haunted by the image of Stepan Razin. The subject of one of the writer's
earliest stories ("Sten'ka Razin," written in 1960) and the tragic hero of a
film script (1968) and a full-length novel (first published as a book shortly
after Shukshin's death in 1974), Razin frames in an important way the entirety of the writer's career. Shukshin spent the greater part of a decade and
a half researching, pondering, and writing about the rebel leader, and his
wish to make an epic film on the ataman became a virtual obsession. Besides the story, script, and novel, Razin figures directly or indirectly in nine
other works, including four of Shukshin's five films and four novellas.[1] More
than any other single figure, Razin dominated Shukshin's imagination and,
in one way or another, permeated his work.

In his childhood, Shukshin learned of Razin from folk songs and Soviet
textbooks. He was the terrible ataman who looted cities at will and flung a
beautiful princess overboard because she had come between him and his
men; he was also the class-conscious leader of a peasant revolt and forerunner of Bolshevik rebels. Later, as the son of an enemy of the people—
moreover, one accused of inciting an uprising against Soviet power during
collectivization—Shukshin would perceive Razin's vague outline in the ab-
sent figure of his own father, a kinship with the Cossack hero born of the injustice dealt his own family by the state. Indeed, commentators have seen
features of the artist himself as well as his father in Shukshin's Razin.[2]

But for all of his love of the folklore surrounding Razin and for all of
his own historical research on the ataman, Shukshin set out to write neither
a colorful legend nor a historical account of the Cossack leader, this despite
the fact that Shukshin's portrayal of Razin won strong endorsements from

the historians who read his script for Gorky Film Studio.[3] The irony here is that Shukshin's script and novel are hardly concerned with the facts of the ataman's life or the history of his peasant rebellion, nor does his Razin behave anything like the mythic figure from Russian folklore. Rather, Shukshin's Razin serves very specific personal and artistic ends. His novel rereads the personality of the folk hero and historical personage in terms of the search for *volia* (freedom from constraint or obligation, liberation), thus underscoring the importance of this notion for Shukshin's art and cultural critique.

Razin in particular and the myth of the Cossack in general appealed to Shukshin, as he did to other writers in the history of Russian literature, as both a symbol of freedom and a means of achieving it in art. The unfettered freedom inherent in the Cossack way of life and the creative liberty craved by Russian artists through two centuries of imperial and Soviet censorship merged in the Cossack ethos and the men who embodied it. The appeal of the Cossack myth, according to Judith Kornblatt, is that it "allows the author to proclaim not only that he is like the Cossack in a general sense, but that he shares the particular Cossack pursuit of freedom in a restricted world."[4]

Such are Marina Tsvetaeva's conclusions in her essay about Aleksandr Pushkin and the Cossack rebel Emel'ian Pugachev, in which she claims that Pushkin's Pugachev represents, among other things, "poetic freedom."[5] As artists, however, neither Pushkin nor Shukshin nor the many others captivated by the Cossack myth ever translated "passion for rebellion" or "passion for the transgressor" into open revolt. All the same, writing about rebels in an authoritarian state was a delicate business, especially during the Brezhnev period. As Kornblatt writes, "The flood of Cossacks in Russian literature diminished after Stalin's death, perhaps because writers, or more likely editors and censors, finally perceived the political volatility, if not artistic inconsistency, of a hero both loyal and rebellious."[6]

The tension between a narrative of revolt and real-life conformity is not, of course, unique to writers whose heroes are rebels. In twentieth-century Russian literature, such protagonists—especially Cossacks—have largely been put in the safe contexts of socialist revolution or Socialist Realism. This is particularly true of Sten'ka Razin, who figures in classics of Soviet literature written by Aleksei Chapygin (*Razin Stepan,* 1926) and Stepan Zlobin (*Stepan Razin,* 1951). Both novelists are guilty of endowing Razin with modern motivations, and both view Razin's uprising as but the prehistory of the 1917 revolution. Zlobin's novel was so orthodox in content and style that it even garnered a Stalin Prize the year it appeared. Indeed, Kornblatt singles out Zlobin's novel as a prime example of how the Cossack myth in Russian culture—that of "free and expansive, wild and energetic, uncompromised and unbounded" men—died during the Stalinist period as it was being recast in terms of a newer Soviet mythology. At that time, she

172

argues, the unfettered ethos of the Cossack was "finally and inescapably bounded" by the "aesthetic and moral norms of a centralized authority."[7]

Kornblatt's "postmortem" of the Cossack myth in Soviet literature, however, is premature. By concluding with Evgenii Evtushenko's treatment of Razin in his 1965 poem *Bratskaia GES,* where Razin is remade into an "ideal socialist image" and converted "into a rebel for the proletariat cause,"[8] Kornblatt stops short of Shukshin's novel *I Have Come to Give You Freedom* (*Ia prishel dat' vam voliu*), in which the Cossack myth is rediscovered, restored, and revitalized by an artist with a personal and creative stake in the expansive and boundless image of the Cossack Stepan Razin. The title of Shukshin's novel—uttered by Razin but also associated with the author because his name appears on the cover—already suggests a crucial difference in Shukshin's approach to his "rebellion personified by one individual." Shukshin's Razin seeks *volia,* and as such not only serves as a vessel for poetic freedom but resurrects the free, unbounded, and unrestrained Cossack nature precisely when it seemed to have disappeared for good—during the long days of the Brezhnev-era stagnation.

Unlike Zlobin's portrait of Sten'ka Razin, Shukshin's novel is no socialist bildungsroman in which "the hero matures from rebellious adolescent to sophisticated ideologue" and represents "Soviet values of order."[9] Shukshin avoids endowing his rebel protagonist with historical prescience or class consciousness. On the contrary, his reworking of the Cossack myth serves personal polemical ends, bound up with the artist's own history as well as that of his country, an outcome that points to the figure's contemporary significance for the artist. The intercessor for the peasantry during the consolidation of serfdom in the seventeenth century, Shukshin's Razin also stands as an indictment of the wrongs of collectivization in the twentieth century. The defender of Cossack independence in the Don region, Razin reflects Shukshin's own desire for "provincial autonomy," a desire that conditioned the style and setting of his works and that led to his decision—expressed shortly before he died—to leave Moscow for his *malaia rodina* in Siberia. By burning imperial decrees and ordinances in his war with "Lord Document" (*Gospozha Bumaga*), Razin also raises questions about the depersonalizing effects of government bureaucracy, questions particularly relevant to contemporary Soviet reality. Finally, when Razin's bid to give people *volia* is defeated by apathy, complacency, and careerism, and when he is betrayed by his own men for the sake of an easy life serving the government, he becomes a tragic and very contemporary figure with whose plight Soviet readers living under Brezhnev could easily sympathize.

Shukshin's reworking of the key terms of the Cossack myth—according to Kornblatt, the Cossack's boundlessness, timelessness, and epic affinities—in the service of his own artistic program and cultural critique constitutes a central operation for the artist and an appropriate conclusion to the present study. We will look first at the important concept of *volia* in Shukshin's novel and its relation to the Cossack myth, then trace the close links between Shukshin's Cossacks and the folk aesthetic so vital to the novel and his own art, and end by seeing in Razin's fate a reflection of Russia's own. Ultimately, *I Have Come to Give You Freedom* resurrects the Cossack myth as an important narrative for the Soviet 1960s and 1970s, those crucial decades of high hopes and dashed expectations in which the opposition between personal freedom and government authority—personified in the trials of Brodsky, Daniel, and Sinyavsky; dramatized in the Soviet crushing of the Prague Spring; and epitomized in the public hounding and eventual expulsion of Solzhenitsyn—became an emblem of the Brezhnev era.

VOLIA, COSSACK FREEDOM, AND LORD DOCUMENT

I Have Come to Give You Freedom chronicles the last two years of Razin's life and, unlike Chapygin's and Zlobin's novels, focuses exclusively on Razin's campaign to reach Moscow, which began in August 1669 and ended on June 6, 1671, when Razin was executed.[10] The novel is divided into three parts. "Vol'nye kazaki" ("Free Cossacks") describes the aftermath of Razin's successful series of raids on Persian cities along the Caspian Sea. It concludes with Razin's decision to "move on Moscow." The second part, "Mstites', brat'ia!" ("Take Vengeance, O My Brothers!"), relates the height of Razin's campaign: his successful capture of Astrakhan' and Tsaritsyn and the growing popular support for his revolt. The book concludes with "Kazn'" ("Execution"), in which Razin meets defeat at Simbirsk, fails to rally a second campaign, is turned over to the tsar by the Don Cossacks centered in Cherkassk, and is tortured in Moscow, then drawn, quartered, and beheaded.

The novel's title proposes *volia* as a "key word" in Shukshin's lexicon,[11] what one critic describes as the "'golden thread' of his entire mature *oeuvre*."[12] *Volia* (meaning primarily "will") is freedom in the sense of nonconstraint, release, liberation, doing whatever one likes: a kind of anarchic freedom. Russians have long observed an important distinction between this kind of liberty and that represented by the other Russian word for freedom, *svoboda*. In the post-Soviet period in particular, the two words have been used contrastively to explain the state of the transition in Russia to a market economy and democratic political system. While commentators noted an ample quantity of *volia* in post-Soviet Russia—that is, the freedom to do or say what one pleased—there was little *svoboda*, the rule of law that insures taxes are paid and laws are evenly enforced.[13]

"The effete *svoboda* can sometimes have overtones of an almost Western liberal concept of freedom, including elements of reciprocity and individual purpose, fulfillment, and discipline."[14] *Volia*, on the other hand, "was the peasant's word for 'freedom' in its broadest and most appealing sense: a life without obligation to others."[15] It is therefore distanced from the narrower, civic meanings attached to the idea of *svoboda* and reflects, instead, a much more vague and emotional concept, one as broad and inexplicable as the expanses of central Russia and Siberia where the peasant made his home. *Volia* in this sense is a bit of a folk liberty, and as such it is tied to the peasant's desire to overcome the burdens he has carried from time immemorial.

In his own use of the term, Shukshin considerably expands what *volia* encompasses. His use of the word speaks to three distinct themes in the novel: liberation from physical constraint, liberation from legal compulsion (the rule of law and the dominance of bureaucracy), and liberation from the worldly and the material. Taken together, these aspects of *volia* in *I Have Come to Give You Freedom* propose a rereading and rejuvenation of the Cossack myth as a meaningful cultural narrative for the late Soviet period, where physical constraint (in the form of impassable borders, internal passports, and prison camps), legal compulsion (aided and abetted by the absence of legal redress and the lack of separation among political, economic, and cultural spheres in Soviet society), and dialectical (as well as consumeristic) materialism all made up the realities of daily living. We will turn first to the idea of *volia* as a spatial freedom.

Dmitrii Likhachev defines *volia* as "freedom plus wide expanses. . . . *Volia* is broad planes where you can walk without end, wander, sail great distances on big rivers, inhale the free air of open places, breathe in the wind, feel the sky above your head, and move in whatever direction you want."[16] In Shukshin's novel *volia* also reflects an important spatial relationship, for it expresses "the ancient peasant dream of . . . escape from serfdom and drudgery into the open borderlands inhabited by brigands and Cossacks."[17] The wide steppe of the Don region, like the broad expanses of Siberia elsewhere in Shukshin's fiction, is a haven of freedom, not only for its Cossack masters, whose expansive nature it reflects, but for runaway serfs as well. The Cossacks have a "sacred ordinance": *s Dona vydachi net* ("there is no handing over [of refugee serfs] from the Don" [4:333]). Indeed, Razin despises the Don Cossack leader Kornei Iakovlev because of the latter's willingness to go back on this sacred ordinance for the sake of the tsar's continued *zhalovanie* (the "salary" or "payment"—in foodstuffs and ammunition—that the tsar paid the Cossack host for its willingness to guard the empire's frontiers from Asian invaders).

This erosion of Cossack *volia* and the encroachment of government authority into the Cossack homeland are among the important issues in *I Have Come to Give You Freedom,* where the traditional boundlessness of Cossack life is being threatened by a very real physical and legal infringement on Cossack territorial sovereignty. In fact, Razin's campaign to bring *volia* to the downtrodden is as much about restoring and preserving the

Prodigal Son

Cossack's territorial integrity—and through it, the expansiveness of their very nature—as it is about peasant rebellion.

If the notion of *volia* in Shukshin's novel is linked to the wide expanses of the steppe in the Don and Volga Cossack regions, then to impinge upon that *volia* is, first and foremost, a *spatial* infringement. As Likhachev puts it in his essay on *volia*, if freedom is linked to open expanses, then "to oppress someone is . . . to deprive him of space."[18] Like Likhachev, Shukshin favors the verb *pritesniat'/pritesnit'* to describe this oppression, whose root, *-tes-*, has the connotation of "crowding, pressure, squeezing, tightness,"[19] rather than the verb *ugnetat'*, which also means "to oppress." For instance, when the tsar orders taverns to charge the Cossacks an exorbitant amount for liquor, the Cossacks complain to Razin, "Pritesniaiut, bat'ka!" ("They're oppressing us, Father!" [4:342]). Razin's peasant advisor, Matvei Ivanov, describes the boyars as *pritesniteli* (oppressors), in this case bypassing the more common *ugnetatel'* (4:453). Elsewhere *volia* is explicitly contrasted to *tesnota*, "a cramped state" (4:372).

In a confrontation with Kornei Iakovlev later in the novel, Razin affirms this important link between *volia* and broad expanses when he declares that the true Cossack home is not in the earthen dugouts of Cherkassk, where the tsar wants to contain the Cossack host as on a reservation. The true Cossack home is "in the open field," where the Cossacks can roam and raid for a living: "It's a big house, the ceiling is high . . . It has many inhabitants," Razin proclaims (4:396). In so doing, Razin fully evokes the myth of the unbounded, uncompromised Cossack, for whom "space is Edenlike— primal, pure, and unrestricted."[20] Indeed, Shukshin builds on this myth as he describes the end of Razin's Persian campaign and his subsequent move on Moscow. As cities fall and rebel followers increase, the growing amount of captured territory matches Razin's ever expanding *volia*. During this stage of the campaign, Razin is free and uncompromised. But as the campaign starts to fall apart, as the Cossack governments he installs in his conquered cities fall into corruption and popular disfavor, and especially after he abandons the peasant forces at Simbirsk, Razin loses his aura of invincibility as well as his expansive character. He becomes compromised. As he retreats, Razin's *volia* diminishes in proportion to his conceded territory, which shrinks to the Don region, then to his home base of operations in Kalagal'nik, then finally to his earthen dugout, where he is captured by Kornei and the Don Cossacks faithful to the tsar.[21]

As Razin's *volia* contracts, Moscow's authority expands, reflecting the historical conflict "pitting the expanding center against the retreating frontier."[22] Razin's true enemy, it turns out, was never the tsar (despite his desire to pull the tsar by the beard). In fact, Tsar Aleksei is barely depicted in the novel. Razin's true enemy is Moscow,[23] the metonymic reference for government and the seat of centralized authority, where serfdom was being "clamped down more firmly than ever and the last vestiges of popular freedom and local autonomy" were being "trampled underfoot."[24] In the novel, as in Shukshin's life, this center/periphery dichotomy is symbolic of a deeper polemic—that over the relationship between the powerful, authoritarian, and privileged (Moscow) and the disempowered, disenfranchised, and backward (the frontier: the Don, Siberia).

> [T]here had arisen on Russian soil some large, dark power—moreover, this power was not [the Astrakhan' officials] Ivan Prozorovskii, not Semen L'vov, not the old Church metropolitan. It was somehow not them, but something more ominous, not the tsar even, not his musketeers—they were people, why fear people? [. . .] This power remained unclear, huge, inevitable, but just what it was—that they couldn't understand. And this angered Stepan, tormented him, enraged him. His most intense rage was channeled toward one thing—the boyars. But when he really thought about it, he understood that it actually wasn't about the boyars at all, but something else. [. . .] And while this power existed, there would be no peace, this Stepan understood in his heart. [. . .] That power, which the muzhiks could not realize or fix a word to, that power was called—GOVERNMENT. (4:374–75)

It is government that opposes Shukshin's *volia,* government that, because of its laws and its bureaucracy, hems in the expansive nature of the Cossacks and pulls tight the peasants' bonds. In this aspect of his novel, Shukshin departs significantly from his predecessors, for the government which his Razin opposes is pointedly disassociated from the usual targets of Soviet historical depiction: the oppressive tsar, his troops, and the landowning boyars. Shukshin's enemy is a generalized image of the government, ambiguous in its referents and therefore ahistorical. Government in general is the main threat to Cossack *volia* and peasant autonomy, an anarchic notion whose applicability to Soviet times explains in part why the novel and especially the film project were viewed with distrust by the cultural establishment.

In thus designating Moscow as the source of the spatial infringement on Cossack autonomy, Shukshin also discovers a second threat to *volia,* that of legal constraint, embodied in the novel by that quintessential symbol of government, governmental bureaucracy. The chief weapon of the bureaucracy in Shukshin's novel—one capable of destroying a man's life as surely as if he had been cleaved in two by a Cossack saber—is the dreaded *bumaga* (literally "paper," here government documents). In a striking, almost existentialist twist—one that deepens the novel's modern-day resonance—it is the bureaucrat and his *bumaga* who, it turns out, are the ultimate foils for the saber-wielding Cossack. The ink, quill, government seal of official edicts, and Church pronouncements represent a power to be reckoned with, one that nearly exceeds the ability of the (significantly) illiterate Cossacks to resist. Repeatedly throughout the novel Shukshin casts his central conflict in terms of this opposition between *volia*—as intangible, formless, and free as the air itself—and the bureaucrat's *bumaga,* which is binding, anesthetizing, and ossified.

The very text of *I Have Come to Give You Freedom* is framed by two of the more dramatic examples of the power of the *bumaga:* it opens with the Russian Orthodox Church's anathema of Razin and closes with the death sentence pronounced at Razin's execution.[25] Both of these inclusions by Shukshin rely on the original documents the writer had read during the course of his research for the novel. Interesting in and of themselves as historical texts, the documents are reproduced with all of their spelling and grammatical irregularities intact.[26] Parts Two and Three of the novel also open with examples of the hated *bumagi.* Official letters from different *voevody* (governors) and imperial *gramoty* (edicts) from the tsar are reproduced in the text, most of them apparently Shukshin's own adaptations of actual documents (see 3:360, 399–402, 511–14).

Razin's hatred of these papers knows no bounds. Even before his Moscow campaign begins, he dramatically rips up the tsar's decrees before the eyes of his own men and a detachment of royal musketeers (4:339–40). In both Tsaritsyn and Astrakhan' he orders all official documents to be gathered into a heap and burned (4:447, 493). In Astrakhan', this "trial of the papers" turns into a heathen celebration as Razin and his Cossacks are joined by townspeople forming an "ancient merry circle" of dancers around the bonfire, while the bells of the city ring out. "Apparently there lived—there burned—in the blood of these people vestiges of paganism: it was, of course, a holiday, the burning of the repulsive, hated, evil idol—the almighty document. The people rejoiced" (4:494). Unlike scenes in Zlobin's novel, where the burning of government documents is a class-conscious blow against the tsar and the boyars that signals the destruction of "the old life" and the end of the "untruths of the rich and powerful,"[27] Shukshin's document burning is an exercise in anarchic volition. It is an elemental celebration of pure Cossack *volia.*

The endless red tape (*volokita* [4:354, 358]), the tyranny of bureaucratic procedure, and the paper trail of decrees and instructions emanating from Moscow in the novel all point to Shukshin's own preoccupation with the faceless, powerful, and arbitrary bureaucracy of his own day. Indeed, two-thirds of the way through the novel, it is as if the tsar and his troops have all but been supplanted by the powerful *bumaga,* which, in the following passage, has become the main enemy bearing down on Razin and his men.

No, it was not in vain that Stepan Timofeich so fiercely hated bureaucratic documents: they had already stirred to life, and a ripe threat was even now gathering against him. There, on the Volga, you had to thunder, lop off heads, take cities, shed blood . . . Here, in Moscow, you had to skillfully and punctually make haste with documents, and a power would rise up that would go forth and overwhelm that force on the Volga. For Government by that time had already drawn mankind into its heavy, slow, hopeless cycle: the document, like a snake, had built up its paralyzing strength. Edicts. Decrees. Lists . . . O, how terrible they are! When those documents which Razin burned on the town square in Astrakhan' cried out, moaned, hissed oaths, and prayed for mercy, these Moscow documents rose up with a vengeance and got down to business coolly and efficiently. Nothing is as terrible in Rus' as Lord Document. He makes some people powerful, others weak and helpless. [. . .] God help you, Stepan! God grant you success and bless your warlike arts. With your saber, bring happiness, bring freedom [*voliu*] to the hapless, the beaten, the long-suffering. Give them liberty [*voliu*]! (4:514)

Here the intrusion into the text of the narrator's own voice further blurs the line between historical account and contemporary commentary.

As the novel moves toward its climax, the number of papers (letters, documents, and so on) flowing to and from Moscow increases dramatically. "They wrote to the great sovereign" (4:399) becomes "They wrote and wrote to Moscow" (4:511), and finally "documents traveled, poured, streamed to the tsar" (4:520). As the number of these documents and the speed with which they move increase, Razin's *volia*—and Cossack boundlessness—is diminished. When the anathema is read again in one of the closing episodes of the novel, we are reminded once more of the power of the document. Again the narrator's voice intrudes to say: "Here it is—here's the document for you!" (4:573). And when Razin's sentence is pronounced, his voice is heard one last time in the narration: "Here's where the document shows its full strength! Here's how it takes its vengeance!" (4:586).

It turns out that the biggest threat to Cossack freedom is not political, military, or ideological in nature but derives from the deeper implications of this opposition between *volia* and *bumaga*. As in many other works by Shukshin, bureaucracy is the surface manifestation of a deeper complacency, an avoidance of taking personal responsibility for one's actions, a shallow privileging of the material over the spiritual, and, as we read in the novel, "an ability to run to someone and complain and inform on people" (4:531). Bureaucracy breeds servility: people who live "in order to stuff their guts" and who "suffocate the living movement of the soul," as we learn in one passage toward the end of the novel (4:573). Here is where the Cossack myth meets metaphysics, where *volia* becomes a quest not only for physical and personal freedom but also for a higher, spiritual emancipation, a theme most prominently developed in two important passages.

When Razin criticizes his former comrade, Frol Minaev, for defecting from his movement, he first mentions the spiritual side of the quest for *volia* by pointing out how Frol is tied down to things of this world.

"I don't understand one thing, Frol: how's life so dear to you that you're saving it and pitying it like a new bride? That kind of a life is vile! . . . What are you so sorry to give up? Sleeping with women? Stuffing your face? Why are

179

you clinging on so? You were nothing before you were born, you'll be nothing when you die. But now that you've been born you're scared about croaking [. . .] You're not sorry to give your life for junk [that is, Cossack booty], but for *volia* you come up short." (4:431–32)

The two meet again as Razin is being taken to Moscow in chains. Frol asks the inevitable question: "So what's come of all this?"

"What's come of all this? I gave the people freedom [*voliu*]," Stepan said staunchly.
    "How's that?"
    "I gave the people freedom . . . Take it!"
    "But you're in chains! 'I gave them freedom!' . . ."
    "I did. You still don't get it?" (4:578)

Razin has in mind the larger ideal behind the Cossack ethos of a free, fully realized, uncompromised life. It is an inner, moral freedom, that of living for more than just this world or Cossack loot. It is, ultimately, a metaphysical freedom, one that reveals the kinship between Razin and Shukshin's idealistic oddballs, who also seek perfection in a compromised world. As Valentin Rasputin writes, in this passage "there can be no doubt that [Razin] is talking about spiritual freedom, about inner emancipation, about driving the slave out of oneself and realizing one's individuality."[28]

Cossack boundlessness in Shukshin's reading, as in the Cossack myth, is thus not to be understood in only the physical sense; by reinterpreting it in terms of *volia*, Shukshin elevates it to the philosophical and spiritual plane. The central place of *volia* in Shukshin's novel—announced on the title page and explicated in Razin's own quest for freedom—reasserts the ontological freedom and essential liminality of the Cossack ethos for post-Stalinist culture. In restoring the ideal of the "free and expansive, wild and energetic, uncompromised and unbounded" Cossack hero to Soviet literature, Shukshin is also proposing the Cossack myth as a viable narrative of opposition to constraint of any kind, whether physical, legal, or metaphysical, a narrative particularly relevant to the Soviet 1960s and 1970s. Moreover, the concept of *volia* helps Shukshin free Razin—and the Cossack myth—from the historical purposefulness of Socialist Realist depictions. Both here and elsewhere in his works, it serves as a strong affirmation of Shukshin's "drive towards the transcendental," which, as Hosking points out, "Marxism denied and Socialist Realism distorted."[29]

RAZIN, THE FOLK AESTHETIC, AND EPIC AFFINITIES

By this point it has become clear that *I Have Come to Give You Freedom* intertwines past and present in an unresolved but highly productive dialectic involving, on the one hand, seventeenth-century Russian history and twentieth-century Soviet reality, and, on the other hand, the Cossack myth and Shukshin's contemporary rereading of it. The effect is to blur the boundary between past and present, myth and history, fact and fiction, leading some commentators to see little difference between Shukshin's Razin and the modern-day heroes of the writer's short stories. Mikhail Geller writes, "Doubting, torn by contradictory thoughts, tormented by grief, drowning his grief in vodka, Shukshin's Stepan Razin presents a tragic and contemporary image."[30]

Shukshin was well aware of the distorting effect of the double lens he used on his material. Nor did he particularly try to conceal the very contemporary resonance of his interpretation of Razin. When Shukshin told one interviewer that "to understand the present you need to understand the past," he was not just repeating a truism; he was laying bare the essence of his work on Razin. "The film about people of the seventeenth century," he stated, "will be addressed to the people of the twentieth century. That's the whole formula."[31] Boris Eikhenbaum called this kind of approach "the science of double vision":

> History is, in effect, a science of complex analogies, a science of double vision: the facts of the past have meanings for us that differentiate them and place them, invariably and inevitably, in a system under the sign of contemporary problems. Thus one set of problems supplants another, one set of facts overshadows another. History in this sense is a special method of studying the present with the aid of the facts of the past.[32]

Obviously, this much may also be said of Chapygin and Zlobin, each of whose novels likewise view the Don Cossack through their own kind of "double vision." Thus we move from the "contrived atheistic and antitsarist attitudes" of Chapygin's Razin,[33] a portrayal written in the flush of revolutionary romanticism in the 1920s, to Zlobin's Stalin-era depiction of an overly class-conscious ataman who, in one critic's words, was "turned into an illustration for a [Soviet] history textbook."[34] Shukshin's representation of Razin, however, works its double vision through the lens of the author's own lyric "I"; his interpretation is intensely personal, more interesting and meaningful because its layers of artistic "distortion" and conjecture lead us to the writer's own personality and his creative program.

Shukshin's inclusion in the novel of his own autobiographical legend— the story of the *skomorokh* from the village of Shuksha—directly links his Cossack subject matter to his own artistic development.[35] It also affirms the importance of the folk aesthetic in Shukshin's own art while revealing the relevance of the folk imagination for Razin and his Cossacks. What is important, Shukshin emphasizes, is not that Razin should behave as he does in folk songs and legends but that the folk imagination should be seen as an integral component of his worldview. Shukshin makes this connection in the novel possible by emphasizing the peasant origins of not only much of the Cossack host but also of Razin himself. "I . . . brought closer together his kinship with the peasants, the muzhiks of the Voronezh region. I saw the possibility for doing so in some documents," he stated, adding that many of the Don and Volga Cossacks were historically runaway peasants.[36] Indeed, in *I Have Come to Give You Freedom* Shukshin calls Razin's Cossacks "yesterday's muzhiks" (4:309) and identifies central Russian cities as their original homelands (4:353).

Shukshin's emphasis on Razin's folk outlook and his liberal inclusion of inserted folk genres (from folk songs and sayings to folk charms and riddles) lend the novel an epic timelessness by conveying a sense of the Cossacks' mythic, cyclical life, thereby allowing Shukshin to transcend the very specific historical setting in which the novel is placed as well as elude the petrified clichés of Soviet historical interpretation. In fact, of all of Shukshin's works, *I Have Come to Give You Freedom* is the one most saturated with examples of folk culture, folk poetic devices, and folk satiric constructs, all of which lend the text the eternal quality of folk culture itself.

The power of folk genres is affirmed in the novel when Razin's Cossacks, like heroes out of Russian folk tales and *byliny* (oral epic poems), taunt their enemies with riddles designed to foretell their fate. One such riddle makes creative use of a list of body parts, deformed to look like the names of villages:

> I caught a little cow
> in a dark forest;
> I led the little cow
> through Lobeville [*Lobkovo*]
> through Browville [*Brovkovo*]
> through Eyeville [*Glazkovo*]
> through Noseville [*Noskovo*]
>
> . . . .
> through Chestville [*Grudkovo*]
> through Handville [*Ruchkovo*]
> through Shoulderville [*Plechikovo*];
> I led the little cow
> to Toenailville [*Nogotkovo*]
> and there I did
> the little cow in. (4:440–41)

The trail of the "little cow" obviously describes the path of the Cossack's saber through his enemy's body. In other places in the novel, folk tales are told (4:289–90, 385–86) and folk charms are reproduced with impressive authenticity (4:410–11).

In addition, folk songs or folk improvisations are sung on some eleven occasions in the novel.[37] The function of these songs in the text varies. They inspire restful contemplation (4:248–49), or aid the Cossacks' rhythm when they row their *strugi* (the boats, carrying fifteen to thirty men each, in which they carry out their raids on the Don, Volga, and Caspian Sea [4:252–53]). Folk songs are also sung to mourn fallen comrades (4:463, 521–22). Most of the inserted folk songs, however, are directly linked to and evocative of Cossack celebrations. Here, Shukshin follows Gogol''s example from his Cossack epic *Taras Bul'ba*, where he "unites the freedom and wildness of the Cossacks' dance, music, and drinking with the Cossacks themselves."[38]

After Razin's host makes its triumphant entrance into Astrakhan', they settle down to spend their booty, drink, and carouse. In this instance, the singing of folk songs is tied to the Cossacks' *moguchii zagul* (mighty drinking spree) and the elemental passions it releases (4:271). Later, Razin organizes a *zastolitsa* (bout of friendly drinking) that begins with a song about the death of a brave Cossack captain and is followed by several more rounds of drinking and singing (4:277–78). Razin purposefully works his men up into a state of extreme agitation, yet does not give the word for which the assembled host is waiting: to begin the dances. Finally, he rises up, flings his hat onto the ground, and shouts: "Have at it!" (4:279). The ensuing frenzy of song and dance simultaneously affirms the *volia* of elemental Cossack life and confirms the Cossacks' bond as men, for the spectacle is likened in military and sexual terms to "a lightning military strike" and "the reckless caresses of a woman" (2:279). As in a later passage (4:292), folk songs and heavy drinking are the two ways the Cossacks recharge their batteries, while at the same time affirming their unbounded natures.

One of the most interesting folk songs in the novel is the one Razin commissions from a traveling *skomorokh* who shows up in the Cossacks' camp. The song is at the center of one of the main episodes in the novel: the story of Astrakhan' governor Prozorovskii's sudden and obsessive desire to possess Razin's sable coat. Here the satiric qualities of the *skomorokh's* art—that of the gleeful inversion of hierarchies—lay bare the similar effects of Shukshin's use of folk constructs in his works. The vivid contrast between two opposite world orders—Cossack ethos versus government precepts—engendered by the *skomorokh's* art also reveals the power of the folk genres that are inherent in the daily lives of peasants and Cossacks and that constitute an important part of Shukshin's art. The incident with the fur coat has entered into the folklore surrounding Sten'ka Razin and was immortalized by Pushkin in the second of his "Pesni o Sten'ke Razine" ("Songs of Sten'ka Razin," 1826).[39] Its inclusion in Shukshin's novel thus endows his Cossacks with the aura of popular legend.

As part of his ploy to escape to the Don with the plunder and weapons from his raid on Persia intact, Razin showers the tsar's officials in Astrakhan'— its governor, Prozorovskii, in particular—with generous gifts, then retires to his camp outside the city to plan his withdrawal from the region before the government officials realize what he is doing. Prozorovskii catches on, however, and visits Razin to demand that he hand over his weapons and the loot he stole from government trade caravans as well as submit to a government registration of all of his men. These demands, of course, are anathema to the Cossack soul. For them, looting is a way of life, bureaucratic procedures are loathsome, and there is "no such thing as an unarmed Cossack" (4:306). Razin, a crafty manipulator of circumstances, decides to put Prozorovskii's demands to his men. Emerging from his conference tent with the *voevoda*, Razin sends word to have the entire Cossack host assembled. Sensing Razin's treachery, Prozorovskii warns him, "Ty skomoroshnichaesh', ataman" ("You're acting the part of the jester, ataman" [4:313]). The appearance of hundreds of angry Cossacks, however, soon convinces the governor to withdraw, but not before he repeatedly hints to Razin how much he would like to have Razin's sable coat for himself ("You'll just lose it drinking," he tells Razin [4:315]). Razin promises to send it.

That very evening, a procession of some three hundred Cossacks, with the sable coat on a cross at the head, winds its way through Astrakhan' to the accompaniment of an irreverent, bawdy song (spread over four pages of text) sung by the *skomorokh*. The song is about how the fur coat is "on its way to wed and bed" the *voevoda*. The Cossacks tell the delighted townspeople "Stepan Timofeich's fur coat is getting married. To the governor. It really caught his eye. He dropped to his knees, begged for it. So our *bat'ka* is giving her away. He's a good man, after all" (4:318). The governor, livid at the humiliation, sends his agents to lure the *skomorokh* and his companions away from the Cossacks. The *strel'tsy* (government musketeers) cut the *skomorokh*'s tongue out and kill one of Razin's men. When he learns of the deed, Razin sends a party of Cossacks to rescue the folk jester and to kill as many government troops as possible in the process. The rescue and the killings are Razin's first steps toward open revolt against Moscow.

While the spectacle surrounding the presentation of the coat is clearly meant to cast Razin in a favorable light in contrast to the corrupt and greedy government officials, Shukshin also reveals the powerful resonance of folk forms of art in his polemic with centralized authority. Prozorovskii threatens Razin with letters to Moscow (4:315); Razin counters with folk art. The outcome, however, is as foreboding as it is symbolic. In a literal sense, the *skomorokh* is mutilated to avenge the *voevoda*, but in a figurative sense, he stands for the artist deprived by the government of his right to pursue his art freely. For Shukshin, this is an especially important side to the story.

Later in the novel, Razin exacts personal revenge for the *skomorokh* by publicly executing the *voevoda* himself, but only after another "performance," this one deadly. After asking Prozorovskii how the fur coat is getting along, Razin forces the governor to wear it as he is tossed from a tower in full view of the townspeople: "They brought the fur coat. The same one the *voevoda* had bothered Stepan about. And Stepan wanted it to be the same one. The performance with the fur coat had to be finished in front of everyone—the last performance, and then, the end" (4:491). It is not just the *skomorokh* who is being avenged here; the *skomorokh*'s irreverent folk art is also being vindicated through the spectacle of the governor's execution. It, too, is a means toward achieving *volia*. Indeed, Razin himself had previously indulged in skomorokhian carnival earlier in the novel, when he put on a performance for his men in which his veteran lieutenant, Styr', playing the role of the tsar, wound up astride Razin, who as a Don stallion took him in search of *volia* (4:435–38). The scene recalls a similar instance of carnival discrowning in a prior episode, where two of Razin's officers lampoon royal arbitrariness (4:416–18).

Yet, for all of the novel's dependence on folk genres, Shukshin's Razin, paradoxically, is *not* a folk hero. With the exception of Razin's drowning of the Persian princess (Shukshin's incorporation into his novel of the famous episode in the ballad he had loved since childhood), Shukshin rejects the image of the ataman popularized in Russian folklore.[40] While he renews and restores the Cossack myth and endows his Cossack heroes with epic qualities, Shukshin divests Razin himself of his mythic aura. Why? To answer that question, we must return to the problem of the novel's double vision and its implied critique of contemporary Soviet reality.

RAZIN'S FATE AND RUSSIA'S

Unlike the way the Cossack Razin was typically portrayed in Russian folk songs and legends, Shukshin's hero is a flawed, contradictory, more believable, and more interesting character. He is a hero with whom Shukshin's contemporary readers could sympathize: someone chafing against the constraints of an autocratic authority who must make difficult decisions and compromise his beliefs. Shukshin even confessed that Razin was "dearer" to him precisely as a "compromised figure."[41] To that end, his Razin is marked on the one hand by his "morbid conscientiousness and ability to feel another's suffering"[42] and on the other by a ruthless, violent megalomania. He is both a betrayer in abandoning his peasant army during his defeat at Simbirsk[43] and a victim of betrayal at the hands of his fellow Cossacks, who have sold out to Moscow. He is a coward (when he begs a former trusted lieutenant to help him escape while being taken in chains to Moscow) and a hero (enduring torture and quartering without complaint). Yet this flawed and compromised figure allows Shukshin to propose a new reading of both the epic and the historical ataman, one whose message is most relevant to Shukshin's contemporaries. His interpretation of Razin also helps to explain the rather marginal role in the novel played by the peasantry, whose cause Razin is supposedly championing. As it turns out, in

Shukshin's novel Razin's revolution has little to do with Russian history or class revolt.

The only peasant who gets to speak is Matvei Ivanov, Razin's wise peasant advisor, a figure many critics found unrealistic. Ivanov serves two functions. First, he gives voice to the plight of the peasants and their helplessness to do anything about it. As Matvei reminds Razin, "You Cossacks live a privileged life. The estate owners don't bend your backs, don't tan your hide, don't take your wives and daughters from their beds at night for their own enjoyment. [. . . But y]ou can knock our muzhik forty times upside the head before he'll stir (the devil take him!), before he'll run and break himself off a picket" (4:419). Razin's refusal to march on Moscow by way of the Don and the central Russian towns and villages heavily populated by peasants (where, as Matvei assures him, he could pick up many adherents [4:420]); his selfish abandonment of the peasants at Simbirsk; and his refusal to return to the Volga after that defeat to support the independent, popular peasant revolts that sprang up in the wake of his withdrawal to the Don—all doom the peasants to defeat and harsh reprisals. It is Matvei's function in *I Have Come to Give You Freedom* to articulate these aspects of the drama.

But Matvei serves another important purpose in Shukshin's novel. By endowing Matvei rather than Razin with historical prescience, Shukshin avoids the trap into which Chapygin and especially Zlobin fell: his Razin, unlike that of his predecessors, is free of any political or historical "purposefulness" prescribed by the demands of revolutionary romanticism or Socialist Realism. If Matvei is a prophetic, righteous representative of the interests of the peasantry who comes close to endowing Razin's movement with an ideology uncomfortably similar to that prescribed later for the ataman by Soviet historians, then Shukshin brusquely rejects that ideology by having Lar'ka Timofeev, Razin's most loyal Cossack lieutenant, lure the peasant advisor away and brutally murder him (4:558–59). When Razin learns what has happened, he nevertheless pushes on with his own Cossack agenda, for, after Simbirsk, he considers the peasants to be "a stone around the neck" of his Cossack host (4:562).

Unlike Zlobin, who privileges "peasant truth" over "Cossack truth,"[44] Shukshin rejects peasant truth in favor of the Cossack myth. In doing so, however, he is not betraying his own peasant heritage or the leitmotif of his art.[45] On the contrary, he is liberating the history of the peasantry from Soviet dogma by favoring the ideal of ultimate individual freedom, personified in Razin and the Cossack ethos, over the ideology of class struggle. The "Russian muzhik in search of freedom," whom Geller claims as Shukshin's hero,[46] must first liberate himself from the slave within. Revolution is meaningless as a mass manifestation; such revolutionaries turn into bureaucrats.[47] This is Shukshin's message to his contemporaries, and it is a heretical indictment of Soviet historical dogma. Razin thus becomes much more than an epic folk hero or ideological standard bearer: he becomes a flawed but compelling incarnation of an individual's search for inner freedom, for liberation from falsehood, complacency, and compromise.

Accordingly, Shukshin's Razin chooses not to rally again to the peasant cause, but instead rides fruitlessly around the Don region, trying desperately to attract another Cossack host to ride once more against Moscow in the cause of *volia*, this time outside of any peasant agenda. What he encounters, however, is *volia*-killing complacency—Cossacks who refuse to rise against the tsar because, as one Cossack puts it, "he feeds me and dresses me" (4:563). When Kornei Iakovlev and his host loyal to the tsar take over Razin's home base, Kalagal'nik, Razin understands that the end is near. But he chooses not to flee to Siberia. Instead, he rides to Kalagal'nik to die "poliudski" ("like a human being"), meaning like a real Cossack (4:567). Any other death is repugnant to Razin.

Shukshin is careful, however, not to idealize Razin's last days. In pointed contrast to Razin's idealistic attempts to rally a second host, Shukshin includes a scene after Razin is captured in which he suddenly begs his traitorous former lieutenant to cut his chains.

". . . Cut them, Frol, we'll fly away, they'll never find us again. [. . .] Frol, my friend," Stepan kept looking at Frol, and wept. The devil only knows what kind of weak moment had seized him, but he wept. Light drops fell from his lashes onto his cheeks, his beard, and from his beard they trembled and dropped. "I'll never forget it. Are those Moscow boyars really dearer to you? We'll leave . . . We'll go wherever you like. We'll have a big host again!" (4:578)

This passage, coming significantly after Razin delivers his speech to Frol about how he gave the people *volia,* at once reveals Razin's human weakness and his Cossack nature, his desire to ride again as a free warrior. More important, it replaces an overtly ideological speech in the *Sibirskie ogni* version in which Razin proudly tells Frol not to pity him because people would later understand what Razin had truly given the people, what idea he had sown in people's minds: "You can't put *that* notion [of *volia*] in chains, the one I've carried with me. You can't cut *its* head off, brother."[48] Shukshin apparently, and correctly, sensed that this speech smacked too much of the dead ideology weighing down previous Razin novels, the kind of ideology against which he was writing his version in the first place. His revision—as does the bulk of his depiction of Razin—favors the flawed, contradictory Cossack over the prescient revolutionary hero.

As the end draws near, Razin offers his brother, Frol Razin (who also has been arrested and taken to Moscow), a final Cossack consolation: "Endure, brother! [. . .] We had a good romp, now we have to put up with it"

(4:582). Razin suffers all of the torments of the tsar's torturers and undergoes "the execution of the wicked"—quartering and beheading—without uttering a sound (true to historical accounts).[49] His brother, on the other hand, betrays Razin at the last moment by crying out, "Gosudarevo slovo i delo!" ("The Sovereign's word and deed!" [4:588]), an official phrase designating that the condemned wished to put off the execution to divulge important information.[50] Even though Razin's moment of *volia* is thus tainted and in so telling a fashion—by a bureaucratic maneuver of none other than his own brother and fellow Cossack—his final moments are not in vain. The assembled crowd of common folk is silent as they listen to his sentence ("Slushal narod moskovskii. Molchal" [4:587]), just as their descendants are quiet when they listen to the anathema against Razin repeated each year by the Church. And as Shukshin states at the beginning of the novel, "If you tried to understand looking at them there whether it was pain and horror or hidden pride and sympathy for him who 'disdained his mortal hour' you couldn't tell for sure. They were quiet" (4:236). Hence the common folk's inscrutable attitude toward the rebel figure—one of fear as well as pride.

As for the Cossack host, Shukshin paints a different picture. They ultimately carry no "seeds of revolt" within them whatsoever, a departure from typical Soviet depictions. Quite the contrary. In *I Have Come to Give You Freedom,* Shukshin shows how the Cossacks' complacency has led to the loss of their Cossack independence, how they have sold out to central authority. In doing so, Shukshin sounds a strong warning to his contemporaries about the insidious power of bureaucracy and self-satisfied materialism, the unlikely vanquishers of the wild Cossack breed and the ultimate destroyer of the Cossack ethos. It is irrelevant that in the novel, as in history, it is the tsar to whom the Cossack host has sold its freedom. Shukshin's double lens allows for a contemporary interpretation of central authority as well.

Shukshin's novel, then, is at once a personal interpretation of a historical figure and a contemporary critique of Soviet Russian society. His rereading of the Cossack myth in terms of Razin's search for *volia* indicates that the Cossack myth in Russian culture survives well into the present day as an ideal of an unbounded, uncompromised life—the kind of life Shukshin doubtless craved for himself. As an artist, Shukshin also saw in Razin a potent symbol of artistic independence, as irreverent and subversive as the satiric folk constructs at the base of the *skomorokh*'s art so prominently featured in the novel. As we have seen, however, Shukshin's ultimate conclusions are ambiguous, for while Razin is associated with the ideal of *volia*, he also represents the reality of betrayal and compromise. In the end, Shukshin's Razin seems to embody the paradox that inheres in the search for *volia* in *any* society, what Joseph Brodsky calls the "disheartening idea that a freed man is not a free man, that liberation is just the means of attaining freedom and is not synonymous with it."[51] Shukshin—and his Sten'ka Razin—understood this truth, even as they both attempted nevertheless to communicate their ideal of *volia* to a public unable or unwilling to heed them.

Shukshin's friends and critics often testify that the artist behaved "like Razin" in real life. According to V. Fomin, Shukshin "not only thought 'like Razin,' but in both his own life and his art often behaved 'like Razin.' . . . With the same frenzied bitterness, absolutely not sparing himself or thinking about the consequences, he fought, through his art, anything that threatened or could threaten the moral health of the common folk."[52] Writing shortly after Shukshin's death, Fomin overstates the connection between the two. Razin, after all, was a true rebel who carried out a bloody rebellion and paid the ultimate price; Shukshin was not. Still, there is some evidence that Shukshin the actor did sometimes wear the masks of his characters in real life, including that of Razin. Egor Prokudin, for instance, personified issues of such private importance to Shukshin that during the shooting of *Kalina krasnaia* he continued to wear the Prokudin costume and act "in character" even after the cameras stopped rolling.[53]

One interesting example of Shukshin's donning of a Razin mask can be found in a letter Shukshin wrote to Gleb Goryshin, an editor of the journal *Avrora*. According to Goryshin, Shukshin would sometimes recommend new writers to him: "Having discovered in this or that manuscript the signs of talent, a faithfulness to life, and, the main thing, the writer's impertinence [*derzost'*], his difference from others, [Shukshin] would get all excited, and write recommendation letters." In one such letter, Shukshin asks Goryshin to excuse him for sending a copy of a writer's manuscript that had been sent to other journals: "Time can't wait. I took the responsibility on myself before the author and before you—I want to 'outgallop' the 'fat' Moscow boyars."[54] The boyars Shukshin had in mind are, of course, the editors of the "thick" (*tolstye*, the word also means fat, hence Shukshin's pun in his letter) Moscow literary journals, the "rivals" of Goryshin's Leningrad magazine.

Goryshin's response to Shukshin's Razin-inspired analogy is interesting. As if reassuring an alarmed tsarist readership about the tone of Shukshin's language, Goryshin feels compelled to soften Shukshin's pronouncement about "'fat' Moscow boyars." In doing so, he brings up a central polemic of the artist's life: the question of whether he was a country boy or a Muscovite, a Siberian Neanderthal or an urban *intelligent*. Goryshin wastes no time in claiming Shukshin for the capital. "It goes without saying," he writes, "that Vasilii Shukshin in no way intended to humiliate the Moscow literary journals just because they were *Moscow* journals. After all, he himself had become a Muscovite in the highest degree, and was a bearer of the capital's mark of quality."[55]

Not all of Shukshin's Moscow friends agreed. The actor Georgii Burkov,[56] for instance, argues the opposite point: "Vasilii Makarovich never considered himself to be a Muscovite. It pained him that Moscow, and other large cities, lured people away from the countryside and bled the villages dry."[57] Originating in the polemics that erupted over the city/country theme in Soviet literature in the 1960s, this debate about Shukshin's "identity crisis" was never resolved, either by the artist himself or in critical assessments of him.

The image of Razin in Shukshin's novel, however, suggests its own clarification of the writer's professional and personal identity. Shukshin, perhaps, is neither a country rube nor a member of the cultural elite. Rather, he, like Razin, is a transgressor, a trespasser striving to cross cultural and social boundaries. Such is Goryshin's implication when he likens Shukshin to the "troublemaker" Sten'ka Razin. In his justification of the writer's desire to tweak the noses of the Moscow "literary boyars," Goryshin writes: "Shukshin, too, wanted at times to 'outgallop' these 'fat Moscow boyars.' That is, he wanted to play—unconsciously, instinctively. He was one of the great actors of our time, and played in his creative imagination one after another of the most varied roles, trying out the 'pros' and 'cons,'" which enabled him to see more clearly the "negative sides of the capital's literary and peripheral literary environment."[58]

Shukshin's swipe at the "Moscow literary boyars" betrays the artist's own *derzost'*, the same impertinence that Goryshin claims was the "main thing" Shukshin valued in the writers whom he helped to get published. It was this *derzost'* that served Shukshin so well during his VGIK entrance exams and that later drove his program as an artist. It was also a conspicuous quality of the central hero of his creative life, Stepan Razin. Indeed, it comes as no surprise that Shukshin wrote into Razin's character and Razin's cause not only his own *derzost'* but many other of his concerns as an artist, too. When Shukshin told friends, "Sten'ka's my whole life,"[59] he was but announcing this important connection between the issues of his art and those of his biography.

The Shukshin Legend Revisited

> It's not old age by itself that is worthy of respect,
> but a life fully lived. If there was one.
> —Vasilii Shukshin, from a working note

VASILII SHUKSHIN'S SUDDEN DEATH in 1974 at age forty-five was followed by an outcry of national grief. His funeral was a huge public event, attracting thousands of mourners. Within a month, some 160,000 letters poured in to television studios, the Committee for Cinematography, the editorial offices of newspapers and journals, and the writer's apartment.[1] The ensuing "Shukshin boom" included memoir literature, nostalgic critical reviews, and tributes by poets like Andrei Voznesenskii, Evgenii Evtushenko, and Vladimir Vysotskii.[2] Author and critic Gleb Goryshin quipped that "after the death of the author [. . .] the only people who did not write about Shukshin were those too lazy to write at all."[3]

Within two years of the writer's death, annual "Shukshin readings" were inaugurated in the writer's home village of Srostki in the Altai region commemorating his July birthdate. Within four years the first museum dedicated to his life and works was opened in the Srostki home Shukshin bought his mother with the royalties from his first novel. It was the first such museum to be erected so soon after the death of a Soviet cultural figure, and it attracts thousands of visitors each year.

Partly because of the immense popularity of his final film and partly because that success never led to any openly rebellious posture on Shukshin's part, the Soviet government found no reason to temper the meteoric posthumous rise in Shukshin's fame and stature. On the contrary, there was every incentive to claim the writer for the Soviet literary establishment and to capitalize on his popularity. Mikhail Geller notes the large print runs of posthumous publications of the writer's works—200,000 copies of a two-volume collection, 300,000 copies of a one-volume anthology, the dedication of two issues of *Roman-gazeta* (editions of two million each) to his stories, all within a year of the writer's death—as one sign of "the interest the leaders of Soviet culture had in the work of Vasilii Shukshin."[4]

This interest also helps explain why the annual "Shukshin readings" and the opening of the Shukshin museum in Srostki followed so soon after the writer's death. As John Dunlop argues, "Shukshin was allowed to become a cult figure after his death. This could not have occurred unless this gifted writer, actor and film producer had enjoyed powerful support in the highest ranks of the Party."[5] The idea, perhaps, was to put any controversial aspects of Shukshin's fiction and film into an acceptable context. Andrei Tarkovsky explains the situation in the following way: "It seems to me that he was somehow feared, that they expected something dangerous or explosive from him. And so when he died, everyone began to thank him for the fact that the explosion never took place."[6]

Not only did that explosion never occur, but, in the years following his death, Shukshin was turned into something of a Soviet classic. It was not difficult for the Soviet cultural establishment to appropriate Shukshin's works, for rarely in his prose do we bump up against what Carl and Ellendea Proffer call the "unmentionable backdrop" of "totalitarian society cut off from the larger world by the Russian Great Wall," an outcome that makes Shukshin, in their assessment, "one of the best and truest practitioners of Socialist Realism."[7] Although this assertion is overstated—Shukshin's fiction and films, as we have seen, were clearly not conformist works infused with Party ideology—his art, with few exceptions, did not stray far from what was thematically and stylistically possible at the time.

Still, there was an independent and truthful air about Shukshin, detectable in his stories and most apparent in his publicistic writing, which was collected and published posthumously in 1981 and which, according to Igor' Zotov, "had the sweet aftertaste of opposition."[8] In that volume we find the following passage from an essay Shukshin wrote at the midpoint of his creative career:

> A sober and reasonable man, of course, always and everywhere ultimately understands his time and knows the truth, and if circumstances are such that it is better for the time being to be silent about it (the truth), then he is silent. An intelligent and talented man will somehow find a way to reveal the truth, be it through a hint or through half-uttered words, otherwise [the truth] will torment him, otherwise it will seem to him that his life will pass in vain. A genius will rain down all of the truth with lightning and thunder upon the heads and souls of people. The circumstances might kill him but he will accomplish his task. As for a man who is simply talented, he will precisely reflect his time (in song, in his actions, in his longing, in a novel), perhaps himself not understanding it, but he will open the eyes of the thinking and the intelligent.[9]

Shukshin gives no indication which of these positions is closest to his own, but the acknowledgment that the truth is something that the artist reveals at his own peril is an obvious enough indictment of the constraints imposed on art in a totalitarian state.

In the last few years of his life, Shukshin often spoke of himself as an encoded writer. In conversations with his friend and fellow actor Georgii

Burkov, Shukshin would talk of finally "deciphering" himself. According to Burkov, Shukshin "had arrived at the conclusion that there comes a time in the life of any creative person when you are simply obligated to reveal yourself completely, 'to decode yourself' and tell about everything that you love and hate, loudly and clearly, without beating around the bush, and even to await proudly future attacks and accusations."[10] If Burkov is to be believed, it would seem that Shukshin was preparing to confront once and for all the conflicting sides of his personality, where the son of an enemy of the people cohabited with the rank-and-file Communist Party member and the country hick bumped up against the Moscow artist.

Burkov hints that Shukshin planned to accomplish his decoding through the Razin movie and through the role of Razin himself. If true, the "secret warrior" and the "undecoded other" whom Shukshin once confessed he kept buried secretly in his consciousness all of his life would thus turn out to be Sten'ka Razin, whose quest for *volia* would also match Shukshin's quest for the ultimate reconciliation of his private conflicts.[11] Burkov wrote in 1983 that Shukshin planned to put more of himself into the Razin film than into any of his previous films. In moments of anxiety over the film, Shukshin would repeatedly ask the actor: "Are you capable of completely decoding yourself?" According to Burkov, "decoding" was Shukshin's favorite word.[12]

We can only speculate about the extent to which Shukshin actually would have "decoded" himself in his Razin film and how that might have changed the movie and its reception. In the wake of the success of *Kalina krasnaia*, much was expected of Shukshin. Andrei Tarkovsky was known to have remarked that once the Razin movie was finished, Shukshin "would be our number one director."[13] Although Shukshin was unable to complete the film, the script and the novel have nevertheless contributed in an important way to the writer's legacy. This is an outcome confirmed in articles written on the sixtieth jubilee of Shukshin's birth in 1989. As the image of Egor Prokudin receded in the public's memory over the fifteen years since Shukshin's death, the writer's beloved Sten'ka Razin was increasingly viewed as a more important artistic and biographical emblem for Shukshin.

This result initially had much to do with the politics of the early glasnost period of national and cultural reevaluation. The occurrence of Shukshin's sixtieth jubilee during this period proved to be a case of fateful coincidence. At a time when heated political and literary debates were being waged in journals and newspapers among liberals, Slavophiles, Russophiles, nationalists, neo-Stalinists, and others, Shukshin's anniversary presented an opportunity to inject the artist's name and works into the polemics. The major outcome of this reawakened interest in Shukshin, however, was that scholars, critics, and the public at large all exhibited a renewed curiosity about Sten'ka Razin, the rebel whose life had had such resonance for Shukshin.

Rebels, of course, are especially significant during "revolutionary" times, hence the appeal of Shukshin's Razin at the height of the political storms caused by Mikhail Gorbachev's policies of glasnost and perestroika. The nationalist writer and critic Genrikh Mitin spoke in 1989 of the failures of Gorbachev's perestroika and of a "nostalgia for a revolution 'from below,'" identifying Shukshin's Razin as the true "hero of our time," someone capable of "rising up against stagnation."[14] An anniversary article on Shukshin printed in *Iskusstvo kino* that year also concentrated on Razin, relating Shukshin's attempt to finalize an agreement for the film.[15] Shukshin's novel about Razin even made the list of the hundred best books of 1989—fourteen years after its initial publication—according to a reader's poll conducted by the publishing industry's weekly paper, *Knizhnoe obozrenie.*[16] Two newspapers—*Izvestiia* and *Sovetskaia Rossiia*—went so far in their glasnost-inspired rereadings of the artist as to call 1989 "the year of Shukshin."[17]

The rise in Russian nationalist sentiment that began in the late 1960s and that exploded onto the cultural scene in the mid-1980s also affected how Shukshin was reread at this time. Some writers and critics routinely invoked Shukshin's name as a symbol of specifically Russian national culture at a time when the influence of Western culture was at an unprecedented high.[18] A more troubling appropriation of Shukshin's name in the cause of Greater Russian nationalism can be glimpsed in the founding by Georgii Burkov and others of the V. M. Shukshin Center of Russian Art and Culture (Russkii tsentr iskusstva i kul'tury imeni V. M. Shukshina) in 1989. According to Burkov—himself rumored to have been a member of the ultranationalist group Pamiat'—the center's goal is "the rebirth of the culture of our vast Fatherland and the transmittal to the entire world of its values, produced over the centuries, in order to make them the property of our common world culture."[19]

This was not the first time the writer's name had been linked to the nationalist cause. In his 1979 monograph on postwar Soviet culture, Grigorii Svirski accused Shukshin of associating with anti-Semitic "pseudo-Slavophiles" from the Rodina (Motherland) group, which he claims was a "front for the KGB."[20] Svirski offers no proof for his allegation, but Shukshin's case is not helped when we realize that three of his closest friends at the end of his life—Georgii Burkov, Vasilii Belov, and his main cameraman, Anatolii Zabolotskii—were all suspected or avowed Russian ultranationalists. I have already mentioned Burkov's alleged links to Pamiat'. Belov, on the other hand, was a longtime personal friend who gained notoriety during glasnost as a vehement anti-Semite and xenophobe for his novel *Everything Lies Ahead* (*Vse vperedi*, 1986) and for his public pronouncements about the state of Soviet society. As for Zabolotskii, his 1993 reminiscences make Shukshin out to be a defender of the Russian character from the forces—mainly Soviet—bent on destroying it. He also claims that Shukshin had read—and accepted as true—Sergei Nilus's Russian edition of the infamous *Protocols of the Elders of Zion,* a document purporting to outline a secret Jewish conspiracy to take over the world.[21]

Shukshin's death a decade before glasnost—when he might have clarified his own position on these issues—prevents us from drawing any definitive conclusions. Though there is little in his films, fiction, or publicistic writings that betrays the virulent nationalism latent in Vasilii Belov or alleged by Svirski or Zabolotskii, Shukshin's premature death may nevertheless have saved his reputation from a later "decoding" that might have revealed an altogether less attractive picture of the artist. Some claim that a less appealing side to Shukshin's personality is already to be found in stories such as "Regards to Gray Hairs!" "Friends for Fun and Games," and the novella *Till the Cock Crows Thrice,* where the writer takes swipes at the pernicious effects of Western popular culture on Soviet youth. For the most part, however, in these and other works, Shukshin singles out fad, fashion, and materialism for criticism rather than Western culture as a whole. (In *Pechki-lavochki,* Shukshin takes the urban collectors of antique samovars and icons to task for much the same reason.) Where Russian culture is under threat elsewhere in his works, it is invariably Soviet ideology that appears to be the culprit, as in *The Liubavin Family* novels and the stories "On Sunday an Old Mother" ("V voskresen'e mat'-starukha," 1967), "The Master," and "Tough Guy." Still, there can be no ironclad guarantee that, despite its absence in his fiction and films, Shukshin might not have eventually revealed a stronger strain of nationalism had he lived longer.

One glimpse of a possible nationalist "decoding" came at a dinner hosted by Mikhail Sholokhov for the cast of Bondarchuk's film *They Fought for Their Motherland,* where Shukshin spoke out against the toll Soviet hegemony had taken on Russia. "We've let our nation go," Shukshin stated. "Now we have a difficult task ahead—to gather it together. To gather a nation together again is much more complicated than to let it go."[22] Here Shukshin comes as close as he ever would to betraying an allegiance to a Greater Russian agenda. In the end, however, it is impossible to predict whether Shukshin's nationalist sentiment was aimed solely at the Soviet dominance of Russian culture or whether it would have turned into the kind of intolerant Russian chauvinism his friend Belov would later espouse during glasnost and afterward.

With few exceptions, most commentators agree that it is hard to find in Shukshin's works the kind of hatred for the city, idealization of the countryside, or anti-intellectual stance in which the worst strains of Russian nationalism thrive. Viktor Nekrasov offers the following insight:

Many people considered him a *pochvennik* [native-soil conservative], a Russophile, and an anti-intellectual. They suspected him of the most terrible sin—anti-Semitism. But no, nothing of this sort was in him. There was love for the village, for its way of life, and its patriarchy. He considered himself to be something of a traitor, a betrayer, for supposedly trading the village for the city. And he castigated himself over it. And eventually made the city his home.[23]

This last point is important. Having made it in the capital, Shukshin could never really turn back. For one thing, Moscow had changed him. "I could hardly have become a writer if it weren't for Moscow or VGIK," he once told an interviewer.[24] His life in Moscow and his work in the cinema expanded his personal and professional horizons, exposing him to a wide variety of people and ideas. He moved in broad and varied circles, and this helped broaden the artist's worldview more than is generally acknowledged. At the same time, Shukshin was fiercely independent and, as Dunlop notes, "indifferent, even hostile to ideology."[25] Evgenii Evtushenko neatly captured the essence of the writer's personality when he said, "[T]his was a blunt man but at the same time a man free of any kind of group mentality when it comes to literature."[26] Significantly, Evtushenko made this remark at a meeting at the Central House of Writers three years after the artist's death in which he defended Shukshin's reputation from those trying to use his name as an ideological weapon.

In outlook and intellectual interests, Shukshin was most at home in the city and even confessed on several occasions that he would not be able to live again in the village. "I fear the provinces," he wrote in a letter to Belov. "Personally, I'd take to drink there."[27] This, of course, led to intense feelings of guilt, but these guilt feelings did not translate into any submerged nationalist resentment over the irretrievable loss suffered by rural Russia, for Shukshin never saw preserving village life as the solution to Russia's problems. Despite the significance of the provincial setting to his artistic program and despite his vow to abandon the cinema and move back to Srostki, it is unlikely that Shukshin would ever really have given up his life in Moscow or the pleasures and rewards of movie-making. After all, Shukshin knew that much of his appeal and visibility came from his movie career. Moreover, moving back to Siberia would essentially have unraveled the legend the artist had obviously cultivated and would have tainted the "success story" he had come to embody, for it would have been seen as a retreat from the demands and price of the fame for which he so ardently longed. "My salvation is in fame," he once wrote to his sister. "I'm stubbornly striving after it. And I'll get it if I don't die first."[28] As it turned out, Shukshin died with both his fame and his legend intact.

In the years since 1974, the Shukshin legend has been read in diverse and at times diametrically opposed ways. It has been understood as a triumph of natural or "folk" talent over the cultural constraints of the Brezhnev era and as the victory of an anti-intellectual and rural bigot. Viktor Gorn represents the first approach:

The cultured world will always have a need for the man "in tarpaulin boots," the man who returns to words and deeds their original meaning. This man somehow contrives a way not to accept the "rules of the game" that were established before his time. He attentively listens, willingly agrees that he's a "homespun hick," a "country bumpkin," that he's not against learning a little sense, but deep down he hides the sneer of the "undeciphered" warrior.[29]

A samizdat obituary attributed to the writer Fridrikh Gorenshtein offers a radically different interpretation:

> So what did this prematurely deceased idol represent? He had the worst features of the Altai provincial—which he brought with him and retained—mixed with the worst features of the Moscow intellectual inculcated by his foster fathers [in the capital]. . . . He had an inborn lack of culture and a hatred for culture in general, along with the Siberian peasant cunning of a Rasputin and the pathological hatred of everything different from him, which accordingly led him to an unusually extreme anti-Semitism.[30]

Both of these interpretations suffer from their own excesses and distortions, so I would like to offer a third reading, one in a sense suggested by Shukshin himself. In many ways, Shukshin's legend and his life echo those of the American writer Jack London, whose semiautobiographical *Martin Eden* (1909) was a favorite book from Shukshin's youth. The novel, which for years has appealed to aspiring writers, tells the story of how low-born and poorly educated Martin Eden becomes an acclaimed writer through sheer effort and determination. A strong-willed, "natural" talent from the common folk who moves into the cultured circles of society only to ultimately reject that establishment, he embodied many aspects of Shukshin's own life.

Shukshin often mentioned London's novel to friends and acquaintances. Navy buddies from Shukshin's days as a sailor remember his great love for the book.[31] Director Aleksandr Mitta claims Shukshin brought up *Martin Eden* during his interview with Romm while trying to matriculate to VGIK.[32] Writer Leonid Chikin reports that when he met Shukshin in 1959, he spoke only of London's works when he spoke of literature.[33] Ignatii Ponomarev recalls discussing *Martin Eden* with Shukshin in the 1960s.[34] Iurii Skop quotes the writer as hoping "a Jack London will be born in Siberia,"[35] an event Nikolai Zadornov, in a review of Shukshin's collection *Tam, vdali*, claims has already happened in the person of Shukshin himself.[36] Shukshin mentions *Martin Eden* as late as 1974, calling the book's hero a "person of incredible volition" and comparing his suicide with the murder/suicide of Egor Prokudin from his own movie *Kalina krasnaia*.[37]

It is easy to understand why Martin Eden was such an attractive figure for Shukshin. Like Martin Eden—and like Jack London himself—Shukshin was a self-educated latecomer to the world of art who suffered from the excesses of his own merciless drive to prove his talents and to succeed against his better-educated, more highly cultured rivals. Indeed, Paul Watkins's analysis of London is equally applicable to Shukshin: "London, like all people driven by their creativity to the point of self-destruction, was struggling to overcome the tragedies and injustices experienced in his youth. He sought to earn with his writing the social credibility he lacked and to reinvent the birthright he so desperately craved."[38] Such was Shukshin's struggle; also like Jack London and his Martin Eden, Shukshin died a relatively young man while in the middle of that struggle.

In an episode almost straight out of *Martin Eden,* Viktor Nekrasov reports a meeting with Shukshin in the late 1960s during which Shukshin complained that he had no one to talk to. Having quit drinking, he could no longer slip into the dingy beer halls he used to frequent, where he found inspiration for his stories and renewed his sense of kinship with the class from which he himself sprang. No one would talk to a sober person in such a place; indeed, such a person might even be taken for an informer. But talking to the likes of Sergei Gerasimov—the cream of the Soviet cultural establishment—did not appeal to him either.[39] Like Martin Eden, he missed the rough crowd of his younger days to which he could not return and yet felt like an outsider in the social circles opened up to him by his cultural success. This in-betweenness is, of course, the leitmotif of his art, and although it did not kill the artist the way success killed Martin Eden and Jack London, its explication became Shukshin's abiding contribution to Soviet culture. As one critic notes, Shukshin's central problem was that of "adaptation":

> How can a person live in this world who is unable or unwilling to adapt himself to it, whether this be the change from a rural way of life to that of the city, the pressure of scientific and technological progress, the temptation of consumerism, or the measured monotony of an existence without the spiritual.[40]

Indeed, the theme of marginality, which dominates the film and fiction of post-Soviet Russia, was significantly influenced by Shukshin in the years following the Thaw. He gave voice to an important stratum of Soviet society and embodied their sense of dislocation and protest. To understand Shukshin—his life and his work—is to understand the millions of disaffected and rootless people who only yesterday were peasants but who migrated to the cities in search of a better lot in life.

Andrei Siniavskii once stated, "Deep in his gut, the writer longs not for freedom, but for *liberation,* as someone who understands that mechanism once said. The very act of writing is a liberation . . . The point is to open a valve, and for that to be done the valve must first of all be pretty firmly shut."[41] Shukshin, who in a similar way sought *volia* (liberation) and not *svoboda* (freedom), might have appreciated Siniavskii's paradoxical statement.

His life was bound up not so much with achieving *svoboda*—he was clearly no dissident—but with finding *volia*, that release from constraint that goes beyond political interpretations and enters into the realm of the philosophical, the spiritual, and the psychological. Here is where we can locate the attractions of his art for the Soviet public of his day. He opened a valve, and it released a lot of built-up pressure.

His village eccentrics, urban grotesques, misfits, the recidivist-thief Egor Prokudin, the Don Cossack Sten'ka Razin taken together comprise the composite hero Shukshin proposed for his times, at once a rebellious fool and a foolish rebel. This hero was comic and tragic and, like his creator, was stranded between the city and the country, stagnation and thaw, constraint and freedom. His search for *volia* reflected the quest of the last generation of Soviet peasants, a lost generation whose physical and metaphysical transience Shukshin captured in stories and films that were as popular as they are important for understanding the shape of Soviet Russian culture after Stalin.

Notes

PREFACE

1. Kathleen Parthé, *Russian Village Prose: The Radiant Past* (Princeton, N.J.: Princeton University Press, 1992), ix–x.
2. This is Dora Shturman's term. See her "Kem byl Iurii Trifonov: chem otlichaetsia pisatel' sovestkoi epokhi ot sovetskogo pisatelia," *Literaturnaia gazeta*, 22 October 1997.
3. Evgenii Sidorov, "The Short Story Today," *Soviet Literature* 6 (1986): 4.
4. In a *Nezavisimaia gazeta* poll about the best and worst television programs and the "most outstanding television personality" for the week of May 27 to June 3, 1998, three of the eleven respondents named *Kalina krasnaia* (which aired May 31) the best movie, while one designated Shukshin as the week's "outstanding personality." See "Ia russkii by vyuchil . . . ," *Kollektsiia NG* [supplement to *Nezavisimaia gazeta*] 9 (June 1998): 4.
5. One recent article, for instance, examines Shukshin in light of postmodernism, while another looks at Shukshin and the writer Andrei Platonov as the two "geopolitical axes" of Russian Soviet literature. See, respectively, Raul' Eshel'man, "Epistemologiia zastoia: o postmodernistskoi proze V. Shukshina," *Russian Literature* 35 (1994): 67–92, and Aleksei Varlamov, "Platonov i Shukshin: geopoliticheskie osi russkoi literatury," *Moskva* 2 (1998): 167–74. The ongoing publications of the Shukshin Center at Altai State University in Barnaul (Tsentr issledovanii zhizni i tvorchestva V. M. Shukshina) are also evidence of continued scholarly investigation into his works.

INTRODUCTION

1. Vasilii Shukshin, "'Pered mnogomillionoi auditoriei,'" in *Voprosy samomu sebe* (Moscow: Molodaia gvardiia, 1981), 168–69.
2. See Maya Turovskaya's remarks in her book on Andrei Tarkovsky, *Tarkovsky: Cinema as Poetry*, trans. Natasha Ward, ed. Ian Christie (London: Faber and Faber, 1989): "it is important to remember the strict hier-

archy within which the arts in Russia have always been regarded, and the fact that literature still ranks much higher in prestige than the cinema" (32).

3. Donald Rayfield, "Cussedly Independent," *Times Literary Supplement,* 8 August 1997, 28 (review of Vasily Shukshin, *Stories from a Siberian Village,* trans. Laura Michael and John Givens [DeKalb: Northern Illinois University Press, 1996]).

4. *Kirkus Reviews,* 1 August 1996 (review of Shukshin, *Stories from a Siberian Village*).

5. Eduard Yefimov, *Vasily Shukshin,* trans. Avril Pyman (Moscow: Raduga, 1986), 190–91.

6. Edward J. Brown, *Russian Literature since the Revolution* (Cambridge, Mass.: Harvard University Press, 1982), 311.

7. Vysotskii's tribute to Shukshin, "Eshche—ni kholodov, ni l'din," written shortly after the latter's death, was first published in the famous *Metropol'* literary almanac that appeared illegally in the Soviet Union in 1979. For an English translation, see "On the Death of Shukshin," trans. H. William Tjalsma, in *Metropol Literary Almanac,* ed. Vasily Aksyonov et al. (New York: W. W. Norton, 1982), 168–69.

8. Mikhail Ivanov writes:

There could be few better contrasts to Russia's corrupt bureaucrats than Vasilii Shukshin. . . . When many of today's bureaucrats were still children, Shukshin, a gifted writer and film maker, was an uncompromising artist whose soul was as clean as the nature in his native Altai region. . . . It is interesting to consider what Shukshin would say if he were alive now, when Russia's "orphans of reform" are sucked into massive criminality, begging or drug addiction. He would probably rail on the "sick" children of Russian democracy, just as he railed on Soviet ideologues who did their utmost to prevent his truthful books and films from seeing the light of day.

See Ivanov, "Mother Russia's 'Difficult Kids,'" *Russian Life* 6 (1997): 2.

9. The reader is referred to the following sources: Anatolii Bocharov, "Counterpoint: The Common and the Individual in the Prose of Iuryi Trifonov, Vasilii Shukshin, and Valentin Rasputin," *Soviet Studies in Literature* 20, no. 1 (Winter 1983–84): 25 (translation of "Kontrapunkt. Obshchee i individual'noe v proze Iu. Trifonova, V. Shukshina, V. Rasputina," *Oktiabr'* 7 [1982]: 190–99); I. I. Plekhanova, "Priroda nravstvennogo soznaniia v traktovke V. Shukshina, Iu. Trifonova, V. Rasputina," *Sever* 5 (1980): 82–98, and her "Osobennosti siuzhetoslozheniia v tvorchestve V. Shukshina, Iu. Trifonova, V. Rasputina: k probleme khudozhestvennoi uslovnosti," *Russkaia literatura* 4 (1980): 71–88. See also W. Bruce Lincoln, *Between Heaven and Hell: The Story of a Thousand Years of Artistic Life in Russia* (New York: Viking, 1998), 439–44.

10. Anatoly Vishevsky, *Soviet Literary Culture in the 1970s: The Politics of Irony* (Gainesville: University Press of Florida, 1993), 7–8.

11. Richard Stites, *Russian Popular Culture: Entertainment and Society since 1900* (New York: Cambridge University Press, 1992), 5.

12. Katerina Clark, *The Soviet Novel: History as Ritual* (Chicago: University of Chicago Press, 1985), 43.

13. J. H. Bater, *The Soviet City—Ideal and Reality* (London: Arnold, 1980), 64; cited in Nicole Christian, "Manifestations of the Eccentric in the Works of Vasilii Shukshin," *Slavonic and East European Review* 75, no. 2 (April 1997): 202–3.

14. Hedrick Smith, *The Russians* (New York: Ballantine, 1976), 275.

15. Petr Vail' and Aleksandr Genis, *60-e: Mir sovetskogo cheloveka* (Ann Arbor, Mich.: Ardis, 1989), 33.

16. Stites, *Russian Popular Culture*, 168–69.

17. Ol'ga Berggol'ts, "Razgovor o lirike," *Literaturnaia gazeta*, 16 April 1953; Vladimir Pomerantsev, "Ob iskrennosti v literature," *Novyi mir* 12 (1953): 218–45.

18. *Stiliagi* were Russian youth who wore modified zoot suits, smoked American cigarettes, and donned kitschy ties with cowboys and cactuses on them while listening to American jazz. Their rereading of artifacts of American popular culture was not only "cool"; it also signified their rejection of Soviet values and middle-class mores in general. The writer Vasilii Aksenov goes as far as to call the *stiliagi* the Soviet Union's "first dissidents" in his own recollections of the time. See Vassily Aksyonov, *In Search of Melancholy Baby: A Russian in America*, trans. Michael Henry Heim and Antonina W. Bouis (New York: Vintage, 1987), 18. For more on the *stiliagi*, see Stites, *Russian Popular Culture*, 124–28.

19. See Kathleen Parthé, *Russian Village Prose: The Radiant Past* (Princeton, N.J.: Princeton University Press, 1992).

20. Anatoly Gladilin, *The Making and Unmaking of a Soviet Writer: My Story of the "Young Prose" of the Sixties and After*, trans. David Lapeza (Ann Arbor, Mich.: Ardis, 1979), 43.

21. Ibid.

22. These characterizations of Shukshin and his stories are from Raul' Eshel'man, "Epistemologiia zastoia: o postmodernistskoi proze V. Shukshina," *Russian Literature* 35 (1994): 68.

23. The most recent study of Shukshin's favorite character type is by Nicole Christian, "Manifestations of the Eccentric in the Works of Vasilii Shukshin," *Slavonic and East European Review* 75, no. 2 (April 1997): 201–15.

24. Carl and Ellendea Proffer, "Introduction: Russian Writing into the Eighties," in *Contemporary Russian Prose*, ed. Carl and Ellendea Proffer (Ann Arbor, Mich.: Ardis, 1982), xxii.

25. Diane Nemec Ignashev, "Song and Confession in the Short Prose of Vasilij Makarovič Šukšin: 1929–1974" (Ph.D. diss., University of Chicago, 1984), 119.

26. Virginia Woolf, "Jane Austen at Sixty," *Nation*, 15 December 1923, 433; cited in John Halperin, *The Life of Jane Austen* (Baltimore: Johns Hopkins University Press, 1984), 50, whose paraphrase I've adapted.

27. Donald Rayfield, *The Cherry Orchard: Catastrophe and Comedy* (New York: Twayne, 1994), 3.

28. V. Kardin, "Sekret uspekha," *Voprosy literatury* 4 (1986): 102.

29. Proffer and Proffer, "Introduction," xxiii

30. Joseph Brodsky, *Less than One* (New York: Farrar Straus Giroux, 1986), 300; Gennadii Ziuganov, "Rossiia—strana slova," interview with Vladimir Bondarenko, *Aprel'* 17 (1996): 3.

CHAPTER ONE

1. See, respectively, I. Kramov, *V poiskakh sushchnosti: literaturno-kriticheskie stat'i, literaturnye portrety* (Alma-Ata: Zhasushy, 1980), 252; Vsevolod Sakharov, "Vlast' kanona: zametki o rasskaze," *Nash sovremennik* 1 (1977): 163; and B. M. Iudalevich, "Khudozhnik i ego geroi: k 60-letiiu so dnia rozhdeniia V. M. Shukshina," *Izvestiia Sibirskogo otdeleniia Akademii nauk SSSR: Seriia istorii, filologii i filosofii* 3 (1989): 55.

2. Both are quoted in Aleksandr Ovcharenko, *Bol'shaia literatura: osnovnye tendentsii razvitiia sovetskoi khudozhestvennoi prozy 1945–85 godov. Semidesiatye gody* (Moscow: Sovremennik, 1988), 371, 321, respectively.

3. Igor' Dedkov, *Vozvrashchenie k sebe: literaturno-kriticheskie stat'i* (Moscow: Sovremennik, 1978), 129.

4. Veniamin Kaverin, "Shukshin's Stories," *Soviet Studies in Literature* 14, no. 3 (1978): 60; translation of "Rasskazy Shukshina," *Novyi mir* 6 (1977): 261–66.

5. Sakharov, "Vlast' kanona," 163.

6. V. Serdiuchenko, "O Shukshine segodnia: nadeznost' traditsii," *Novyi mir* 9 (1980): 237–38.

7. Kathleen Parthé, *Russian Village Prose: The Radiant Past* (Princeton, N.J.: Princeton University Press, 1992), xi.

8. See especially M. Klimakova, "Zhivet takoi paren'," *Moskovskii komsomolets,* 7 June 1964; "Vasilii Shukshin," *Iskusstvo kino* 6 (1965): 46; N. Zhelezniakova, "'Zolotoi lev'—prostomu parniu," *Ogonek* 36 (1964): 29; T. Osipov, "Est' takoi paren'. . . ," *Uchitel'skaia gazeta,* 5 December 1964, 4; Ia. Varshavskii, "Dobro pozhalovat' na komediiu!" *Komsomol'skaia pravda,* 24 June 1964, 4; I. Vasil'iev, "S podkupaiushchei iskrennost'iu," *Volga,* 8 December 1964.

9. Iurii Skop, "V Sibiri dobro—sibirskoe: v gostiakh u Shukshina," *Literaturnaia gazeta,* 3 July 1968, 3.

10. Nicholas Galichenko, *Glasnost—Soviet Cinema Responds,* ed. Robert Allington (Austin: University of Texas Press, 1991), 12. My thanks to Greg Miller for bringing this passage to my attention.

11. Aleksandr Mitta, "Kak o nem napisat'?" *Iskusstvo kino* 1 (1971): 114.

12. Aleksandr Pankov, "'Kharaktery i rezkaia kartina nravov,'" *Sibirskie ogni* 4 (1978): 179.

13. Anninskii's comments are from his brochure *Vasilii Shukshin* (Moscow: Biuro propagandy sovetskogo kino, 1976), 1.

14. This fact is mentioned in passing by Vladimir Korobov in *Vasilii Shukshin* (Moscow: Sovremennik, 1988), 30.

15. The famous Soviet director Sergei Gerasimov mentions Shukshin's Party membership while talking about the latter's entrance into VGIK. See Gennadii Bocharov, "Esli govorit' o Shukshine," *Komsomol'skaia pravda,* 24 November 1974, 4.

16. Vasilii Shukshin, "Mne vezlo na umnykh i dobrykh liudei . . . ," in *Voprosy samomu sebe* (Moscow: Molodaia gvardiia, 1981), 151–52.

17. Boris Tomashevskii, "Literature and Biography," trans. Herbert Eagle, in *Readings in Russian Poetics: Formalist and Structuralist Views,* ed. Ladislav Matejka and Krystyna Pomorska (Ann Arbor: University of Michigan Press, 1978), 47, 55.

18. Ibid., 55.

19. Svetlana Boym, *Death in Quotation Marks: Cultural Myths of the Modern Poet* (Cambridge: Harvard University Press, 1991), 24.

20. The most conspicuous example is M. Klimakova's feature "Zhivet takoi paren'," which appeared in the 7 June 1964 issue of *Moskovskii komsomolets* and contains all of the essential elements of the VGIK legend: Shukshin's lack of formal education; how he made up for three years of schooling in six months; his brief stint as the head of a rural night school; his trip to Moscow and unlikely acceptance into the film institute; his reputation as "an original thinker" and "a unique and independent" talent at school; his homesickness and late-night work habits; his nervous temperament and down-to-earth style as a director ("he works without any posing, without playing the 'maestro'"); and his humility in light of his film's success. The detail and focus of Klimakova's account suggest a biographical legend in the making, although it is impossible to know for sure how much Shukshin himself might have influenced the final shape of the article.

21. Viktor Gorn, *Vasilii Shukshin: lichnost', knigi* (Barnaul: Altaiskoe knizhnoe izdatel'stvo, 1990), 39–40.

22. I. Solov'eva and V. Shitova, "Svoi liudi—sochtemsia," *Novyi mir* 3 (1974): 246.

23. Ibid.

24. See, for example, Vladimir Korobov, *Vasilii Shukshin: tvorch-estvo, lichnost'* (Moscow: Sovetskaia Rossiia, 1977), 47–50; its revised second edition, *Vasilii Shukshin* (Moscow: Sovremennik, 1988), 26–36; Viktor Gorn, *Kharaktery Vasiliia Shukshina* (Barnaul: Altaiskoe knizhnoe izda-tel'stvo, 1981), 27–31; its revised second edition, *Nash syn i brat: problemy i geroi prozy V. Shukshina* (Barnaul: Altaiskoe knizhnoe izdatel'stvo, 1985), 20–25; its revised third edition, *Vasilii Shukshin: lichnost', knigi* (Barnaul: Altaiskoe knizhnoe izdatel'stvo, 1990), 11–45; Valentina Karpova, *Talantli-vaia zhizn': Vasilii Shukshin—prozaik* (Moscow: Sovetskii pisatel', 1986), 14–21; Galina Binova, *Tvorcheskaia evoliutsiia Vasiliia Shukshina* (Brno: Univerzita J. E. Purkyne, 1988), 14, 62; Evgenii Vertlib, *Vasilii Shukshin i russkoe dukhovnoe vozrozhdenie* (New York: Effect, 1990), 16–27. Besides articles previously cited, see V. Ivanova, "Talant Vasiliia Shukshina," *Zaria vostoka,* 24 October 1973, 4; Vsevolod Sakharov, "Zhizn', oborvavshaisia na poluslove . . .: neskol'ko mysli vslukh o Vasilii Shukshine," *Moskva* 6 (1975): 206, 209; Nina Koptiug, "Geroi nashego vremeni," *Sibirskie ogni* 11 (1988): 143.

25. Gennadii Bocharov, *Nepobezhdennyi* (Moscow: Molodaia gvar-diia, 1978), 133.

26. Ibid., 136.

27. Leonid Kuravlev, "Kak berezy . . . ," in *O Shukshine: ekran i zhizn',* ed. L. N. Fedoseeva-Shukshina and R. D. Chernenko (Moscow: Iskusstvo, 1979), 223–24.

28. Valerii Ginzburg, "Uchenicheskaia tetrad' v kolenkorovom pere-plete," in *O Shukshine,* 214.

29. Evgenii Lebedev, "Chuvstvoval on cheloveka," in *O Shukshine,* 241.

30. Sergei Vikulov, "A Human Being on Earth," in "Shukshin: Week-days and Holidays: Pages from Recollections," *Soviet Studies in Literature,* 16 (Winter 1979–80): 92; translation of "Chelovek na zemle," in "Shukshin: Budni i prazdniki: stranitsy vospominanii," *Literaturnaia gazeta,* 25 July 1979, 6.

31. Shukshin, "Mne vezlo na umnykh i dobrykh liudei . . . ," 152.

32. Mikhail Bakhtin, "Forms of Time and Chronotope in the Novel," in *The Dialogic Imagination: Four Essays,* trans. Caryl Emerson and Michael Holquist, ed. Michael Holquist (Austin: University of Texas Press, 1981), 159.

33. Ibid., 163.

34. Ibid., 159.

35. Like the name of the fictional village of Shuksha, the stress of Shukshin's own name was also originally on the first syllable. He changed it shortly after arriving in Moscow in order to sound less provincial. See V. Novikov, "Vstrechi v Srostkakh," *Sibirskie ogni* 7 (1975): 138; cited in

Diane Nemec Ignashev, "Song and Confession in the Short Pieces of Vasilij Makarovič Šukšin: 1929–1974" (Ph.D. diss., University of Chicago, 1984), 47.

36. M. Vaniashova asserts that "[t]he uniqueness of Shukshin's works will remain an enigma until the organic tie between the characters of his stories and the popular art of the *skomorokhi* is recognized. The creative act of laughter [*smekhotvorchestvo*] and folk buffoonery are always secretly present in Shukshin's prose." See her "Zhanrovoe svoeobrazie rasskazov V. Shukshina," in *Problemy estetiki i poetiki: mezhvuzovskii sbornik nauchnykh trudov*, no. 160 (Iaroslavl': Iaroslavskii gosudarstvennyi pedagogicheskii institut, 1976), 113. Galina Belaia concurs, stating, "It is no coincidence that Shukshinian eccentricity should evoke in our memory the traditions of the art of folk humor." See her *Khudozhestvennyi mir sovremennoi prozy* (Moscow: Nauka, 1983), 105. Gorn, too, discovers that Shukshin's works are "literally saturated with *skomoroshestvo* and theatricality, which reflect one of the characteristics of the Russian common folk" (*Vasilii Shukshin*, 227–28).

37. For a brief overview of the *skomorokhi*, see Russell Zguta, "Skomorokhi: The Russian Minstrel-Entertainers," *Slavic Review* 31 (1972): 297–313.

38. Valentin Rasputin, "Your Son, Russia, and Our Passionate Brother: On Vasily Shukshin," in *Siberia on Fire*, trans. Gerald Mikkelson and Margaret Winchell (DeKalb: Northern Illinois University Press, 1989), 204.

39. John Dunlop, "Russian Nationalist Themes in Soviet Film of the 1970s," in *The Red Screen: Politics, Society, Art in Soviet Cinema*, ed. Anna Lawton (London: Routledge, 1992), 232.

40. Grigori Svirski, *A History of Post-War Soviet Writing: The Literature of Moral Opposition*, trans. and ed. Robert Dessaix and Michael Ulman (Ann Arbor, Mich.: Ardis, 1981), 299.

41. Viktor Nekrasov, "Vzgliad i nechto," pt. 2, *Kontinent* 12 (1977): 118.

42. Anatoly Gladilin, *The Making and Unmaking of a Soviet Writer: My Story of the "Young Prose" of the Sixties and After*, trans. David Lapeza (Ann Arbor, Mich.: Ardis, 1979), 129.

43. Evgenii Chernykh, "Komu nado bylo?" *Ekspress gazeta* 28 (October 1996): 5. Fedoseeva's article "Ego ubili!" is on page 4, the first of the two-page spread devoted to the murder theory. My thanks to Brian Oles for discovering the exposé and sending it to me.

44. "Shukshinskii bum." This is Gleb Goryshin's term from an article marking the sixtieth anniversary of Shukshin's birth. See Goryshin, "'Glubokho i po-nastoiashchemu zhit' . . . ,'" *Avrora* 7 (1989): 73.

45. Vasilii Shukshin, "Monolog na lestnitse," in *Voprosy samomu sebe*, 36.

46. Vasilii Shukshin, "Kommentarii" to "'Esche raz vyveriaia svoiu zhizn' . . . ,'" in *Voprosy samomu sebe*, 243–44.

47. Anatolii Bocharov, "Counterpoint: The Common and the Individual in the Prose of Iuryi Trifonov, Vasilii Shukshin, and Valentin Rasputin," *Soviet Studies in Literature* 30, no. 1 (Winter 1983–84): 25.

48. V. Perevedentsev, "Nauchnyi pokhod? Neobkhodim!" *Literaturnoe obozrenie* 5 (1978): 22; cited in David C. Gillespie, *Valentin Rasputin and Soviet Russian Village Prose* (London: Modern Humanities Research Association, 1986), 7.

49. So marked is this sense of difference that, according to Gleb Goryshin, the inhabitants of the Altai region of Siberia say "in Russia" or "out West" when referring to European Russia. See his *Zhrebii: Rasskazy o pisateliakh* (Leningrad: Sovetskii pisatel', 1987), 137.

50. Ignashev, "Song and Confession," 45.

51. A. Sarantsev, "Vernost': k 60-letiu so dnia rozhdeniia Vasiliia Shukshina," *Moskva* 7 (1989): 198.

52. Ignashev, "Song and Confession," 45.

53. This quote is taken from a selection of Shukshin's letters to his mother and sister published by Boris Iudalevich, "Rodnaia moia . . . ," in *Shukshinskie chteniia,* ed. V. Gorn (Barnaul: Altaiskoe knizhnoe izdatel'stvo, 1984), 189. I have translated *otvetstvennye rabotniki* as "executives."

54. Sarantsev, "Vernost'," 198.

55. This information comes from an autobiographical fragment published fifteen years after Shukshin's death. See "Solnechnye kol'tsa," ed. Lidiia Fedoseeva-Shukshina, *Sovetskaia Rossiia,* 12 July 1989, 4; reprinted in Vasilii Shukshin, *Sobranie sochinenii,* 5 vols. (Moscow: Panprint, 1996), 5:210–14.

56. The essay, "Kity, ili O tom, kak my priobshchalis' k iskusstvu," was reprinted in Shukshin's *Voprosy samomu sebe* in the commentary to "Mne vezlo na umnykh i dobrykh liudei . . . ," 152–56.

57. Ignashev, "Song and Confession," 32.

58. Quoted in V. I. Fomin, *Peresechenie parallel'nykh* (Moscow: Iskusstvo, 1976), 295–96.

59. Kuravlev, "Kak berezy . . . ," 224.

60. See the biography of Tarkovsky in the first chapter of Vida T. Johnson and Graham Petrie, *The Films of Andrei Tarkovsky: A Visual Fugue* (Bloomington: Indiana University Press, 1994).

61. Mikhail Romm, *Ustnye rasskazy* (Moscow: Soiuz kinematografistov SSSR, 1991), 14.

62. Neya Zorkaya, *The Illustrated History of Soviet Cinema* (New York: Hippocrene Books, 1989), 275–77.

63. Ignashev, "Song and Confession," 45.

64. Vasilii Shukshin, "'Eshche raz vyveriaia svoiu zhizn','" in *Voprosy samomu sebe,* 232–33.

65. Boris Pankin, "Shukshin about Himself: Notes on the Collection *Morality Is Truth,*" *Soviet Studies in Literature* 17, no. 1 (1980–81): 43;

translation of "Shukshin o samom sebe: zametki o sbornike *Nravstvennost'* *est' Pravda,*" *Druzhba narodov* 6 (1980): 212–19.

66. Bella Akhmadulina, "Ne zabyt'," in *O Shukshine*, 331.

67. See Shukshin's 1967 essay " 'Tol'ko eto ne budet ekonomicheskaia stat'ia . . . ,' " in *Voprosy samomu sebe*, 25–31, for details of Shukshin's own mishaps on a trip back to Siberia.

68. Kathleen Parthé, "Shukshin at Large," in Vasily Shukshin, *Stories from a Siberian Village*, trans. Laura Michael and John Givens (DeKalb: Northern Illinois University Press, 1996), x.

69. See Marlen Khutsiev's "Krupnyi plan," in *O Shukshine*, 321, and Gennadii Bocharov, *Nepobezhdennyi*, 133. For a detailed account of Shukshin's fistfight and how it nearly resulted in his expulsion from film school, see Evgenii Taranov, "Vse my nemnogo limitchiki," *Vecherniaia Moskva*, 13 May 1998, 2.

70. See Evgenii Sorokin, " 'Nesu rodinu v dushe . . . ,' " *Molodaia gvardiia* 7 (1989): 260–61.

71. John McGowan, "Postmodernism," in *The Johns Hopkins Guide to Literary Theory and Criticism*, ed. Michael Groden and Martin Kreiswirth (Baltimore: Johns Hopkins University Press, 1994), 586.

72. Anatolii Bocharov, "Counterpoint," 25.

73. Dedkov, *Vozvrashchenie k sebe*, 128. The *zavalinka* is a mound of earth surrounding a Russian peasant hut that provides both protection from the weather and a place for sitting outside. An early anonymous assessment of Shukshin's prose also notes its "very simple phrases and elastic dialogue, so familiar and genuine that it seems you've just heard it on the train, on the road, outside." See "Vasilii Shukshin," *Iskusstvo kino* 6 (1965): 46.

74. Ivanova, "Talant Vasiliia Shukshina," 4.

75. Goryshin, *Zhrebii*, 113.

CHAPTER TWO

1. Vasilii Shukshin, " 'Eshche raz vyveriaia svoiu zhizn'. . . ,' " in *Voprosy samomu sebe* (Moscow: Molodaia gvardiia, 1981), 242.

2. Neya Zorkaya, *The Illustrated History of Soviet Cinema* (New York: Hippocrene Books, 1989), 277.

3. Anna Lawton, *Kinoglasnost: Soviet Cinema in Our Time* (Cambridge: Cambridge University Press, 1992), 35.

4. Vasilii Shukshin, "Edin v trekh litsakh" (interview), in *Voskresnye vstrechi*, ed. A. P. Udal'tsov (Moscow: Moskovskii rabochii, 1975), 84. The interview (by S. Vishniakov) originally appeared under the same title in *Moskovskii komsomolets*, 11 March 1973, 3.

5. Quoted in V. I. Fomin, *Peresechenie parallel'nykh* (Moscow: Iskusstvo, 1976), 296; my emphasis.

6. Vasilii Shukshin, "Iz rabochikh zapisei," in *Voprosy samomu sebe,* 249.
7. Vasilii Shukshin, "Kak ia ponimaiu rasskaz," in *Voprosy samomu sebe,* 115.
8. Ibid., 116.
9. L. A. Muratova and L. G. Riabova, "Signaly razgovornosti v khudozhestvennom dialoge i skaze V. M. Shukshina," in *Iazyk i stil' prosy V. M. Shukshina,* ed. A. A. Chuvakin (Barnaul: Altaiskii gosudarstvennyi universitet, 1991), 61, 67.
10. N. A. Kozhevnikova and N. A. Nikolina, "O iazyke V. M. Shukshina," in *Iazyk i stil' prozy V. M. Shukshina,* 7. Kozhevnikova and Nikolina provide the following example of a text formed through "parceling": "Gleb would laugh. And narrow his steely eyes somewhat vindictively. In the village all the mothers of notable people disliked Gleb. They were afraid of him." See Shukshin's story "Cutting Them Down to Size" (2:8). Shukshin's "definition" of the short story is another example of his use of parceling.
11. G. G. Khisamova, "Dialog v rasskazakh V. M. Shukshina," in *Iazyk i stil' prozy V. M. Shukshina,* 47.
12. Vasilii Shukshin, "Vozdeistvie pravdoi," in *Voprosy somomu sebe,* 189.
13. Vasilii Shukshin, "'Pered mnogomillionnoi auditoriei,'" in *Voprosy somomu sebe,* 170, 171. Elsewhere Shukshin notes: "I always perceive the movie theater as a very intelligent person with whom it's very interesting to have a chat" ("Kommentarii" to "Vozdeistvie pravdoi," 193).
14. Shukshin, "Kommentarii" to "'Eshche raz vyveriaia svoiu zhizn' . . . ,'" 240.
15. L. M. Shelgunova, "Dialog i vnutrenniaia rech' personazhei v strukture rasskazov V. M. Shukshina," in *Iazyk i stil' prozy V. M. Shukshina,* 38. Some examples: "Ignakha priekhal" ("Ignakha's Come Home," 2:144–53); "Vania, ty kak zdes'?!" ("Vania, What are *You* Doing Here?!" 2:245–51); "Daesh' serdtse!" ("Let's Conquer the Heart!" 2:385–89); "Mil' pardon, madam!" ("Mille Pardons, Madame!" 2:345–52); "Veruiu!" ("I Believe!" 2:538–46); "Shire shag, maestro!" ("Step Lively, Maestro!" 3:20–31); "Moi ziat' ukral mashinu drov!" ("My Son-in-Law Stole a Truckload of Wood!" 3:112–24); "Vybiraiu derevniu na zhitel'stvo" ("I'm Moving to the Country," 3:302–9); "Privet Sivomu!" ("Regards to Gray Hairs!" 3:413–20); and, of course, Shukshin's novel *Ia prishel dat' vam voliu* (*I Have Come to Give You Freedom*).
16. Shukshin, quoted in Fomin, *Peresechenie,* 296.
17. Shukshin, "Kak ia ponimaiu rasskaz," 116.
18. Ibid., 115, 114, 117.
19. See Shukshin's own account of this period: "Mne vezlo na umnykh i dobrykh liudei . . . ," in *Voprosy samomu sebe,* 151–52.
20. Shukshin, "Kommentarii" to "Vozdeistvie pravdoi," 195.

21. Ibid., 189.

22. Ibid., 195.

23. Vasilii Shukshin, "'Problema iazyka,'" in *Voprosy samomu sebe,* 148.

24. Shukshin, quoted in Fomin, *Peresechenie,* 297.

25. Carl and Ellender Proffer, "Introduction: Russian Fiction into the Eighties," in *Contemporary Russian Prose,* ed. Carl and Ellendea Proffer (Ann Arbor, Mich.: Ardis, 1982), xxiii.

26. See Shukshin's comments in "Vozdeistvie pravdoi," 187–88.

27. See chapter 2 of Diane Nemec Ignashev's "Song and Confession in the Short Prose of Vasilij Makarovič Šuškin: 1929–1974" (Ph.D. diss., University of Chicago, 1984) for a detailed treatment of censorship and Shukshin's texts.

28. Igor' Dedkov, *Vozvrashchenie k sebe: literaturno-kriticheskie stat'i* (Moscow: Sovremennik, 1978), 101.

29. I. Solov'eva and V. Shitova, "Svoi liudi—sochtemsia," *Novyi mir* 3 (1974): 246. Shukshin's response to Solov'eva's and Shitova's reproach is recorded in an exchange between him and *Literaturnaia gazeta* correspondent Grigorii Tsitriniak in "'Eshch raz vyveriaia svoiu zhizn','" 232.

30. Shukshin, "'Eshch raz vyveriaia svoiu zhizn','" 222.

31. M. M. Bakhtin, *Speech Genres and Other Late Essays,* trans. Vern W. McGee, ed. Caryl Emerson and Michael Holquist (Austin: University of Texas Press, 1986), 89.

32. Ibid., 88.

33. Ibid., 95–96.

34. Ibid., 75.

35. Kozhevnikova and Nikolina, "O iazyke V. M. Shukshina," 4.

36. Ibid.

37. Hugh McLean, "Introduction" to Mikhail Zoshchenko, *Nervous People and Other Stories,* trans. Maria Gordon and Hugh McLean (Bloomington: Indiana University Press, 1963), xii.

38. Edward J. Brown, *Russian Literature since the Revolution,* rev. ed. (Cambridge, Mass.: Harvard University Press, 1982), 187.

39. Solov'eva and Shitova, "Svoi liudi—sochtemsia," 245.

40. Aleksandr Ovcharenko, "Rasskazy Vasiliia Shukshina," *Don* 1 (1976): 159.

41. Mikhail Lobanov, "Znanie i mudrost'," *Volga* 1 (1978): 159.

42. Vladimir Korobov, *Vasilii Shukshin,* 2d ed. (Moscow: Sovremennik, 1988), 218.

43. E. Kuz'mina, "Prochnaia osnova," *Novyi mir* 4 (1964): 244.

44. Ia. El'sberg, "Dva stila," *Literaturnaia Rossiia,* 17 July 1964, 10.

45. *Smena* 15 (1958): 6–7.

46. This little-known story was published by Shukshin in the newspaper *Turkmenskaia iskra,* 22 July 1962, 4. It has never appeared in any

anthologies nor has it been republished in any form, although Shukshin alludes to its plot in his *kinopovest'* "Brat moi" ("My Brother," 5:361).

47. Shukshin, "Iz rabochikh zapisei," 249.

48. V. V. Vinogradov, "Zametki o stilistike sovremennoi sovetskoi literatury," *Literaturnaia gazeta,* 19 October 1965, 2. See the responses by V. Khabin, "Zhivet takoi khudozhnik," *Literaturnaia Rossiia,* 12 November 1965, 14; F. Vasil'eva, "Diskussii prekrashchaiutsia, problemy ostaiutsia: o rabote nad slovom," *Sibirskie ogni* 10 (1966): 168; and Viktor Gura, "Ot rasskazov k romanu," *Literaturnaia gazeta,* 27 November 1965, 3. Khabin, though defending Shukshin's style, agrees that he had oversaturated the speech of his characters with "dissonant dialectal elements and vulgarisms" due to "the lack of experience characteristic of beginning novelists." Vasil'eva admits that Shukshin had "exceeded poetic license" in communicating the colorful speech of his characters, but acknowledged that "a writer can't make a remote Siberian village of the 1920s speak a correct literary language, smooth and 'neutral.'" Gura is unapologetic in his defense of Shukshin's style. He notes that "in the speech of his heroes there are quite a few subtle verbal tones, and we have no right to impose on him a puritanical attitude toward language."

49. Gura mentions this debate and how it affected critical reception of Shukshin's novel in his article "Ot rasskazov k romanu." With Youth Prose fading from the literary scene and Village Prose growing as a movement, the language deformation and stylistic innovation so important to both schools remained a hot topic in the literary press, both in 1965 and throughout the second half of the decade.

50. Years later, Shukshin would parody the language debate surrounding his novel in, appropriately enough, the novel's sequel. In Book Two of *The Liubavin Family,* a teacher is sent to Siberia *po raspredeleniiu,* that is, on a post-college obligatory work assignment, and decides to win fame and fortune by writing a book about his three years "in exile." The book will include descriptions of his passage across the divide between Europe and Asia, reflections on his first Siberian acquaintances, confessions of his homesickness, and depictions of his first difficult days teaching unruly, "ignorant" Siberian children. Most important, it will also showcase his friendship with "Babka Akulina" ("Granny Akulina"), who will drop pearls of wisdom in a folksy, semigrammatical, dialectal speech. In an obvious parody of his own battles with censors, Shukshin reports how the teacher will insist that his future publisher keep intact every one of her *temnye vyrazheniia* (illiterate expressions) in his text so that he can later tell all his friends how each word was defended (3:468). Here, the battle for substandard style is obviously insincere and superficial, an instance in which Shukshin shows his awareness of the "fashionable" side to the use of common parlance.

51. Vasilii Shukshin, "Nravstvennost' est' Pravda," in *Voprosy samomu sebe*, 55.

52. V. Serdiuchenko, "O Shukshine segodnia: nadeznost' traditsii," *Novyi mir* 9 (1980): 239.

53. Bakhtin, *Speech Genres*, 97.

54. M. Chudakova, "Notes on the Language of Contemporary Prose," *Soviet Studies in Literature* 1 (Winter 1972–73): 41; translation of "Zametki o iazyke sovremennoi prozy," *Novyi mir* 1 (1972): 214.

55. Viktor Shklovskii, *Literatura i kinematograf* (Berlin: Russkoe universal'noe izdatel'stvo, 1923), 27. An interesting application of Shklovskii's and Bakhtin's ideas in the context of the works of Liudmila Petrushevskaia can be found in Nina Kolesnikoff, "The Generic Structure of Ljudmila Petruševskaja's *Pesni vostočnyx slavjan*," *Slavic and East European Journal* 37 (1993): 220–30, from which I learned of the Shklovskii work.

56. See Galina Belaia, *Zakonomernosti stilevogo razvitiia sovetskoi prozy 20-kh godov* (Moscow: Nauka, 1977), and her article "Rozhdenie novykh stilevykh form kak protsess preodoleniia 'neitral'nogo' stilia," in *Teoriia literaturnykh stilei. Mnogoobrazie stilei sovetskoi literatury. Voprosy tipologii,* ed. N. K. Gei et al. (Moscow: Nauka, 1978), 460–85. See pages 479–85 of the latter for her assessment of Shukshin's contribution to stylistic change in Russian literature of the 1960s.

57. Shukshin, quoted in Fomin, *Peresechenie*, 296.

58. Vasilii Shukshin, "Esli by znat'. . . ," in *Voprosy samomu sebe*, 215.

59. Shukshin, "Kak ia ponimaiu rasskaz," 115–16.

60. See Wolfgang Iser, *The Implied Reader* (Baltimore: Johns Hopkins University Press, 1974) and *The Act of Reading* (Baltimore: Johns Hopkins University Press, 1979).

61. Quoted in Julian Connolly, "The Nineteenth Century: Between Realism and Modernism, 1880–95," in *The Cambridge History of Russian Literature,* rev. ed, ed. Charles A. Moser (Cambridge: Cambridge University Press, 1992), 363.

62. Shukshin, "Vozdeistvie pravdoi," 188, 193.

63. Shukshin, "Iz rabochikh zapisei," 247. A different notion of cinematic co-authorship is described by Andrei Tarkovsky:

> The method whereby the artist obliges the audience to build the separate parts into a whole and to think on, further than has been stated, is the only one that puts the audience on a par with the artist in their perception of the film. And indeed from the point of view of mutual respect only this kind of reciprocity is worthy of artistic practice.

See Tarkovsky, *Sculpting in Time,* trans. Kitty Hunter-Blair (Austin: University of Texas Press, 1991), 21.

64. Shukshin, "'Pered mnogomillionoi auditoriei,'" in *Voprosy samomu sebe,* 178.

65. This definition of a script is used by Shukshin on several separate occasions; see *Voprosy samomu sebe,* 145, 150, 169, 229.

66. Kathleen Parthé's discussion of improvisation in the works of the Village Prose writers has relevance for my discussion here. She writes:

> In Russian folklore, there were set themes, plots, and character-functions— as Vladimir Propp had explained—but there were also countless ways in which the same basic tale could be varied in the telling. The balance between set themes and opportunities for improvisation was of great interest to a number of Village Prose writers; however, it is a subject they approached not out of theoretical interest, but because they had heard as children, and taken note of as writers, so much living folk speech.

Parthé, *Russian Village Prose: The Radiant Past* (Princeton, N.J.: Princeton University Press, 1992), 32.

67. Vasilii Shukshin, "Voprosy samomu sebe," in *Voprosy samomu sebe,* 13.

68. Shukshin, "Vozdeistvie pravdoi," 188. A case can be made that Shukshin turned to the theater shortly before his death precisely because it allowed for more improvisation (conceivably, in every performance) as well as more intimate contact with the viewer. Earlier Shukshin had claimed that the play was a literary form he could not bring himself to read: "I've tried— I can't," he stated in a questionnaire for *Voprosy literatury* in 1967. See Shukshin, "'Problema iazyka,'" 150.

69. Shukshin, "'Eshche raz vyveriaia svoiu zhizn' . . . ,'" 230; see also pp. 144 and 240.

70. Ibid., 227.

71. Ibid. See also Bondarchuk's account of working with Shukshin on the movie, "Pervorodstvo," in *O Shukshine: ekran i zhizn',* ed. L. N. Fedoseeva-Shukshina and R. D. Chernenko (Moscow: Iskusstvo, 1979), 193–94. Theater director Georgii Tovstonogov also recalls Shukshin's skill at improvisation during rehearsals of Shukshin's play *Energetic People (Energichnye liudi).* See his "Golos Shukshina" in *O Shukshine,* 305.

72. See L. L. Salagaeva, "Nekotorye osobennosti dialoga v rasskazakh V. M. Shukshina," in *Russkoe iazykoznanie,* vol. 6, ed. D. T. Tursunov (Alma-Ata: Kazakhskii pedagogicheskii institut, 1976), 69–70; Viktor Gorn, "Zhivoi iazyk Vasiliia Shukshina," *Russkaia rech'* 2 (1977): 28; E. M. Pul'khritudova, "Vasilii Makarovich Shukshin: zhizn' i tvorchestvo," in *Literatura i stranovedenie,* ed. F. F. Kuznetsov and E. M. Pul'khritudova (Moscow: Russkii iazyk, 1978), 29–30; T. N. Damitio-Il'ina, "Iskusstvo slovesnoi ostroty i nekotorye osobennosti dialogicheskoi rechi v proizvedeniiakh V. M. Shukshina," in *Dutch Contributions to the Eighth International Congress of Slavists: Zagreb, Ljubljana, September 3–9, 1978,* ed. Jan M. Meijer (Amsterdam: John Benjamins, 1979), 179; N. Zhilina, "Slovo av-

tora i slovo geroia v rasskazakh V. Shukshina," in *O zhanrovo-stilevom svoeobrazii: sbornik nauchnykh trudov* (Tashkent: Tashkentskii gosudarstvennyi universitet, 1985), 30.

73. Pul'khritudova, "Vasilii Makarovich Shukshin," 30.

74. A. Marchenko, "Iz knizhnogo raia," *Voprosy literatury* 4 (1969): 64–65, 69.

75. Solov'eva and Shitova list among the "temptations" of Shukshin's early prose (which he was in the process of overcoming as a mature writer) the tendency to write stories as if he were fulfilling acting improvisation assignments: "This is how they set up situations at acting class: 'A father comes to visit his son at the dormitory. You're the son, you're the father: act it out.'" See their "Svoi liudi—sochtemsia," 246.

76. Pul'khritudova, "Vasilii Makarovich Shukshin," 30.

77. Yuri Olesha, "Speech to the First Congress of Soviet Writers," in *Envy and Other Works*, trans. Andrew R. MacAndrew (New York: W. W. Norton, 1981), 213.

78. Shukshin, "Iz rabochikh zapisei," 254.

79. For a more detailed discussion of discourse types, see Bakhtin's chapter "Discourse in Dostoevsky" in his *Problems of Dostoevsky's Poetics*, trans. and ed. Caryl Emerson (Minneapolis: University of Minnesota Press, 1984), 181–269, and Gary Saul Morson and Caryl Emerson, *Mikhail Bakhtin: Creation of a Prosaics* (Stanford, Calif.: Stanford University Press, 1990), 146–71.

CHAPTER THREE

1. I. Kramov, *V poiskakh sushchnosti: literaturno-kriticheskie stat'i, literaturnye portrety* (Alma-Ata: Zhasushy, 1980), 260.

2. Zhores Medvedev, *Soviet Agriculture* (New York: W. W. Norton, 1987), 321–23.

3. Mikhail Bakhtin, "Forms of Time and of the Chronotope in the Novel," in *The Dialogic Imagination: Four Essays*, trans. Caryl Emerson and Michael Holquist, ed. Michael Holquist (Austin: University of Texas Press, 1981), 84.

4. Galina Belaia, "Rozhdenie novykh stilevykh form kak protsess preodoleniia 'neitral'nogo' stilia," in *Teoriia literaturnykh stilei. Mnogoobrazie stilei sovetskoi literatury. Voprosy tipologii*, ed. N. K. Gei et al. (Moscow: Nauka, 1978), 470.

5. Lev Anninskii, "Put' pisatelia," in *O Shukshine: ekran i zhizn'*, ed. Lidiia Fedoseeva-Shukshina and R. D. Chernenko (Moscow: Iskusstvo, 1979), 119.

6. L. Belova, "Tri rusla odnogo puti: o tvorchestve Vasiliia Shukshina," *Voprosy kinoiskusstva*, vol. 17 (Moscow: Nauka, 1976), 139.

7. Ibid.

8. L. Mikhailova, "Pronitsatel'nost' talanta," *Literaturnoe obozrenie* 1 (1975): 31.

9. Anninskii, "Put' pisatelia," 119.

10. A. Klitko, "Osmyslenie kazhdodnevnosti," *Sibirskie ogni* 7 (1972): 163.

11. V. Kochetov, "Vremia bol'shikh nadezhd," *Komsomol'skaia pravda*, 16 November 1962, 3.

12. See Chapter Six for a more detailed discussion of Shukshin's relationship with the critics.

13. See, in particular, Leonid Emel'ianov, *Vasilii Shukshin: ocherk tvorchestvo* (Leningrad: Khudozhestvennaia literatura, 1983), 14–43; Diane Nemec Ignashev, "Song and Confession in the Short Prose of Vasilij Makarovič Šukšin: 1929–1974" (Ph.D. diss., University of Chicago, 1984), 398–99; Viktor Gorn, *Vasilii Shukshin: lichnost', knigi* (Barnaul: Altaiskoe knizhnoe izdatel'stvo, 1990), 49; Galina Pavlovna Binova, *Tvorcheskaia evoliutsiia Vasiliia Shukshina* (Brno: Univerzita J. E. Purkyně v Brně, 1988), 26.

14. Petr Vail', "Smert' geroia," *Znamia* 2 (1992): 229.

15. Diane Nemec Ignashev was the first to make this link explicit. See her "Song and Confession," especially 298–313.

16. Although sweet and sentimental, "Stepan in Love" was actually Shukshin's first controversial story, evoking a polemic in *Literaturnaia Rossiia* involving the critics Genrikh Mitin, Vadim Kozhinov, and Lev Anninskii. Mitin began the debate in his "Zakon est' zakon" (13 December 1963, 14–15) and "Liubvi poryvy . . ." (19 June 1964, 14–15); in the latter article, he ridiculed the story's premise: "All a guy needs are arms and legs and he can take any girl he wants? And any girl would marry him? All you've got to do is make a match?" (15). Anninskii and Kozhinov defended the story on artistic grounds. Anninskii ("Nechto o sostiazanii zhanrov," 7 August 1964, 10–11) argues that the matchmaking ritual is an example of how Shukshin likes to put his characters in extreme situations in order to get at the moment of truth (11). (These extreme situations become more numerous and more explosive in later stories.) Kozhinov takes a similar stand, asserting that the "language of art" is not always meant to be read literally: the inappropriateness of the matchmaking ritual is only meant to emphasize—to us and to the teacher—the depth of Stepan's love ("Iazyk iskusstva," 25 September 1964, 18–19).

17. In his deprecating depiction of wives, Shukshin seems to be continuing a tradition prominent in Soviet literature of the Stalin period. According to Vera Dunham, the "fever for possessions is a key trait" of *meshchanstvo*, which, in many ways "is a familial and feminine affair." See her *In Stalin's Time: Middle-Class Values in Soviet Fiction* (Cambridge: Cambridge University Press, 1976), 19–20.

18. Lyndall Morgan, "Shukshin's Women: An Enduring Russian Stereotype," *Australian Slavonic and East European Studies* 1, no. 2 (1987): 140, 146.

19. We learn only in the film version of the story included in *Your Son and Brother* that Moscow is the unidentified city where Ignakha now lives.

20. Two prominent stories on this theme, which appeared before "Ignakha priekhal," are Nikolai Zhdanov's "A Trip Home" ("Poezdka na rodinu," 1956) and Kazakov's "The Smell of Bread" ("Zapakh khleba," 1961).

21. Elizabeth Pond, *From the Yaroslavsky Station: Russia Perceived* (New York: Universe Books, 1981), 266.

22. O-o-ekh, volia, moia volia!
    Volia vol'naia moia.
    Volia—sokol v podnebes'i,
    Volia—milye kraia . . .

23. In the film version, Pasha's last name is changed to Kolokol'nikov.

24. Belova, "Tri rusla odnogo puti," 142.

25. "Pasha Kolokol'nikov ne porazhaet, konechno, intellektom," Shukshin admitted, describing him as being "stikhiinogo obraza zhizni" ("Posleslovie k fil'mu 'Zhivet takoi paren'," in *Voprosy samomu sebe* [Moscow: Molodaia gvardiia, 1981], 114, 112).

26. Ibid., 113.

27. Belova, "Tri rusla odnogo puti," 142.

28. Pashka uses *sfotografirovano* (literally, "photographed") to mean "got it"; *piramidon,* a popular remedy for fever and headache, sounds vaguely like the French "mille pardons."

29. Eduard Yefimov calls both *There's This Guy* and Shukshin's fourth film, *Pechki-lavochki,* essays in the picaresque form and likens them to Cervantes's *Don Quixote* and Gogol''s *Dead Souls* in literature and John Ford's *Stagecoach* and Federico Fellini's *La Strada* in film. See his *Vasily Shukshin* (Moscow: Raduga, 1986), 104–5.

30. Ignashev, "Song and Confession," 63.

31. "Posleslovie k fil'mu 'Zhivet takoi paren'" first appeared in *Iskusstvo kino* 9 (1964): 52–53; collected in *Voprosy samomu sebe,* 111–14.

32. Shukshin, "Posleslovie," 113.

33. Vasilii Shukshin, "Nravstvennost' est' Pravda," in *Voprosy samomu sebe,* 59.

34. Mikhail Bakhtin, "Discourse in the Novel," in *The Dialogic Imagination,* 406.

35. Gary Saul Morson and Caryl Emerson, *Mikhail Bakhtin: Creation of a Prosaics* (Stanford, Calif.: Stanford University Press, 1990), 352–53.

36. Shukshin, "Posleslovie," 111.

37. Bakhtin, "Discourse in the Novel," 404.

38. Vasilii Shukshin, "Kak ia ponimaiu rasskaz," in *Voprosy somomu sebe,* 117.

39. Leonid Emel'ianov, "Edinitsa izmereniia: zametki o proze Vasiliia Shukshina," *Nash sovremennik* 10 (1973): 183.

CHAPTER FOUR

1. Geoffrey Hosking, *Beyond Socialist Realism: Soviet Fiction since Ivan Denisovich* (London: Granada, 1980), 164.

2. *The Oxford Russian-English Dictionary* (Oxford: Oxford University Press, 1992), 890; *Slovar' sovremennogo russkogo literaturnogo iazyka*, vol. 17 (Moscow: Nauka, 1965), 1166.

3. Lev Anninskii identifies Shukshin's "compassion for people in the wrong" (*sochuvstvie nepravomu*) as his central theme. See his "Put' pisatelia," in *O Shukshine: ekran i zhizn'*, ed. Lidiia Fedoseeva-Shukshina and R. D. Chernenko (Moscow: Iskusstvo, 1979), 120, 127.

4. Andrei Siniavskii, *Ivan-Durak: ocherk russkoi narodnoi very* (Paris: Sintaksis, 1991), 36.

5. Vasilii Shukshin, untitled introduction to "Rasskazy" by Evgenii Popov, *Novyi mir* 4 (1976): 164.

6. Lev Anninskii, "Tak prosto, chto ne veritsia," *Voprosy literatury* 10 (1965): 30–45; part of the roundtable discussion "Kto on, geroi sovremennogo rasskaza?" (30–85).

7. See the editorial summation, "Ot redaksii," *Voprosy literatury* 10 (1965): 82–84.

8. Mikhail Lobanov, "Znanie i mudrost'," *Volga* 1 (1978): 157.

9. Vasilii Shukshin, interview with K. Liasko, "Nasushchnoe, kak khleb," *Sovetskaia kul'tura*, 18 January 1968, 4.

10. Ibid.

11. Vasilii Shukshin, "Kommentarii" to "'Pered mnogomillionoi auditoriei,'" in *Voprosy samomu sebe* (Moscow: Molodaia gvardiia, 1981), 181.

12. Vasilii Shukshin, "Moia glavnaia tema—krasota liudei," *Trud*, 18 August 1968, 3.

13. See Chapter Six for a detailed discussion.

14. Hosking, *Beyond Socialist Realism*, 170.

15. I. Loshchits, "Est' takie parni," *Uchitel'skaia gazeta*, 24 September 1968, 4.

16. Between 1914 and 1939, the number of Russian Orthodox churches declined from over 54,000 to merely several hundred. See Timothy Ware, *The Orthodox Church*, rev. ed. (London: Penguin, 1993), 162.

17. Mikhail Geller, "Vasilii Shukshin: v poiskakh voli," *Vestnik russkogo khristianskogo dvizheniia* 120 (1977): 166.

18. Aleksandr Solzhenitsyn writes that "Shukshin appears to have been much agitated by the question of religion, and [in the early 1970s] was making a strenuous effort to justify himself in a way that seemed specifically

hostile to religion yet was not without inner concessions to it." See Solzhen-itsyn, *Invisible Allies*, trans. Alexis Klimoff and Michael Nicholson (Washington, D.C.: Counterpoint, 1995) 111.

19. Carl and Ellendea Proffer, "Introduction: Russian Fiction into the Eighties," in *Contemporary Russian Prose*, ed. Carl and Ellendea Proffer (Ann Arbor, Mich.: Ardis, 1982), xxiii.

20. Enid Welsford, *The Fool: His Social and Literary History* (London: Faber and Faber, 1935), 321.

21. Mikhail Bakhtin, *Rabelais and His World*, trans. Hélène Iswolsky (Bloomington: Indiana University Press, 1984), 10; my emphasis.

22. Vladimir Solov'ev, "Vasilii Shukshin: maniia pravdoiskatel'stva," *Novoe russkoe slovo* 25 (July 1989): 6.

23. Vasilii Shukshin, quoted in N. Lordkipanidze, "Shukshin snimaet *Kalinu krasnuiu*," *Iskusstvo kino* 10 (1974): 115.

24. Vasilii Shukshin, "Nravstvennost' est' Pravda," in *Voprosy samomu sebe*, 54.

25. Ibid., 55–56.

26. Ibid., 54.

27. Dmitrii Likhachev, *Zametki o russkom*, 2d rev. ed. (Moscow: Sovetskaia Rossiia, 1984), 15.

28. Mikhail Bakhtin, "Forms of Time and of the Chronotope in the Novel," in *The Dialogic Imagination: Four Essays*, trans. Caryl Emerson and Michael Holquist, ed. Michael Holquist (Austin: University of Texas Press, 1981), 164.

29. They are first described in his "'Tol'ko eto ne budet ekonomich-eskaia stat'ia . . . ,'" in *Voprosy samomu sebe*, 26–29, an unfinished article Shukshin was commissioned to write by the newspaper *Pravda* about the flight of youth from the village.

30. Ibid., 29.

31. Liudmila Shepelova, *Nravstvennye iskaniia v sovremennoi sovet-skoi proze o derevne: uchebnoe posobie k spetskursu* (Cheliabinsk: Cheliabinskii gosudarstvennyi pedagogicheskii institut, 1984), 52.

32. According to the commentaries to the stories, "Kliauza" was written in December 1973, "Van'ka Tepliashin" in May 1972 (2:579, 584).

33. Shukshin's self-accusation was missed by the majority of readers and critics who first read "A Slander" in 1974. As Diane Nemec Ignashev reports, many considered it "bad form" for him, a "well-known personality with power and connections in the press," to victimize the admittedly "despicable" but "uncultured" and "poor" concierge, who "is just another unfortunate thorn in the side of advancing socialist society." See Ignashev, "Song and Confession in the Short Prose of Vasilij Makarovič Šukšin: 1929–1974" (Ph.D. diss., University of Chicago, 1984), 487. Reader response was so great that some of the letters were collected by a sociologist and

published. See V. Kantorovich, "Chitatel'skie pis'ma," *Sibirskie ogni* 9 (1975): 157–68.

34. Iu. Smelkov, "Strannye liudi Vasiliia Shukshina," *Komsomol'skaia pravda*, 16 September 1970, 2.

35. Vasilii Shukshin, "Kommentarii" to "'Pered mnogomillionnoi auditoriei,'" in *Voprosy samomu sebe,* 182.

36. Vladimir Solov'ev, "Fenomenon Vasiliia Shukshina," *Iskusstvo kino* 10 (1975): 18.

37. Mikhail Bakhtin, *Problems of Dostoevsky's Poetics,* trans. and ed. Caryl Emerson (Minneapolis: University of Minnesota Press, 1984), 233.

38. Galina Belaia, "Paradoksy i otkrytiia Vasiliia Shukshina," in *Khudozhestvennyi mir sovremennoi prozy* (Moscow: Nauka, 1983), 101.

39. Bakhtin, *Problems of Dostoevsky's Poetics,* 125.

40. Diane Nemec Ignashev elaborates on Gleb's thespianism in "Vasily Shukshin's *Srezal* and the Question of Transition," *Slavonic and East European Review* 66 (July 1988): 343.

41. See L. Geller, "Opyt prikladnoi stilistiki: rasskaz V. Shukshina kak ob"ekt issledovaniia s peremennym fokusnym rasstoianiem," *Wiener Slawistischer Almanach* 4 (1979): 95–123; Ignashev, "Vasily Shukshin's *Srezal,*" 337–56; and Svetlana Mikhailovna Kozlova, *Poetika rasskazov V. M. Shukshina* (Barnaul: Altaiskii gosudarstvennyi universitet, 1993), 118–37. These three treatments are the best discussions of the story to date.

42. N. N. Sobolevskaia, "Komicheskoe kak forma proiavleniia narodnogo soznaniia v rasskazakh V. Shukshina," in *Tendentsii razvitiia russkoi literatury Sibiri v XVIII–XX vv.,* ed. L. P. Iakimova (Novosibirsk: Nauka, 1985), 104.

43. See Ignashev, "Vasily Shukshin's *Srezal,*" 339–40, and Viktor Gorn, *Vasilii Shukshin: lichnost', knigi* (Barnaul: Altaiskoe knizhnoe izdatel'stvo), 71–77, for summaries of the critical response to "Cutting Them Down to Size."

44. Vasilii Shukshin, "'Ia rodom iz derevni . . . ,'" in *Voprosy samomu sebe,* 205.

45. This is the Proffers' complaint. In comparing the two terms for freedom, they lament that "Shukshin never felt strongly called to deal with the larger question of liberty which obviously faces everyone who lives in the USSR." See their "Introduction: Russian Fiction into the Eighties," xxxiii.

46. Iu. Nikishov wrote that in Shukshin's third collection, his "heroes are presented outside of the collective concerns so important for Soviet people." See Nikishov, "Ot ulybki do ironii," *Literaturnaia Rossiia,* 28 May 1971, 11.

47. Thomas Moore, *Care of the Soul* (New York: HarperCollins, 1992), xiii.

48. See Diane Nemec Ignashev, "The Art of Vasilij Šukšin: *Volja* through Song," *Slavic and East European Journal* 32 (1988): 415–27, especially 424–26.

49. See Joseph Campbell, *The Hero with a Thousand Faces* (Princeton, N.J.: Princeton University Press, 1969), 128–30 n. 46.

50. N. Leiderman, "Trudnaia doroga vozvysen'ia: o novykh proizvedeniiakh Vasiliia Shukshina," *Sibirskie ogni* 8 (1974): 166, 169.

51. N. A. Bilichenko, "Shukshin's Hero through the Eyes of the Critics," *Soviet Studies in Literature* 17, no. 1 (Winter 1980–81): 50; translation of "Geroi V. Shukshina v otsenkakh kritiki," *Russkaia literatura* 2 (1980): 218–27.

52. Ibid., 66.

CHAPTER FIVE

1. This fact has been noted by critics. In a 1971 overview, V. Kantorovich describes Shukshin's characters as a "gallery of types" who "are brought out on stage with their own direct speech, which reveals the type of thinking characteristic of them." See his "Novye tipy, novyi slovar', novye otnosheniia," *Sibirskie ogni* 9 (1971): 176. In their 1974 review of *Kharaktery*, "Svoi liudi—sochtemsia," I. Solov'eva and V. Shitova call Shukshin's stories "a study of types, Russian types, such as they have arisen over the years and such as they live today" (*Novyi mir* 3 [1974]: 248). Deming Brown writes that "the main function of Shukshin's stories is to display characters in large numbers, constituting, it would seem, a gallery of types and curiosities." See his *Soviet Russian Literature since Stalin* (Cambridge: Cambridge University Press, 1978), 294. A. E. Balikhin speaks of "a whole encyclopedia of contemporary types" created by the writer in his "Vasily Makarovich Shukshin: His Life and Work," trans. V. I. Korotkii, introduction to Vasilii Shukshin, *Rasskazy* (Moscow: Russkii iazyk, 1984), 23. Galina Belaia notes that Shukshin—"perhaps alone" among prose writers in the 1960s and 1970s—"painted a gallery of various national *types*" ("The Crisis of Soviet Artistic Mentality in the 1960s and 1970s," trans. Lesley Milne, in *New Directions in Soviet Literature: Selected Papers from the Fourth World Congress for Soviet and East European Studies, Harrogate, 1990*, ed. Sheelagh Duffin Graham [New York: St. Martin's Press, 1992], 14).

2. Anatoly Vishevsky, *Soviet Literary Culture in the 1970s: The Politics of Irony* (Gainesville: University Press of Florida, 1993), 5.

3. V. Frolov, *Muza plamennoi satiry: ocherk sovetskoi komediografii (1918–86)* (Moscow: Sovetskii pisatel', 1988), 310.

4. The comparison to Anderson is actually very appropriate. Anderson, like Shukshin, wrote about the lives of marginalized and isolated rural eccentrics. In his most famous collection of short stories, *Winesburg, Ohio* (1919), Anderson calls these eccentrics "grotesques," a characterization that

falls somewhere between Shukshin's notion of the *chudik* and his later satiric types.

5. Lev Anninskii, "Put' pisatelia," in *O Shukshine: ekran i zhizn'*, ed. Lidiia Fedoseeva-Shukshina and R. D. Chernenko (Moscow: Iskusstvo, 1979), 123.

6. Aristarkh Andrianov, "Eshche raz o 'strannykh' geroiakh Vasiliia Shukshina," *Molodaia gvardiia* 10 (1973): 311.

7. Solov'eva and Shitova, "Svoi liudi—sochtemsia," 250.

8. Morris Bishop, "La Bruyère (1645–1696)," in *The Middle Ages to 1800*, vol. 1 of *A Survey of French Literature* (New York: Harcourt Brace Jovanovich, 1965), 270.

9. Cited in ibid.

10. Andrianov, "Eshche raz o 'strannykh' geroiakh Vasiliia Shukshina," 311.

11. Northrop Frye, "Satire," in *The Harper Handbook to Literature*, ed. Northrop Frye, Sheridan Baker, and George Perkins (New York: Harper and Row, 1985), 415.

12. These are Enid Welsford's descriptions of the comic writer and the satirist, respectively. See Welsford, *The Fool: His Social and Literary History* (London: Faber and Faber, 1935), 325.

13. Translations from "Petia" will be cited with slight revisions from Vasilii Shukshin, "Petia," trans. Robert Daglish, *Soviet Literature* 12 (1971): 102–8. Citations to this text will be given parenthetically after the Russian reference in the following manner: (2:32/103).

14. In its fixation on the unpleasant details of Petia's morning toilet, the passage calls to mind the opening pages of Iurii Olesha's *Envy* (*Zavist'*, 1927), which Shukshin might have read when it was republished, for the first time since 1936, in the late 1950s.

15. "Petia" was published in *Literaturnaia Rossiia*, 16 October 1970, 12–13, together with "Boots." "The Three Graces" was published there a year later: 24 December 1971, 14–15.

16. An excerpt from Book One of *The Liubavin Family* appeared 16 July 1965. "The Cosmos, the Nervous System, and a Hunk of Fatback" was published 29 July 1966.

17. See the entries *"Literaturnaya gazeta"* and *"Literaturnaya Rossiya"* in Wolfgang Kasack, *Dictionary of Russian Literature since 1917* (New York: Columbia University Press, 1988), 222–23.

18. Vishevsky, *Soviet Literary Culture of the 1970s*, 9–10.

19. Vasilii Shukshin, "Esli by znat' . . . ," in *Voprosy samomu sebe* (Moscow: Molodaia gvardiia, 1981), 217.

20. In his commentary to the collected works, Lev Anninskii cites a 24 January 1966 interview with Shukshin in *Moskovskaia kinonedelia* and an announcement in *Literaturnaia Rossiia*, 17 February 1967, about the

reading ("Kommentarii," in V. M. Shukshin, *Sobranie sochinenii,* 3 vols. [Moscow: Molodaia gvardiia, 1984–85], 1:659–60).

21. Sveltana Boym, *Commonplaces: Mythologies of Everyday Life in Russia* (Cambridge, Mass: Harvard University Press, 1994), 124.

22. Frye, "Satire," 415.

23. Valerii Geideko, *Postoianstvo peremen: sotsial'no-nravstvennye problemy sovremennoi sovetskoi prozy* (Moscow: Sovremennik, 1978), 200.

24. This irreverence was also one reason why the journal *Nash sovremennik* turned the manuscript down, citing the play's "provocative content." See "'Odno znaiu—rabotat' . . .': pis'ma Vasiliia Shukshina Vasiliiu Belovu," *Literaturnaia Rossiia,* 21 July 1989, 7. The play was never staged during Shukshin's lifetime.

25. Brown, *Soviet Russian Literature since Stalin,* 295.

26. D. S. Mirsky, *A History of Russian Literature from Its Beginnings to 1900* (New York: Vintage, 1958), 161.

27. Geoffrey Hosking, *Beyond Socialist Realism: Soviet Fiction since Ivan Denisovich* (London: Granada, 1980), 177.

28. V. Frolov was the first to discuss Shukshin's use of the classical unities in his *Muza plamennoi satiry: ocherk sovetskoi komediografii (1918–86)* (Moscow: Sovetskii pisatel', 1988), 312.

29. Hosking, *Beyond Socialist Realism,* 178.

30. Leonid Ershov, *Pamiat' i vremia* (Moscow: Sovremennik, 1984), 262.

31. M. Vaniashova, "Shukshinskie litsedei," *Literaturnaia ucheba* 4 (1979): 167.

32. Ibid.

33. Mikhail A. Pozin, "Vasilii Shukshin, the Writer and His Times," (Ph.D. diss., University of Illinois at Urbana-Champaign, 1991), 155–57.

34. Diane Nemec Ignashev was the first to speak at length about this aspect of Shukshin's life and art, both with respect to *Do tret'ikh petukhov* and other works. See her "Song and Confession in the Short Prose of Vasilij Makarovič Šukšin: 1929–1974" (Ph.D. diss., University of Chicago, 1984), especially 1–124, 541–44, 614–67.

35. Shukshin had moved into his own four-bedroom apartment in 1972, shortly before writing *Energetic People.*

36. Mikhail Epstein, "After the Future: On the New Consciousness in Literature," trans. Gene Kuperman, in *Late Soviet Culture: From Perestroika to Novostroika,* ed. Thomas Lahusen with Gene Kuperman (Durham, N.C.: Duke University Press, 1993), 261.

37. Victor Erofeyev, "Russia's *Fleurs du Mal,*" trans. Andrew Reynolds, introduction to *The Penguin Book of New Russian Writing: Russia's Fleurs du Mal,* ed. Victor Erofeyev and Andrew Reynolds (London: Penguin, 1995), ix–xxx.

38. Epstein, "After the Future," 261.
39. Ibid., 262.
40. Ibid., 261.
41. G. Tsvetov, "Literaturnaia sud'ba shukshinskikh 'chudikov,'" in *V. M. Shukshin: zhizn' i tvorchestvo*, vol. 2, ed. S. M. Kozlova and A. A. Chuvakin (Barnaul: Altaiskii gosudarstvennyi universitet, 1992), 67–69.
42. Ibid., 69.
43. Diane Nemec Ignashev, "Vasily Shukshin's *Srezal* and the Question of Transition," *Slavonic and East European Review* 66 (1988): 356.
44. Epstein, "After the Future," 261.
45. This is Isaiah Berlin's succinct summation from his *Russian Thinkers* (London: Penguin, 1978), 143.
46. The interview is from the newspaper *Moskovskaia kinonedelia*, 24 January 1966, reprinted in the commentary to the novella in Shukshin's three-volume collected works (*Sobranie sochinenii*, 3:660). This line has been left out of the commentary to the novel in the five-volume Literaturnoe nasledie collected works.
47. Vasilii Shukshin, "Kommentarii" to "Monolog na lestnitse," in *Voprosy samomu sebe*, 48.

CHAPTER SIX

1. Lev Anninskii, "Put' pisatelia," in *O Shukshine: ekran i zhizn'*, ed. Lidiia Fedoseeva-Shukshina and R. D. Chernenko (Moscow: Iskusstvo, 1979), 121.
2. N. A. Bilichenko, "Shukshin's Hero through the Eyes of the Critics," *Soviet Studies in Literature* 17, no. 1 (Winter 1980–81): 47.
3. Kathleen Parthé, *Russian Village Prose: The Radiant Past* (Princeton, N.J.: Princeton University Press, 1992), 81.
4. Mikhail Geller and Vladimir Maksimov, "Vasilii Shukshin: besedy o sovremennykh russkikh pisateliakh," *Strelets* 3 (1987): 25.
5. Alexander Gordon, "Student Years," trans. Paula Garb, in *About Andrei Tarkovsky*, ed. Marina Tarkovskaya (Moscow: Progress, 1990), 35–36.
6. Vida T. Johnson and Graham Petrie, *The Films of Andrei Tarkovsky: A Visual Fugue* (Bloomington: Indiana University Press, 1994), 11.
7. Andrey Tarkovsky, *Sculpting in Time: Reflections on the Cinema*, trans. Kitty Hunter-Blair (Austin: University of Texas Press, 1991), 165.
8. Johnson and Petrie, *The Films of Andrei Tarkovsky*, 25.
9. Vasilii Shukshin, "Iz rabochikh zapisei," in *Voprosy samomu sebe* (Moscow: Molodaia gvardiia, 1981), 252.
10. Iurii Mal'tsev, "Promezhutochnaia literatura i kriterii podlinnosti," *Kontinent* 25 (1980): 285–331. See also his *Volnaia russkaia literatura* (Frankfurt: Possev, 1976).

11. Josephine Woll, *Invented Truth: Soviet Reality and the Literary Imagination of Iurii Trifonov* (Durham, N.C.: Duke University Press, 1991), 14.

12. Shukshin, "Iz rabochikh zapisei," 252.

13. This is Woll's characterization in *Invented Truth*, 2.

14. Aleksandr Solzhenitsyn, *The Oak and the Calf: Sketches of Literary Life in the Soviet Union*, trans. Harry Willetts (New York: Harper Colophon, 1979), 521.

15. The films are: Boris Barnet's *Alenka*, Lev Kulidzhanov's *When the Trees Were Tall* (*Kogda derev'ia byli bol'shimi*), Iurii Egorov's *Business Trip* (*Komandirovka*), and Iurii Pobedonostsev's *Mishka, Serega, and I* (the first movie by Mosfilm; the latter three all by Gorky Film Studio).

16. Vasilii Shukshin, "Mne vezlo na umnykh i dobrykh liudei . . . ," in *Voprosy samomu sebe*, 152.

17. Mark Volotskii, "Logika sluchainostei," *Literaturnoe obozrenie* 7 (1989): inside front and back covers. The stories were "O materi" ("About Mother"), "Muzhchina i zhenshchina" ("A Man and a Woman"), and "Opozdal" ("Late"). The last seems to be an earlier version of "Stepan in Love" ("Stepkina liubov'"), while the second appears to be a version of a storyline that would repeat in Shukshin's diploma film *Iz Lebiazh'ego soobshchaiut* (*News from Lebiazhii*) and the novella *There, in the Distance*.

18. Andreev, "Ob avtore," preface to Vasilii Shukshin, *Sel'skie zhiteli* (Moscow: Molodaia gvardiia, 1963), 3.

19. Ol'ga Rumiantseva, "Govorit' pravdu, tol'ko pravdu," in *O Shukshine*, 263–64.

20. Ibid., 264–65. Shukshin was willing to make small changes in his stories (Rumiantseva uses the verb *dorabotat'*, "to add finishing touches") but refused to rewrite "Sten'ka Razin." The board wanted him to cut out the description of the statue, which tells the story of Stepan's betrayal. Rumiantseva writes: "The whole scene was full of such dynamic, quickly changing action that it would be impossible to depict it all in a sculpture. This struck us as far-fetched, unnatural" (264). Shukshin withdrew the story, only to publish it, unchanged, two years later in the journal *Moskva*.

21. Grigori Svirski, *A History of Post-War Soviet Writing: The Literature of Moral Opposition*, trans. and ed. Robert Dessaix and Michael Ulman (Ann Arbor, Mich.: Ardis, 1981), 235.

22. Anatolii Zabolotskii, "Shukshin v kadre i za kadrom," *Moskva* 1 (1993): 145. The other two students whom Romm placed at Mosfilm were Aleksandr Gordon and Aleksandr Mitta. Shukshin, on the other hand, was offered a position at a studio in the provinces, in Sverdlovsk (Ekaterinburg today).

23. Anatolii Zabolotskii, Shukshin's main cameraman for his last two films, insists that Shukshin told him that a different member of the exami-

nation committee—the Siberian actor Nikolai Okhlopkov (Buslai in Sergei Eisenstein's *Alexander Nevsky*)—and not Romm was responsible for Shukshin's admission to VGIK ("Shukshin v kadre i za kadrom," *Moskva* 1 [1993]: 145). But Zabolotskii's account, which suffers from its author's anti-Semitic and Russian chauvinist biases (Romm was Jewish), conflicts with Shukshin's own version, where Romm is unequivocally credited. See Shukshin's "Mne vezlo na umnykh i dobrykh liudei . . . ," 151–52.

24. Viktor Nekrasov, "Vzgliad i nechto," pt. 2 *Kontinent* 12 (1977): 117.

25. Svirski, *A History of Post-War Soviet Writing*, 293–94.

26. Anatoly Gladilin, *The Making and Unmaking of a Soviet Writer: My Story of the "Young Prose" of the Sixties and After*, trans. David Lapeza (Ann Arbor, Mich.: Ardis, 1979), 35.

27. Nekrasov, "Vzgliad i nechto," 115.

28. Vladimir Korobov reports that Shukshin's residence permit was one of several that Kochetov arranged at the end of 1962 for young writers publishing in *Oktiabr'*. Ol'ga Rumiantseva let Shukshin use her address in his permit, although he never lived with her family, staying instead with friends and living on location while shooting films until late 1964, when he received his own apartment. See Korobov, *Vasilii Shukshin*, 2d ed. (Moscow: Sovremennik, 1988), 75 n. 1. This period of "homelessness" (1960–64) explains Shukshin's comment in 1974 that he "struggled five years to get his Moscow residence permit" ("Kommentarii" to "'Eshche raz vyveriaia svoiu zhizn'," in *Voprosy samomu sebe*, 242). He had the permit in a little over two years, but the apartment would come only after the success of the film *There's This Guy*.

29. Svirski, *A History of Post-War Soviet Writing*, 245.

30. V. Sofronova, "Talant dushi," *Znamia* 1 (1964): 244–45.

31. Katia Shukshina was born in February 1965. Shukshin officially established paternity on 4 March 1972 (interview with Viktoriia Sofronova, Moscow, 27 March 1992). See Korobov, *Vasilii Shukshin*, 2d ed., 133–35, for letters Shukshin wrote to Sofronova about Katia. A more detailed, sensationalist treatment of this topic can be found in Tamara Ponomareva, "On prishel izdaleka," *Altai* 2 (1989): 3–79.

32. *Vshivaia sovetskaia vlast', vshivyi Lenin*. Sofronova, interview, 27 March 1992.

33. Ibid. Sofronova pointed out that not many Soviet men would have insisted that she go through with the pregnancy. Shukshin did; he was adamantly opposed to an abortion.

34. Vasilii Shukshin, "Komentarii" to "Monolog na lestnitse," in *Voprosy samomu sebe*, 53.

35. Nekrasov, "Vzgliad i nechto," 118.

36. Gladilin, *The Making and Unmaking of a Soviet Writer*, 129.

37. See Vasilii Shukshin, "Kommentarii" to "Predlagaiu studii . . . ,"
in *Voprosy samomu sebe*, 110, and Diane Nemec Ignashev, "Song and Confession in the Short Prose of Vasilij Makarovič Šukšin: 1929–1974" (Ph.D.
diss., University of Chicago, 1984), 107–8.

38. The letters were published by G. Rassokhin from the Saratov
Fedin Museum as "Iz ekspozitsii gosudarstvennogo muzeia K. A. Fedina,"
Volga 2 (1982): 151.

39. Shukshin writes that same year (1967): "By all appearances, only
our long-range artillery works (Solzhenitsyn). And this is good!" ("Iz rabochikh zapisei," 232).

40. Another example of this skewed moral scale can be found in
Shukshin's story "A Wife Saw Her Husband Off to Paris," where Kol'ka
commits suicide in order to avoid telling his mother that he is divorcing his
wife and leaving his child. In the village it was considered "a big sin to leave
your own child" (2:100). As Anatolii Bocharov points out, however, surely
suicide is a bigger sin than a divorce that separates you from your children
("Counterpoint: The Common and the Individual in the Prose of Iuryi Trifonov, Vasilii Shukshin, and Valentin Rasputin," *Soviet Studies in Literature*
20, no. 1 [Winter 1983–84]: 47).

41. A. Marchenko, "Iz knizhnogo raia . . . ," *Voprosy literatury* 4
(1969): 70.

42. Georgii Burkov defended Shukshin's Party membership as the
artist's attempt to fight for reform within the system: "Why was he, someone
so alien to careerism, in the ranks of the Party? For the simple reason that
he thought we should be in the Party, too, and not just 'them.' There should
be as many of us there as possible." See his "V dal' svetluiu, k vole . . . ,"
Trud, 23 July 1989, 4.

43. L. Belova, "Tri rusla odnogo puti: O tvorchestve Vasiliia Shukshina," in *Voprosy kinoiskusstva*, vol. 17 (Moscow: Nauka, 1976), 148. Anninskii expresses similar sentiments in his "Put' pisatelia," 120.

44. N. Zhelezniakova, "'Zolotoi lev'—prostomu parniu," *Ogonek* 36
(1964): 29; L. Pogozheva, "Svoia tema," *Sovetskii ekran* 18 (1964): 2–3.

45. N. Ignat'eva, "Vasilii Shukshin i ego geroi," *Nedelia* 45 (1964): 18.

46. "Iskusstvo i GAI," *Sovetskii ekran* 6 (1965): 12.

47. I. Storiia, "Zhivet takaia devushka: radioocherk," *Voprosy literatury* 3 (1965): 242.

48. N. Tumanova, "Pashka Kolokol'nikov i drugie," *Sovetskaia kul'tura*,
25 March 1965; Larisa Kriachko, "Boi za dobrotu," *Oktiabr'* 3 (1965): 175–84.

49. Ignashev, "Song and Confession," 77.

50. Bilichenko, "Shukshin's Hero through the Eyes of the Critics,"
47–48.

51. Kriachko, "Boi za dobrotu," 180.

52. Ibid., 179.

53. Tumanova, "Pashka Kolokol'nikov i drugie," 3.

54. Kriachko, "Boi za dobrotu," 180.

55. Ibid., 180–81.

56. In a contemptuous samizdat mock obituary of Shukshin attributed by Anatolii Zabolotskii to the writer Fridrikh Gorenshtein, this phrase (*terror nizov*) describes the threat posed by the official endorsement of the Russian nationalist aspects of Shukshin and the Village Prose writers. See Zabolotskii, "Shukshin v kadre i za kadrom," *Moskva* 2 (1993): 155.

57. Larissa Kriachko, "Sut' i vidimost'," *Oktiabr'* 2 (1966): 186.

58. Viktor Orlov, "Strela v polete," *Literaturnaia gazeta,* 10 March 1966, 3.

59. M. Bleiman, "Rezhissura-eto professiia," *Sovetskii ekran* 7 (1966): 5.

60. Korobov, *Vasilii Shukshin,* 2d ed., 137.

61. Shukshin, "Kommentarii" to "Monolog na lestnitse," 46. Viktor Gorn reports that Nekrasov's poem "The Schoolboy" ("Shkol'nik") was Shukshin's lifelong favorite (*Vasilii Shukshin: lichnost', knigi* [Barnaul: Altaiskoe knizhnoe izdatel'stvo, 1990], 43–44). The poem is about Lomonosov's now-legendary rise from poor peasant to become, in Pushkin's words, "the first Russian university." The line "znai, rabotai, da ne trus'" ("know, work, and do not fear") from the poem is quoted in "Monologue on a Staircase" (see *Voprosy samomu sebe,* 38). The part of the poem that includes this line is sung in *Kalina krasnaia* by Shukshin's longtime VGIK friend Aleksandr Sarantsev during the *zastol'e* (bout of friendly drinking and singing) at the Baikalovs' house (see Korobov, *Vasilii Shukshin,* 2d ed., 251; see also Korobov, *Vasilii Shukshin: tvorchestvo, lichnost'* [Moscow: Sovetskaia Rossiia, 1977], 40–41).

62. Shukshin, "Kommentarii" to "Monolog na lestnitse," 46–47.

63. Lev Anninskii, "Ne v etom delo, tiatia!" *Iskusstvo kino* 7 (1966): 15–20.

64. N. Klado, "Tak v chem delo?" *Iskusstvo kino* 7 (1966): 21–25.

65. Bilichenko, "Shukshin's Hero through the Eyes of the Critics," 48.

66. Vasilii Shukshin, "Voprosy samomu sebe," in *Voprosy samomu sebe,* 11.

67. Shukshin, "Monolog na lestnitse," 34.

68. Ibid., 36, 34, 35.

69. Shukshin, "Voprosy samomu sebe," 12.

70. Ibid., 18, 14.

71. Ibid., 12.

72. Shukshin, "Monolog na lestnitse," 41.

73. Vasilii Shukshin, "'Ia rodom iz derevni . . . ,'" in *Voprosy samomu sebe,* 198.

74. See Kathleen Parthé's detailed treatment of these elements in the first chapter of *Russian Village Prose.*

75. Deming Brown, *Soviet Russian Literature since Stalin* (Cambridge: Cambridge University Press, 1979), 293.

76. Geoffrey Hosking, "The Twentieth Century: In Search of New Ways, 1953–80," in *The Cambridge History of Russian Literature*, rev. ed., ed. Charles A. Moser (Cambridge: Cambridge University Press, 1992), 565.

77. Marchenko, "Iz knizhnogo raia . . . ," 68.

78. Shukshin, "Monolog na lestnitse," 31.

79. Vasilii Shukshin, "'Tol'ko eto ne budet ekonomicheskaia stat'ia . . . ,'" in *Voprosy samomu sebe*, 25–26.

80. See Natal'ia Zinovieva's reminiscences in *On pokhozh na svoiu rodinu*, ed. V. I. Ashcheulov and Iu. G. Egorov (Barnaul: Altaiskoe knizhnoe izdatel'stvo, 1989), 26.

81. Anninskii, "Put' pisatelia," 123.

82. Galina Belaia, "The Crisis of Soviet Artistic Mentality in the 1960s and 1970s," trans. Lesley Milne, in *New Directions in Soviet Literature: Selected Papers from the Fourth World Congress for Soviet and East European Studies, Harrogate, 1990*, ed. Sheelagh Duffin Graham (New York: St. Martin's Press, 1992), 9.

83. Ibid., 12.

84. L. Muravinskaia, "Khronika zhizni i tvorchestvo V. M. Shukshina v dokumentakh, pis'makh, vospominaniiakh," in *On pokhozh na svoiu rodinu*, 223.

85. Anatolii Bocharov, "Counterpoint: The Common and the Individual in the Prose of Iuryi Trifonov, Vasilii Shukshin, and Valentin Rasputin," *Soviet Studies in Literature* 20, no. 1 (Winter 1983–84): 47.

86. Ibid., 32.

87. B. M. Iudalevich, "Khudozhnik i ego geroi: k 60-letiiu so dnia rozhdeniia V. M. Shukshina," *Izvestiia Sibirskogo otdeleniia Akademii nauk SSSR: Seriia istorii, filologii i filosofii* 3 (1989): 57.

88. Shukshin writes in a letter to the Village Prose author Vasilii Belov at this time: "*Novyi mir* no longer accepts anything for publication, I've withdrawn my stories from them." See "'Odno znaiu—rabotat' . . .': pis'ma Vasiliia Shukshina Vasiliiu Belovu," *Literaturnaia Rossiia*, 21 July 1989, 7.

89. This information has been summarized from Catharine Theimer Nepomnyashchy, "*Our Contemporary* and the Development of the Rural Prose Tradition," *Ulbandus Review* 1, no. 2 (Spring 1978): 58–73.

90. "'Odno znaiu—rabotat' . . . ,'" 7. The novella Shukshin is referring to is probably *Point of View*, which came out in the July issue of *Zvezda* that year.

91. Ia. E. El'sberg, "Smena stilei v sovetskom russkom rasskaze 1950–1960-kh godov: Sergei Antonov, Iurii Kazakov, Vasilii Shukshin," in *Smena literaturnykh stilei: na materiale russkoi literatury XIX–XX vekov*, ed. V. V. Kozhinov (Moscow: Nauka, 1974), 191.

92. L. Anninskii, "'Shukshinskaia zhizn,'" and Vl. Gusev, "Imenno zhizn', a ne chto drugoe . . . ," *Literaturnoe obozrenie* 1 (1974): 50–55.

93. V. Chalmaev, *Obnovlenie perspektivy* (Moscow: Sovremennik, 1978), 117. See also Chalmaev's article by the same name in *Moskva* 12 (1975): 191.

94. Vsevolod Sakharov, "Vlast' kanona: zametki o rasskaze," *Nash sovremennik* 1 (1977): 163.

95. Aleksandr Ovcharenko, *Bol'shaia literatura: osnovnye tendentsii razvitiia sovetskoi khudozhestvennoi prozy 1945–85 godov. Semidesiatye gody* (Moscow: Sovremennik, 1988), 324.

96. Solov'eva and Shitova, "Svoi liudi—sochtemsia," 246, 247.

97. Ibid., 246, 248.

98. Ibid., 250.

99. Boris Pankin, "Shukshin about Himself: Notes on the Collection *Morality Is Truth,*" *Soviet Studies in Literature* 17, no. 1 (1980–81): 40.

100. Lev Anninskii, "Shukshin-publitsist," introduction to Vasilii Shukshin, *Nravstvennost' est' Pravda,* comp. L. Fedoseeva-Shukshina (Moscow: Sovetskaia Rossiia, 1979), 4.

101. See, respectively, Shukshin's essays "Monolog na lestnitse," "Nravstvennost' est' Pravda," and "'Eshche raz vyveriaia svoiu zhizn','" in *Voprosy samomu sebe,* 46, 56, 229.

102. Pankin, "Shukshin about Himself," 40–41.

103. Viktor Kamianov, *Doverie k slozhnosti: sovremennost' i klassicheskaia traditsiia* (Moscow: Sovetskii pisatel', 1984), 307.

104. Konstantin Rudnitskii, "Proza i ekran," in *O Shukshine,* 93.

105. Eduard Yefimov, *Vasily Shukshin,* trans. Avril Pyman (Moscow: Raduga, 1986), 104.

106. Zhores Medvedev, *Soviet Agriculture* (New York: W. W. Norton, 1987), 323.

107. Vasilii Shukshin, "Kommentarii" to "Slovo o maloi rodine," in *Voprosy samomu sebe,* 71.

108. See Zabolotskii's account in the first part of his reminiscences, "Shukshin v kadre i za kadrom," *Moskva* 1 (1993): 152–58.

109. Ibid., 158.

110. Val S. Golovskoy with John Rimberg, *Behind the Soviet Screen: The Motion-Picture Industry in the USSR: 1972–1982* (Ann Arbor, Mich.: Ardis, 1986), 47–53.

111. Zabolotskii, "Shukshin v kadre i za kadrom," *Moskva* 2 (1993): 151.

112. They saw the movie at a closed showing at Gorky Film Studio. See Zabolotskii, "Shukshin v kadre i za kadrom," pt. 1, 153.

113. Yefimov, *Vasily Shukshin,* 103.

114. Shukshin, "Kommentarii" to "Slovo o maloi rodine," 71.

115. Iu. Khaniutin, "'Da' i 'net' Vasiliia Shukshina," *Sovetskii ekran* 12 (1973): 4.

116. Ibid.

117. R. Irenev, "Talant obeshchaet mnogoe," *Iskusstvo kino* 12 (1973): 103. See also Iu. Khaniutin, "'Da' i 'net' Vasiliia Shukshina," *Sovetskii ekran* 12 (1973): 4–5; Vladimir Solov'ev, "Eshche raz o kino," *Neva* 9 (1973): 199–202; L. Pogozheva, "Tri muzy Vasiliia Shukshina," *Literaturnaia gazeta*, 13 September 1972, 8; V. I. Fomin, "Doma i v gostiakh: 'Pechki-lavochki,'" in *Ekran 73/74* (Moscow: Iskusstvo, 1975), 28–31.

118. V. A. Iavinskii, "A vremena meniaiutsia . . . ," *Altaiskaia pravda*, 15 April 1973.

119. Shukshin quotes the letter in "Slovo o maloi rodine," 64. The essay was translated into English by Avril Pyman as "The Place Where I Was Born," in V. Shukshin, *Articles*, ed. Eduard Yefimov (Moscow: Raduga, 1986), 215–24.

120. V. I. Fomin, *Peresechenie parallel'nykh* (Moscow: Iskusstvo, 1976), 311.

121. Vasilii Shukshin, "Priznanie v liubvi," *Smena* 2 (1974): 12–17.

122. Shukshin, "Slovo o maloi rodine," 65–66; "The Place Where I Was Born," 216–17.

123. Shukshin, "Slovo o maloi rodine," 70; "The Place Where I Was Born," 224.

124. V. I. Fomin hailed *Pechki-lavochki* as the best of Shukshin's first four films; see his "Doma i v gostiakh" 31.

CHAPTER SEVEN

1. Some of the letters are reproduced in the following sources: R. Pliatt and M. Bulgakova, "Fil'm vzial za zhivoe," *Sovetskii ekran* 13 (1974): 1–2; V. I. Fomin, *Peresechenie parallel'nykh* (Moscow: Iskusstvo, 1975), 312; I. Levshina, *Liubite li vy kino?* (Moscow: Iskusstvo, 1978), 89–112; Iurii Vorontsov and Igor Rachuk, *The Phenomenon of Soviet Cinema* (Moscow: Progress, 1980), 357–68.

2. Pliatt and Bulgakova, "Fil'm vzial za zhivoe," 1–3; "Zhiznennyi material, poisk khudozhnika, avtorskaia kontseptsiia (obsuzhdaem *Kalinu krasnuiu:* kinopovest' i fil'm Vasiliia Shukshina)," *Voprosy literatury* 7 (1974): 28–90. A partial English translation of the latter was published as "Reality and the Writer's Vision," trans. Margaret Wettlin, *Soviet Literature* 9 (1975): 123–38.

3. See the editor's introduction to N. Lordkipanidze, "Shukshin snimaet 'Kalinu krasnuiu,'" *Iskusstvo kino* 10 (1974): 113–32.

4. "In Brief," *Soviet Literature* 9 (1975): 122.

5. Iurii Tiurin, *Kinematograf Vasiliia Shukshina* (Moscow: Iskusstvo, 1984), 225.

6. Hedrick Smith, *The Russians* (New York: Ballantine, 1977), 510.

7. This incisive formulation was suggested by one of the anonymous reviewers of the article version of this chapter, who pointed out the similarities between Khrushchev's and Brezhnev's interventions as well as the similar themes of Solzhenitsyn's novel and Shukshin's film.

8. Smith, *The Russians*, 511. Shukshin's main cameraman for the movie, Anatolii Zabolotskii, also reports that the film was approved from on high: "And then the film was viewed at the dachas and it became known that someone there had liked it." See part 2 of his reminiscences: "Shukshin v kadre i za kadrom," *Moskva* 2 (1993): 147.

9. Deming Brown, *Soviet Russian Literature since Stalin* (Cambridge: Cambridge University Press, 1979), 295. See also Geoffrey Hosking, *Beyond Socialist Realism: Soviet Fiction since Ivan Denisovich* (London: Granada, 1980), 166–68, and Edward J. Brown, *Russian Literature since the Revolution*, rev. ed. (Cambridge, Mass.: Harvard University Press, 1982), 312, who come to similar conclusions. Sergei Zalygin characterizes the story as one of "crime and punishment," as does Nina Tolchenova. See Zalygin, "Opiraias' na traditsiiu," in "Zhiznennyi material, poisk khudozhnika, avtorskaia kontseptsiia (obsuzhdaem *Kalinu krasnuiu:* kinopovest' i fil'm Vasiliia Shukshina)," *Voprosy literatury* 7 (1974): 46–53, and Tolchenova, *Slovo o Shukshine* (Moscow: Sovremennik, 1982), 43–52. Vera Apukhtina calls the film a "sociopsychological drama" about a man who was lured off the right path in life by evil people. See V. A. Apukhtina, *Proza V. Shukshina*, 2d. rev. ed. (Moscow: Vysshaia shkola, 1986), 40–45. Iurii Tiurin sums up the socially oriented view of the film by arguing that it represents "the pain of all of our postwar life, of all of the countryside" ("Fil'm, kotoryi potriasaet," *Trud*, 2 August 1986).

10. Donald M. Fiene, "Vasily Shukshin's *Kalina krasnaia*," in Vasily Shukshin, *Snowball Berry Red and Other Stories*, trans. Donald M. Fiene et al., ed. Donald M. Fiene (Ann Arbor, Mich.: Ardis, 1979), 206.

11. Robert Mann, "St. George in Vasilij Šukšin's 'Kalina krasnaja,'" *Slavic and East European Journal* 28, no. 4 (1984): 445–54.

12. See Shukshin's comments about the popular cinema in the interview "'Pered mnogomillionnoi auditroiei,'" in *Voprosy samomu sebe* (Moscow: Molodaia gvardiia, 1981), 168–82. Shukshin's phrase "mnogomillionnaia auditoria" is an allusion to Boris Shumiatskii's notion of "cinema for the millions" (*kinematografiia millionov*), the title of his 1935 book.

13. Vasilii Shukshin, "Vozrazhenie po suchshestvu," in *Voprosy samomu sebe*, 162. This essay first appeared as Shukshin's response to the *Voprosy literatury* roundtable in "Zhiznennyi material, poisk khudozhnika, avtorskaia kontseptsiia," 84–88.

14. The only prefilm assessment of the novella that I could find is in Aristarkh Andrianov, "Eshche raz o 'strannykh' geroiakh Vasiliia Shukshina," *Molodaia gvardiia* 10 (1973): 309–11.

15. V. Kisun'ko, "Vstrecha 'vtoroi' i 'tretei' zhizni," in "Zhiznennyi material, poisk khudozhnika, avtorskaia kontseptsiia," 75. See also Diane Nemec Ignashev, "Song and Confession in the Short Prose of Vasilij Makarovič Šukšin: 1929–1974" (Ph.D. diss., University of Chicago, 1984), 119.

16. Eduard Yefimov, *Vasily Shukshin*, trans. Avril Pyman (Moscow: Raduga, 1986), 190.

17. These are B. Runin's characterizations from "Dialektika kharaktera i eklektika stilia," in "Zhiznennyi material, poisk khudozhnika, avtorskaia konseptsiia," 32.

18. Richard Stites, *Russian Popular Culture* (Cambridge: Cambridge University Press, 1992), 142, 170.

19. Shukshin, "Vozrazhenie po suchshestvu," 163.

20. Konstantin Rudnitskii was the first to identify this theme in the movie in "Prostye istiny," *Iskusstvo kino* 6 (1974): 45.

21. Vladimir Solov'ev, "Vasilii Shukshin: maniia pravdoiskatel'stva," *Novoe russkoe slovo,* 25 July 1989, 6.

22. See, respectively, Evgenii Gromov, "Zhizn' i smert' Egora Prokudina," *Literaturnaia gazeta,* 27 February 1974, 8, and Neia Zorkaia, *Fol'klor, lubok, ekran* (Moscow: Iskusstvo, 1994), 147–51.

23. The *lubki* were simple drawings, usually lacking perspective and scale, colored by hand in three or four bright tones. They depicted Bible scenes and folk tales, and were often used to instruct children. See Suzanne Massie, *Land of the Firebird: The Beauty of Old Russia* (New York: Touchstone, 1980), 191–92.

24. M. Kuznetsov, "Obraz. Kharakter. Sud'ba," *Komsomol'skaia pravda,* 23 March 1974.

25. Ibid.

26. S. Borovikov, "Shukshin minus Shukshina," *Volga* 12 (1989): 181.

27. See especially Runin, "Dialektika kharaktera i eklektika stilia," 33–34, and K. Vanshenkin, "Nekotorye proschety," 72–74, both in "Zhiznennyi material, poisk khudozhnika, avtorskaia kontseptsiia."

28. L. Anninskii, "Mezh dvukh opor," in "Zhiznennyi material, poisk khudozhnika, avtorskaia kontseptsiia," 62–70.

29. Carl and Ellendea Proffer, "Introduction: Russian Fiction into the Eighties," in *Contemporary Russian Prose,* ed. Carl and Ellendea Proffer (Ann Arbor, Mich.: Ardis, 1982), xxi–xxii.

30. Shukshin's widow, Lidiia Fedoseeva, recalls singing the song with Shukshin in 1964 "when it had just appeared." They were on the way to film the movie *Kakoe ono, more?* (*What Is the Sea Like?*) with Soviet director E. Bocharov. It was during the filming of this movie that the two fell in love. See Lev Sidorovskii, "Serdtse Shukshina," *Literaturnaia Rossiia,* 10 October 1980, 16.

31. Vasilii Shukshin, "Esli by znat' . . . ," in *Voprosy samomu sebe,* 207.

32. Richard M. Gollin, *A Viewer's Guide to Film* (New York: McGraw-Hill, 1992), 131.

33. See part 2 of Zabolotskii's reminiscences, "Shukshin v kadre i za kadrom," 147.

34. "Vechernii zvon" is included in the collection *Russkie narodnyi pesni*, ed. A. M. Novikova (Moscow: Khudozhestvennaia literatura, 1957), 371.

35. My thanks to the anonymous reader of the article version of this chapter for this and other observations on which the following discussion is based.

36. According to the anonymous reader of the article version of this chapter, several Soviet film historians speculated ("in conversations rather than in print") that the "active use of problematic music material"—in this instance, the criminal songs—was one of the chief difficulties the film encountered in the world of Soviet cinema bureaucracy.

37. Fomin, *Peresechenie parallel'nykh*, 348–49.

38. The danger was great that a Soviet audience would reject Egor as a sympathetic hero. Kuznetsov anticipates this objection in his review "Obraz. Kharakter. Sud'ba": "We can hear those opposed to the film. First: what kind of hero is this? A criminal! And the whole picture is an idealization of such a loathsome phenomenon as criminal activity." His fears turned out to be well founded: nearly all of the letters published objecting to the film did so on the grounds of its inappropriate criminal subject. See note 1 to this chapter for references for these letters.

39. Kuznetsov, "Obraz. Kharakter. Sud'ba." See also Runin, "Dialektika kharaktera i eklektika stilia," 32.

40. V. Baranov, "Vragi Egora Prokudina," in "Zhiznennyi material, poisk khudozhnika, avtorskaia kontseptsiia," 54.

41. S. Gerasimov, "Pravda zhizni," *Sovetskaia kul'tura*, 9 April 1974, 3. See also Anninskii, "Mezh dvukh opor," 64; Pliatt and Bulgakova, "Fil'm vzial za zhivoe," 3; Kuznetsov, "Obraz. Kharakter. Sud'ba"; Iu. Smelkov, "'Kalina krasnaia': novaia kartina V. Shukshina," *Trud*, 14 April 1974; Gromov, "Zhizn' i smert' Egora Prokudina," 8; and especially G. Kapralov, "Berezy Egora Prokudina," *Pravda*, 1 April 1974, translated as "Life and Death of Egor Prokudin," *Sovetskii fil'm* 7 (1975): 14. In the latter piece, Kapralov states: "There is no dearth of superb actors in the Soviet cinema. Yet Shukshin's performance as Egor stands apart from all other screen roles of recent years."

42. Kapralov, "Life and Death of Egor Prokudin," 14.

43. Galina Belaia, "Rozhdenie novykh stilevykh form kak protsess preodoleniia 'neitral'nogo' stilia," in *Teoriia literaturnykh stilei. Mnogoobrazie stilei sovetskoi literatury. Voprosy tipologii*, ed. N. K. Gei et al. (Moscow: Nauka, 1978), 482.

44. Ignashev, "Song and Confession," 645.

45. Here and in all citations to the movie I am relying on the transcription of the film done by Robert Mann in cooperation with Lidiia Fedoseeva-Shukshina, *Kalina krasnaia: transkriptskiia fil'ma.* My thanks to Robert Mann for sharing this transcript with me.

46. Cited in Fomin, *Peresechenie parallel'nykh,* 342.

47. The portrait seems to be at once an indication of a theme (Egor's estrangement) and possibly a swipe at the provincial custom of hanging reprints of classic paintings as a sign of cultural sophistication. Zabolotskii reports that he and set designer Ippolit Novoderezhkin came up with the idea of using the painting. See part 2 of Zabolotskii's memoirs, "Shukshin v kadre i za kadrom," 143.

48. This analogy is not as far-fetched as it may seem. Just before Dmitrii peers in his father's window, he is suddenly distracted by the light falling on a kalina bush: "He was standing behind a bush in the shadow; the front part of the bush was lighted from the window. 'Kalina berries, how red they are! [*Kalina, iagody, kakie krasnye!*]' he whispered, not knowing why." Indeed, the scene from book 8, chapter 4 of Dostoevskii's *Brothers Karamazov* may have been an inspiration for Shukshin. The quotation (which I have modified slightly) is from Fyodor Dostoevsky, *The Brothers Karamazov,* trans. Richard Pevear and Larissa Volokhonsky (San Francisco: North Point Press, 1990), 391.

49. Shukshin, "Vozrazhenie po suchshestvu," 165.

50. The plowed field is itself symbolic, though not in a way obvious to the average viewer. According to Yuri Glazov, thieves refer to honest labor by using the verb "to plow," which is precisely what Egor is doing when Fat Lip catches up with him. Furthermore, any thief who betrays the brotherhood by returning to an honest life is subject to immediate and harsh punishment, usually death. Thus, what many critics called a poorly motivated murder is actually exactly in keeping with the rules of the criminal underworld. See Glazov, *The Russian Mind since Stalin's Death* (Dordrecht, Holland: D. Reidel, 1985), 38, 45, and Valerii Chalidze, *Ugolovnaia Rossiia* (Moscow: Terra, 1990), 83. In this light, the theme of betrayal in *Kalina krasnaia* is twofold: Egor is guilty of betraying both his mother and his criminal gang.

51. Vasilii Shukshin, "'Ia rodom iz derevni . . . ,'" in *Voprosy samomu sebe,* 197–98.

52. Neia Zorkaia goes as far as to assert that the "saturation of 'Sovietness'" in the film is a "precursor to sots-art." See Neia Zorkaia and Elena Stishova, "Rekviem po gumanizmu: O novykh istochnikakh energii v starykh sovetskikh fil'makh," *Kulisa* [supplement to *Nezavisimaia gazeta*] (December 1997): 2.

53. See Fomin, *Peresechenie parallel'nykh,* 347.

54. Mikhail Lobanov, "Znanie i mudrost'," *Volga* 1 (1978): 160.

55. *Prokuda* is the Russian root of Egor's last name. It designates a mischievous, roguish person; *prokudit'* is the verb form. The words are considered to be *prostorechie,* or colloquial terms. See the *Slovar' sovremennogo russkogo literaturnogo iazyka,* vol. 11 (Moscow: Akademiia nauk, 1961), 1167. The noun *prokuda* appears elsewhere in Shukshin's works, in the story "Men of One Soil" ("Zemliaki," 1968), where it is used to describe an old man who visits his brother in the village one last time before he dies.

56. Elizabeth Pond, *From the Yaroslavsky Station: Russia Perceived* (New York: Universe Books, 1981), 267.

57. This translation, adapted from Donald Fiene's translation of the novella in order to match the film version, is from Vasily Shukshin, "Snowball Berry Red," in *Contemporary Russian Prose,* 79.

58. Vasilii Shukshin, "Monolog na lestnitse," in *Voprosy samomu sebe,* 43.

59. Dar'ia Faleeva, who lived in Srostki since 1945 and knew Shukshin and his mother, states in her reminiscences that Mariia Sergeevna

> told her son many stories—about life in the past, their distant ancestors who settled in the Altai from the Volga and the Don, simple everyday stories about life. He eagerly listened to all of this. I think you could say, without exaggerating, that Mariia Sergeevna was for Shukshin what Arina Rodionovna was for Pushkin.

Nadezhda Iadykina states:

> In general, Vasilii Makarovich drew on the life of the common folk for his subjects and characters. His mother—dear Mariia Sergeevna—helped him in this. In the evenings she would tell him various tales, folk superstitions, and he soaked them up like a sponge. And the words peculiar to our Siberian dialect also came from the lips of his mother, he grew up with them.

See *On pokhozh na svoiu rodinu,* ed. V. I. Ashcheulov and Iu. G. Egorov (Barnaul: Altaiskoe knizhnoe izdatel'stvo, 1989), 105, 87–88 respectively.

60. Vasilii Shukshin, "Vot moia derevnia . . . ," in *Voprosy samomu sebe,* 77.

61. V. Kichin and N. Savitskii, "Podvig sovetskogo naroda na ekrane," in *Sovetskoe kino 70-e gody: osnovnye tendentsii razvitiia,* ed. V. Baskakov et al. (Moscow: Iskusstvo, 1984), 45.

62. For two eyewitness accounts of the making of *Kalina krasnaia* in which details are given about the strain the movie placed on Shukshin, see Fomin, *Peresechenie parallel'nykh,* 329–52, and N. Lordkipanidze, "Shukshin snimaet *Kalinu krasnuiu,*" *Iskusstvo kino* 10 (1974): 113–32.

63. Shukshin, "Kommentarii" to "Vozrazhenie po suchshestvu," 166.

64. Vasilii Shukshin, "Ia staralsia rasskazyvat' pro dushu . . . ," *Literaturnaia Rossiia,* 26 September 1975, 15. Shukshin made these comments

before a showing of his movie *Pechki-lavochki* in Belozersk during the first days of the filming of *Kalina krasnaia.*

65. Shukshin, quoted in Fomin, *Peresechenie parallel'nykh,* 342.

66. Vasilii Shukshin, "Slovo o maloi rodine," in *Voprosy samomu sebe,* 65; Vasily Shukshin, "The Place Where I Was Born," in *Articles,* trans. Avril Pyman (Moscow: Raduga, 1986), 216–17 (translation modified).

67. Shukshin, quoted in Fomin, *Peresechenie parallel'nykh,* 344.

68. Ibid., 245.

69. Shukshin notes: "Meeting Liuba, it was as if Egor met himself. And was drawn toward himself. This is the key to everything. Encountering goodness can turn your whole life around" (ibid., 345).

70. The episode about how Raika, the family cow, was run through with a pitchfork for wandering into someone else's field and eating their hay was first recounted in the story "Gogol' and Raika" ("Gogol' i Raika") in the cycle "From the Childhood Years of Ivan Popov."

71. See Fomin, *Peresechenie parallel'nykh,* 293–94.

CHAPTER EIGHT

1. Jerome H. Buckley, *The Turning Key: Autobiography and the Subjective Impulse since 1800* (Cambridge, Mass.: Harvard University Press, 1984), 115; cited in Galya Diment, *The Autobiographical Novel of Co-consciousness: Goncharov, Woolf, and Joyce* (Gainesville: University Press of Florida, 1994), 53.

2. Diane Nemec Ignashev, "Song and Confession in the Short Prose of Vasilij Makarovič Šukšin: 1929–1974" (Ph.D. diss., University of Chicago, 1984), 438.

3. Here another link with "Ignakha's Come Home" is evident: in that story, Ignakha is the "showpiece" and Vasia the more worthy "workhorse."

4. Ignashev, "Song and Confession," 557.

5. Vasilii Shukshin, "Nravstvennost' est' Pravda," in *Voprosy samomu sebe* (Moscow: Molodaia gvardiia, 1981), 63.

6. John B. Dunlop, "The Search for Peace," *Times Literary Supplement,* 30 June 1978, 739; review of Vasilii Shukshin, *Izbrannye proizvedeniia v dvukh tomakh* (Moscow: Molodaia gvardiia, 1975).

7. Ibid.

8. Only the posthumously published fragmentary additions to the cycle, published as "Solnechnye kol'tsa" by Shukshin's widow, Lidiia Fedoseeva-Shukshina, in *Sovetskaia Rossiia,* 12 July 1989, 4, bring up the fate of his father. These additions were published as "Samye pervye vospominaniia" ("Earliest Memories") in the 1996 five-volume collected works (5:210–16); a translation that incorporates these additions into the cycle "From the Childhood Years of Ivan Popov" can be found in Vasily Shukshin, *Stories*

from a Siberian Village, trans. Laura Michael and John Givens (DeKalb: Northern Illinois University Press, 1996), 209–39.

9. V. Ogryzko, "Dusha stremitsia k ladu. Obzor sovremennoi prozy," *Russkaia literatura XX veka: ocherki, portrety, esse. Kniga dlia uchash-chikhsia 11 klassa srednei shkoly,* ed. F. F. Kuznetsov, 2 vols. (Moscow: Prosveshchenie, 1991), 2:306. This statement, coming as it does from the pages of a two-volume textbook for eleventh-graders with a press run of one million copies, will undoubtedly help to establish the importance of this part of Shukshin's biography for all of his works.

10. Viktor Gorn, *Vasilii Shukshin: lichnost', knigi* (Barnaul: Altaiskoe knizhnoe izdatel'stvo, 1990), 31.

11. Ignashev, "Song and Confession," 30 n. 69.

12. Only two stories allude to these issues. Both have to do with men who have done time in Stalin's labor camps for political crimes. In "The Boss" ("Nachal'nik," 1967) we learn that the work brigade leader Ivan Ser-geevich was sent to a camp for "116 over two" ("sto shestnadtsat' popolam" [1:291]), popular parlance for Article 58-10 of the Soviet Criminal Code ("slandering Soviet reality")—the article used primarily to arrest political prisoners. The hero of "The New Arrival" was also a political prisoner un-der Stalin, having been "repressed in 1943" and rehabilitated and released in 1954. The story is about how that former prisoner is reunited with his daughter, whom he had not seen for some twenty years. As such it is a dis-tinct, but distant, allusion to Shukshin's own struggle to come to terms with his fatherlessness. The many differences between the situation described in the story and Shukshin's own, however, make "The New Arrival" only re-motely autobiographical. Not only is the reunion not one between a father and a son, but Igor' Aleksandrovich is arrested in the 1940s, not during the rural purges (as Shukshin's father had been).

"The New Arrival" was written between 1969 and 1972, at the same time as the script for *Pechki-lavochki* (they share a tall tale about flying trains), but it was first published posthumously in the journal *Avrora* in June 1975. In that version the political references are softened. Instead of being repressed, the story's hero, Igor' Aleksandrovich, "wound up in prison." The first uncensored version of the story was published by Shukshin's widow in an illustrated collection, *Rasskazy* (Moscow: Moskovskii rabochii, 1980), 239–49. In the story, Igor' Aleksandrovich has finally tracked down his for-mer wife, who has remarried, and his daughter, whom he last saw as a one-and-a-half-year-old infant and who had never been told the truth about her father. After a tense moment of revelation and confrontation—during which his daughter's stepfather remarks that Igor' Aleksandrovich's prison stint may have been deserved ("1943 was not the same thing as 1937," he hints darkly [1:492])—Igor''s daughter, Ol'ga, tells him to leave. Ol'ga fol-lows him to the bus station, however, and promises to come live with him, admitting that she had always felt he existed. The story ends on a note of reconciliation. Saccharine and melodramatic, the story is interesting mainly as testimony of Shukshin's great need to deal with this aspect of his own biography—the fate of his father and its effect on the artist—and of his equally great need to disguise his private history in his fiction about it.

13. Diment, *The Autobiographical Novel of Co-consciousness*, 4.

14. See Kathryn B. Feuer, *Tolstoy and the Genesis of War and Peace*, ed. Robin Feuer Miller and Donna Tussing Orwin (Ithaca, N.Y.: Cornell University Press, 1996), 23–24, 119–21.

15. Diment, *The Autobiographical Novel of Co-consciousness*, 9.

16. Ibid., 52.

17. William C. Spengemann, *The Forms of Autobiography: Episodes in the History of a Literary Genre* (New Haven, Conn.: Yale University Press, 1980), 132; cited in Diment, *The Autobiographical Novel of Co-consciousness*, 54.

18. In relying on Diment's theory of autobiographical co-consciousness, I depart from Diane Nemec Ignashev, who also sees an autobiographical "bifurcation" in Shukshin's heroes but who defines that split differently. For Ignashev, the division occurs not between characters but within them. (The "brother complex" in her analysis is also understood to be only remotely autobiographical.) Ignashev sees each autobiographical "fictional persona" as possessing two aspects—"one that of reporter, the other that of actor"—through which "Shukshin could re-enact phases of his own life" by means of shared discourse. In other words, Ignashev emphasizes not co-conscious protagonists but a *dual*-conscious protagonist, who can serve as a "functional alter ego" for the author. See her "Song and Confession," 614.

19. In his commentary to the novel, Lev Anninskii conjectures that it was finished "by the end of the sixties" ("Kommentarii," to Vasilii Shukshin, *Sobranie sochinenii v trekh tomakh* [Moscow: Molodaia gvardiia, 1984–85], 3:528).

20. Josephine Woll, *Invented Truth: Soviet Reality and the Literary Imagination of Iurii Trifonov* (Durham, N.C.: Duke University Press, 1991), 11.

21. Anninskii, "Kommentarii," 3:523.

22. Ibid., 3:523–25.

23. John Givens, "Provincial Polemics: Folk Discourse in the Life and Novels of Vasilii Shukshin" (Ph.D. diss., University of Washington, 1993), 201.

24. Cited in Lev Anninskii, "*Liubaviny* v nasledii V. M. Shukshina," in Vasilii Shukshin, *Sobranie sochinenii*, 5 vols. (Moscow: Panprint, 1996), 1:553.

25. S. I. Gimpel' writes: "All of the Liubavins, the father and his four sons, are hardworking, handsome, and independent people, only very evil" ("Problema lichnosti v romane V. Shukshina *Liubaviny*," *Izvestiia sibirskogo*

otdeleniia Akademii nauk SSSR: seriia obshchestvennykh nauk 2 [1974]: 127). Evgenii Gromov states that "they deeply love their home, their allotment of land, their region. . . . The Liubavins are the most diligent of laborers, the hardiest of landlords" ("Poetika dobroty," in *O Shukshine: ekran i zhizn'*, ed. Lidiia Fedoseeva-Shukshina and R. D. Chernenko [Moscow: Iskusstvo, 1979], 22). According to A. Klitko, "they are picturesque, all five of them, especially in the first chapters—'calm, sullen, with squinting, mocking eyes'" ("Osmyslenie kazhdodnevnosti," *Sibirskie ogni* 7 [1972]: 158). Vladimir Voronov, critical of the characterization of other personages in the novel, singles out Egor Liubavin as the only successful (and sympathetic) character: "he picked his wife from a poor family and he loves her geniunely" ("Samostoiatel'nost' khudozhnika," *Voprosy literatury* 2 [1966]: 56).

26. See V. A. Apukhtina, *Proza V. Shukshina*, 2d ed. (Moscow: Vysshaia shkola, 1986), 79; N. N. Ianovskii, "Vasilii Shukshin: ocherk tvorchestva," in *Stat'i i vospominaniia o Vasilii Shukshine*, comp. N. N. Ianovskii (Novosibirsk: Novosibirskoe knizhnoe izdatel'stvo, 1989), 82–83; Igor' Motiashov, "Put' k rodnikam: zametki o proze 1965 goda," *Moskva* 1 (1966): 198; N. Lagino, "Surovye gody," *Znamia* 3 (1966): 250–52; V. Khabin, "Zhivet takoi khudozhnik," *Literaturnaia Rossiia*, 12 November 1965, 14; V. Serganova, "Konets Liubavinykh," *V mire knig* 6 (1966): 30, among others.

27. Serganova, "Konets Liubavinykh," 30.

28. Evgenii Vertlib, *Vasilii Shukshin i russkoe dukhovnoe vozrozhdenie* (New York: Effect, 1990), 41.

29. Boris Riasentsev, *Spasibo, Sibir'! Vospominaniia i razmyshleniia* (Leningrad: Sovetskii pisatel', 1987), 246.

30. Vasilii Shukshin, "Kommentarii" to "'Otdavaia roman na sud chitatelia,'" in *Voprosy samomu sebe*, 125; my emphasis.

31. Vasilii Shukshin, "Kommentarii" to "Zaviduiu tebe . . . ," in *Voprosy samomu sebe*, 97.

32. One account of brawling is related by Marlen Khutsiev, who directed Shukshin's acting debut, *The Two Fedors*. See his "Krupnyi plan" in *O Shukshine*, 321. On Shukshin's little-known marriage to Masha Shumskaia (one of his home village's local beauties), see V. Ia. Riabchikov's and A. M. Kalachnikov's accounts in *On pokhozh na svoiu rodinu*, ed. V. I. Ashcheulov and Iu. G. Egorov (Barnaul: Altaiskoe knizhnoe izdatel'stvo, 1989), 55 and 67–68 respectively.

33. For a more detailed discussion of Shukshin's complicated attitude toward his "little homeland," see my "Siberia as *Volia*: Vasilii Shukshin's Search for Freedom," in *Between Heaven and Hell: The Myth of Siberia in Russian Culture*, ed. Galya Diment and Yuri Slezkine (New York: St. Martin's Press, 1993), 171–84.

34. Ivan later changes his mind, on the recommendation of his Uncle Popov.

35. Vasilii Shukshin, "Slovo o 'maloi rodine,'" in *Voprosy samomu sebe*, 65.

36. Shukshin, "Slovo o 'maloi rodine,'" 67; Vasily Shukshin, "The Place Where I Was Born," in *Articles*, trans. Avril Pyman (Moscow: Raduga, 1986), 220.

37. Vasilii Shukshin, "Monolog na lestnitse," in *Voprosy samomu sebe*, 34.

38. Shukshin, "Slovo o 'maloi rodine,'" 69; "The Place Where I Was Born," 223.

39. The kulak Liubavin family in Book One also live in a large *krestovyi dom;* thus Ivan completes a circle of sorts in constructing his own.

40. Ol'ga Rumiantseva, "Govrit' pravdu, tol'ko pravdu," in *O Shukshine*, 268.

41. The *lichnyi listok po uchetu kardov* and its accompanying autobiographical statement were documents every citizen had to fill out in order to apply for a job, admission to a university, and so on. They were little short of political litmus tests on all levels of Soviet society, for they required individuals to divulge their nationality, social origin, Komsomol or Communist Party membership, education and employment history, and information on the national and social status of their parents. In conjunction with the infamous *trudovye knizhki* (literally, "labor books," a record of one's work signed by all of one's previous employers), these records essentially fashioned their own "bureaucratic biographies" of Soviet citizens.

42. Shukshin's white lies also had to do with the fate of his father and the status of his mother. For more on this topic, see my detailed discussion in "Provincial Polemics," 29–48.

43. Gorn, *Vasilii Shukshin: lichnost', knigi*, 187.

44. Shukshin, "Kommentarii" to "Monolog na lestnitse," 47.

45. Shukshin, "Nravstvennost' est' Pravda," 56.

46. See the conclusion to Chapter Two, where the following quote is first introduced: "They praise an actor for living his part, for being 'completely in his role.' And yet this is bad! You have to be above the role. Like a writer above his material" (Vasilii Shukshin, "Iz rabochikh zapisei," in *Voprosy samomu sebe*, 254).

47. Shukshin writes: "Here are the kinds of stories there should be: 1. The story as fate. 2. The story as character type. 3. The story as confession. The smallest story there can be is the story as anecdote" (ibid., 246).

CHAPTER NINE

1. In chronological order, these works are: (1) the film *Zhivet takoi paren'* (*There's This Guy*, 1964), where Pashka Kolokol'nikov several times sings two lines from the ballad about Sten'ka Razin, "Iz-za ostrova na

strezhen'." The lines are "I za bort ee brosaet / v nabezhavshuiu volnu" ("and he tosses her overboard into the oncoming waves"). (2) Two different lines from the same song are also sung in *Tochka zreniia* (*Point of View*, written in 1966): "Grianem, brattsy, udaluiu / na pomin ee dushi" ("let's strike up a bold song in memory of her soul"). (3) In the novella *Tam, vdali* (*There, in the Distance*, 1968), the character Ol'ga wonders how the teacher with whom she is having an affair would talk about Sten'ka Razin with his students. (4) Shukshin's short story "Sten'ka Razin" was included in his 1969 film *Strannye liudi* (*Strange People*). (5) In "Zabuksoval" ("Stuck in the Mud," written in 1971) a character wonders how Gogol's *Dead Souls* would be different if in place of the swindler Chichikov it were Stepan Razin flying into space in the *troika-Rus'* at the end of the novel. (6) A dream sequence excised from the film *Pechki-lavochki* (1972) featured the movie's main protagonist in the role of Stepan Razin while the ballad "Iz-za ostrova na strezhen'" plays in the background. (7) In Shukshin's novella and film *Kalina krasnaia* (*Red Kalina Berry*, 1972, 1974) Egor Prokudin is likened to Sten'ka Razin by old man Baikalov. (8) The first four lines of "Iz-za ostrova na strezhen'" are sung by the black marketeers in *Energichnye liudi* (*Energetic People*, 1974), where a character also likens himself to a brave Cossack. (9) Razin's features are discernible in the figure of the unnamed ataman from the novella *Do tret'ikh petukhov* (*Till the Cock Crows Thrice*, 1974).

2. See Lev Anninskii, G. Kostrova, and L. Fedoseeva-Shukshina, "Kommentarii" to Shukshin's *Ia prishel dat' vam voliu*, in *Sobranie sochinenii*, 5 vols. (Moscow: Panprint, 1996), 4:595, 600; G. Kozhukhova, "Imia sobstvennoe: Vasilii Shukshin: pisatel', rezhisser, akter," *Literaturnaia gazeta*, 31 March 1976, 8; Gleb Goryshin, "Pogovorit' s Shukshinym," *Literaturnaia gazeta*, 26 July 1989, 6; Georgii Burkov, "V dal' svetluiu," *Trud*, 23 July 1989, 4.

3. The historians were A. Zimin, A. Sakharov, V. Pashuto, and S. Shmidt. See Lev Anninskii, "Kommentarii," in Vasilii Shukshin, *Sobranie sochinenii v trekh tomakh* (Moscow: Molodaia gvardiia, 1984–85), 1:694. Pashuto claimed Shukshin's film would be of "major historical significance." See Mark Volotskii's commentary to Vasilii Shukshin, "Sten'ka dlia menia—vsia zhizn'," *Iskusstvo kino* 7 (1989): 92–93. Shmidt praised Shukshin's knowledge of historical details and called the script a "masterful work of fiction" ("O literaturnom stsenarii V. Shukshina *Ia prishel dat' vam voliu*," unpublished review, Moscow, 1966; my thanks to Mark Volotskii for sharing a photocopy of this review from the archives of the Gorky Film Studio Museum). In his introduction to a special edition of *I Have Come to Give You Freedom* as part of a series of books devoted to the history of seventeenth-century Russia, historian V. S. Shul'gin singled out Shukshin's novel from those of his predecessors for having a "real factual basis" and for avoiding "one-sidedness" in his depiction of Razin. See his "Predislovie," in *Bun-*

tashnyi vek: Vasilii Shukshin. Ia prishel dat' vam voliu. Iz sochineniia Grig-oriia Kotoshikhina (Moscow: Molodaia gvardiia, 1983), 10.

4. Judith Deutsch Kornblatt, *The Cossack Hero in Russian Literature: A Study in Cultural Mythology* (Madison: University of Wisconsin Press, 1992), 16.

5. Marina Tsvetaeva, "Pushkin i Pugachev," in *Izbrannye proizvedeniia v dvukh tomakh: 1917–1937*, 2 vols. (New York: Russica Publications, 1979), 2:364.

6. Kornblatt, *The Cossack Hero in Russian Literature*, 172.

7. Ibid., 3, 170–71, 96 respectively.

8. Ibid., 173.

9. Ibid., 170–71.

10. For an interesting analysis and comparison of the three different novels on Razin, see Viktor Petelin's "Stepan Razin—lichnost' i obraz" in his *Miatezhnaia dusha Rossii: spory i razmyshleniia o sovremennoi russkoi proze* (Moscow: Sovetskaia Rossiia, 1986), 13–58. This piece, which originally appeared in the journal *Volga* 3 (1972): 157–83, was one of the earliest reviews of Shukshin's novel.

11. Mikhail Geller, "Vasilii Shukshin: v poiskakh voli," *Vestnik russkogo khristianskogo dvizheniia* 120 (1977): 162. Geller was the first to make the important distinction between the two Russian words for "freedom" (*svoboda* and *volia*) with regard to Shukshin's thematics. Elsewhere, academician Dmitrii Likhachev devotes a section of his *Zametki o russkom* to a discussion of the difference between the two words and its significance to Russian culture and the Russian worldview. See *Zametki o russkom,* 2d rev. ed. (Moscow: Sovetskaia Rossiia, 1984), 10–12. Shukshin apparently based the title of his novel on the account by the Dutch seaman Jan Struys, an eyewitness to Razin's successful taking of the southern city of Astrakhan', in which Struys records Razin's appeal to the local population: "I have come to give all of you freedom and deliverance" ("Ia prishel dat' vsem vam svobodu i izbavlenie"). See V. M. Solov'ev, *Stepan Razin i ego vremia* (Moscow: Prosveshchenie, 1990), 69. Russian historians translate "freedom" here as *svoboda;* Shukshin substitutes the word *volia* instead.

12. Diane Nemec Ignashev, "Song and Confession in the Short Prose of Vasilij Makarovič Šukšin: 1929–1974" (Ph.D. diss., University of Chicago, 1984), 85.

13. At the Colloquium on Russian National Identity, held June 11–12, 1998, at the New Jerusalem Monastery near Moscow, Aleksandr Yakovlev—Gorbachev's chief ideologist during the reform period known as glasnost—remarked that the anarchy in Russian civil life was a sign that Russia had achieved *volia* but not *svoboda,* a sentiment shared by other colloquium participants. My thanks to Kathleen Parthé—co-organizer with James Billington, Librarian of Congress, of the colloquium—for this insight.

14. Elizabeth Pond, *From the Yaroslavsky Station: Russia Perceived* (New York: Universe Books, 1981), 266.

15. Daniel Field, *Rebels in the Name of the Tsar'* (Boston: Unwin Hyman, 1989), 31.

16. Likhachev, *Zametki o russkom*, 10.

17. Geoffrey Hosking, "The Twentieth Century: In Search of New Ways, 1953–80," in *The Cambridge History of Russian Literature*, rev. ed., ed. Charles Moser (Cambridge: Cambridge University Press, 1989), 566.

18. Likhachev, *Zametki o russkom*, 10.

19. Catherine A. Wolkonsky and Marianna A. Poltoratzky, *Handbook of Russian Roots* (New York: Columbia University Press, 1961), 360; George Z. Patrick, *Roots of the Russian Language: An Elementary Guide to Wordbuilding* (Lincolnwood, Ill.: Passport Books, 1989), 194.

20. Kornblatt, *The Cossack Hero in Russian Literature*, 72.

21. Gorn, *Vasilii Shukshin: lichnost', knigi*, 228–29.

22. Paul Avrich, *Russian Rebels, 1600–1800* (New York: W. W. Norton, 1976), 116.

23. Shukshin told the Gorky Studio Artistic Council: "Moscow is the personification of the enemy." See Shukshin, "Sten'ka dlia menia—vsia zhizn'," 95–96.

24. Avrich, *Russian Rebels*, 118.

25. Tsar Aleksei ordered Patriarch Ioasaf to anathematize Razin and his cohorts in a solemn ceremony at the Kremlin in March 1671, three months before Razin's execution, apparently to counter the great popularity Razin had garnered among the common folk and the lower clergy of the Church. This popularity was so great during the uprising that priests themselves joined in Razin's movement, inciting peasants and helping to write seditious letters for the largely illiterate Cossack leaders. Patriarch Ioasaf eventually had to issue a circular to every parish, rural and urban, "not to be allured by the enticements of the bandit and traitor Stenka Razin and his comrades." In addition, the patriarch issued a charter in September 1670 condemning Razin as a "desecrator of the cross" and a betrayer of the Church and the "Great Sovereign." See ibid., 92–94, 112.

26. Shukshin relied primarily on the three-volume collection of documents on Razin's uprising published by the Soviet Academy of Sciences between 1954 and 1962: *Krest'ianskaia voina pod predvoditel'stvom Stepana Razina: sbornik dokumentov* (vol. 1, 1954; vol. 2, part 1, 1957; vol. 2, part 2, 1959; vol. 3, 1962). He constantly cited this set of source materials, unavailable to previous writers, as one of the reasons a "new" Razin was necessary in Russian literature. See Iu. Gal'perin, "U mikrofona Vasilii Shukshin," *Literaturnaia Rossiia*, 1 August 1975, 14; Vasilii Shukshin, "'Ia rodom iz derevni . . . ,'" in *Voprosy samomu sebe* (Moscow: Molodaia gvardiia, 1981), 204, and "Edin v trekh litsakh," in *Voskresnye vstrechi: besedy s interesnymi*

liud'mi, ed. A. P. Udal'tsov (Moscow: Moskovskii rabochii), 81. Shukshin's documentary accuracy was noted by the critics; see, for example, Valentina Karpova, *Talantlivaia zhizn': Vasilii Shukshin, prozaik* (Moscow: Sovetskii pisatel', 1986), 186, and A. Filatova, "V vekakh proslavlennyi," *Ural* 4 (1972): 126, among others.

27. Stepan Zlobin, *Stepan Razin*, 2 vols. (Moscow: Khudozhestvennaia literatura, 1978), 2:163.

28. Valentin Rasputin, "Your Son, Russia, and Our Passionate Brother: On Vasily Shukshin," in *Siberia on Fire*, trans. Gerald Mikkelson and Margaret Winchell (DeKalb: Northern Illinois University Press, 1989), 216.

29. Geoffrey Hosking, *Beyond Socialist Realism Soviet Fiction since Ivan Denisovich* (London: Granada, 1980), 179.

30. Geller, "Vasilii Shukshin: v poiskakh voli," 163.

31. Shukshin, "Edin v trekh litsakh," 78, 81.

32. Boris Ejxenbaum, "Literary Environment," trans. I. R. Titunik, in *Readings in Russian Poetics: Formalist and Structuralist Views*, ed. Ladislav Matejka and Krystyna Pomorska (Ann Arbor: University of Michigan Press, 1978), 56.

33. Wolfgang Kasack, "Chapygin, Aleksey Pavlovich," in *Dictionary of Russian Literature since 1917*, trans. Maria Carlson and Jane T. Hedges, rev. Rebecca Atack (New York: Columbia University Press, 1988), 74.

34. Petelin, *Miatezhnaia dusha Rossii*, 28.

35. See Chapter One for a more detailed discussion of this topic.

36. Shukshin, "'Ia rodom iz derevni . . . ,'" 204–5.

37. See 4:248–49, 252–53, 271, 276–78, 280, 292, 316–19, 355, 463, 521–22, 583–84.

38. Kornblatt, *The Cossack Hero in Russian Literature*, 56.

39. The line most quoted from Pushkin's poem is "Voz'mi sebe shubu / da ne bylo b shumu" ("Take the coat if you must / so there won't be a fuss"). According to Filatova, the first question Tsar Aleksei put to Razin in his personal interrogation was one concerning the coat. See "V vekakh proslavlennyi," 126.

40. Despite his love of the song, Shukshin nevertheless included the incident with the princess only because he felt he had to do so. "How, for example, could I get around the episode with the princess? If I took it out of the film, we wouldn't be forgiven. So let the princess be there, but resolve the episode in passing—it's not the main thing." See Vasilii Shukshin, "Stepan Razin, legenda i byl'," interview in *Literaturnaia gazeta*, 4 November 1970, 8. In his review of the novel, Lev Anninskii points out how, indeed, the legend is treated "with demonstrative hastiness." See Anninskii "Volia. Put'. Rezul'tat," *Novyi mir* 12 (1975): 263.

41. Shukshin, "Sten'ka dlia menia—vsia zhizn'," 97.

42. Vasilii Shukshin, "Iz rabochikh zapisei," in *Voprosy samomu sebe*, 251.

43. Shukshin was very critical of the Razin novels by Chapygin and Zlobin, who both gloss over this not-so-heroic aspect of Razin's campaign. Unlike them, Shukshin did not want to "pass over in silence" (as Chapygin did) or "through some trick" (as in Zlobin's version, in which an unconscious Razin is unaware that the Cossacks are leaving the peasants to their doom) Razin's betrayal at Simbirsk of the peasant masses who had rallied to his rebellion. See Vasilii Shukshin, "Predlagaiu studii . . . ," in *Voprosy samomu sebe*, 107.

44. Kornblatt, *The Cossack Hero in Russian Literature*, 171.

45. Shukshin once stated in an interview: "The main theme of my art is the peasantry." See "Edin v trekh litsakh," 78.

46. Geller, "Vasilii Shukshin: v poiskakh voli," 162.

47. Shukshin writes in a working note appearing only in the five-volume *Sobranie sochinenii:* "In our society the bureaucrat–bean counter has vanquished the Communist-revolutionary" (5:233).

48. See the Biblioteka *Sibirskikh ognei* series publication of Shukshin's novel, *Ia prishel dat' vam voliu (Stepan Razin)* (Novosibirsk: Novosibirskoe knizhnoe izdatel'stvo, 1989), 305–6.

49. See Avrich, *Russian Rebels*, 113.

50. See Shul'gin's commentary ("Predislovie") to the *Buntashnyi vek* edition of *Ia prishel dat' vam voliu*, 552.

51. Joseph Brodsky, "The Condition We Call Exile," in *On Grief and Reason* (New York: Farrar Straus Giroux, 1995), 34.

52. V. I. Fomin, *Peresechenie parallel'nykh* (Moscow: Iskusstvo, 1976), 358.

53. Fomin, who observed much of the filming of *Kalina krasnaia*, reports: "It seemed that he did not part not only with his costume but with the hero himself. He had so profoundly entered into his role, so become one with it, that even apart from the filming of scenes, it was at times hard to determine who was Shukshin and who was Prokudin." See ibid., 334.

54. Gleb Goryshin, *Zhrebii: rasskazy o pisateliakh* (Leningrad: Sovetskii pisatel', 1987), 113.

55. Ibid.

56. Burkov played major roles in Shukshin's last two films, *Pechkilavochki* and *Kalina krasnaia*. He was also slated to play the part of Matvei Ivanov in *Ia prishel dat' vam voliu*. The two men became close friends and acted together in Sergei Bondarchuk's *Oni srazhalis' za rodinu*. It was Burkov who discovered that Shukshin had died in his sleep on board the steamship *Dunai*, where the actors and crew of that film were being housed.

57. Georgii Burkov, "V dal' svetluiu, k vole . . .: k 60-letiiu so dnia rozhdeniia V. M. Shukshina," *Trud*, 23 July 1989, 4.

58. Goryshin, *Zhrebii*, 113–14.

59. See Iurii Skop, "V Sibiri dobro—sibirskoe: v gostiakh u Shukshina," *Literaturnaia gazetam* 3 July 1968, 3, and Ol'ga Rumiantseva, "Govorit' pravdu, tol'ko pravdu," in *O Shukshine: ekran i zhizn'*, ed. Lidiia Fedoseeva-Shukshina and R. D. Chernenko (Moscow: Iskusstvo, 1979), 272.

CONCLUSION

1. Vladimir Korobov, *Vasilii Shukshin*, 2d ed. (Moscow: Sovremennik, 1988), 277–78.

2. Andrei Voznesenskii, "Shukshin," *Iunost'* 4 (1976) 28; Evgenii Evtushenko, "'V iskusstve uiutno . . . ,'" *Literaturnaia Rossiia*, 11 October 1974, 11; Vladimir Vysotskii, "'Eshche—ni kholodov, ni l'din . . . ,'" published "illegally" in the now famous literary almanac *Metropol'* in 1979. Vysotskii's poem was published in English as "On the Death of Shukshin," in *Metropol Literary Almanac*, ed. Vasily Aksenov et al. (New York: W. W. Norton, 1982), 168–69.

3. Gleb Goryshin, "'Gluboko i po-nastoiashchemu zhit' . . . ,'" *Avrora* 7 (1989) 73. Shukshin's close personal friend and fellow writer Vasilii Belov confirms this sentiment:

> It was almost within two days of Vasilii Makarovich Shukshin's death that claims [announcing intended books on him] appeared at three Moscow publishing houses. People who neither loved nor published Shukshin, who had seen him only on the screens of movie theaters, suddenly wished to quickly write whole books about him.

See Belov's introduction to "'Odno znaiu—rabotat' . . .': pis'ma Vasiliia Shukshina k Vasiliiu Belovu," *Literaturnaia Rossiia*, 21 July 1989, 6.

4. Mikhail Geller, "Vasilii Shukshin: v poiskakh voli," *Vestnik russkogo khristianskogo dvizheniia* 120 (1977): 159.

5. John Dunlop, "The Search for Peace," *Times Literary Supplement*, 30 June 1978, 739.

6. Andrei Tarkovsky, "Dlia menia kino—eto sposob dostich' kakoi-to istiny," interview in *Sovetskaia Rossiia*, 3 April 1988, 4.

7. Carl and Ellendea Proffer, "Introduction: Russian Fiction into the Eighties," in *Contemporary Russian Prose*, ed. Carl and Ellendea Proffer (Ann Arbor, Mich.: Ardis, 1982), xxiii.

8. Igor' Zotov, "Vorishki na klirose: Vasilii Shukshin kak predvestnik nashikh porazhenii," *Knizhnoe obozrenie*, literary supplement to *Nezavisimaia gazeta*, 22 May 1997, 2.

9. Vasilii Shukshin, "Nravstvennost' est' Pravda," in *Voprosy samomu sebe* (Moscow: Molodaia gvardiia, 1981), 53–54.

10. Cited in Vladimir Korobov, *Vasilii Shukshin: tvorchestvo, lichnost'* (Moscow: Sovetskaia Rossiia, 1977), 55.

11. Vasilii Shukshin, "'Eshche raz vyveriaia svoiu zhizn','" in *Voprosy samomu sebe,* 232–33. See also Chapter One.

12. Georgii Burkov, "Pri Shukshine vsegda byla tetradochka," *Literaturnaia Rossiia,* 9 September 1983, 17.

13. Cited by Anatolii Kovtun, "Mgnoveniia zhizni," in Vasilii Shukshin, *Mgnoveniia zhizni,* comp. G. Kostrova and L. Shukshina (Moscow: Molodaia gvardiia, 1989), 54.

14. Genrikh Mitin, "Na strezhen'! O Shukshinskikh dniakh na Altae," *Literaturnaia Rossiia,* 15 September 1989, 9.

15. See Vasilii Shukshin, "Sten'ka dlia menia—vsia zhizn',"" *Iskusstvo kino* 7 (1989): 92–98, a transcription of Shukshin's appearance at the 16 February 1971 official discussion before the Gorky Studio Artistic Council (*Khudozhestvennyi sovet*) of his proposed film on Razin. The article is prefaced by Gorky Film Studio Museum director Mark Volotskii. These "discussions" were part of the torturous censorship process all films in the Soviet Union underwent. See also a transcription of Shukshin's appearance before that same committee on 11 February 1971, published as "'Nado imet' muzhestvo'" in *Voprosy samomu sebe,* 81–85. The latter vividly captures Shukshin's frustration with the endless bureaucratic hoops through which filmmakers had to jump to produce their movies in the former Soviet Union.

16. "100 luchshikh knig 1989 goda," *Knizhnoe obozrenie,* 17 August 1990, 9.

17. O. Galina, "Shukshinskaia skhodka," *Sovetskaia Rossiia,* 25 July 1989, 4; Larisa Iagunkova, "Slovo o Shukshine," *Izvestiia,* 17 September 1989, 4.

18. One example can be found in the introduction to an article on Shukshin in the December 1988 issue of *Nash sovremennik:*

> Recently, the literary games of the critics, who have been creating new idols nearly every six months, have virtually pushed aside this remarkable Russian writer into the secondary stratum of literature. The professional organizers of the literary processes, who decide who is to be alive and praised, prefer not to remember Shukshin. But the people remember him.

Editor's introduction to Evgenii Chernosvitov, "Narodnye kharaktery Shukshina: o 'chudikakh,' chudachestve i russkoi traditsii v proizvedeniiakh Shukshina," *Nash sovremennik* 12 (1988): 179.

19. Georgii Burkov, "V dal' svetluiu, k vole . . .: k 60-letiiu so dnia rozhdeniia V. M. Shukshina," *Trud,* 23 July 1989, 4. Due to lack of financial support, the V. M. Shukshin Center has yet to open.

20. See Grigorii Svirski, *Na lobnom meste: literatura nravstvennogo soprotivleniia (1946–76)* (London: Novaia literaturnaia biblioteka, 1979), 396–97. Svirski's accusation did not appear in the English translation published by Ardis in 1981.

21. See the second part of Zabolotskii's memoirs, "Shukshin v kadre i za kadrom," *Moskva* 2 (1993): 150.

22. This quote, previously unpublished during Soviet times, is reproduced in the five-volume *Sobranie sochinenii*, 5:236, as a working note.

23. Viktor Nekrasov, "Vzgliad i nechto," pt. 2 *Kontinent* 12 (1977): 116.

24. Vasilii Shukshin, "Edin v trekh litsakh," in *Voskresnye vstrechi: besedy s interesnymi liud'mi*, ed. A. P. Udal'tsov (Moscow: Moskovskii rabochii), 84.

25. Dunlop, "The Search for Peace," 739.

26. "Klassika i my," the transcript of a meeting of writers and critics held at the Central House of Writers on 21 December 1977, *Moskva* 1 (1990): 199.

27. "'Odno znaiu—rabotat'. . . .:' pis'ma Vasiliia Shukshina Vasiliiu Belovu," 6. See also Vasilii Shukshin, "Iz rabochikh zapisei," in *Voprosy samomu sebe*, 249, where the author states: "I can't live in the village. But I like to visit there—it warms my heart."

28. Cited in Korobov, *Vasilii Shukshin*, 2d ed., 65.

29. Viktor Gorn, *Vasilii Shukshin: lichnost', knigi* (Barnaul: Altaiskoe kniznoe izdatel'stvo, 1990), 44.

30. Cited in Zabolotskii, "Shukshin v kadre i za kadrom," pt. 2, 155.

31. See Vasilii Grishaev, *Shukshin. Srostki. Piket.* (Barnaul: Altaiskoe knizhnoe izdatel'stvo, 1994), 98.

32. Aleksandr Mitta, "Kak o nem napisat'?" *Iskusstvo kino* 1 (1971): 114. See also Chapter One.

33. Leonid Chikin, "Zemliak, tovarishch . . . ," *Sibirskie ogni* 1 (1978): 132.

34. Ignatii Ponomarev, "Shukshin," *Nash sovremennik* 3 (1981): 97.

35. Iurii Skop, "V Sibiri dobro—sibirskoe: v gostiakh u Shukshina," *Literaturnaia gazeta*, 3 July 1968, 3.

36. Nikolai Zadornov, "Retsenziia na sbornik Vasiliia Shukshina *Tam, vdali*," *Daugava* 12 (1984): 101.

37. Vasilii Shukshin, "Esli by znat'. . . ," in *Voprosy samomu sebe*, 208.

38. Paul Watkins, "A Surfeit of Manly Virtues," *Times Literary Supplement*, 8 August 1997, 25; review of Alex Kershaw, *Jack London: A Life* (New York: HarperCollins, 1997).

39. See Nekrasov, "Vzgliad i nechto," 116–17.

40. Anatolii Bocharov, "Counterpoint: The Common and the Individual in the Prose of Iurii Trifonov, Vasilii Shukshin, and Valentin Rasputin," *Soviet Studies in Literature* 20, no. 1 (Winter 1983–84): 35.

41. Andrei Sinyavsky (Abram Tertz), "The Literary Process in Russia," in *Kontinent* (New York: Anchor, 1976), 84.

Select Bibliography

The two most detailed bibliographies of works by and about Shukshin published to date are Geoffrey Hosking's "Preliminary Bibliography," published in Vasily Shukshin, *Snowball Berry Red and Other Stories*, ed. Donald M. Fiene, trans. Donald M. Fiene et al. (Ann Arbor, Mich.: Ardis, 1979), 237–49; and *Vasilii Makarovich Shukshin (1929–1974): Bibliografīcheskii ukazatel'*, 3d rev. ed., ed. M. L. Bortsova et al. (Barnaul: AO Poligrafist, 1994). Both contain original publication data for all of Shukshin's stories, novellas, plays, scripts, novels, and anthologies. As these two bibliographies are each exhaustive for the time periods they cover, the present bibliography will limit itself to Shukshin's major publications and the more important of the critical studies on Shukshin cited in this work. It will also include important critical studies published since 1994.

PRIMARY SOURCES

Works in English Translation

"Stories." Trans. Ralph Parker. *Soviet Literature* 5 (1964): 82–114.
"Inner Content." Trans. Avril Pyman. *Soviet Literature* 6 (1968): 138–45.
"Stories." Trans. Robert Daglish. *Soviet Literature* 12 (1971): 102–15.
I Want to Live: Short Stories. Trans. Robert Daglish. Moscow: Progress, 1973.
"The Obstinate One." Trans. Natasha Johnstone. *Soviet Literature* 10 (1974): 3–17.
"Short Stories." Trans. Hilda Perham, H. Perham, Robert Daglish, and Keith Hammond. *Soviet Literature* 9 (1975): 3–56.
"The Red Guelder Rose." Trans. Robert Daglish. *Soviet Literature* 9 (1975): 56–122.
"The Brother-in-Law." Trans. D. M. Fiene and B. N. Peskin. *Russian Literature Triquarterly* 12 (1975): 168–74.
"The Odd-Ball." Trans. Margaret Wettlin. *Soviet Literature* 10 (1976): 130–38.

Snowball Berry Red and Other Stories. Ed. Donald M. Fiene. Trans. Donald M. Fiene, Boris Peskin, Geoffrey A. Hosking, George Gutsche, George Kolodziej, and James Nelson. Ann Arbor, Mich.: Ardis, 1979.

"Snowball Berry Red." Trans. Donald M. Fiene. In *Contemporary Russian Prose,* ed. Carl and Ellendea Proffer, 57–126. Ann Arbor, Mich.: Ardis, 1982.

"Makar Zherebtsov." Trans. Marguerite Mabson. In *The Barsukov Triangle, the Two-Toned Blond, and Other Stories,* ed. Carl R. Proffer and Ellendea Proffer, 149–55. Ann Arbor, Mich.: Ardis, 1984.

Roubles in Words, Kopeks in Figures and Other Stories. Trans. Natasha Ward and David Iliffe. London: Marian Boyars, 1985, 1994.

Articles. In Eduard Yefimov, *Vasily Shukshin.* Trans. Avril Pyman. Moscow: Raduga, 1986.

"Stories." Trans. Andrew Bromfield, Holly Smith, Robert Daglish, and Kate Cook. *Soviet Literature* 3 (1990): 3–106.

Short Stories. Trans. Andrew Bromfield, Robert Daglish, Holly Smith, and Kathleen Mary Cook. Moscow: Raduga, 1990.

Stories from a Siberian Village. Trans. Laura Michael and John Givens. DeKalb: Northern Illinois University Press, 1996.

Major Publications in Russian

Sel'skie zhiteli. Moscow: Molodaia gvardiia, 1963.

Zhivet takoi paren'. Moscow: Iskusstvo, 1964.

Liubaviny. Moscow: Sovetskii pisatel', 1965.

Tam, vdali. Moscow: Sovetskii pisatel', 1968.

Zemliaki. Moscow: Sovetskaia Rossiia, 1970.

Kharaktery. Moscow: Sovremennik, 1973.

Ia prishel dat' vam voliu. Moscow: Sovetskii pisatel', 1974.

Besedy pri iasnoi lune. Moscow: Sovetskaia Rossiia, 1974.

Brat moi. Moscow: Sovremennik, 1975.

Izbrannye proizvedeniia v dvukh tomakh. Moscow: Molodaia gvardiia, 1975.

Kinopovesti. Moscow: Iskusstvo, 1975. Rev. ed. 1988, 1991.

Nravstvennost' est' Pravda. Moscow: Sovetskaia Rossiia, 1979.

Voprosy samomu sebe. Moscow: Molodaia gvardiia, 1981.

Sobranie sochinenii v trekh tomakh. Moscow: Molodaia gvardiia, 1984–85.

Liubaviny: roman (kniga pervaia i vtoraia). Moscow: Knizhnaia palata, 1988.

Ia prishel dat' vam voliu (Stepan Razin): Roman. Rasskazy. Comp. A. U. Kitainik. Vol. 1 of *Biblioteka Sibirskikh ognei.* Novosibirsk: Novosibirskoe knizhnoe izdatel'stvo, 1989.

Mgnoveniia zhizni. Moscow: Molodaia gvardiia, 1989.

Sobranie sochinenii v piati tomakh. Seriia "Literaturnaia nasledie." Moscow: Panprint, 1996.

SECONDARY SOURCES

Andrianov, Aristarkh. "Eshche raz o 'strannykh' geroiakh Vasiliia Shukshina." *Molodaia gvardiia* 10 (1973): 308–12.

Anninskii, Lev. "Kommentarii" to V. M. Shukshin, *Sobranie sochinenii,* 3 vols., 1:683–701. Moscow: Molodaia gvardiia, 1984–85.

———. "Put' pisatelia." In *O Shukshine: ekran i zhizn',* ed. Lidiia Fedoseeva-Shukshina and R. D. Chernenko, 113–39. Moscow: Iskusstvo, 1979.

———. "Shukshin-publitsist." Introduction to V. M. Shukshin, *Nravstvennost' est' Pravda,* 3–20. Moscow: Sovetskaia Rossiia, 1979.

———. "Shukshinskaia zhizn'." *Literaturnoe obozrenie* 1 (1974): 50–55.

———. "V poiskakh otvetov." Introduction to V. M. Shukshin, *Voprosy samomu sebe,* 3–9. Moscow: Molodaia gvardiia, 1981.

———. "Volia. Put'. Rezul'tat." *Novyi mir* 12 (1975): 262–64.

Anninskii, Lev, and Lidiia Fedoseeva-Shukshina. "Kommentarii" to V. M. Shukshin, *Sobranie sochinenii,* 3 vols., 2:577–89, 3:651–69. Moscow: Molodaia gvardiia, 1984–85.

Anninskii, Lev, G. Kostrova, and L. Fedoseeva-Shukshina. "Kommentarii" to V. M. Shukshin, *Sobranie sochinenii,* Seriia "Literaturnaia nasledie," 5 vols., 1:545–55, 2:573–89, 3:523–30, 4:591–600, 5:429–56. Moscow: Panprint, 1996.

Apukhtina, V. A. *Proza V. Shukshina.* 2d ed. Moscow: Vysshaia shkola, 1986.

Ashcheulov, V. I., and Iu. G. Egorov, eds. *On pokhozh na svoiu rodinu: zemliaki o Shukshine.* Barnaul: Altaiskoe knizhnoe izdatel'stvo, 1989.

Belaia, Galina. "Antimiry Vasiliia Shukshina." *Literaturnoe obozrenie* 5 (1977): 23–26.

———. "The Crisis of Soviet Artistic Mentality in the 1960s and 1970s." Trans. Lesley Milne. In *New Directions in Soviet Literature: Selected Papers from the Fourth World Congress for Soviet and East European Studies, Harrogate, 1990,* ed. Sheelagh Duffin Graham, 1–17. New York: St. Martin's Press, 1992.

———. "Fars ili tragediia?" *Literaturnoe obozrenie* 3 (1979): 58–60.

———. "Iskusstvo est' smysl." *Voprosy literatury* 7 (1973): 62–94.

———. "Paradoksy i otkrytiia Vasiliia Shukshina." In *Khudozhestvennyi mir sovremennoi prozy,* 93–118. Moscow: Nauka, 1983.

———. "Rozhdenie novykh stilevykh form kak protsess preodoleniia 'neitral'nogo' stilia." In *Teoriia literaturnykh stilei. Mnogoobrazie stilei sovetskoi literatury. Voprosy tipologii,* ed. N. K. Gei et al., 460–85. Moscow: Nauka, 1978.

Belov, Vasilii. Introduction to "'Odno znaiu—rabotat' . . .': pis'ma Vasiliia Shukshina k Vasiliiu Belovu." *Literaturnaia Rossiia*, 21 July 1989, 6–7.

Belova, L. "Tri rusla odnogo puti: o tvorchestve Vasiliia Shukshina." *Voprosy kinoiskusstva*, vol. 17 (Moscow: Nauka, 1976), 136–62.

Bilichenko, N. A. "Shukshin's Hero through the Eyes of the Critics." *Soviet Studies in Literature* 17, no. 1 (Winter 1980–81): 45–69. [Translation of "Geroi V. Shukshina v otsenkakh kritiki." *Russkaia literatura* 2 (1980): 218–27.]

Binova, Galina Pavlovna. *Tvorcheskaia evoliutsiia Vasiliia Shukshina.* Brno: Univerzita J. E. Purkyně v Brně, 1988.

Bocharov, Anatolii. "Counterpoint: The Common and the Individual in the Prose of Iuryi Trifonov, Vasilii Shukshin, and Valentin Rasputin." *Soviet Studies in Literature* 20, no. 1 (Winter 1983–84): 21–48. [Translation of "Kontrapunkt. Obshchee i individual'noe v proze Iu. Trifonova, V. Shukshina, V. Rasputina." *Oktiabr'* 7 (1982): 190–99.]

Brown, Deming. *Soviet Russian Literature since Stalin.* Cambridge: Cambridge University Press, 1979.

Brown, Edward J. *Russian Literature since the Revolution.* Rev. ed. Cambridge, Mass.: Harvard University Press, 1982.

Burkov, Georgii. "Pri Shukshine vsegda byla tetradochka . . ." *Literaturnaia Rossiia*, 9 September 1983, 16–17.

———. "V dal' svetluiu, k vole . . .: k 60-letiiu so dnia rozhdeniia V. M. Shukshina." *Trud,* 23 July 1989, 4.

———. "Zhivoi Shukshin." In *Shukshinskie chteniia: stat'i, vospominaniia, publikatsii,* ed. Viktor Gorn, 104–13. Barnaul: Altaiskoe knizhnoe izdatel'stvo, 1984.

Chalmaev, V. "Poryv vetra: molodye geroi i novellisticheskoe iskusstvo Vasiliia Shukshina." *Sever* 10 (1972): 116–26.

Chapygin, A. *Razin Stepan.* Moscow: Sovetskii pisatel', 1948.

———. *Stepan Razin.* Trans. Cedar Paul. London: Hutchinson International Authors, 1946.

Chernosvitov, Evgenii. *Proiti po kraiu. Vasilii Shukshin: mysli o zhizni, smerti i bessmertii.* Moscow: Sovremennik, 1989.

Chikin, L. "Zemliak, tovarishch . . ." *Sibirskie ogni* 1 (1978): 128–71.

Christian, Nicole. "Manifestations of the Eccentric in the Works of Vasilii Shukshin." *Slavonic and East European Review* 75, no. 2 (April 1997): 202–3.

———. "Vasilii Makarovich Shukshin, 1929–1974: Prose Writer, Film Director, and Actor." In *Reference Guide to Russian Literature,* ed. Neil Cornwell and Nicole Christian, 734–36. London: Fitzroy Dearborn, 1998.

———. "Vasilii Shukshin and the Russian Fairy Tale: A Study of *Until the Cock Crows Thrice.*" *Modern Language Review* 92, no. 2 (April 1997): 392–400.

Chudakova, M. "Notes on the Language of Contemporary Prose." *Soviet Studies in Literature* 1 (Winter 1972–73): 37–112. [Translation of "Zametki o iazyke sovremennoi prozy." *Novyi mir* 1 (1972): 212–45.]

Chuvakin, A. A., ed. *Iazyk i stil' prozy V. M. Shukshina.* Barnaul: Altaiskii gosudarstvennyi universitet, 1991.

Condee, Nancy. "Shukshin, Vasily Makarovich (1929–74)." *Handbook of Russian Literature*, ed. Victor Terras, 417–18. New Haven, Conn.: Yale University Press, 1985.

Desiatov, V. V., et al., eds. *Tvorchestvo V. M. Shukshina: opyt entsiklopedicheskogo slovaria-spravochnika.* Barnaul: Altaiskii gosudarstvennyi universitet, 1997.

Diment, Galya. *The Autobiographical Novel of Co-consciousness: Goncharov, Woolf, and Joyce.* Gainesville: University Press of Florida, 1994.

Dunlop, John B. "The Search for Peace." *Times Literary Supplement*, 30 June 1978, 739.

Emel'ianov, L. I. *Vasilii Shukshin: ocherk tvorchestva.* Leningrad: Khudozhestvennaia literatura, 1983.

Eshel'man, Raul'. "Epistemologiia zastoia: o postmodernistskoi proze V. Shukshina," *Russian Literature* 35 (1994): 67–92.

Fedoseeva-Shukshina, Lidiia, and R. D. Chernenko, eds. *O Shukshine: ekran i zhizn'.* Moscow: Iskusstvo, 1979.

Fiene, Donald M. "Vasily Shukshin's *Kalina krasnaia:* Translator's Notes." In *Snowball Berry Red and Other Stories*, ed. Donald M. Fiene, trans. Donald M. Fiene et al., 200–212. Ann Arbor, Mich.: Ardis, 1979.

Fiene, Donald M., and Boris N. Peskin. "The Remarkable Art of Vasily Shukshin." *Russian Literature Triquarterly* 11 (1975): 174–78.

Fomin, V. I. "Doma i v gostiakh: 'Pechki-lavochki,'" *Ekran 73/74* (Moscow: Iskusstvo, 1975), 28–31.

———. *Peresechenie parallel'nykh.* Moscow: Iskusstvo, 1976.

Freilikh, S. "O stile Vasiliia Shukshina." *Voprosy literatury* 9 (1982): 57–66.

Galichenko, Nicholas. *Glasnost—Soviet Cinema Responds.* Ed. Robert Allington. Austin: University of Texas Press, 1991.

Geller, L. "Opyt prikladnoi stilistiki. Rasskaz V. Shukshina kak ob"ekt issledovaniia s peremennym fokusnym rasstoianiem." *Wiener Slawistischer Almanack* 4 (1979): 95–123.

Geller, Mikhail. "Vasilii Shukshin: v poiskakh voli." *Vestnik russkogo khristianskogo dvizheniia* 120 (1977): 159–82. [Translated as Michel Heller, "Vasily Shukshin: In Search of Freedom." trans. George Gutsche, in *Snowball Berry Red and Other Stories*, ed. Donald M. Fiene, trans. Donald M. Fiene et al., 13–33. Ann Arbor, Mich.: Ardis, 1979.]

Geller, Mikhail, and Vladimir Maksimov. "Besedy o sovremennykh pisateliakh: Vasilii Shukshin." *Strelets* 3 (1987): 25–27.

Givens, John. "Leksiko-semanticheskie osobennosti rasskaza V. M. Shuk-shina 'Srezal' v angliiskom perevode." In *Rasskaz V. M. Shukshina 'Srezal': Problemy analiza, interpretatsii, perevoda*, ed. S. M. Kozlova, 112–22. Barnaul: Altaiskii gosudarstvennyi universitet, 1995.

———. "Osobennosti realizatsii ekzistentsialistskikh idei v proze V. M. Shukshina." In *V. M. Shukshin: filosof, istorik, khudozhnik*, ed. S. M. Kozlova, 11–36. Barnaul: Altaiskii gosudarstvennyi universitet, 1992.

———. "Provincial Polemics: Folk Discourse in the Life and Novels of Vasilii Shukshin." Ph.D. diss., University of Washington, 1993.

———. "Siberia as *Volia:* Vasilii Shukshin's Search for Freedom." In *Between Heaven and Hell: The Myth of Siberia in Russian Culture*, ed. Galya Diment and Yuri Slezkine, 171–84. New York: St. Martin's Press, 1993.

———. "Tvorchestvo Shukshina v Soedinennykh Shtatakh Ameriki (problemy vospriiatiia)." In *Tvorchestvo V. M. Shukshina: Poetika, stil', iazyk*, ed. A. A. Chuvakin, 184–91. Barnaul: Altaiskii gosudarstvennyi universitet, 1994.

———. "Vasilii Shukshin and the 'Audience of Millions': *Kalina krasnaia* and the Power of Popular Cinema." *Russian Review* 58, no. 2 (April 1999): 268–85.

———. "Vasilii Shukshin's *Liubavin Family* Chronicle and the Autobiographical Novel of Co-consciousness." *a/b: Auto/Biography Studies* 11, no. 2 (1996): 105–24.

———. "Vasily Shukshin." In *Encyclopedia of World Literature in the 20th Century*, vol. 5, ed. Steven R. Serafin, 554–56. New York: Continuum, 1993.

———. "Vasily Shukshin: A Storyteller's Story." Introduction to Vasily Shukshin, *Stories from a Siberian Village*, trans. Laura Michael and John Givens, xv–xliii. DeKalb: Northern Illinois University Press, 1996.

Gladilin, Anatoly. *The Making and Unmaking of a Soviet Writer: My Story of the "Young Prose" of the Sixties and After.* Trans. David Lapeza. Ann Arbor, Mich.: Ardis, 1979.

Gorn, Viktor. *Vasilii Shukshin: lichnost', knigi.* Barnaul: Altaiskoe knizhnoe izdatel'stvo, 1990.

Gorn, Viktor, ed. *Shukshinskie chteniia: stat'i, vospominaniia, publikatsii.* 2 vols. Barnaul: Altaiskoe knizhnoe izdatel'stvo, 1984 and 1989.

Goryshin, Gleb. "Pogovorit' s Shukshinym." *Literaturnaia gazeta.* 26 July 1989, 6.

———. *Zhrebii: rasskazy o pisateliakh.* Leningrad: Sovetskii pisatel', 1987.

Grishaev, V. "Neskol'ko strok v biografiiu Shukshina: zametki arkhivista." *Sibirskie ogni* 4 (1983): 165–68.

———. *Shukshin. Srostki. Piket.* Barnaul: Altaiskoe knizhnoe izdatel'stvo, 1994.

Hosking, Geoffrey. *Beyond Socialist Realism: Soviet Fiction since Ivan Denisovich*. London: Granada, 1980.
————. "The Twentieth Century: In Search of New Ways, 1933–80." In *The Cambridge History of Russian Literature*, rev. ed., ed. Charles Moser, 520–94. Cambridge: Cambridge University Press, 1989.
————. "Vasily Shukshin: A Preliminary Bibliography." In *Snowball Berry Red and Other Stories*, ed. Donald M. Fiene, trans. Donald M. Fiene et al., 237–49. Ann Arbor, Mich.: Ardis, 1979.
Ianovskii, N. N., ed. *Stat'i i vospominaniia o Vasilii Shukshine*. Novosibirsk: Novosibiskoe knizhnoe obozrenie, 1989.
Ignashev, Diane Nemec. "The Art of Vasilij Šukšin: *Volja* through Song." *Slavic and East European Journal* 32 (1988): 415–27.
————. "Song and Confession in the Short Prose of Vasilij Makarovič Šukšin: 1929–1974." Ph.D. diss., University of Chicago, 1984.
————. "Vasily Shukshin's *Srezal* and the Question of Transition." *Slavonic and East European Review* 66 (1988): 337–56.
Kantorovich, V. "Novye tipy, novyi slovar', novye otnosheniia." *Sibirskie ogni* 9 (1971): 176–80.
Karpova, Valentina. *Talantlivaia zhizn': Vasilii Shukshin, prozaik*. Moscow: Sovetskii pisatel', 1986.
Kasack, Wolfgang. *Dictionary of Russian Literature since 1917*. Trans. Maria Carlson and Jane T. Hedges. Rev. Rebecca Atack. New York: Columbia University Press, 1988.
Kaverin, Veniamin. "Shukshin's Stories." *Soviet Studies in Literature* 14, no. 3 (1978): 60. [Translation of "Rasskazy Shukshina." *Novyi mir* 6 (1977): 261–66.]
Klitko, A. "Osmyslenie kazhdodnevnosti." *Sibirskie ogni* 7 (1972): 157–66.
Kornblatt, Judith Deutsch. *The Cossack Hero in Russian Literature: A Study in Cultural Mythology*. Madison: University of Wisconsin Press, 1992.
Korobov, Vladimir. *Vasilii Shukshin: tvorchestvo, lichnost'*. Moscow: Sovetskaia Rossiia, 1977.
————. *Vasilii Shukshin*. 2d rev. ed. Moscow: Sovremennik, 1988.
————. *Vasilii Shukshin: veshchee slovo*. 3d rev. ed. Seriia "Zhizn' zamechatel'nykh liudei." Moscow: Molodaia gvardiia, 1999.
Kozhevnikova, N. A., and N. A. Nikolina. "O iazyke V.M. Shukshina." In *Iazyk i stil' prozy V. M. Shukshina*, ed. A. A. Chuvakin, 4–13. Barnaul: Altaiskii gosudarstvennyi universitet, 1991.
Kozlova, Svetlana Mikhailovna. *Poetika rasskazov V. M. Shukshina*. Barnaul: Altaiskii gosudarstvennyi universitet, 1993.
————. "Politicheskie 'apokrify' V. M. Shukshina ('Krysha nad golovoi' i 'Shtrikhi k portretu')." In *Tvorchestvo V. M. Shukshina: problemy, poetika, stil'*, ed. S. M. Kozlova, 72–101. Barnaul: Altaiskii gosudarstvennyi universitet, 1991.

———. "Regial'naia kontseptsiia natsional'nogo vozrozhdeniia v proze V. M. Shukshina." In *Tvorchestvo V. M. Shukshina: Poetika, stil', iazyk*, ed. A. A. Chuvakin, 3–17. Barnaul: Altaiskii gosudarstvennyi universitet, 1994.

———. "Sud'ba narodnoi pesni v proze V.M. Shukshina." In *Kul'turnoe nasledie Altaia*, ed. T. M. Stepanskaia, 3–24. Barnaul: Altaiskii gosudarstvennyi universitet, 1992.

———. "Tsikl 'Vnezapnye rasskazy.' K probleme tvorcheskogo sinteza." In *Tvorchestvo V. M. Shukshina: metodika, poetika, stil'*, ed. S. M. Kozlova et al., 45–60. Barnaul: Altaiskii gosudarstvennyi universitet, 1997.

Kozlova, S. M., et al., eds. *Tvorchestvo V. M. Shukshina: metodika, poetika, stil'*. Barnaul: Altaiskii gosudarstvennyi universitet, 1997.

Kuliapin, A. I., and O. G. Levashova. *V. M. Shukshin i russkaia klassika*. Barnaul: Altaiskii gosudarstvennyi universitet, 1998.

Kuz'muk, V. A. "Vasilii Shukshin and the Early Chekhov (An Essay in Typological Analysis)." *Soviet Studies in Literature* 14, no. 3 (1978): 61–78. [Translation of "Vasiliii Shukshin i ranii Chekhov (Opyt tipologicheskogo analiza)," *Russkaia literatura* 3 (1977): 198–205.]

Le Fleming, Stephen. "Vasily Shukshin: A Contemporary Scythian." In *Russian and Slavic Literature: Selected Papers in the Humanities from the First International Slavic Conference*, ed. R. Freeborn, R. R. Milner-Gulland, and Charles A. Ward, 449–66. Cambridge, Mass.: Slavica, 1977.

Likhachev, Dmitrii. *Zametki o russkom.* 2d rev. ed. Moscow: Sovetskaia Rossiia, 1984.

Lordkipanidze, N. "Shukshin snimaet *Kalinu krasnuiu.*" *Iskusstvo kino* 10 (1974): 113–32.

Mann, Robert. "St. George in Vasilij Šukšin's '*Kalina krasnaja.*'" *Slavic and East European Journal* 28, no. 4 (1984): 445–54.

Marchenko, A. "Iz knizhnogo raia." *Voprosy literatury* 4 (1969): 49–71.

McMillin, Arnold. "Chekhov and the Soviet Village Prose Writers: Affinities of Fact and Fiction." *Modern Language Review* 93, no. 3 (July 1998): 754–61.

Morgan, Lyndall. "Shukshin's Women: An Enduring Russian Stereotype." *Australian Slavonic and East European Studies* 1, no. 2 (1987): 137–46.

———. "The Subversive Sub-text: Allegorical Elements in the Short Stories of Vasilii Shukshin." *Australian Slavonic and East European Studies* 5, no. 1 (1991): 59–76.

Nekrasov, Viktor. "Vzgliad i nechto." Part 2. *Kontinent* 12 (1977): 112–19.

Ovcharenko, Aleksandr. "Rasskazy Vasiliia Shukshina," *Don* 1 (1976): 155–66.

Pankin, Boris. "Shukshin about Himself: Notes on the Collection *Morality Is Truth.*" *Soviet Studies in Literature* 17, no. 1 (1980–81): 28–44. [Translation of "Shukshin o samom sebe: zametki o sbornike *Nravstvennost' est' Pravda*," *Druzhba narodov* 6 (1980): 212–19.]

———. "Vasilii Shukshin and His 'Cranks.'" *Soviet Studies in Literature* 14, no. 2 (1978): 16–37. [Translation of "Vasilii Shukshin i ego 'chudiki.'" *Iunost'* 6 (1976): 74–80.]

Pankov, Aleksandr. "'Kharaktery i rezkaia kartina nravov.'" *Sibirskie ogni* 4 (1978): 177–85.

Parthé, Kathleen. *Russian Village Prose: The Radiant Past.* Princeton, N.J.: Princeton University Press, 1992.

Ponomarev, I. "Shukshin." *Nash sovremennik* 3 (1981): 76–113.

Popov, Ivan. "Brat: pis'ma V. Shukshina." In *Shukshinskie chteniia: stat'i, vospominaniia, publikatsii,* ed. Viktor Gorn, 176–85. Barnaul: Altaiskoe knizhnoe izdatel'stvo, 1984.

Pozin, Mikhail A. "Vasilii Shukshin, the Writer and His Times." Ph.D. diss., University of Illinois at Urbana-Champaign, 1991.

Rasputin, Valentin, "Your Son, Russia, and Our Passionate Brother: On Vasily Shukshin." In *Siberia on Fire,* trans. Gerald Mikkelson and Margaret Winchell, 202–18. DeKalb: Northern University Press, 1989.

Red'ko, A. V., comp. *Vasilii Makarovich Shukshin (1929–1974): bibliograficheskii ukazatel'.* 2d rev. ed. Barnaul: Altaiskoe knizhnoe izdatel'stvo, 1981.

Serdiuchenko, V. "O Shukshine segodnia: nadeznost' traditsii." *Novyi mir* 9 (1980): 237–38.

Shvyrev, Iurii. "K tvorcheskoi istorii neosushchestvlennogo zamysla V. M. Shukshina." *Kinostsenarii* 3 (1989): 156–57.

Sidorov, Evgeni. "The Short Story Today." *Soviet Literature* 6 (1986): 3–4.

Skop, Iurii. "V Sibiri dobro—sibirskoe: v gostiakh u Shukshina." *Literaturnaia gazeta,* 3 July 1968, 3.

Sobolevskaia, N. N. "Komicheskoe kak forma proiavleniia narodnogo soznaniia v rasskazakh V. Shukshina." In *Tendentsii razvitiia russkoi literatury Sibiri v XVIII–XX vv.,* ed. L. P. Iakimova, 91–107. Novosibirsk: Nauka, 1985.

Solov'ev, V. "Fenomen Vasiliia Shukshina." *Iskusstvo kino* 10 (1975) 16–29; 12 (1975): 33–43.

Solov'eva, I., and V. Shitova. "Svoi liudi—sochtemsia." *Novyi mir* 3 (1974): 245–50.

Svirski, Grigori. *A History of Post-War Soviet Writing: The Literature of Moral Opposition.* Trans. and ed. Robert Dessaix and Michael Ulman. Ann Arbor, Mich.: Ardis, 1981.

Tarkovskii, Andrei. "Dlia menia kino—eto sposob dostich' kakoi-to istiny." *Sovetskaia Rossiia,* 3 April 1988, 4.

Tiurin, Iu. *Kinematograf Vasiliia Shukshina.* Moscow: Iskusstvo, 1984.

Tolchenova, Nina. *Slovo o Shukshine.* Moscow: Sovremennik, 1982.

———. *Vasilii Shukshin—ego zemlia i liudi.* Barnaul: Altaiskoe knizhnoe izdatel'stvo, 1978.

Tsvetov, G. "Literaturnaia sud'ba shukshinskikh 'chudikov.'" In V. M. Shuk-shin: zhizn' i tvorchestvo, vol. 2, ed. S. M. Kozlova and A. A. Chuvakin, 67–69. Barnaul: Altaiskii gosudarstvennyi universitet, 1992.

Vaniashova, M. "Shukshinskie litsedei." Literaturnaia ucheba 4 (1979): 160–68.

———. "Zhanrovoe svoeobrazie rasskazov V. Shukshina." In Problemy estetiki i poetiki: mezhvuzovskii sbornik nauchnykh trudov, no. 160, 106–14. Iaroslavl': Iaroslavskii gosudarstvennyi pedagogicheskii institut, 1976.

Varlamov, Aleksei. "Platonov i Shukshin: geopoliticheskie osi russkoi literatury," Moskva 2 (1998): 167–74.

Vertlib, Evgenii. Vasilii Shukshin i russkoe dukhovnoe vozrozhdenie. New York: Effect Publishing, 1990.

Vishevsky, Anatoly. Soviet Literary Culture in the 1970s: The Politics of Irony. Gainesville: University Press of Florida, 1993.

Vorontsov, Yuri, and Igor Rachuk. The Phenomenon of the Soviet Cinema. Moscow: Progress, 1980.

Woll, Josephine. Invented Truth: Soviet Reality and the Literary Imagination of Iurii Trifonov. Durham, N.C.: Duke University Press, 1991.

Yefimov, Eduard. Vasily Shukshin. Trans. Avril Pyman. Moscow: Raduga, 1986.

Zabolotskii, Anatolii. "Shukshin v kadre i za kadrom." Moskva 1 (1993): 142–58; 2 (1993): 141–58.

"Zhiznennyi material, poisk khudozhnika, avtorskaia kontseptsiia (obsuzhdaem Kalinu krasnuiu: kinopovest' i fil'm Vasiliia Shukshina)," Voprosy literatury 7 (1974): 28–90. [A partial English translation by Margaret Wettlin was published as "Reality and the Writer's Vision," Soviet Literature 9 (1975): 123–38.]

Zlobin, St. Stepan Razin. 2 vols. Moscow: Sovetskii pisatel', 1952.

Zorkaya, Neya. The Illustrated History of Soviet Cinema. New York: Hippocrene Books, 1989.

Zorkaya, Neya, and Elena Stishova, "Rekviem po gumanizmu: O novykh istochnikakh energii v starykh sovetskikh fil'makh." Kulisa (supplement to Nezavisimaia gazeta) (December 1997): 2.

Filmography

MOVIES WRITTEN AND DIRECTED
BY VASILII SHUKSHIN

Iz Leb"iazhego soobshchaiut (*Report from Lebyazhe*). Diploma Film at VGIK, 1960.

Zhivet takoi paren' (*There's This Guy*). Gorky Film Studio, 1964.

Vash syn i brat (*Your Son and Brother*). Gorky Film Studio, 1966.

Strannye liudi (*Strange People*). Gorky Film Studio, 1969.

Pechki-lavochki (*Stoves and Benches*). Gorky Film Studio, 1972.

Kalina krasnaia (*Red Kalina Berry*). Mosfilm, 1974.

ACTING ROLES

Dva Fedora (*The Two Fedors*). Odessa Film Studio, 1959. Director: M. Khutsiev.

Zolotoi Eshelon (*The Golden Echelon*). Gorky Film Studio, 1959. Director: I. Tiurin.

Iz Leb"iazhego soobshchaiut (*Report from Lebyazhe*). Shukshin's Diploma Film at VGIK, 1960.

Prostaia istoriia (*A Simple Story*). Gorky Film Studio, 1961. Director: Iu. Egorov.

Kogda derev'ia byli bol'shimi (*When the Trees Were Tall*). Gorky Film Studio, 1962. Director: L. Kulidzhanov.

Alenka (*Alyonka*). Mosfilm, 1962. Director: B. Barnet.

Mishka, Serega i ia (*Mishka, Seryoga, and I*). Gorky Film Studio, 1962. Director: Iu. Pobedonostsev.

Komandirovka (*Mission*). Gorky Film Studio, 1962. Director: Iu. Egorov.

My, dvoe mushchin (*We Two Men*). Dovzhenko Film Studio, 1963. Director: Iu. Lysenko.

Kakoe ono, more? (*What's It Like, the Sea?*). Gorky Film Studio, 1965. Director: E. Bocharov.

Zhurnalist (*The Journalist*). Gorky Film Studio, 1967. Director: S. Gerasimov.

261

Filmography

Tri dnia Viktora Chernysheva (Three Days in the Life of Viktor Cherny-shev). Gorky Film Studio, 1968. Director: M. Osep'ian.
Muzhskoi razgovor (Man Talk). Gorky Film Studio, 1969. Director: I. Shatrov.
Liubov' Iarovaia (Lyubov Yarovaya). Lenfilm, 1971. Director: V. Fetin.
U ozera (By the Lake). Gorky Film Studio, 1971. Director: S. Gerasimov.
Dauriia (Dauriya). Lenfilm, 1972. Director: V. Tregubovich.
Osvobozhdenie (Liberation). Mosfilm, 1972. Director: Iu. Ozerov.
Pechki-lavochki (Stoves and Benches). Gorky Film Studio, 1972. Director: V. Shukshin.
Kalina krasnaia (Red Kalina Berry). Mosfilm, 1974. Director: V. Shukshin.
Esli khochesh' byt' schastlivym (If You Want to Be Happy). Mosfilm, 1974. Director: N. Gubenko.
Oni srazhalis' za rodinu (They Fought for Their Motherland). Mosfilm, 1975. Director: S. Bondarchuk.
Proshu slova (May I Have a Word?). Lenfilm, 1976. Director: G. Panfilov.

SCRIPTS

Ia prishel dat' vam voliu (I Have Come to Give You Freedom). Originally published in *Iskusstvo kino* 5 (1968): 144–87; 6 (1968): 132–85. Reprinted in Vasilii Shukshin, *Kinopovesti*, rev. ed. (Moscow: Iskusstvo, 1988).
Prishel soldat s fronta (Back from the Front). Based on stories by Sergei Antonov. Mosfilm, 1972. Director: N. Gubenko. Originally published as *Ivan Stepanovich, Iskusstvo kino* 1 (1971): 169–92.
Zemliaki (Fellow Countrymen). Mosfilm, 1975. Director: V. Vinogradov. Originally published as *Brat moi . . . (My Brother), Iskusstvo kino* 7 (1974): 169–92. Reprinted in *Sobranie sochinenii v piati tomakh* (Moscow: Panprint, 1996), 5:341–85.
Pozovi menia v dal' svetluiu (Call Me to the Bright Beyond). Mosfilm, 1977. Director: G. Lavrov and S. Liubshin. Originally published in *Zvezda* 6 (1975): 3–38. Reprinted in *Sobranie sochinenii v piati tomakh* (Moscow: Panprint, 1996), 4:50–100.

262

Index

Index

Index